Liberty!
THE AMERICAN REVOLUTION ℠

On July 9, 1776, after the Declaration of Independence was read to George Washington's army, the people of New York celebrated by pulling down the gilded lead statue of George III on Bowling Green. The torso was shipped to Connecticut to be melted down for bullets. The head was given to the soldiers, who set it up on a spike in the Blue Bell Tavern, near present-day 181st Street and Broadway.

Liberty!
The American Revolution ℠

THOMAS FLEMING

Viking

Viking
Published by the Penguin Group
Penguin Putnam Inc., 375 Hudson Street, New York, New York 10014, U.S.A.
Penguin Books Ltd, 27 Wrights Lane, London W8 5TZ, England
Penguin Books Australia Ltd, Ringwood, Victoria, Australia
Penguin Books Canada Ltd, 10 Alcorn Avenue, Toronto, Ontario, Canada M4V 3B2
Penguin Books (N.Z.) Ltd, 182–190 Wairau Road, Auckland 10, New Zealand

Penguin Books Ltd, Registered Offices: Harmondsworth, Middlesex, England

First published in 1997 by Viking Penguin, a member of Penguin Putnam Inc.

1 3 5 7 9 10 8 6 4 2

Illustration credits appear on pages 391–92.

Cataloging in Publication Data is available from The Library of Congress.
ISBN 0-670-87021-8

This book is printed on acid-free paper.

Printed in Hong Kong by Toppan Printing Company
Produced and designed by Amy Janello and Brennon Jones, Jones & Janello

Contents

Introduction
FACE TO FACE WITH HISTORY   1

Chapter One
THE PATRIOT KING   8
"I am not sorry that blows must decide."

Chapter Two
OVER THE EDGE   90
"I am not a Virginian but an American!"

Chapter Three
SOLDIERS OF LIBERTY   178
"Are these the men with which I am to defend America?"

Chapter Four
YEAR OF THE HANGMAN   226
"A sovereign cordial to the dying."

Chapter Five
PROTRACTED VICTORY   276
"The play, sir, is over."

Chapter Six
LIBERTY VERSUS UNION   344
"Let us raise a standard to which the wise and honest can repair."

Coda
OPENING THE EYES OF THE WORLD   382

Index   385
Picture Credits   391
Acknowledgements   393

Face to Face with History

The portraits on the next five pages of this book are an instant summary of the American Revolution. Each tells us something about that world-transforming event—and simultaneously reminds us that individuals transcend as well as personify the forces of history. Take a long look at these faces. Doesn't King George III seem to be confronting the millions of eyes he knows are out there watching him? Behind him loom a fleet and army that had conquered an empire and a nation whose burgeoning factories were producing unparalleled wealth. His gaze speaks power—and puzzlement. He never understood how his personality coalesced with history to drive the Americans into rebellion.

George Washington's resolute mouth and unillusioned eyes seem to be challenging generations of Americans to imitate his calm courage and astute judgment. This diffident soldier became a man for all American seasons by reaching deep within himself to discover a genius for leadership.

Benjamin Franklin, who was seventy when he helped Thomas Jefferson write the Declaration of Independence, emanates a different kind of strength. It is a blend of shrewdness and wisdom that enabled him to win a war of wits with Europe's sophisticated diplomats.

The other two faces tell different stories. James Lafayette was born a slave named Jim. In 1781, when the Marquis de Lafayette was defending Virginia against a British invasion, Jim's owner lent him to the young French nobleman as a combination valet and groom. Jim volunteered to infiltrate the British army's camp at Yorktown, pretending to be a runaway, and brought back valuable information. After the war, a grateful Lafayette persuaded Virginia to free him. Jim adopted the Marquis's last name and spent the rest of his life as James Lafayette.

Abigail Adams faces us as the far-from-submissive spokesperson of the silent majority of the Revolution—the women who ran the farms and raised the children while their men fought the war. They coped with raging inflation, scarcity and the constant threat of angry enemy soldiers blundering into their lives. Somehow, Abigail found time to write innumerable letters to her missing husband, Congressman John Adams. In a voice charged with love and vivid with intelligence, she recorded the women's side of the struggle.

For all these people, the American Revolution was more than a war. It was a cause. The pride on James Lafayette's face tells us better than any words that the essence of the cause was liberty. That is why the word is the title and central idea of this book, and of the PBS series the book celebrates.

George III believed in liberty, too. But it was British liberty, granted by the government and hedged with demands for subordination and submission. In the Declaration of Independence, liberty became a birthright that every person could claim, no matter what any government said. In that great leap forward, the United States of America became more than a country; it became an idea, a heritage open to people of every race and creed.

Liberty is as relevant to modern Americans as it was to the men and women of 1776. We live in a world webbed and sustained by the liberties they won at terrific cost in an agonizing eight-year ordeal. The freedom to speak our minds, to worship in the churches of our faith, to vote for the political leaders of our choice, to pursue our careers, to manage our individual lives in a hundred different ways, depends on American liberty as it was enunciated and defined in the crisis years of the Revolution.

Ultimately, these faces tell us that behind the rhetoric and gunfire of 1776 is a galaxy of vivid, fascinating men and women who are not as different from contemporary Americans as their knee breeches and long skirts sometimes suggest. *Liberty!* wants to restore the revolutionary generation to our national consciousness. It is not merely a sentimental journey, an exercise in retroactive patriotism. The men and women of 1776 created the nation we inhabit with varying degrees of enthusiasm today.

Our goal, on both film and paper, is to help us understand that explosive word, liberty—and appreciate the tremendous human drama that gave it life and substance in America. Join us for one of the most important journeys of your life.

King George III

George Washington

Benjamin Franklin

James Lafayette

Abigail Adams

The Patriot King

Thirty-six English lords came to a special meeting of the Privy Council to hear George III's solicitor general call Benjamin Franklin a liar and a thief.

"I am not sorry that blows must decide."

—George III

George III ascends the throne as a patriot King. Americans lecture him on the importance of liberty. He is more interested in subordination and ignores the corruption of British liberty. Parliament's attempt to tax Americans without their consent sparks fierce resistance. America becomes an issue in British politics. The family quarrel veers toward war.

On October 25, 1760, King George II—the short, thick-bodied seventy-seven-year-old ruler of England, Wales, Scotland, Ireland, the Duchy of Hanover, and numerous imperial colonies and plantations in Africa, India, the West Indies and North America—arose as usual at six in Kensington Palace and drank his morning cup of chocolate. At a quarter after seven, a royal page heard a thud. Dashing in, he found the King dead on the floor.

Word of the King's death was rushed to Kew House, the palace on the outskirts of London where George II's grandson, twenty-two-year-old George, the Prince of Wales, was living with his mother, Princess Augusta, and his numerous brothers and sisters. He immediately set out for London and before nightfall was conferring with his grandfather's chief ministers, Secretary of State William Pitt and First Lord of the Treasury Thomas Pelham-Holles, the Duke of Newcastle.

George III's attitude toward these two men, who were in the process of winning the Seven Years War, one of the greatest conflicts the world had yet seen, was somewhat peculiar. In the new King's lexicon, the tall, stooped, perpetually anxious-to-please Newcastle was "my grandfather's knave and counselor." The hawk-nosed Pitt, known as the Great Commoner for his electrifying oratory in the House of Commons, had rescued England from the brink of humiliating defeat by transforming the war with France into a struggle for an "empire of liberty." Nevertheless, to the new King, Pitt was "the blackest of hearts," "a true snake in the grass" and "the most dishonorable of men."

Only a few people were aware of these opinions: the two most important were George's mother, Princess Augusta, and his former tutor, the handsome Scottish peer, John Stuart, the Earl of Bute. For several years George had been fuming over the failure of Pitt and Newcastle to pay any attention to Bute's spasmodic attempts to give them advice. This tendency to mingle the personal and the political in dark conspiratorial terms was not a good omen.

Everyone in fashionable London believed Bute (pronounced "boot") was Princess Augusta's lover. This rumor, of which Horace Walpole, the son of a

ABOVE *The mythical gryphon—half lion, half eagle—was often used by Americans as a symbol of England.*

LEFT *George III poses in his coronation robes. Two years before he became King, he said: "Though I act wrong in most things, I have too much spirit to accept the crown and be a cipher."*

previous prime minister, was "as convinced as if I had seen them together," was almost certainly untrue. But it was another indication that George III's reign was likely to be turbulent.

"George, be a King!" his mother had reportedly told her oldest son as he grew to manhood in her straitlaced custody. Modern historians scoff at the story, but his father, Frederick, who had died when George was thirteen, had unquestionably issued similar exhortations to his son. In a forlorn testament that Augusta read to George after her husband's death, Frederick urged George to "retrieve the glory of the throne…I shall have no regret never to have wore [sic] the crown if you but fill it worthily."

Along with this personal entreaty, Frederick left a book, *The Idea of a Patriot King*, which one of his followers had dedicated to him. Whether or not George III read this turgid tome is a moot point, but there is no doubt that he absorbed its basic idea: that England needed such a monarch to rescue the throne from the dominance of "factions." What the author really meant was the dominance of Parliament. He yearned for the days when Parliament danced to the King's tune and not vice versa. England had fought a civil war in the previous century to establish Parliament's independence from royal control.

The Earl of Bute had reinforced this summons to battle by describing George II as an old fool easily manipulated by his mistresses and his cabinet ministers—and portraying Parliament as an institution in the grip of

politicians who constantly put their own corrupt interests ahead of the nation's welfare. There was some truth to Bute's criticism of Parliament. In 1760 it was a largely closed corporation, ruled by the descendants of the noblemen who had ousted King James II in the Glorious Revolution of 1688 because they suspected he was plotting with his fellow Catholics to create an absolute monarchy. These so-called "Whig" lords had gained even more power in 1714, when Queen Anne died without heirs and they invited the German Protestant rulers of the Duchy of Hanover to the British throne. Owing their crowns to the men who had created them, and frequently threatened by James II's ousted descendants, George I and George II were in no position to exert much royal authority. As England became an imperial mercantile state, the Whig noblemen had felt free to enrich themselves from its wars and conquests. They maintained control of Parliament thanks to an antiquated electoral system that permitted only two percent of the population to vote.

A patriot King was not the answer to this large problem. An aristocrat himself, the King would be unlikely to appeal to the people to help check the power of the Whig nobles. All he could do was attempt to bend the Whigs to his will with the same devices they used to stay in power: bribery, patronage and favors. Yet Bute repeatedly assured George that he could redeem the realm

by reigning as this idealized monarch—with Bute at his side, dispensing sage advice. Eventually, Bute promised him, George would reign as a beloved father of his country—the ultimate title that a paternalistic age bestowed on a good King. The young Prince grew to worship his self-assured, seemingly all-wise tutor. The moment George learned of his grandfather's death, he rushed a letter to his "dearest friend," stating he would "wait till I hear from you to know what further must be done."

Year of Miracles

People called 1759, the year preceding George III's ascension, the *annus mirabilis*—the year of miracles. It began with news of a victory in Goree, West Africa, clearing the French out of that continent and giving England a virtual monopoly in the immensely lucrative slave trade. Then a British amphibious assault captured Guadeloupe, richest of the French West Indian sugar islands. Next General James Wolfe ousted France from North America with his conquest of the fortress city of Quebec. In Europe British and Hanoverian infantry shattered a huge French army at the battle of Minden, while Prussia, operating on a British subsidy of almost £1 million a year, kept Russia and Austria at bay. In the Mediterranean the British navy smashed the French Toulon fleet, and at Quiberon Bay virtually annihilated King Louis XV's Atlantic squadron. In India Robert Clive continued the string of triumphs he had begun in 1757, destroying the French as an Asian power in a final victory at Pondicherry as 1760 began. By spending money on an unprecedented scale and choosing his generals and admirals for their talent rather than their political connections, William Pitt had created an awesome war machine.

ABOVE *John Stuart, the Earl of Bute, rose from George III's tutor to prime minister but soon resigned, whining: "The Angel Gabriel could not at present govern this country." He was accused of having an affair with George III's mother.*

FAR LEFT *Front-row seats in Westminster Abbey cost ten guineas when George III was crowned in 1761. The twenty-three-year-old King was England's youngest monarch since Queen Elizabeth I.*

"Victories come so tumbling over one another from distant parts of the globe that it looks like the handiwork of a London romance writer," a breathless Horace Walpole told one of his many correspondents. "The Romans were 300 years conquering the world. We subdued [it] in three campaigns," he gasped to another friend.

In the aura of these triumphs, George III's youth, his apparent eagerness to serve his people and his avowed pride in being English unleashed a tidal wave of enthusiasm and hope throughout the empire. Not since 1558, when Elizabeth I was crowned, had England seen such a young monarch. To many people, George seemed to herald the dawn of a golden age. "One hears nothing of the King," wrote the poet Thomas Gray to a friend, "but what gives one the best opinion of him imaginable."

This was by no means the view of the politicians who were dealing with the King face to face. The young monarch informed the Duke of Newcastle, who presided over dispensing the jobs, government contracts and favors that

THE SLAVE TRADE

The average English slave ship carried 200-300 slaves. Sanitation was nonexistent, dysentery rampant. Once, when water ran short, 131 slaves were thrown overboard. The Solicitor General of England argued no crime had been committed because the blacks were property.

The African slave trade was a major British industry for 100 years before the Revolution. It began even earlier, in 1562, when Captain John Hawkins, backed by London money and royal approval, descended on Sierra Leone and obtained 300 Africans, whom he sold to the Spanish colonies in the Americas. Soon other Englishmen were in this lucrative business, which the Spanish and Portuguese had hitherto controlled, shipping no fewer than 1.6 million Africans to the new world before 1700.

Most of those slaves were captured in wars among rival African states. Slavery was a very old African institution. Captives had been sold into slavery to the Moslem world for centuries. After 1700, however, most slaves were kidnapped. Entire African kingdoms, such as Dahomey, devoted virtually all their resources to seizing young men and women deep in the interior and marching them to the coast for sale.

Overall, an estimated 2 million Africans were transported to British colonies. Most British slave ships carried their human cargoes to England's West Indies sugar plantations. To Jamaica alone went 610,000 slaves.

Another half-million were sold to French and Spanish colonies. The ports of Liverpool and Bristol grew rich on the trade. In one ten-year period, the value of slaves carried by 878 Liverpool ships was more than £15 million. Returns of 100 to 200 percent per voyage were common. New England merchants and ship captains also participated in the trade, drawn by its astonishing profits.

The first African slaves came to Virginia in 1619, brought by a Dutch ship. Throughout most of the seventeenth century, however, white indentured servants were more numerous in the American colonies than African slaves. In 1660, there were only 1,700 blacks in Maryland—compared with 20,000 in Barbados. In another decade the number on that island had leaped to 40,000 . After 1680 the supply of indentured white labor began to diminish, and the owners of large mainland plantations in the South and manors in New York and New Jersey turned to Africa for manpower.

By 1759 an English visitor was writing: "The number of Negroes in the southern colonies is upon the whole nearly equal, if not superior, to that of white men; and they propagate and increase even faster."

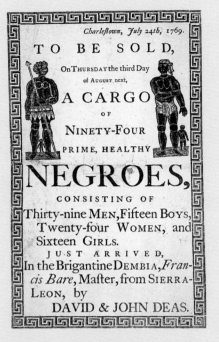

This broadside advertised a cargo of slaves to be sold in Charleston, South Carolina. A slaver sometimes took two months to sell a cargo. By 1740 there were 40,000 Africans in South Carolina.

By 1775 Virginia and Maryland were exporting 220 million pounds of tobacco a year, and the British West Indies were producing 100,000 tons of sugar using black labor. In the four centuries of the slave trade's existence, historians estimate 11,698,000 Africans were exported to North and South America.

This model of a slave ship suggests how the shipowners stacked their cargo below decks. Each slave was allotted about ten square feet and was allowed on deck once a day. On some voyages the death rate was 30 percent.

kept him and Pitt in office, that henceforth he would take his orders from Lord Bute. Too much in love with power to quit, Newcastle swallowed the humiliation in comparative silence.

In the first full cabinet meeting on the night of George II's death, George III attempted to browbeat Pitt in similar fashion. The new King read to his ministers a statement written by Lord Bute. The brief paragraph declared George's "tenderest affection for this my native country" and his determination to "preserve and strengthen the Constitution." It closed with his hope that "the bloody and expensive war" would soon be terminated.

Pitt was no Newcastle. He took instant umbrage at this comment on the Seven Years War and told Bute that it had to be changed to "expensive but just and necessary war" before the text was made public. Bute crumpled before the mere threat of Pitt's wrath and persuaded an extremely reluctant George III to make the change in his own handwriting. It was another omen of trouble to come.

American Liberty

By now, one thing should be obvious. Neither George III nor his ministers gave more than a passing thought to America when he ascended the throne. Nevertheless, the new monarch was hailed with enthusiasm by his distant subjects. For them, the victory won at Quebec in 1759 had ended 150 years of bloody strife over who would rule America. Patriotism mingled with gratitude to produce continental euphoria.

Massachusetts, second-largest of the thirteen colonies, led the chorus of praise. Samuel Cooper, minister of the Brattle Street Church in Cambridge, contributed a poem to a volume produced by Harvard College, *Pietas et Congratulo*. "Silver-tongued Sam," as Cooper was called, hailed the young King as "the Heaven-inspir'd youth."

All the poems reeked of the same adulation. But the preface to the book struck a very different tone. The writer lectured George III on liberty. The King was urged to pay heed to "the miserable effects of despotic power" in Europe and to found his empire on maintaining "the freedom of the people." This stern exhortation was far more typical of these descendants of the English puritans than the fawning poetry. In the 1630s they had left a Mother Country they considered hopelessly corrupt to create a way of life in America in which the liberty to do "that which is good, just, and honest"—what one historian has called "ordered liberty"—was the centerpiece. The words of their first governor, John Winthrop, still resounded in their souls: "This liberty you are to stand for, with the hazard not only of your goods but of your lives if need be."

By interesting coincidence, liberty was the centerpiece of a legal drama that was unfolding in Boston while George III and Lord Bute were beginning their duel for power with William Pitt. The death of George II had forced the

The capture of Quebec in 1759 marked a crucial turning point in relations between England and America. The event is dramatized in this painting of the death of the British commander, General James Wolfe. The victory forced France to surrender Canada. No longer fearful of French and Indian attack, Americans became less hesitant about disagreeing with their British rulers.

A KING IN LOVE

In this fanciful painting, Lady Sarah Lennox is dressed as a Roman aristocrat sacrificing to the Graces. She was only fifteen when George III fell in love with her.

George III devoted not a little of the year 1761 to finding a wife. The first choice of the young King's heart was Lady Sarah Lennox, a saucy fifteen-year-old who was described by one admirer as "different from and prettier than any other girl I ever saw." She had "the finest complexion, the most beautiful hair...with a sprightly and fine air...and remarkably fine teeth." Moreover, Lady Sarah had royal blood: She was the great-great-granddaughter of Charles II by his favorite mistress.

George wrote a swooning letter to his ex-tutor, Lord Bute, confessing that his "passion has been increased" every time he had seen Sarah. "She is everything I can form lovely," he virtually moaned on paper. "I am daily grown unhappy, sleep has left me." When he heard that the young Duke of Marlborough

was invading Sarah's affections, the King fled to his bedroom and "remained [there] for several hours in the depths of despair."

When Bute read this letter, he rushed to show it to George's mother. Sarah's brother-in-law was Henry Fox, one of the most aggressive, ambitious, avaricious politicians in Parliament. This wily gentleman was well aware of George's passion for Sarah, and he shrewdly advised his sister-in-law on how to augment it. He saw himself and his family with ineradicable access to political power. Lady Sarah cheerfully joined the game. One day, when the King came to visit and could not take his eyes off her, she remarked: "I almost thought myself prime minister."

Bute and Princess Augusta descended on George and told him that marrying anyone from the English aristocracy was out of the question. He would be far better advised to choose his wife from Germany. This would not only make him immune to undue influences from in-laws but would also reassure the citizens and nobility of his Duchy of Hanover, who might have become a little unsettled by his fervent protestations about being an Englishman.

Swallowing hard, George agreed that it was his duty to marry a German, if his mentors could find one that did not give him dyspepsia. While he was sighing over Lady Sarah, several Princesses from the numerous little duchies and principalities of Germany had been presented to him—and all had gotten the royal negative. The problem with the Princess of Darmstadt, George plaintively concluded, was her size. The Princess of Schwedt was reported as stubborn and ill-tempered. Finally his Hanoverian searchers recommended seventeen-year-old Princess Charlotte of Mecklenberg-Strelitz. She was no beauty, but George gloomily concluded she was preferable to the immense Princess of Darmstadt. "I am resolv'd to fix here," he told Lord Bute, presuming that his mentor too was "satisfied" with the choice.

George left himself no time for second thoughts. He and Charlotte were married after supper on the day she arrived in London. Among the ten bridesmaids was Lady Sarah Lennox.

Historians, a group chary of psychological explanations, have seldom asked what impact this experience had on George III's personality. It seems more than reasonable to assume that the young monarch, having surrendered one of the supreme privileges every man has in life—selecting a wife of his choice—resolved deep in his soul that he was going to get something out of being a King. Henceforth, power, not pleasure, would be the supreme value in George III's life.

customs officials of Massachusetts to apply for new writs of assistance in the name of George III. These search warrants, frequently used in England and elsewhere in the empire, gave a customs inspector the right to break into a man's ship, his shop, his warehouse or his home—to go, in short, wherever he suspected smuggled goods might be hidden.

With the Seven Years War virtually over in America, royal officials in London had begun urging a tighter enforcement of the customs laws to bring in more revenue. William Pitt's global conflict, which even he admitted was expensive, had run up the national debt to £133 million. But Americans in general and Bostonians in particular had seldom obeyed these complicated laws, which were designed to keep the empire's trade in British channels, with the Mother Country's merchants making most of the profits.

Particularly reprehensible in London's eyes was trade with the French, Dutch or Danish West Indies. But the Americans blithely continued to do business with these foreigners, whose sugar and molasses were far cheaper than British brands. New Englanders used molasses to make rum. As early as 1750, Massachusetts was exporting more than 2 million gallons a year. Newport, Rhode Island, alone had thirty profitable distilleries. The British islands could not absorb all the salt fish, rum and other products such as lumber that New England produced. Over the course of several decades, the West Indies trade had become an economic necessity, winked at by most customs inspectors once their palms were crossed with a little silver.

The merchants of Boston had gone to court to block the new writs of assistance and—by implication—the customs service's get-tough policy. They ran into a wall of official intransigence. The royal governor, Francis Bernard, needed money and stood to pocket (legally) a third of all the fines imposed on smugglers unlucky enough to get caught. Complicating matters, the office of chief justice of the colony was open due to the recent death of the incumbent. Everyone expected the job to go to Colonel James Otis of Barnstable, speaker of the Massachusetts assembly. Several previous royal governors had promised it to him. But Governor Bernard wanted a safer man than the mercurial Otis, and he appointed Thomas Hutchinson, who already held the office of lieutenant governor and several other government jobs. It was a mistake that would have large consequences.

Infuriated, James Otis Jr., the colonel's son, resigned his job as prosecutor in the colony's vice-admiralty court, where he had been successfully convicting smugglers, and took the merchants' case. A passionate, headstrong man, much like his father, Otis announced he would accept no fees for his services. In February 1761, he sat silent while two older lawyers argued the case against the writs citing precedents back to the

RIGHT *Lumber was an important export of the four New England colonies. Shipbuilding was also a major source of wealth.*

reign of Charles II. In the packed courtroom sat a young admirer of James Otis Jr., an attorney from nearby Braintree named John Adams. Sensing something important was in the wind, he began taking notes as Otis rose to speak.

Otis began his argument with an electrifying sentence: "This writ is against the fundamental principles of laws." With blazing rhetoric, Otis traced the history of Englishmen's struggle against arbitrary power. He denounced the writs as "destructive to English liberty." They would give every petty customs official in Massachusetts the right to invade any citizen's home, on the mere suggestion of an informer. Even if Parliament itself passed a law specifically endorsing writs of assistance, Otis thundered, the statute would be void because it violated that great unwritten charter of liberty, the English Constitution.

For three hours, Otis held his audience enthralled—or in some cases appalled—by his headlong argument. Chief Justice Hutchinson, alarmed by the emotions swirling through his courtroom, hastily continued the case into the next judicial term and declared he would write to England for instructions. That night young John Adams wrote in his diary: "Every man appeared to me to go away, as I did, ready to take arms against writs of assistance." In May the town of Boston elected James Otis Jr. one of its four representatives to the colony's legislature.

The Old Dominion

In Virginia, the largest of the thirteen colonies, Francis Fauquier, the royal governor, proclaimed the new King in Williamsburg on February 12, 1761. Present were members of the governor's council, the colony's legislature (known as the House of Burgesses), and a company of local militia. "Proclamations of His Majesty's right to the crown of these realms," the governor wrote to his superiors in England, "were read, amidst the joyful acclamations of the people, at the capital, the market place and the college [of William and Mary], each proclamation followed by a discharge of small arms." The governor added that not all the councilors or burgesses were present, because of "the inclemency of the season." Among those who missed the ceremony was the twenty-eight-year-old burgess from Frederick County, Colonel George Washington.

LEFT *William Pitt was the Winston Churchill of his time, the man who rescued England from defeat in the Seven Years War. He was a magnetic orator, immensely popular with the people of London. He opposed taxing America.*

ABOVE RIGHT *James Otis stirred Boston with his protest against British writs of assistance, which empowered customs officers to search anywhere, even in private houses, for smuggled goods.*

LIFE IN THE THIRTEEN COLONIES

Well-to-do colonial families spent a great deal of money on clothes and education for their children. Families were large. Eight children was not unusual. There were few public schools outside New England, and tuition at private schools was high.

Most modern Americans have the impression that Americans of the revolutionary era were poor. On the contrary, they enjoyed the highest per-capita income of any people in the civilized world of their time. Another impression is that they were more or less equal. In fact, in each of the thirteen colonies, a highly stratified, class-conscious society already existed. In the northern colonies, the wealthiest 10 percent of the population owned about 45 percent of the property. In many parts of the South, 10 percent of the taxpayers possessed 75 percent of the wealth. This was

hardly surprising. The colonies had been in existence for 150 years when the Revolution began—more than enough time for the talented and ambitious to acquire money and land.

In the 1770s George Washington was a typical member of the upper class, thanks in part to his marriage to wealthy Martha Dandridge Custis. He owned 12,463 acres of Virginia farmland and 24,103 unimproved acres in the western wilderness along the Kanawha and Ohio rivers. On his farms he kept 130 horses and maintained 135 slaves, and earned as much as £3,213 a year from his various

crops—a fortune compared with a landless laborer's income of £30 a year.

Wealth was also dispersed widely through the rest of the population. About 40 percent of the people were independent farmers who lived in considerable comfort. A typical northern farmer owned ten head of cattle, sixteen sheep, six pigs, two horses and a team of oxen—and was usually able to sell two-fifths of his crops for cash. When artisans, shopkeepers and the like were added to this group, they made up a thriving middle class whose members typi-

Newspapers were full of ads for slaves who had run away. Rewards were offered for their capture. Indentured servants also ran away regularly.

cally owned property worth about £400.

Colonial Americans fretted over the cost of living as much as their modern descendants. One prosperous craftsman in Charleston, South Carolina, spent £313 a year to live in genteel fashion and educate his two sons at a private school. It took about £500 a year for a family to feel well-to-do. Skilled workers such as carpenters earned from £45 to £90 a year. Schoolteachers were wretchedly paid—as little as £30 a year—unless, like Nathan Hale, they taught at an academy or private school. Harvard paid its professors £100 a year—one-eighth the salary of a judge. Yale paid its president £150 a year, considerably less than the owner of a prosperous tavern made. Ministers did somewhat better, as did doctors. Near the top of the economic pyramid were lawyers. Boston attorneys often made £2,000 to £3,000 a year. At the very top were merchants, who spent money as freely as they made it. One Baltimore merchant laid out £600 a year for, among other things, dancing lessons for his children, membership in a fishing club and losses at cards.

The ultimate sign of wealth, similar to the ownership of a yacht or private airplane today, was an "equipage"—a coach drawn by four matched horses, with servants in livery riding outside. There were no fewer than eighty-four of these elaborate vehicles in Philadelphia—thirty of them owned by supposedly unworldly Quakers.

Adino Paddock of Boston was the premier colonial coach manufacturer. Beginning as a chaise maker in 1758, he displayed modern sales techniques early, advertising six secondhand chaises at an "under their value" sale in 1759. He was soon employing a large force of workers making luxury coaches for £200. In another modern touch, his ads informed customers he would take old chaises and coaches "in part pay for new."

Some American businesses reached remarkable size. Isaac Zane Jr., son of a wealthy Philadelphia Quaker, ran an ironworks on Cedar Creek, near Winchester, Virginia, that produced six tons of iron a week and employed 150 hands. Numerous other ironworks were busy in Pennsylvania, New Jersey and other colonies. By 1775 Americans were producing one-seventh of all the iron in the world. In Connecticut, Christopher Leffingwell's Norwich Paper Manufactory supplied paper for all the state's newspapers. Another Connecticut Yankee, Simon Huntington, annually produced 5,000 pounds of chocolate, using waterpower. In Massachusetts John Adam Dagyr, a Welsh shoemaker who settled in Lynn, turned out 80,000 pairs of ladies' footwear a year. By 1775 the thirteen colonies had an economy two-fifths the size of England's. It was seventeen times as large as it had been in 1700 and was clearly on its way to surpassing that of the Mother Country.

Not only were colonial Americans big spenders, but they were also often in debt. In Kent, Connecticut, 140 people owed money to the local storekeeper. A Beaufort, South Carolina, merchant claimed that 500 persons owed him a total of £20,000. If a man could not pay his debts, he often went to prison until he or someone else came up with the money. One writer found more than fifty men in a single room in New York's debtors' prison, many of them ragged and emaciated. One historian has estimated that the Americans owed English merchants almost £6 million on the eve of the Revolution.

Rural cornhusking bees were also songfests, and when a fiddler arrived, the dancing began. The English Dancing Master, *listing 918 dances, was one of the most popular books in America.*

LIFE IN THE THIRTEEN COLONIES

In the cities, indigents and men temporarily out of work were placed in almshouses. In New England, "going on the town" was considered a catastrophe among the poor. At the town meeting, the selectmen "bid off" the indigent to whoever would hire them—a procedure almost as humiliating as a slave auction.

Already a Melting Pot

Recent studies of American origins have forced historians to revise the conventional picture of the colonists as English. Only 60.9 percent of colonial Americans came from the Mother Country. Another 14.3 percent were Scots and Scotch-Irish from Northern Ireland, 8.7 percent were German, 5.8 percent were Dutch, 3.7 percent southern Irish and 6.6 percent miscellaneous. Added to this surprising non-English total were 540,000 blacks, most of them slaves, 20 percent of the total population of 2,640,000.

Religion was equally varied. America boasted 749 Congregational churches, 485 Presbyterian, 457 Baptist, 406 Anglican, 328 Dutch or German Reformed, 240 Lutheran and 56 Catholic. There were also 200 Quaker meetinghouses and 5 synagogues. Not a few of these denominations were hostile to each other. Catholics were tolerated only in Maryland and Pennsylvania. Quakers were not welcomed in most of New England. Presbyterians regarded Anglicans as a threat to their religious freedom because they talked of bringing bishops to America to set up an established church as in England.

Music Makers

Music was the favorite American recreation. Young Thomas Jefferson practiced his violin three hours a day. Benjamin Franklin played the guitar, the harp and the violin. Patrick Henry played the violin, the lute, the flute and the piano. George Washington paid $1000 (the equivalent of $50,000 today) for a spinet for his granddaughter, Nelly Custis. When New Jerseyan Philip Vickers Fithian went to Virginia in 1774 to tutor the children of Robert Carter at Nomini Hall, he found the mansion contained a guitar, a harpsichord, a piano, violins, flutes and an organ and was amazed to discover that Carter could play them all.

Like the Americans themselves, the music came from many countries: England, Ireland, Germany, France, Italy and Africa. The violin was the most popular instrument, followed closely by the flute and the recorder, which the colonists called the German flute. These were played mostly by men. Women played the harpsichord and the piano. Another favorite was the ten-string guitar, a predecessor of the modern six-string instrument, with a flat back and teardrop shape.

Musical theater was very popular. In fact, almost every play had musical interludes within it or between the acts. Concert-going was also popular. A visiting Bostonian said a performance at the concert house of the St. Cecilia Society in Charleston, South Carolina, was "the best [music] he ever heard." He noted "there were upwards of two hundred and fifty ladies present, and it was called no great number." The Society paid its first violinist, a newly arrived Frenchman, £525 a year. Boston, New York and Philadelphia all had subscription concerts.

The Americans of the Revolutionary era loved to sing as well as play music. Philip Vickers Fithian told of being delayed by bad weather in the mountains and hearing two young women singing while they sat at their spinning wheels. "They sung well. In perfect unison," he wrote in his journal. "They sung deliberately. Not one long note or pause did either of them hurry over. They were young. Both were handsome. There is something harmonious in a well turned face. But when it is improved by real sound, surely there is then intrinsic harmony."

Stage music often became widely popular. One of the favorites was "Over the Hills and Far Away." Beginning as a folk song, this plaintive air

This quilt portrait of a Connecticut lady in her parlor has the charm of a primitive painting. Quilting was a favorite pastime for women.

became one of the hits of John Gay's *The Beggar's Opera*, which debuted in America in the 1750s. The rich harmonies of Scottish songs were also popular. A favorite was "When Bidden To the Wake or Fair." As these melodies traveled from place to place, new words were often written for them. Equally popular were ballads, sung in taverns or at private parties. One of the most rousing was "Brave Wolfe," a tribute to General James Wolfe, the conqueror of Quebec.

Francis Hopkinson of Philadelphia published the first American song, in 1759—"My Days Have Been So Wondrous Free." He played the harpsichord beautifully and for many years was the center of musical life in Philadelphia. He was also a signer of the Declaration of Independence. He wrote graceful, romantic music. "Come, Fair Rosina, Come Away"; "Enraptured I Gaze when my Delia is By"; "My Gen'rous Heart Disdains, the Slave of Love To Be" are some of his other titles.

Another talented musician was James Lyon, from Newark, New Jersey. Philip Vickers Fithian called him "a great master of music" and in his journal told of spending an evening singing many of his "tunes" with him. Lyon sang with "his usual softness and accuracy," Fithian remarked. One of his best-known songs was "Friendship." After Lyon became a Presbyterian minister, he wrote a number of powerful hymns.

The most important song writer in America was William Billings, who was born in Boston in 1746. Blind in one eye, with a short leg and a withered arm, this eccentric genius transformed American vocal music with his 1770 book, *The New England Psalm Singer*. It was the first published collection of entirely original American music. All told, this remarkable book contained 126 tunes, multiplying by ten the number of new songs available for singers and audiences.

Some of Billings's music was rich in political defiance as well as new har-

In the 1770s "heads" reached ridiculous heights. A hairdresser uses a sextant to measure the altitude of this creation.

monies. His tune "Chester" soon rivaled "Yankee Doodle" as the favorite song of the Revolution:

> Let tyrants shake their iron rod
> And slav'ry clank her galling chains
> We fear them not we trust in God
> New England's God forever reigns.

Dancing Up a Storm

Dancing was as popular as concert-going and singing. The book *The English Dancing Master*, listed no less than 918 dances. Among the favorites were minuets, reels, jigs and country dances, which were the forerunners of square dances.

Philip Vickers Fithian described a typical night of southern dancing at Nomini Hall: "There were upwards of 70 at the ball...About seven the ladies & gentlemen began to dance in the ball-room...the music was a French horn and two violins—the ladies were dressed gay, and splendid, and when dancing their skirts & brocades rustled and trailed behind them!"

European visitors were dismayed by the energy required to do an American jig or reel. "These dances are without method or regularity," one complained. "A gentleman and a lady stand up, and dance about the room, one of them retiring and the other pursuing, then perhaps meeting in an irregular fantastical manner..." Such exertions tested "at every turn the respective strength of their sinews."

Best Bib and Tucker

Both men and women dressed in styles that would dazzle their modern descendants. One New York fashion plate ordered a suit of "superfine" scarlet plush and a vest of light blue plush. Claret-colored duffel coats were equally popular. George Washington rode to hounds in a black velvet hunting cap and a waistcoat of scarlet cloth and gold lace. A newspaper described wealthy John Hancock's at-home costume: "He wore a red velvet cap within which was one of fine linen...a blue damask coat, lined with velvet, a white stock, a white satin embroidered waistcoat, black satin small clothes, white silk stockings and red Morocco slippers."

For women, small waists were the fashion, and corsets were laced to the brink of asphyxiation. Women began wearing these whalebone monstrosities as early as eleven years of age. The hoop skirt, the prevailing fashion, stretched out on each side from six inches to two feet. To enter a room a woman had to turn sideways. It often took a half-day for a hairdresser to "permanent" a lady's hair for a ball. Hair styles became extreme in the 1770s, with women sporting towers of real and artificial hair up to twenty-four inches in height.

The Beauty Business

Although moralists decried the practice, women spent a great deal of money to preserve the sheen of youth. They bought "paints" from China, a lip salve from India. From Greece came "Jerusalem washballs" and the "Bloom of Circassia," which supposedly gave their cheeks a rosy

LIFE IN THE THIRTEEN COLONIES

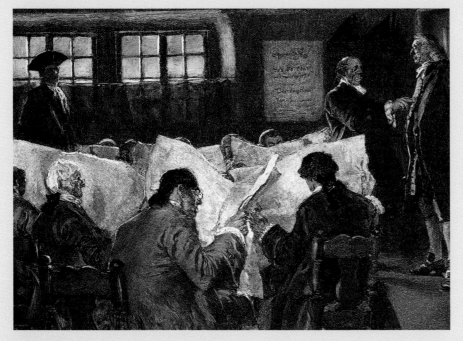

Men went to taverns to read the latest newspapers and talk politics. The tavern-keeper was often the local political boss. A well-run tavern made as much as £1,000 a year.

hue that defied perspiration. Maryland's sprightly Molly Tilghman summed up the prevailing feminine opinion when she told her cousin Polly Pearce: "Wisdom says beauty is a fading flower, but...it attracts more admiration than wit, goodness or anything else in this world."

Increase and Multiply

One reason the number of Americans doubled every twenty-five years was the custom of early marriage. An English traveler in the backcountry remarked: "It is not uncommon to see a mother of 13 or 14 years of age, and it is rare to see a maid unmarried at 18." Americans elsewhere married almost as young. In New England courtship was often hastened by the custom of bundling: allowing a suitor to share a young woman's bed—with a centerboard down the middle of it. Houses were small, and families large; this was the only way to give a courting couple some privacy. But the custom had its dangers. In some churches a bride and groom confessed their sins before the ceremony.

Almost half the couples admitted they had become lovers.

Money was frankly accepted as a significant item in a marriage. Newspapers regularly stated the amount of a bride's estate. Elizabeth Stith of Virginia, for instance, was described as "a very amiable lady with a fortune of a thousand pounds sterling." Cash was frequently the reason for mingling youth and age. When fifteen-year-old Betsy Hanford of Virginia married fifty-one-year-old John Cam, one of her friends explained: "She is to have a chariot and there is to be no padlock put upon her mind."

The ultimate in this department may have been reached on March 15, 1771, when *The Virginia Gazette* announced: "Yesterday was married, in Henrico, Mr. William Carter, third son of Mr. John Carter, age 23, to Mrs. Sarah Ellyson, relict [widow] of Mr. Gerald Ellyson, aged 85, a sprightly old tit with 3,000 pounds fortune."

Family life was full of affection, though the expression of feeling was usually restrained and formal. Colonel Thomas Jones addressed his fiancée,

Elizabeth Cock, a widow, as Madam or Dearest Madam when they were courting. After their wedding, however, his letters usually began "My dearest life." He told of reading one of her letters twenty times and wished while she slept his heart could take flight and whisper to her "the truth of my soul"—that she "bless[ed] the earth" with her presence.

Nevertheless, essays and letters about unhappy marriages frequently appeared in the newspapers. One correspondent in *The Virginia Gazette* claimed that the cause was a loss of respect for matrimony. He blamed this on women who spent too much of a man's money on luxury and on men who for the sake of beauty or wealth, married "a fury" or an "ideot [sic]."

Independent Women

Except for private tutors, women had almost no educational opportunities. Divorce was seldom granted by the courts, and a woman's property was legally controlled by her husband. But a surprising number of colonial women managed their own affairs. Mrs. Sueton Grant ran her husband's gunpowder-manufacturing company in Rhode Island for thirty years after he was killed by an explosion in 1744. Anna Marie Hoyland of Charlestown, Massachusetts, informed the public that she was doing "any kind of braziery and tinwork as [her] mother used to do." Elizabeth Shaw advertised in *The Boston Post Boy* that she "mend[ed] men's shoes in the neatest manner." The first woman undertaker, Lydia Darragh, opened her business in Philadelphia in 1766.

At nineteen, Eliza Lucas of South Carolina experimented with raising figs on her family's plantation and confided to a friend that she "loved the vegitable world extreamly." When her father, a British officer, went off to fight for the King, she began raising indigo and ginger and cotton on the plantation and succeeded so well with indigo, it became one of the most profitable crops in South Carolina. After she married Charles Pinckney, she imported silkworms that produced enough silk to make three handsome gowns.

Some women speculated briskly in land. Abigail Bromfield joined John Hancock, Samuel Adams and other VIPs in buying thousands of acres in Maine. In 1771 Marcy Cheese advertised for sale "the small island of Chopoquidic, adjoining Martha's Vineyard."

The amazing thing is that women accomplished anything at all, considering the basic chores they had to perform. Abigail Foote of Connecticut summed up one day's work in her diary:

Fix'd gown for Prude—Mend Mother's riding hood—spun short thread—fix'd two gowns for Welsh's girls—carded tow—spun linen—worked on cheese—hatchel'd flax with Hannah, we did 51 lbs apiece—pleated and ironed—read a sermon of Doddridge's—spooled a piece—milked the cows—spun linen, did 50 knots—made a broom of Guinea wheat straw—spun thread to whiten—set a red dye—had two scholars from Mrs. Taylor's—carded two pounds of whole wool—spun harness twine—scoured the pewter.

Food and Drink

Practically all the foods available today were on the colonial table. Tomatoes, however, were not considered edible, and only passing references to cucumbers can be found. Ham was by far the favorite meat, with Virginia ham conceded to be the best—though New Jerseyans strenuously disagreed. William Byrd, who built the great Virginia mansion West-over, considered ham so important he had his recipe for cooking it on the flyleaf of his Bible.

It was common to begin the day with a stiff drink, even in Quaker Philadelphia. The favorite potion was hard cider, with rum a close second. Almost every deed, will and property inventory in Lexington and Concord contained references to a supply of cider. In 1767, 33,436 barrels were produced in Middlesex County, Massachusetts—seven barrels for each family, or 1.1 per person. One writer has remarked that colonial Americans drank enough hard cider in a single day to make modern Americans "woozy for a week."

Taverns of Liberty

This fondness for a "glass" was one of several reasons why the tavern was second only to the church as the cen-

"After breakfast we all retired to the dancing room." This painting hangs in the Governor's Palace in Colonial Williamsburg. It illustrates Americans' fondness for dancing even when the orchestra consisted of only one instrument.

LIFE IN THE THIRTEEN COLONIES

ter of colonial American life. Wrote one early Boston commentator: "They [taverns] were the resort at once of judge and jury, the clergy and the laity, the politician and the merchant, where royal governors and distinguished strangers were entertained with the humblest wayfarer and the meanest citizen; where were held the carousals of roistering redcoat officers and the midnight plottings of stern-lipped patriots."

Medical Men

There were some 3,500 practicing doctors in America on the eve of the Revolution. Fewer than 200 had medical degrees—all from abroad. Even the best doctors relied on drugs such as calomel, mercury and quinine, often in doses so large they did more harm than good. Some used Indian remedies. All practiced "strenuous medicine"—bleeding the sick, dipping them in cold water, sweating and blistering them, evacuating them with laxatives. A jingle attributed to a Quaker doctor aptly summed up medical practice:

When patients come to I
I physics, bleeds and sweats 'em
Then if they choose to die
What's that to I—I lets 'em.

American dentists were nonexistent. Only a handful of British surgeon dentists visited the colonies occasionally. This was unfortunate, because Americans, thanks to their fondness for sugary desserts and heaps of sugar in their tea and coffee, had very bad teeth. Milk was not a popular beverage. No one knew about calcium deficiency. It was not uncommon for women to lose half their teeth by the age of thirty.

In the 1760s craftsmen such as silversmith Paul Revere developed techniques for making false teeth. They were usually fashioned from hippopotamus teeth, which kept their color, and were attached to adjacent teeth by a silver or gold thread.

Getting Around

Stagecoaches began running between New York and Philadelphia in 1764, making the ninety-mile trip in three days. When the trip was cut to two days, the coaches were called "flying machines." The fare was twenty shillings to ride on top, thirty shillings inside the coach. There was a great deal of road building between 1763 and 1776. A traveler had the choice of four routes from Boston to New Haven.

The standard mode of transportation for most people was the horse. Men were as fussy about their horses as modern Americans are about their cars. In Virginia "even the most indigent person has his saddle horse," one visitor observed, "which he rides to every place and on every occasion." The Indians were amused at the way Virginians avoided walking. "Two legs are are not enough for such lazy people," they said. "They cannot visit their next neighbor without six."

In 1775 a good horse sold for £20, half a year's salary for a laboring man. Horses were also expensive to maintain. They ate many pounds of hay and oats a day. Horse thieves were numerous. George White was among the cleverest. He often stole a horse and

This Connecticut tavern sign also achieved the level of folk art. The tavern keeper was the second most important person in a town, after the minister.

sold it in the next town. A few hours later he would steal it again and sell it the next day in another town. The following day he would steal the animal again and return it to its original pasture, where it may never have been missed.

Sexy Novels Sell

Samuel Richardson's *Pamela* was by far the most popular novel in colonial America. The story of a servant girl's rise to high position proved that virtue is rewarded, and simultaneously delivered titillating descriptions of a young woman agonizing over sexual desire. The novel created a minor industry of *Pamela* fans and *Pamela* engravings. Equally popular was *Pamela's* successor, *Clarissa*, which showed the sad end of a young woman who succumbed to a scoundrel's blandishments before she got a wedding ring.

Lingo

Americans continued to use words that had dropped out of circulation in England. "Burly," "catercornered," "deft" and "scant" are examples. The English stopped calling boys "Bub" in the seventeenth century but the word was still in wide use in America. When an American invented a word, it was usually direct and descriptive—"popcorn," "eggplant," "cold snap," "skunk" (an Indian word). A boat that leaped out of the water in a strong wind became a "catboat," and one that glided gracefully along became a "schooner."

Land of Promise

Between 1760 and 1775, the idea of America as a good place to live swept the British Isles. More than 55,000 Protestant Irish and 40,000 Scots emigrated to the colonies. The British were vastly alarmed by this massive outflow, which represented 3 percent of the population of Scotland and 2.3 percent of the population of Ireland.

London's *Gentleman's Magazine* wrung its editorial hands over a story

A typical Northern farmer owned 10 head of cattle, 16 sheep, 6 pigs, 2 horses and a team of oxen—and was usually able to sell two-fifths of his produce for cash. Americans had the highest per-capita incomes in the world.

reporting that 43,720 emigrants sailed from five Irish ports between 1769 and 1774. Almost as alarming was the emigration of more than 30,000 Englishmen in the same period. The government created a Register of Emigration in 1773 to find out why people were leaving the British Isles.

Insiders knew the answer before they started the investigation. Wills Hill, the Earl of Hillsborough, the haughty aristocrat who served as secretary of state for America from 1768

to 1772, had already informed Parliament that multitudes were flocking there "for no other reason but because they hope to live better, or to earn more money...than they can at home."

Hillsborough thought England should not tolerate such ambitions among the "lower sort." For the public good, Parliament ought to "lay a restraint upon poor people leaving the place of their birth without leave [permission] from the magistrates of the place." Benjamin Franklin, who

had many dealings with Lord Hillsborough, most of them unpleasant, succinctly explained what the noble Lord meant by the public good. He was "terribly afraid of dispeopling Ireland" because most of his income came from the vast estates he owned in that oppressed country.

Even before the Revolution began, America had become a beacon of hope for those who yearned for a decent life.

The colonel had far more English blood in his veins than George III. In the seventeenth century, the Washingtons had been a distinguished family in the county of Northampton. Like many of the English who emigrated to Virginia, they had supported King Charles I in the English Civil War of 1642-48 and had been hounded into obscurity and relative poverty by the Puritan winners. John Washington, who arrived in Virginia in 1657, had worked his way across the Atlantic as a mate on a ship. He had married well and swiftly displayed the energetic acquisitive spirit that was to characterize his descendants.

Like George III, George Washington lost his father, Augustine Washington, at an early age—in his case, eleven. But he was far more fortunate in the substitute father that fate bestowed on him. Lawrence Washington, Augustine's son by his first marriage, more or less adopted the gangling boy when he turned fourteen. Lawrence invited George to Mount Vernon, the estate he had inherited from Augustine, and encouraged him to become a surveyor and thus earn enough money to escape his virago of a mother, Mary Ball Washington.

Through Lawrence, George Washington met the Fairfaxes, owners of Belvoir, the estate adjoining Mount Vernon. The first Lord Fairfax had defended English liberty against Charles I in the Civil War. He was one of the commanders of the army that shattered the forces of that arrogant King in the battle of Marston Moor. But he had no sympathy with the dictatorship that

BELOW *George Washington inherited Mount Vernon from his half-brother, Lawrence. Washington enlarged the original one-and-a-half-story house and expanded the property until it included more than 8,000 acres.*

Oliver Cromwell set up in the wreckage of the monarchy. The Fairfaxes found their inspiration in the great figures of the ancient Roman republic, men of high principles and unflinching courage, such as Cincinnatus, who spurned the chance to become a dictator and went back to his farm after winning his military victories.

Lawrence Washington shared these ideals. He had been educated in England and had served with distinction in a previous colonial war, winning a captain's commission in an expedition against the South American treasure city of Cartagena. He had named his estate Mount Vernon in honor of the British admiral who commanded the expedition. The admiral in turn had given him a lantern from his flagship to decorate the hall.

The Fairfaxes and Lawrence saw life in terms of duty and honor, both personal and public. No duty was higher, no honor more glorious, than service to one's country. A man could not hope to perform this service well without achieving self-mastery. These ideals were summed up in the tragedy *Cato*, by Joseph Addison. This tale of a Roman hero who refused to surrender his liberty to a tyrannical Julius Caesar was one of the favorite plays of the eighteenth century. It was often part of the amateur theatricals performed at Belvoir, in which young George Washington eagerly joined.

In the character of Cato, the play describes the spiritual stature that a man who has achieved self-mastery can attain.

> Turn up thy eyes to Cato!
> There may'st thou see to what a godlike height
> The Roman virtues lift up mortal man
> While good and just and anxious for his friends
> He's still severely bent against himself
> Renouncing sleep and rest and food and ease.

Impossibly noble? It may sound that way in our cynical era. But this philosophy gave young George Washington goals he would pursue all his life. It opened his eyes to a world beyond the horse races, fox hunts, dances and girls that absorbed other Virginians his age. Cato was a supreme example of a man who was prepared to sacrifice everything, even his life, for his country's liberty.

Virginia's liberty was very different from the ordered, morality-driven liberty to which the Puritans of Massachusetts were devoted. Virginia was closer to the traditional English idea of liberty—a right to rule, to have one's own way—and not to be ruled arbitrarily by the will or whims of others. In this view of life, the world was a harsh place that did not apportion liberty equally. Some men had more than others, and some had none at all—which explains why George Washington and his fellow Virginians saw no conflict between being fervent devotees of liberty and owners of slaves.

At the end of these formative years came tragedy. Lawrence, the debonair

TOP RIGHT *Lawrence Washington was fourteen years older than George Washington. He became a surrogate father who helped George escape from his sharp-tongued mother. Lawrence died of tuberculosis in 1752.*

soldier and thoughtful substitute father, was stricken with tuberculosis and wasted away before the eyes of his grief-stricken family. He was as generous to his half-brother in death as he had been in life. Lawrence made modest provisions for his infant daughter and his wife, who soon remarried—and he bequeathed George the Mount Vernon estate.

Thus the fatherless boy grew up to become a member of the Virginia aristocracy. Their huge plantations and opulent mansions, their frank enjoyment of expensive clothes, good wines and all the other pleasures of life, made the men and women of Virginia and the rest of the South so different from the people of New England that it was hard to believe they lived in the same country.

Throughout the American colonies, in their 150 years of growing population and mounting prosperity, a tradition of deference had grown up, a sort of shadowy imitation of British aristocracy, in which certain wealthy families were acknowledged to be the leaders of a city or district. Nowhere was this more pronounced than in Virginia, where an elite composed of Randolphs, Carters, Byrds, Lees and other "First Families" came to be acknowledged as rulers of the colony. Young George Washington aspired to join this upper echelon. After he inherited Mount Vernon, he began his climb up the social ladder by winning election as a burgess from Frederick County, in western Virginia, where he had made his reputation as a soldier.

Chief among Washington's legislative concerns at the time of George III's ascension was an issue of considerable moment to the residents of the town of Winchester: "to preserve the water for the use of the inhabitants...by preventing hogs from running at large therein." The roaming hogs had developed a habit of relaxing in the town's springs and fouling the ground around the wells. Can there be a better illustration of the contrast between the two Georges—and between England and America—in 1761?

Yet Colonel Washington, in spite of his parochial concern with unpenned hogs, was not a provincial nobody. He could say with considerable truth that he had started the global war with France about which George III, Lord Bute and William Pitt were arguing so vehemently. In the late fall of 1753, as a twenty-one-year-old militia major, George had trekked through 250 miles of wintry woods to carry a warning from the royal governor of Virginia to the French to clear out of the Ohio Valley, where they were building forts and forging alliances with local Indian tribes. The French had bluntly informed Major Washington that they claimed this vast domain and would do no such thing. To prove that the French had been given fair warning, the governor arranged for publication in London of Washington's journal of his harrowing trek, during which he survived an accidental plunge into the icy Allegheny River and an Indian's attempt to kill him at point-blank range.

A few months later, back on the frontier at the head of a regiment, Washington had exchanged the first shots of the war with a French patrol, killing ten of them. He wrote to his brother Jack: "I heard the bullets whistle, and believe me, there is something charming in the sound." The royal governor of Virginia, even prouder of his protégé, sent this letter to England too, and it was published in *The London Magazine*. George II reportedly read it and grunted: "He would not say that if he had been used to hear many."

For a twenty-two-year-old, Washington was displaying a remarkable

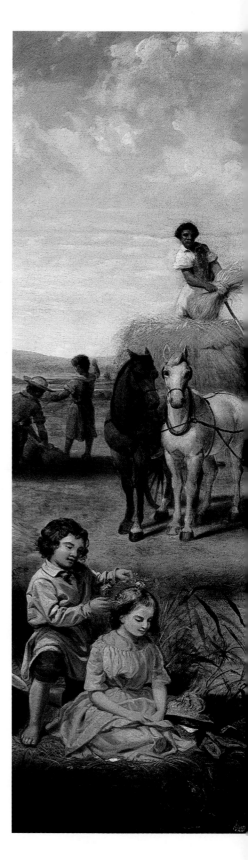

ABOVE *Washington struggled to make Mount Vernon profitable, but the soil was mediocre, and the price of tobacco declined steadily. He owned more than 100 slaves but favored a policy of gradual manumission after the Revolution. In his will, he freed all his slaves.*

ability to win international attention. A few months after his victorious skirmish, however, he won public notice of a less enjoyable kind. Colonel Washington was forced to surrender his outnumbered regiment to the counterattacking French and their Indian allies. His name became synonymous in some English circles with American military incompetence.

Washington spent the next five years as a soldier, fighting in what the Americans called the French and Indian War. In 1755 he served as an aide to General Edward Braddock when that unlucky commander led two British regiments to slaughterous defeat on the site of present-day Pittsburgh. Later he served with the British army that drove the French from the Ohio Valley. But for most of the war, Washington was a much-harassed provincial colonel guarding the frontier against French and Indian incursions with Virginia soldiers who were inclined to do as little fighting as possible. When Washington resigned his commission in 1759, the burgesses unanimously endorsed a resolution to grant the colonel "the thanks of the House" for "his brave and steady behavior." Aware of his shortcomings as a public speaker, Washington acknowledged the tribute with a wordless blush—a frequent reaction when he felt deep emotion. There is little doubt that it was a deeply satisfying moment for the young soldier—a sign that he had achieved a modicum of the honor for which Lawrence Washington had taught him to strive.

That same year, the chestnut-haired, six-foot-three-inch warrior capped his public career by marrying pert, plump Martha Dandridge Custis, one of the richest widows in Virginia. He resided with Martha and her two children by her first marriage at Mount Vernon, which he began busily expanding and

BELOW *In 1755 French-led Indians ambushed a British army led by General Edward Braddock on the site of present-day Pittsburgh. Braddock was shot from his horse. The aide trying to help him is twenty-three-year-old George Washington.*

redecorating in line with Martha's expensive tastes—and his own. He soon learned what many Virginians and other Southerners were beginning to discover: the economic system that had made the South wealthy was no longer working very well. Tobacco, the great cash crop shipped to England each year, was beginning to glut the market. As prices fell, the cost of English luxuries rose, creating an ever-spiraling burden of debt that troubled—and sometimes angered—an industrious man such as George Washington.

Anglo-American Patriots

After a year of indecision, George III gave up the woman he loved and chose homely Princess Charlotte of Mecklenberg-Strelitz as his Queen. Among the witnesses when they were crowned in Westminster Abbey on September 22, 1761, were two Americans from Philadelphia, Benjamin Franklin and his son, William. They represented another variation on the emerging American character—the people of the so-called Middle Colonies. They were far less homogenous than the society of the South or New England. From Pennsylvania, where Quakers dominated, to New Jersey, where a half-dozen religions and ethnic groups mingled, to New York, with its prosperous urban merchants and Hudson River manor lords, to Maryland and tiny Delaware, where southern traits mixed with brisk business instincts, the Middle Colonies identified more strongly with England than they did with each other.

Certainly that was true of Benjamin and William Franklin. They enjoyed every minute of the magnificent procession of brilliantly uniformed horse guards and nobles in splendid coaches that escorted the new King and Queen to the abbey. Houses along the royal route rented for a thousand guineas to give the wealthy few a chance to ogle. Others paid lesser amounts to peer from booths hastily hammered together by enterprising Londoners.

The front seats in the abbey cost ten guineas each and were distributed only to VIPs and their friends. Among these lucky few was William Franklin—a tribute to the handsome thirty-year-old's ability to ingratiate himself with men in power. William's far more famous father had to be content with a ticket for a streetside booth. The Franklins had been in England since 1757, representing the legislature of Pennsylvania in a dispute with the sons of the colony's founder, William Penn. Both had fallen in love with the Mother Country.

This was hardly surprising. Benjamin Franklin's experiments in electricity had placed him in the front rank of the gentlemen scientists of the age. His findings—above all the discovery that lightning and electricity were identical—had been printed in the proceedings of the Royal Society, England's premier scientific association. He had been made a member of this select body, and from the moment he came to England, the cultured and sophisticated members of English society had virtually adopted him. England's Oxford and Scotland's St. Andrew's universities gave him honorary doctorates. Oxford threw in a master of arts for William because he had assisted his father in many

TOP RIGHT *Martha Dandridge Custis was one of the richest widows in Virginia when she married George Washington in 1759. She had four children by Daniel Parke Custis, two of whom died in infancy. She and Washington were childless.*

experiments—notably the risky feat of flying a kite in a thunderstorm.

Forgotten today is another scientific feat that made Franklin almost as famous in England as his discoveries in electricity. In 1750 he published the first study of the amazing growth of America's population. The numbers in the thirteen colonies were doubling every twenty-five years. He concluded that in a century, there would be "more Englishmen" on the American side of the Atlantic—an idea that struck not a few important people in England as somewhat alarming.

All in all, England was a heady experience for a man who had begun life in 1706 as the son of a Boston soap and candle maker. It was equally satisfying for William. In London he met none of the social rebuffs he frequently encountered in provincial Philadelphia because he was illegitimate. No one has ever learned the identity of his mother. Franklin brought the boy up in his own household, to the not inconsiderable irritation of his formidable wife, Deborah.

The Franklins, like the Washingtons, originally hailed from Northampton, and the blood in their veins was pure English. But in the old country as in the new, they had been part of the laboring classes—in their case, mostly blacksmiths. Benjamin Franklin had risen far beyond this lowly status with a rare combination of genius and geniality.

ABOVE *This painting shows Benjamin Franklin when he was the chief spokesman for the American colonies in London. He also worked hard to win a 20 million-acre land grant to found the colony of Vandalia in Illinois.*

Apprenticed to his older brother James as a printer at the age of twelve, he decamped from Boston to Philadelphia at seventeen and soon started his own newspaper, *The Pennsylvania Gazette*. Next came his equally successful almanac, which he named for his imaginary editor, Poor Richard, and packed full of pithy sayings, many of them borrowed from previous collections. Appointed deputy postmaster general for the colonies, he overhauled the haphazard postal service, turning it into an efficient medium for continental communication—and producing a profit for the first time in its history. At forty-six he had made enough money to retire and indulge his interest in science, one of the approved pursuits of an eighteenth-century gentleman.

Politics came naturally to Franklin. He loved to play a part in various associations, though in most cases he shrewdly let others do the leading—and he had no illusions about how much he could accomplish. As Poor Richard noted in his 1758 almanac: "The first mistake of public business is the going into it." Franklin was more than content to be a man of influence. In this role, he soon found himself at odds with Thomas and Richard Penn, the arrogant sons of William Penn, the founder of Pennsylvania. As proprietors of the colony, the Penns owned huge swaths of the countryside. With a greed that made it clear they disdained their saintly father's Quaker faith, they instructed the governor, whom they appointed, to forbid the legislature to tax their lands.

The quarrel brought both Franklins to London to petition the Privy Council, the group of nobles who served as advisors to the King, and whose backing would win royal attention. The Penns, however, made sure that the president of the council, John Carteret, Earl Granville, was thoroughly prejudiced against the colony's ambassador. They did not have to try very hard. Granville was married to the sister of Thomas Penn's wife. When Franklin went to see the Earl, he got a ferocious lecture on who was running the empire.

"You Americans have wrong ideas on the nature of your constitution," Granville intoned. "The King is legislator for the colonies." That meant proprietors such as the Penns, who ruled in the King's name, had the final say on any and all laws.

Unintimidated by the noble lord, Franklin read him a lecture in return. "This is new doctrine to me. I always understood…that our laws were to be made by our colonial assemblies, to be presented indeed to the King for his royal assent. As the assemblies cannot make permanent laws without his assent, so neither can he make a law for them without theirs."

Lord Granville huffed that Franklin was "totally mistaken." Franklin bowed politely and went back to the rooms he had rented on Craven Street, just off the fashionable Strand, where he wrote down an exact account of the conversation. If the rest of the English nobility thought this way, the future of liberty for Pennsylvanians—and other Americans—was grim.

Liberty had been the bedrock of Franklin's creed for a long time. As a sixteen-year-old journalist writing under a pseudonym for his brother's Massachusetts newspaper, he described himself as a "mortal enemy of arbitrary government and unlimited power." His years in Pennsylvania, where the Quakers saw liberty as a gift of God that every man and woman had a right to exercise, had deepened and broadened his commitment to it.

The Penns, buoyed by Granville's rebuff, refused to negotiate with Franklin. It was one of the worst mistakes of their lives. Franklin hired Richard Jackson, an astute attorney who specialized in colonial law, and opened a publicity offensive. It began with a full-length book on the history of the government of Pennsylvania, which William Franklin researched and Jackson wrote. The most important thing about it was the motto on the title page, which was

RIGHT *Benjamin Franklin created this rattlesnake cartoon to urge the colonies to unite to fight the French and Indian War. The Americans revived it when the Revolution began.*

Benjamin Franklin's contribution: "Those who give up essential liberty, to preserve a little temporary safety, deserve neither liberty nor safety."

Simultaneously, Jackson lobbied (the word was already in active use—professional favor-seekers had been buttonholing MP's in Parliament's lobby for decades) on Franklin's behalf. Franklin's friends, who included Dr. John Pringle, Lord Bute's personal physician, also spoke up on his behalf at St. James's Palace. The coup de grace was a direct appeal to William Pitt himself. The Great Commoner sided emphatically with the Americans. The Penns were soon practically pleading for mercy, and in a final showdown before the chief justice of the King's Bench, they feebly surrendered all their objections and agreed to let their lands be taxed.

Franklin's victory added to his affection for England and deepened his conviction that Americans could play power politics as equals with the English. He saw England and her fecund American colonies as integral parts of an empire that would rule the world. This vision made him especially sensitive to men such as Lord Granville, who seemed to threaten harmony between England and America.

Franklin was almost as nettled by a British officer who published a letter claiming that American soldiers were responsible for most of the British defeats in the Seven Years War. Franklin asked his best friend, the printer William Strahan, publisher of one of the biggest newspapers in the realm, *The London Chronicle*, for a chance to respond.

Franklin compiled a veritable roll call of British defeats in the West Indies and elsewhere before Pitt took charge of the war. In all these disasters, not a single American participated. What a shame, Franklin said. "Our commanders would have been saved the labor of writing long apologies for their conduct. It might have been sufficient to say: 'Provincials were with us!' "

In a soothing final paragraph, Franklin maintained that most Americans admired the bravery of British regulars and that most British officers were willing to allow Americans "their share of merit." In fact, most regular army officers were delighted to discover "the children of Britain retain their native intrepidity to the third and fourth generations in the regions of America, together with that ardent love of liberty, and zeal in its defense, which in every age has distinguish'd their progenitors among the rest of mankind."

Capping his comfortable sense of British-American accord, Franklin used his influence to acquire for William the royal governorship of New Jersey. When he returned to America in the fall of 1762 to see his son installed in this prestigious post, Franklin told William Strahan that he was almost certain he would soon return to his beloved England and settle there "forever."

TOP LEFT *President of the Privy Council Lord Granville told Benjamin Franklin the King was the supreme legislator for the colonies. Franklin bluntly disagreed.*

Power to the Dearest Friend

After much bickering and prodding, George III finally persuaded the Duke of Newcastle and William Pitt to include Lord Bute in the government. He was made a secretary of state (there were two), giving him, in theory at least, power equal to Pitt's. Bute immediately began pressing to end the war with France as quickly as possible. Pitt was infuriated. British intelligence operatives, already the best in Europe, had warned him that the Spanish King had signed a secret compact with his Bourbon cousin in Paris and was preparing to enter the war. Pitt planned a preemptive strike on the Spanish treasure fleet on its annual voyage home, laden with the silver and gold of Peru and Mexico.

Irked by the Scotsman's interference in his plans, Pitt resigned from the cabinet. The news reverberated throughout the empire—especially in America, where Pitt was as popular as he was in London. A King who preferred a Scots nobleman named Stuart to Pitt, the man who had frequently described the American colonies as the capstone of his empire of liberty, could be suspected of being no friend of America—or of liberty.

BELOW *If there was a capital of liberty in pre-revolutionary America, it was Boston. This painting of King Street (now State Street) includes the Old State House, at that time the hated headquarters of His Majesty's Customs. The Boston Massacre took place in 1770 just east of the State House.*

Bute soon discovered that English politics was a rough game. A month after Pitt resigned, the Scotsman's coach was assailed by angry Londoners as he was en route to a dinner at the Guildhall. A barrage of mud covered the uniforms of the coachmen and footmen. Bodyguards hired to protect Bute fled, and the rioters began trying to cut loose his horses. Just in time, a phalanx of city constables fought their way to his rescue.

George III nevertheless pressed ahead with his plan to make Lord Bute his first or "prime" minister. He ousted the Duke of Newcastle, and Bute became First Lord of the Treasury, the usual post held by the leader of the government. Almost instantly, the London newspapers, egged on by Pitt's supporters, opened a ferocious attack on him. Cartoons displayed Bute in the Dowager Princess Augusta's bedchamber. A boot and a petticoat became symbols of the pair, who were frequently burned in effigy. Horace Walpole opined that Bute was more abused in twenty days than his father, Sir Robert Walpole, had been in twenty years as prime minister.

Compounding Bute's troubles, he found speaking for the government in the House of Commons an excruciating ordeal. In the eighteenth century, the House was not the stately chamber it is today. Members met in St. Stephen's Chapel, a remnant of the old palace of Westminster, where they were jammed together like passengers in steerage. The give-and-take was virtually face to face and as savage as the attacks in the press. Bute was neither quick enough nor tough enough to handle these brutal exchanges. He retreated into what Horace Walpole called "haughty ignorance."

Still George III heaped encouragement on his "dearest friend," and in 1763 they negotiated a peace with France and Spain. The Spanish had come into the war as Pitt predicted and had been thoroughly thrashed by British armies and fleets. The peace treaty infuriated the merchants and bankers of London, because it returned almost all the captured West Indian sugar islands

ABOVE LEFT *The peace treaty with France and Spain ending the Seven Years War deeply divided England. Many thought George III and his Prime Minister, Lord Bute, gave too many conquests back to England's traditional enemies.*

to France. These sun-baked sand spits, where black slaves were driven by overseers' whips from dawn to dusk to satisfy Europe's appetite for sweets, were considered far more valuable than the mainland colonies. Not a few Americans were dismayed by two other clauses of the treaty: Cuba, which several hundred Americans had died helping to capture in 1762, was returned to Spain along with the Philippines. Also, the French were permitted to continue fishing on Newfoundland's Grand Banks, competing with New England's sailors. William Pitt, ill and depressed, struggled to the House of Commons and denounced the treaty for three and a half hours.

George III had recruited a politician even more unscrupulous than the Duke of Newcastle to make sure the peace treaty was approved: cherubic, smiling Henry Fox. The patriot King, in his passion to support his dearest friend, had postponed his plans to purify British politics. Wearily he confessed: "We must call in bad men to govern bad men."

As paymaster of the forces, Fox had access to oceans of money. He let Pitt orate and then disbursed more than £25,000 in bribes to ram the peace treaty through the House of Commons by a vote of 319 to 65. George's mother, Augusta, is said to have crowed: "*Now* my son is King of England!" But her euphoria—and George's—was short-lived. Their dearest friend, Lord Bute, informed the stunned King that he wanted to resign.

When Bute rode to the opening of Parliament, his coach had again been

BELOW *The House of Commons met in cramped quarters in the eighteenth century. The chamber in St. Stephen's Chapel was sixty feet long, twenty-eight feet wide and thirty feet high. In a population of 8 million, only 215,000 males could vote.*

BRITISH LIBERTY

The British were proud of their tradition of liberty. Their favorite eighteenth-century song, more popular with people at large than "God Save the King," was "Rule Britannia," with its stirring line "Britons never never never shall be slaves." George III, in the days when he was being tutored by Lord Bute, obediently wrote essays in which he declared, "The pride, the glory of Britain, and the direct end of its Constitution, is political liberty."

A jasperware teapot by Wedgwood.

Englishmen boasted that liberty was making the country an industrial powerhouse. Inventions such as the spinning jenny were revolutionizing the production of cloth, and the steam engine was creating a new source of power. Hand in hand with new machines went a bold spirit of enterprise, which inspired manufacturers such as potter Josiah Wedgwood to build great companies. The leaders of these industries were enlightened men who often called for reforms in the government to bring order to the cities and improve the health and happiness of the millions of English who did not enjoy the nation's imperial prosperity.

But the English political system remained in the grip of the aristocracy. Out of a total population of 8 million, only 215,000 males could vote. Moreover, there were almost incredible imbalances between population and representation. The county of Middlesex, which included London, contained well over 1 million people. They returned eight members to Parliament, while Cornwall, with barely 100,000 country bumpkins, sent forty-four. Major cities—Manchester, Birmingham—had no representatives at all.

In the "pocket borough" of Gatton, there were only seven voters, in Tavistock, ten, and in St. Michael's, seven. On election day these gentlemen usually sold their votes to the highest bidder. Perhaps seventy MP's were returned by thirty-five "rotten boroughs," in which there were no voters whatsoever. The nobleman or merchant who owned the borough moved people into it on election day, gave them lavish amounts of food and drink and a few pounds and they cast their votes as directed. One historian has estimated that 6,000 voters elected enough members to compose a majority in Parliament.

To get an idea of the extent to which Parliament was a closed aristocratic corporation, ponder these statistics: More than 50 percent of those who sat in the House of Commons between 1734 and 1832 had a close blood relative in the Parliament immediately preceding them. There were, for instance, seventeen Townshends and thirteen Grenvilles during these years. Although a nobleman could not sit in the House of Commons, the rule applied only to the 184 peers who held a title. Brothers and sons of nobles could and did seek election in the people's chamber. Much of the time one in four members of the House of Commons was either a baronet (a rank below the highest peers but still hereditary) or the son of a living peer.

American visitors were appalled by the corruption of British elections. John Dickinson of Pennsylvania, in London studying law in 1754, told his father that the Duke of Newcastle, the prime minister in that year's election, had spent more than £1 million to keep himself in power. The opening bid for votes in one pocket borough was 200 guineas. Voters were required to swear that they had not been bribed. "Few people can...refrain from laughing while they take it [the oath]," Dickinson wrote.

Almost half the nation made less than £50 a year. Tens of thousands struggled for survival in gin-soaked city slums that were degrading beyond belief. There was a constant fear of the resentful poor. Between 1740 and 1775, England was shaken by no fewer than 159 major riots. There is little doubt that without the army, the country would have collapsed into anarchy. In 1757, when riots protesting a rise in the price of bread and other basic foods swept London and other cities, twenty regiments were deployed to restore order.

There was another reason to worry about British liberty. Forty miles from England across the Irish Sea lay a country

By the 1760s England was on its way to becoming an industrial powerhouse. Adam Smith's The Wealth of Nations, *the bible of capitalism, was published in 1776.*

Painter William Hogarth satirized the orgiastic eating and drinking in a so-called rotten borough on election day in the 1760s. By 1776 the price of a seat in Parliament had risen to £3,000, perhaps a half-million dollars in today's money.

of 6 million people living under a tyranny more absolute than anything inflicted by Catherine the Great of Russia or Frederick the Great of Prussia. The perpetrators of this tyranny were English. After the Irish chose the losing side in the Glorious Revolution of 1688, most of the nation's leaders were driven into exile, more or less decapitating the country. The Irish Parliament, controlled by England, voted a series of "penal laws" that denied Catholics the right to vote or to own land or any other kind of property worth more than £5. In 1719 the English Parliament issued a Declaratory Act that gave them the right to legislate for Ireland "in all cases whatsoever."

When Benjamin Franklin visited Ireland in 1771, he was appalled by how totally crushed the country was by the ruthless application of English power. "The appearances of general extreme poverty among the lower people are amazing," he wrote a Boston friend. "They live in wretched hovels of mud and straw, are clothed in rags and subsist chiefly on potatoes. Our New England farmers of the poorest sort are...princes when compared to them."

How could a nation supposedly devoted to liberty inflict such oppression on a neighboring people? That was a question asked by not a few Irishmen who came to England in search of a better life. One of the more brilliant of these exiles was Oliver Goldsmith. In the journalism he practiced between his poetry and plays, he gave English liberty a Celtic horselaugh. In one series of sketches, Goldsmith reported on England through the eyes of a Chinese philosopher who found "liberty is echoed in all their assemblies and thousands might be found ready to offer up their lives for the sound, though perhaps not one of all the number understands its meaning."

In his travels, the Chinese philosopher stops by a prison window to hear a debtor, a porter and a prison guard talking about the threat of an invasion from France. The jailed debtor says: "The greatest of my apprehensions is for our freedom; if the French should conquer, what will become of English liberty?" The two listeners, who make a living out of denying Englishmen their freedom, solemnly agree with him.

Later the Chinese philosopher meets an old soldier who has lost a leg fighting the French and is forced to beg for a living. The crippled warrior tells the story of his misfortunes, which include captures, beatings and starvation. But he cheerfully insists it was worthwhile, because it was in defense of English liberty. "O liberty, liberty, liberty! That is the property of every Englishman," he declaims as he lies in the gutter.

assailed by the London mob, and he had to be rescued by the Royal Horse Guards. He accused Pitt of plotting his assassination and moaned that this was only one of the many reasons for "the little time I get for sleep and the little I ever enjoy even when abed." He pleaded that his bowels were in a permanent state of agitation and that his life was literally at stake. To a Scottish friend he whined that "the Angel Gabriel could not at present govern this country."

The King asked another member of the cabinet, George Grenville, to be prime minister. Grenville was William Pitt's brother-in-law, but the connection seems only to have intensified his jealousy of the Great Commoner. Grenville was so hungry for power he accepted the job despite the King's insistence that Lord Bute would distribute the government's patronage and advise George III on all important matters.

Many Whig nobles refused to tolerate Bute's attempt to rule from "behind the curtain." They saw it as a threat to Parliament's right to challenge the King's ministers about the government's policies in open debate. George III, on the other hand, thought he had found the perfect solution to his kingship. He had his "dearest friend" to give him advice on everything—"what few princes can boast of except myself." He spoke of Grenville and the other cabinet ministers with total contempt. "I shall…without regret change my tools whenever they act contrary to my service," he wrote Bute on April 14, 1763. George was on the royal road to arbitrary power, blissfully ignoring that old saw about the highways to hell being paved with good intentions.

The opposition turned to John Wilkes, a dissolute member of Parliament with a reputation for recklessness, and gave him money to start a newspaper. Soon *The North Briton* was on the streets. The title was a common term for Scots, making it a gibe at Bute. The paper relentlessly attacked "the Scotch favorite."

In issue number 45 of *The North Briton*, Wilkes's vituperation reached a climax. He accused George III of lying when he said the treaty of peace was good for the country and declared the treaty had been approved only after massive bribery. This meant the Scotch favorite was still in control of the government and the ministers were "tools of corruption and despotism."

An infuriated George III demanded that Wilkes be prosecuted for seditious libel. In the eighteenth century, it was considered a crime to attack the King in the press, on the grounds that such writing

TOP LEFT *Satirizing Lord Bute (pronounced "boot"), George III's favorite, was a popular British pastime. Glasses and mugs shaped like boots sold briskly. Large paper boots were burned in public.*

LEFT *Henry Fox reportedly spent £25,000 in bribes on George III's behalf to persuade Parliament to approve the peace treaty ending the Seven Years War.*

undermined public order and amounted to treason. Prime Minister Grenville, eager to please his sovereign, went all out. He obtained a general warrant, which entitled the government to investigate anyone suspected of being involved in the publication and distribution of *The North Briton*. Master printers, compositors and booksellers were dragged from their beds in the middle of the night, and their houses were ransacked for evidence. Wilkes himself was arrested and confined to the Tower of London.

The metropolis was outraged. General warrants had been a favorite device of the ousted Stuart Kings. Such tactics could be justified only when the country was fighting a war or investigating a plot to overthrow the government. Wilkes's friends procured a writ of habeas corpus, which restored him to freedom. They took his case before a judge, who declared general warrants illegal and ruled that a member of Parliament could not be arrested for libel in the

BELOW *John Wilkes launched the newspaper* The North Briton *to attack George III's policies. The King ordered him tried for seditious libel. "Wilkes and Liberty!" became the cry of London's mob. Wilkes was financed by William Pitt's wealthy brother-in-law, Lord Temple.*

first place. A huge crowd had assembled outside the courtroom. When Wilkes walked out a free man, they sent up a roar that echoed through the British empire: "Wilkes and Liberty!"

Retiring to France to escape the ruckus he had started, Wilkes met Madame Pompadour, mistress of King Louis XV. She expressed amazement that he had been able to abuse the royal family in print and asked: "How far does liberty of the press extend in England?"

"That is exactly what I'm trying to find out!" Wilkes said.

He found out a few months later, when the House of Commons expelled him for seditious libel and the Court of the King's Bench found him guilty of the same charge and ordered his arrest. Wilkes chose to stay in France and enjoy further conversations with Madame Pompadour. He remained a hero to the people of London. When the public hangman attempted to burn a copy of number 45 of *The North Briton* at the Royal Exchange, a huge mob shouting "Wilkes and Liberty!" attacked him and the sheriff and his deputies, putting them to headlong flight. Instead of *The North Briton*, the crowd burned a gigantic effigy of a boot and a petticoat, restating their hatred of Bute—and their mounting dislike of their patriot King.

American Echoes

Nowhere in the empire was the struggle between George III and Pitt, the supposedly malign influence of Bute and its dramatization by John Wilkes followed with more fascination than in America. One of the least understood aspects of the American Revolution is how closely the colonies and England were linked by the written word. London newspapers were rushed from the presses to ships departing for Boston, New York, Philadelphia and Charleston. For those who did not care to pay transatlantic prices, American papers swiftly excerpted and reprinted the lead stories.

Interest in the uproar over general warrants was especially intense in Boston, where the royal government had advised Chief Justice Thomas Hutchinson that writs of assistance, the customs-service version of general warrants, were legal and could be enforced. James Otis began writing a defiant pamphlet, *The Rights of the British Colonies Asserted and Proved*, which he would publish in 1764. But before Americans realized the full significance of the Wilkes imbroglio, they were distracted by an upheaval on their frontier.

Throughout the French and Indian War, North America's Indians had divided their allegiance between England and France. The Iroquois of New York were Britain's allies, which inclined almost every other tribe in the East to side with the French. No one fought wars with more savagery or had more imperial pretensions than this proud confederacy of six "nations." The Iroquois claimed hegemony over distant tribes such as the Delaware of Pennsylvania and the Shawnee of Ohio, which they enforced by dispatching massive war parties that wiped out whole villages.

On both sides, the Europeans had gained the allegiance of the Indians with gifts of guns, ammunition, blankets, woolen skirts and shirts, kettles and hatchets, hoes for their farms, and jewelry that both Indian men and women liked to wear. Over the course of 150 years, the Indians had become dependent on these commodities. Most no longer had any enthusiasm for wearing clothing made from animal skins; they had largely forgotten how to hunt with bows and arrows.

One of Prime Minister George Grenville's passions was economy. In this respect, he was echoing George III, who had nightmares over the £133 million British national debt. General Jeffery Amherst, the British commander-in-chief in America, was well aware of this worry. He decided to demonstrate that unlike most generals, who specialized in soaking the government, he too could save money. He announced that one of the fruits of victory would be the elimination of presents to the Indians—both the Iroquois and the Shawnee, the Ottawa, and other Canadian and western tribes who had sided with the French. There was no longer a need to purchase any Indian's friendship.

Numerous Americans, in particular the astute northern superintendent of Indian affairs, Sir William Johnson, urged Amherst not to eliminate the presents. They understood that for the Indians, presents were more than mere bribery for services in war. Presents represented proof of a "chain of friendship"

"THE ATLANTIC WAS A GREAT HIGHWAY BY THE MIDDLE OF THE EIGHTEENTH CENTURY. THE ENGLISH AND AMERICANS SENT EACH OTHER BOOKS AND READ EACH OTHER'S PAMPHLETS. ALL SORTS OF CORRESPONDENCE SHUTTLED TO AND FRO."

Colin Bonwick
Professor of
American Studies,
Keele University

between them and the English. To eliminate these gifts was a hostile act—compounded by the fact that the Indians could seldom buy such items themselves. Their only source of income was the fur trade, which was difficult and uncertain.

Many Indians were already disturbed by the flood of settlers moving into the so-called "backcountry"—the western parts of New York, Pennsylvania, Virginia and the Carolinas. Many of these newcomers were unruly, combative Scots and Irish from the borderlands of Scotland and England and from the province of Ulster, where the once-prosperous linen trade had been ruined by laws favoring English manufacturers. Clashes between these settlers and neighboring Indians were frequent and alarming. Now the newcomers eyed the vast region between the Allegheny Mountains and the Mississippi that the expulsion of the French had opened to them. More than a few Indian leaders had begun to fear encroachment on these prime hunting grounds. The abrupt cessation of presents gave these chiefs an opportunity to preach hatred of the white man and call upon the Indians to unite for the first time in an all-out war to drive the whites back to the seacoast.

Historians have called this upheaval Pontiac's Rebellion, but the Ottawa chief whose name survives at General Motors was only one of a number of war chiefs and prophets who spread the flame of revolt through the forests and along the rivers of the West. With stunning ferocity, the Indians launched

BELOW *Quaker William Penn negotiated with chiefs of the Lenni-Lenape, Susquehannock and Shawnee Indian tribes to found the colony of Pennsylvania. The French philosopher Voltaire called it "the only treaty never sworn to [Quakers do not take oaths] and never broken." Few other treaties with the Indians achieved this status.*

coordinated attacks on British forts and American settlers, spreading a thousand-mile swath of terror and slaughter from Canada to the forks of the Ohio. Hundreds of British soldiers and defenseless backcountry settlers died. The stunned Amherst found himself with a mobile reserve of fewer than 600 highland Scots to rescue the two outposts that had survived the onslaught, Fort Pitt and Detroit.

Fortunately, Amherst had a brilliant field commander in his employ, the Swiss-born Colonel Henry Bouquet. Marching to relieve Fort Pitt, Bouquet was attacked by 700 to 1,000 Shawnee and Seneca near a western Pennsylvania creek called Bushy Run. Faking a retreat, he tempted the Indians to emerge from their forest cover, then turned his Highlanders on them with fixed bayonets. The Indians left at least 300 dead on the field, and Pontiac's Rebellion never recovered from the blow. A shaky peace returned to the "Middle Ground"—the stretch of the frontier where whites and Indians mingled. The calm was soon bolstered by hasty promises to resume the giving of presents.

News of this tumult reached London in July 1763. The Grenville ministry, ignoring the way Amherst had triggered the bloodshed, blamed it on the backcountry settlers' greed for Indian land. The government responded with the Proclamation of 1763, which declared that henceforth, no American would be allowed to locate west of the Alleghenies. Only licensed fur traders would be permitted beyond the mountains, and even they were supposed to conduct their business under the severe eyes of British commissaries at the various forts, to make sure fair prices were paid to the Indians.

ABOVE *In 1763 Pontiac, an Ottawa chief, united many tribes in an all-out war on the whites. The Indians were enraged because the British had ended the 100-year-old tradition of presents of guns and cloth. Nine British forts were overrun and their garrisons slaughtered. Isolated settlers were murdered. Fort Detroit, shown here under siege, was among the few strongholds that survived.*

Some historians have opined that this attempt to confine the colonists to the eastern side of the Alleghenies started the American Revolution. It certainly did not please the Irish and Scots of the backcountry, who had their own contentious definition of liberty—born of the strife-ridden worlds from which they had emigrated. But most Americans reacted like George Washington, to whom the Virginia legislature had promised thousands of acres of land west of the mountains in return for his services in the French and Indian War. Virginia maintained that its territory extended westward "from sea to sea"—from the Atlantic to the Pacific.

Washington considered the Proclamation of 1763 "a temporary expedient to quiet the minds of the Indians." He and other Virginians proceeded with plans to form the Mississippi Company and purchase 2.5 million acres from the western tribes, once they had calmed down and accepted the inevitability of American migration. But the bureaucrats in London, ignorant of America's vast distances, took the proclamation more seriously. To keep peace on the frontier, they decided to expand the British army in North America to 7,500 men and station them in a long chain of western forts. The cost of paying, feeding and supplying these soldiers would be £320,000 a year.

The money had to come from somewhere—and Britons were already complaining mightily about how much they paid in taxes. It seemed perfectly reasonable to George Grenville and George III that the Americans should pay some, if not all, of the cost of their "defence." The Americans saw the matter in a somewhat different light. With the pugnacious Scots and Irish borderers in their backcountry and every man on the continent between the ages of sixteen and sixty in the militia and subject to military service, they were perfectly capable of defending themselves against the Indians, whom they outnumbered 20 to 1. The French and Spanish had been reduced to comparative ciphers in North America. The Americans did not want or need these British troops. Was there another more sinister reason for posting this standing army in their midst?

Debate on that question might have been confined to a few worrywarts—if Prime Minister Grenville had figured out some way to raise the money without resorting to two explosive words—"revenue" and "tax." He began with the Sugar Act of 1764. In the preamble, the prime minister frankly stated its purpose: "That a Revenue be raised in Your Majesty's Dominions in America for defraying the expenses of defending, protecting, and securing same."

The new law threatened to destroy—or at least make much less profitable—the business of making rum. In a seemingly reasonable gesture, Grenville lowered the duty on molasses imported from the French or Dutch West Indies from six cents to three cents a gallon. But he announced a new determination to collect this lower charge. A Royal Navy squadron was established at Halifax, Nova Scotia, and empowered to search and seize ships engaged in smuggling. Captains and merchants were required to post bonds and produce carefully detailed invoices of their cargoes. Since few had bothered to pay the previous duty, the new law was a financial shock to the owners of booming distilleries in Massachusetts, Rhode Island, New York and Pennsylvania.

Massachusetts immediately dispatched a protest to London, claiming the Sugar Act "violated the right of levying taxes conferred by the Charter" of the colony. Each colony had a charter—a sort of public contract—with the crown that had been negotiated in its early years. New Yorkers were even more vehement than Massachusetts. In a petition to Parliament, the colony's assembly declared that there could be "no liberty, no happiness, no security" if Parliament had the right to raise money this way. From taxing trade, it was only a short step to taxing land, houses and every other kind of property.

These blunt protests irritated many English officials. The Board of Trade huffily reported to the King that "the acts and resolutions of the legislature of Great Britain are treated with the most indecent respect" by the Americans. Prime Minister Grenville, obsessed with the Treasury's bottom line, ignored these warning signals.

Sons of Liberty

The Sugar Act's duties were expected to raise only £45,000—a long way from the £325,000 that it would cost to maintain a 7,500-man army in America. So, early in 1765, Prime Minister Grenville introduced a stamp tax. Few people saw anything wrong with this idea. Almost everyone in England paid stamp taxes on wills, mortgages, licenses, college diplomas, playing cards and many other items. Stamps were part of the British excise system, which employed a small army of tax collectors to raise almost half of the money that fueled the British imperial state.

Benjamin Franklin, speaking for Pennsylvania, earnestly advised against a stamp tax for America. Pontiac's Rebellion had brought him back to England, determined to oust the Penns for their refusal to vote funds to defend Pennsylvania's frontier. The agents of all the other American colonies joined Franklin in opposing the tax. Grenville ignored them. In Parliament friends of America, most of them followers of William Pitt, echoed the agents. Many urged that the colonists should be allowed to tax themselves. Others said the tax would be an unfair burden on the colonies.

This remark severely annoyed Charles Townshend, the playboy grandnephew of the Duke of Newcastle, known for his tendency to make speeches when drunk. "Champagne Charlie," as he was sometimes called, leaped to his feet and made an incredibly condescending attack on the colonists' patriotism. "And now will these Americans, children planted by our care, nourished up by our indulgence until they are grown to a degree of strength and opulence and protected by our arms, will they grudge to contribute their mite to relieve us from the heavy burden which we lie under?"

Up sprang Irish-born Colonel Isaac Barré, who had fought at Quebec and lost an eye in that fierce clash. He answered Townshend in words that would soon resound through the American colonies even more loudly than "Wilkes and Liberty."

ABOVE LEFT **A tax stamp manufactured for the Stamp Act.**

"They planted by your care? No! Your oppressions planted 'em in America. They fled your tyranny to a then uncultivated and inhospitable country—where they exposed themselves to all the hardships to which human nature is liable, and among others to the cruelties of a savage foe...

"They nourished by your indulgence? They grew by your neglect of 'em: as soon as you began to care about 'em, that care was exercised by sending persons to rule over 'em in one department or another, who were...sent to spy out their liberty, to misrepresent their actions and to prey upon 'em: men whose behavior on many occasions has caused the blood of these sons of liberty to recoil within them...

"They protected by your arms? They have nobly taken up arms in your defence, have exerted a valour amidst their constant and laborious industry for the defence of a country whose frontier, while drench'd in blood, its interior parts have yielded up all its little savings to your emolument...Remember I this day told you so, that same spirit of freedom which actuated these people at first, will accompany them still..."

Grenville did not even bother to answer Barré. Instead, he orated about England's £133 million deficit. Parliament beat down opposition motions by overwhelming numbers—245 to 49 on one vote. The "readings" given the fifty-five resolutions of the Stamp Act were a joke. It became law with scarcely another murmur of opposition.

Even the colonial agents, including Benjamin Franklin, saw no cause for serious alarm in a stamp tax for America. With sighs of resignation they told their constituents they would have to live with it. All the agents accepted Grenville's offer to let them appoint the men who would fill the lucrative post of stamp commissioner in their respective colonies. They would be in charge of distributing the stamps throughout each colony. In return they would collect a nice percentage of the total fees. Franklin got the job for one of his oldest friends, John Hughes.

Amazement, not to say consternation, was general when reports reached London that Americans did not like the Stamp Act. Beginning in the early summer of 1765, as a trickle that was hardly more noticeable than a wavelet splashing against a Thames dock, the news soon assumed the proportions of a roaring tidal wave.

American Voices

The first response came from Virginia. On May 29, 1765, a backcountry firebrand named Patrick Henry introduced a series of resolutions in the House of Burgesses that bluntly denied Parliament's power to levy the stamp tax.

RIGHT *Irish-born Colonel Isaac Barré christened American protesters "Sons of Liberty" in a historic speech in Parliament. He lost an eye fighting the French at Quebec.*

"Caesar had his Brutus, Charles I his Cromwell," Henry reportedly roared. "May George III profit from their example." Although we are unsure of Henry's exact words, Thomas Jefferson, a law student in Williamsburg at the time, was among the spectators and later recalled that Henry seemed to speak "as Homer wrote."

Cries of "Treason! Treason!" from older members of the House of Burgesses forced Henry to apologize and affirm his loyalty to the King. The assembly passed all except one of the resolutions, affirming their refusal to be taxed without their consent. The "Virginia Resolves" were published in newspapers throughout the colonies. General Thomas Gage, commander of the British army in America, considered them "a signal for a general outcry over the continent."

In Massachusetts, resistance swiftly went from outcry to action. Boston had a history of mob violence that almost matched London's. In 1747, protesting the attempt by a British warship to impress citizens for involuntary service in the Royal Navy, a mob had taken over the town and forced the royal governor to retreat to Castle William, an island fortress guarding the entrance to the town's harbor. Modern Americans—and modern Englishmen—regard all kinds of mob violence with abhorrence. In eighteenth-century England, where only a tiny percentage of the people could vote, some mobs had been given a shadowy legitimacy. Bostonians liked to quote a 1737 speech in Parliament that declared: "The people seldom or never assemble in any riotous or tumultuous manner unless they are oppressed." Even the great English jurist, William Blackstone, had declared that there were times when "the voice of society itself" had a right to be heard in the form of a mob when there was no "other tribunal to resort to."

Why Americans loathed the Stamp Act can be glimpsed in a resolution passed during a town meeting of John Adams's village of Braintree: "Considering the scarcity of money…the execution of [this] act for a short space of time would dreign [drain] the Country of Cash, strip multitudes of the poorer people of all their cash and Reduce them to absolute beggary." More than forty Massachusetts towns subscribed to this statement.

The act specified that payment had to be in "hard money," which almost doubled its cost in many colonies where paper money was discounted against the pound sterling. Worse, because the balance of trade was heavily in England's favor, hard money was frequently impossible to find. Worst of all, anyone who violated the Stamp Act would be tried in an admiralty court, which meant there would be no jury. That was the policy of the British excise system, and the reason excisemen were feared and hated throughout England.

On August 14, 1765, people going to work in Boston found two large objects hanging from branches of a stately old elm tree on Orange (now Washington) Street. One was an effigy of Andrew Oliver, who had been appointed stamp commissioner for Massachusetts in addition to his well-paid job as secretary of the province. The other object was a huge boot. Some historians have claimed that the boot proved how out of touch the colonists were with England, since Bute had long since resigned as prime minister. On the contrary, the footwear (which was said to have a "new Grenville sole") showed how closely Bostonians were in touch with London, where rumors still swirled that Bute ruled George III "behind the curtain."

RIGHT *Patrick Henry's denunciation of George III for the Stamp Act marked the emergence of this backwoods lawyer as a major spokesman. He had been a member of the House of Burgesses only nine days when he rose to defend his country's "dying liberty." This is a very romantic version of the scene.*

The sheriff arrived on Orange Street with an order from Andrew Oliver's brother-in-law, Chief Justice Hutchinson, to take down the objects. The growing crowd advised the sheriff not to obey the order if he wanted to keep breathing. The crowd swelled to 5,000 people—almost one-third of Boston's population. At the end of the day, a procession chanting, "Liberty, property and no stamps" carried Oliver's effigy to Fort Hill, near his opulent house, where the protesters beheaded and burned it. Along the way they paused to demolish a building where it was rumored Oliver planned to distribute his stamps. Next the mob decided to look for—and possibly demolish—Oliver. They broke into his house, from which he had prudently fled, and wrecked the place.

The next day Andrew Oliver resigned as stamp commissioner. Not satisfied, crowds continued to seethe and storm around Boston. The leaders were a group of small businessmen known as the "Loyal Nine," who were friendly with Samuel Adams, Boston's tax collector. Adams' accounts were £8,000 in arrears, which did him no harm with the city's voters. Playing favorites on the city's tax rolls was a longstanding way of building political popularity in Boston.

On August 25 Jonathan Mayhew, the minister of the West Church, preached on St. Paul's letter to the Galatians: "I would they were even cut off which trouble you. For brethren, ye have been called unto liberty." A great many Bostonians considered this sermon a benediction on their policy of selective violence.

A day later, a mob attacked the homes of several officials connected to the customs service. The protesters debated whether to assault Governor Francis Bernard's house but decided against it because it would be rebuilt with public

ABOVE *American protests against the Stamp Act were numerous and noisy. In New York rioters demolished the house of a British officer who said he would cram the stamps down American throats at the point of his sword.*

money—their money. Instead, they focused on the man who seemed equally responsible for the hated stamps, writs of assistance and the customs-house clampdown, Chief Justice Hutchinson.

Raw envy added to the mob's rage. The Oliver–Hutchinson clan controlled a baker's dozen of the best government jobs in the colony. There was a long English tradition of the people retaliating against those who "rioted in luxury and power" with riotous action in a more violent style.

On the evening of August 26, 1765, the mob stormed Hutchinson's house. Working through the night with ferocious determination, the rioters smashed doors to splinters, tore the wainscoting off the walls, chopped down the fruit trees in the garden, flung into the street the manuscript of a history of the colony that Hutchinson had been writing for years, destroyed or stole all the books in his library and made off with every piece of furniture, crockery and clothing in the place, plus £900 sterling. Dawn found them trying to tear off the roof. Another hour of darkness and they would have leveled the building. "Such ruins were never seen in America," Hutchinson wailed in a letter to an English friend.

Hutchinson appeared in court the next day, distraught to the point of hysteria, declaiming that he and his family had lost everything but the clothes on their backs. He swore that he had never encouraged the Stamp Act and that he had done everything in his power to persuade the royal government to drop the idea. Governor Bernard, having sought refuge in Castle William in the harbor, wrote bitterly to General Gage, lamenting that he "had no force to oppose" the mob. Cities of this era—including London—had no police departments, beyond part-time constables. They relied on the army to deal with mob action.

Boston's violent protest against the Stamp Act ignited similar crowds in other American cities, from Newport to Charleston. Inspired by Isaac Barré's speech, they called themselves "Sons of Liberty." In Newport, the stamp men and those who supported them had their houses wrecked. In New York, Major Thomas James, commander of the 130-man British garrison at Fort George on the tip of Manhattan, declared he would cram the stamps down American throats at the point of his sword. A mob of 2,000 sacked James's elegant house and burned in effigy Acting Governor Cadwallader Colden, an American. Colden found that "the mob…openly threatened to destroy every thing I had in both town and

ABOVE RIGHT *Even teapots were used to express American defiance of the Stamp Act.*

RIGHT *In many cities, stamp commissioners were hung in effigy from local Liberty Trees. Several had their houses demolished.*

We the Ladys
of Edenton do
hereby Solemnly
Engage not to Conform
that Pernicious Custom
of Drinking Tea, or that we the
aforesaid Ladys will not promote y wear
of any Manufacture from England
untill such time that all Acts
which tend to Enslave this our
Native Country shall be Repealed

AN ENGLISHMAN LOOKS AT AMERICA

No people in the world live more comfortably than the people of America. They are the happiest farmers. The climate is good and hitherto the taxes have been easy. The provisions [food] are under half the value [price] of England. I thought it happy the tenants of this country don't know it. It would soon depopulate England.

Richard Oswald, testifying before Parliament in 1766

LEFT *This British cartoon satirized a group of women in Edenton, North Carolina, who resolved not to drink British tea or wear British-made clothes until all anti-American legislation was repealed by Parliament. Many other groups of American women gathered to spin cloth and issue statements encouraging American resistance.*

TOP RIGHT *This American cartoon graphically expressed local opinion of the Stamp Act.*

country." He decided it might be best to surrender the stamps to the Sons of Liberty, who promptly burned them.

In Virginia the stamp commissioner was George Mercer, a close friend and former aide of Colonel George Washington. The colonel learned that Mercer had scarcely gotten off a ship from London when a crowd assailed him. "The concourse of people," Governor Francis Fauquier later observed, "I would call a mob did I not know it was chiefly if not altogether composed of gentlemen of property." Mercer was soon persuaded to resign as stamp commissioner. Colonel Washington remained aloof from this upheaval, although he made it clear that he considered the Stamp Act "an unconstitutional method of taxation."

In a letter to a London merchant, Washington commented that England would soon regret the measure because it would force Americans to dispense with a great many British luxuries to pay it—and make them realize that the "necessaries of life" could be found in America. Struggling to pay for his purchases in England with the low prices he was getting for his tobacco, Washington was changing Mount Vernon from a tobacco plantation to a farm raising a variety of crops that he could sell locally.

In Philadelphia, Stamp Commissioner John Hughes wrote to Benjamin Franklin: "You are now from letter to letter to suppose each may be the last you will receive from your old friend." Hughes told the astonished Franklin he was barricaded inside his house, with anti-stamp rioters raging on his doorstep. Franklin was even more dismayed by a letter from his former partner, David Hall, who was now editing *The Pennsylvania Gazette*. Hall told him that a great many people had "imbibed the notion" that Franklin had a hand in framing the Stamp Act.

At least as unnerving was a letter from Franklin's wife, Deborah, telling him that she had made one room of their house into a "magazin" and summoned her brother and a cousin to "fech a gun or two" and help her defend the place. Finally came a letter from Franklin's son, William, the royal governor of New Jersey, complaining that the man who had been appointed stamp commissioner in that colony had resigned before the slightest threat was made against him. William went on to denounce the "outrageous conduct" of the Boston mob—an omen of coming trouble between father and son.

In many cities, groups who called themselves Daughters of Liberty appeared in tandem with the men. In Providence, Rhode Island, seventeen young women met to begin spinning and weaving cloth. They hoped their homespun wares would replace imported English wool and brocades. The idea proved so popular that for their second meeting, they had to move to the courthouse, where they set up a veritable factory. Similar groups sprang up in other colonies.

Meanwhile, in response to a call from Massachusetts, a Stamp Act Congress met in New York. Composed of twenty-seven delegates from nine colonies, it included a few firebrands, such as Boston's James Otis and

Charleston's Christopher Gadsden. They elected conservative Timothy Ruggles of Massachusetts as chairman and debated the problem of what to say to London on behalf of all the colonies. They finally produced a set of mild resolutions that reiterated Americans' refusal to be taxed without their consent. Perhaps more important, the Congress rejected sending American representatives to Parliament. Most agreed the distance made it impractical—and their relative handful of delegates would never be able to muster a majority.

On November 1, 1765, the day the Stamp Act was supposed to go into effect, not a single stamp commissioner was in business anywhere in America. The Americans announced that not a ship would sail to England from their ports nor would any British ships be welcomed until the act was repealed. In Virginia, when a merchant named Archibald Ritchie declared he was going to send several cargoes of wheat to London, more than 400 Sons of Liberty assembled outside his house and soon persuaded him to change his mind.

As factories laid off workers in England, the British began learning the hard way what George Washington had predicted in the letter to his London merchant—that the Stamp Act was going to cost them far more in trade than it could ever produce in revenue. For the time being, the retired colonel continued to remain aloof from the struggle, concentrating on trying to make his plantation profitable. But Colonel Washington read the newspapers, and there is little doubt that he was wholly in sympathy with his fellow Virginians in their fierce determination to defend their liberty.

Back from the Brink

George III saw America's violent resistance to the Stamp Act from a somewhat personal viewpoint. He deplored the upheaval, but it was a heaven-sent opportunity to get rid of George Grenville. The King had grown to loathe his pompous prime minister for several reasons. Grenville had forced him to stop consulting Lord Bute and had developed a habit of lecturing the King as if he were a six-year-old. Swallowing his previous denunciations of Pitt, George III tried to persuade the Great Commoner to form a government. But Pitt had begun a sad slide into physical illness and mental depression, and the King had to settle for one of his followers, Charles Watson-Wentworth, the thirty-five-year-old Marquess of Rockingham, one of the richest men in England.

Young Rockingham saw himself as merely holding down the job until Pitt recovered his health. A poor public speaker, the Marquess was far better known for his thoroughbred horses, which won prizes at Newmarket, England's premier racetrack, nearly every year. Besides his money and popularity, his chief asset was a brilliant Irishman, Edmund Burke, whom he brought into Parliament and hired as his private secretary.

With Burke at his elbow, Rockingham made it his first order of business to

"BRITISH ACTIONS— NOT JUST IN AMERICA, BUT ALSO IN IRELAND, THE WEST INDIES AND IN ENGLAND ITSELF— CONTRIBUTED TO THE COLONISTS' CONCLUSION THAT TO REMAIN UNDER THE CROWN WOULD BE TO ACCEPT FOR THEMSELVES AND THEIR CHILDREN THE STATUS OF THE OPPRESSED IRISH."

*Pauline Maier
Professor of History,
Massachusetts Institute
of Technology, School
of Humanities*

TOP LEFT **This British label advertised Virginia tobacco. The Stamp Act boycott cost British merchants millions of pounds.**

A COAT OF TAR AND FEATHERS

Sons of Liberty sometimes resorted to tarring and feathering loyalists who supported the King. The punishment went back to the Middle Ages. It was used in the navy of King Richard the Lionhearted in 1191. The victim was stripped and coated with hot tar, then a bushel of feathers was dumped on him. British mobs used this punishment to intimidate people they feared or disliked, such as tax collectors. Bailiffs who tried to arrest people for debt were sometimes tarred and feathered and taken in a wheelbarrow to the Strand, where they were tied to a Maypole. In Boston, the British also resorted to this unpleasant national pastime. Early in 1775, the soldiers of the 47th Regiment tarred and feathered a peddler who had tried to buy guns from them. They marched him through the streets accompanied by a fifer and drummer playing the Rogue's March—a song traditionally used to escort prostitutes out of town.

These British cartoons look with disapproval on the American adoption of this old national custom. Top left, a tarred and feathered victim is hauled around town in an open cart. Below that is a look at the sort of protest riot that led to the application of the unwelcome pelt. At the right, "Paying the Exciseman" shows five Bostonians pouring tea down the throat of a tarred and feathered tax collector. On the Liberty Tree the Stamp Act hangs upside down. The hot tar could inflict third-degree burns. Victims often took weeks to recover from the ordeal.

repeal the Stamp Act. The betting in London's coffeehouses was heavily against him. Grenville and his followers were rampaging around the city denouncing the Americans. The newspapers were full of snide remarks about selfish, greedy colonists who refused to pay their share of the empire's taxes.

When Parliament reconvened in December 1765, the ousted Grenville immediately introduced a resolution to declare the Americans in rebellion. Several prominent MPs, including two members of the cabinet, supported him. Rockingham managed to stall the motion and sent an emergency call to William Pitt. Almost crippled by gout, Pitt hobbled into Parliament and gave one of the greatest speeches of his career. He declared that he "rejoiced that America has resisted" the Stamp Act. "Three millions of people, so dead to all feelings of liberty as to voluntarily submit to being slaves, would have been fit instruments to make slaves of the rest of us." The Stamp Act, Pitt thundered, had to be repealed "absolutely, totally and immediately."

With Grenville silenced, Edmund Burke decided that Parliament needed information. "Ignorance of American affairs," Burke said later, "had misled Parliament. Knowledge alone could bring it into the right road." At his urging, Rockingham summoned a parade of witnesses to the bar of the House of Commons. Fugitive stamp commissioners, including George Washington's friend George Mercer, testified. London merchants and experts from the Board of Trade told members how much money England made from her exports to America— which the Americans were now boycotting. None of these earnest witnesses seemed to be making much of an impression—until Burke summoned Benjamin Franklin.

Galvanized by the letters from his wife and other Philadelphians, Franklin had been working night and day to support the push for repeal. He had published a barrage of articles in newspapers, refuting various British critics with a nice mixture of facts and sarcasm. One irate Briton had even sneered at the American fondness for Indian corn. Franklin wondered how a man could denounce something he had never tasted. "But why should that hinder you writing upon it?" he asked. "Have you not written even on politics?"

When he was invited to testify, Franklin made sure his performance would have a climactic impact. With the help of several Rockingham supporters, he drew up and rehearsed a list of questions and answers that would refute the Stamp Act once and for all. There would of course be questions from George Grenville and his followers, and from other hostile members, but Franklin was willing to take his chances with them.

On February 13, 1766, Franklin stepped to the bar—a horizontal piece of wood that blocked passage into the well of the House of Commons—and fielded 174 questions, 89 of them unfriendly. With the help of a merchant

ABOVE *Stamp Act protesters sometimes hoisted stamp commissioners or their defenders aloft on liberty poles. Riots in Boston touched off a wave of similar disturbances in other cities. Most commissioners hastily resigned. Only in Georgia did one attempt to officiate. He lasted two weeks. Parliament repealed the act on March 18, 1766.*

RIGHT *Adding to America's Stamp Act woes was an economic slump following the end of the French and Indian War. The* Pennsylvania Journal *summed up the state of things in this glum headline.*

BELOW *Boston's Sons and Daughters of Liberty tried to punish merchants who ignored the boycott against trading with England.*

The·TIMES are Dreadful, Dismal Doleful Dolorous, and DOLLAR-LESS.

WILLIAM JACKSON, an IMPORTER; at the BRAZEN HEAD, North Side of the TOWN-HOUSE, and Opposite the Town-Pump, in Corn-hill, BOSTON.

It is defired that the SONS and DAUGHTERS of LIBERTY, would not buy any one thing of him, for in fo doing they will bring Difgrace upon themfelves, and their Pofterity, for ever and ever, AMEN.

from Coventry, which had been hard hit by the American boycott, he first cleared up the misconception that Americans paid no taxes. He recited a long list of taxes on houses and land; on licenses for all professions; on trades and businesses; on wine, rum and other spirits.

Another friendly member asked Franklin, speaking as deputy postmaster general, to comment on the distribution of the proposed stamps. He replied that the act was not only unjust; it was completely impractical. America was a country of vast distances. In the backcountry, people received no mail and could not get stamps. They could not marry, draw their wills, or buy or sell property without making long journeys, "spending perhaps three or four pounds, that the Crown might get sixpence."

Rockingham's supporters asked Franklin to tell the House what he knew about America's increasing population and how much the colonies imported from England. He chose to dwell on how many men in America between sixteen and sixty could bear arms—300,000. As for imports, Pennsylvania alone spent £500,000 a year on British goods. The implicit point was clear: a war with America would be dangerous—and costly.

On and on the questions and answers went, zigzagging between friendly and hostile voices. One member asked if "anything less than a military force" could make America accept the stamps.

Franklin replied that he did not see any point in sending a military force. If an army was sent, it could not compel people to take stamps. "They will not find a rebellion," he added. "They may indeed make one."

"If the act is not repealed, what do you think will be the consequences?"

"A total loss of the respect and affection the people of America bear to this country, and of all the commerce that depends on that respect and affection."

The Rockinghamites brought down the curtain with two prearranged questions.

"What used to be the pride of the Americans?"

"To indulge in the fashions and manufactures of Great Britain."

"What is now their pride?"

"To wear their old clothes again, till they can make new ones."

A week later the House of Commons voted to repeal the Stamp Act. A wave of euphoria swept the Americans in London—and there was even more exulting in the thirteen colonies. South Carolina voted to erect a statue of William Pitt. New York voted statues of Pitt and George III. Behind the scenes in London, the mood was not so euphoric. Prime Minister Rockingham had grave difficulty extracting George III's agreement to repeal. The King yielded with extreme reluctance. The young nobleman also discovered he had no hope of winning Parliament's consent, even with Franklin's testimony, unless he agreed to propose a Declaratory Act, in which Parliament affirmed its right to tax Americans "in all cases whatsoever." The wording was virtually identical to a 1719 declaration of parliamentary supremacy that had reduced Ireland to an imperial appendage.

Franklin had no illusions that repeal meant an outbreak of British benevolence toward America. On the contrary, he saw all too clearly that the colonies had become an issue in British politics, with points to be gained or lost for politicians who favored or opposed the Americans, depending on the mood of the country and Parliament. To his friend Charles Thomson in Philadelphia, Franklin wrote: "If I live to see you, I will let you know how much we were obliged to what the profane would call luck and the pious, Providence."

A few days later Parliament voted to indemnify the stamp agents and others such as Thomas Hutchinson who had suffered substantial losses for their loyalty to the Crown. Grenville and his followers vehemently insisted the Americans ought to pay these damages. At the very least, Grenville huffed, they should pay for the cost of printing millions of stamps, which were now worthless paper.

An anonymous letter commenting on this proposal soon appeared in a London paper. The writer said it reminded him of a Frenchman who used to accost Englishmen on one of the Seine's bridges, brandishing a red-hot iron. "Pray, Monsieur Anglais," he would say. "Do me the favor to let me have the honor of thrusting this red-hot iron into your backside?"

"Zoons!" the agitated Englishman would cry. "Begone with your iron or I'll break your head."

"Nay Monsieur," replied the Frenchman. "If you do not chuse to do it, I will not insist on it. But at least you will in justice have the goodness to pay me something for the heating of my iron."

The author of this ribald satire was Benjamin Franklin. The controversy over the Stamp Act had transformed his attitude toward England. Never again would he consider himself an Englishman. Henceforth, he was the man who announced himself at the bar of the House of Commons: "Franklin of Philadelphia."

Champagne Charlie Takes Charge

Franklin stayed on in London, acting as the colonial agent for Pennsylvania and later for New Jersey and Georgia. His testimony before Parliament was reprinted in newspapers throughout America, and he soon achieved the status of unofficial ambassador for all the colonies. Optimistic as always, he hoped the Stamp Act was an aberration and concentrated on joining his son, William, and a number of other Americans in a project to found a colony in the West. He brought a number of wealthy Englishmen into the scheme, and for a while prospects seemed promising.

But the anti-Americanism that had infected British politics soon threw obstacles in his way. The situation was not improved by the instability of the British government—caused by this same anti-Americanism as well as the continued absence of William Pitt. George Grenville and his followers, supported

Top Left *When the Stamp Act was repealed, Americans paid tribute to William Pitt's help by striking medals bearing his image. Charleston erected a statue of him.*

by a loose confederation of powerful noblemen who sympathized with them, sniped at the Rockingham administration throughout the spring of 1766, steadily whittling away its support. Even more unsettling was the emergence of a new power center in Parliament, whose members called themselves the King's friends. Many of them had been Lord Bute's friends—mostly because he had given them posts in his brief administration. These gentlemen were as anti-American as the Grenvilleites. Soon Parliament's reigning wit, Charles Townshend, was calling the Rockinghams "a lute-string [a glossy silk cloth] administration, fit only for summer wear."

Still nursing a grudge against Rockingham for repealing the Stamp Act, George III decided to get rid of this ministry of "a few weak boys." The King sent for William Pitt, who reluctantly agreed to form a new government. Watching George III flounder from one prime minister to another, Pitt had become convinced it was his duty to help this troubled, uncertain young monarch. But Pitt was still a visionary loner who disliked the day-to-day business of politics, especially deciding who gets what. He badly needed a fixer such as the Duke of Newcastle. The Great Commoner's health was too fragile to take over the hardest job, first lord of the treasury. Instead, he appointed an utter lightweight, thirty-one-year-old Augustus Fitzroy, Duke of Grafton, to that crucial task. For himself, Pitt chose the presidency of the Privy Council— and revealed a hidden agenda. No longer up to the grueling give-and-take of the House of Commons, Pitt wanted to become a peer and make his speeches in the more relaxed and dignified House of Lords.

BELOW *This British cartoon of industrious Americans with a prosperous city in the distance reveals Britain's underlying fear that colonists would soon surpass the Mother Country. Americans were already producing one-seventh of the world's iron. Their economy was two-fifths the size of England's.*

The King readily agreed to make him Lord Chatham. George's letter of consent revealed not a little of his patriot king psychology: "I know the Earl of Chatham will zealously give his aid towards destroying all party distinctions and restoring that subordination to Government which can alone preserve that inestimable blessing, Liberty, from degenerating into licentiousness."

Pitt had made a serious miscalculation. By becoming a peer, the Great Commoner forfeited most of his popularity with the British man in the street—and with many of his followers in the House of Commons. The reaction offered a glimpse of the simmering resentment many Englishman felt toward the Whig oligarchs who had dominated the nation for most of the century. Stung by bitter comments in the press, such as "Pitt was adored—but Chatham is quite unknown" and by wisecracks behind the scenes—"a fall upstairs"—the one politician with the prestige and personal force to lead Parliament retired to his country estate and sank into melancholia and worsening illness. His rudderless administration was soon on a collision course with America.

Among his many dubious appointments, Pitt had selected Charles Townshend to be chancellor of the exchequer, the man in charge of imperial finances. Champagne Charlie had no loyalty to Pitt and few political principles. He played his own game—one that was tuned to the growing anti-Americanism in the House of Commons. When George Grenville rose to demand that the government raise money in America to pay for British troops there, Townshend airily informed him that he had a plan that he would soon unveil. His fellow cabinet members could only stare at each other in astonishment. Townshend had never so much as mentioned this plan to any of them. The cabinet sent another emergency call to William Pitt.

Pitt rushed to London, but he could find no one to replace Townshend. The crisis triggered a complete nervous breakdown. Pitt was carted off to a country house, where he alternated between depression and raving hysteria. A few days later Townshend proposed a series of what he called "external" taxes on America—import duties on glass, lead, paints, paper, tea and a long list of other items. He was taking advantage of a distinction Franklin and several other Americans had made in attacking the Stamp Act. They said Americans did not object to external taxes—customs duties—used to regulate trade.

To worsen matters, Champagne Charlie added a new system of vice-admiralty courts with sweeping powers to issue general warrants to enforce the new duties. As a final fillip, Townshend specified that some of the revenue would be used to pay the salaries of colonial governors, thereby rendering them immune to pressure from local assemblies. Almost as if he wanted to make his policy completely obnoxious, Townshend parenthetically admitted he saw no difference between internal and external taxes. The Declaratory Act gave Parliament the power to lay any tax it pleased, anywhere in America. The Townshend Acts won massive majorities in Parliament and became law on June 29, 1767.

The acts were popular with the English man in the street. A worried Benjamin Franklin mournfully observed that "every man in England seems to consider himself as a piece of a sovereign over America; seems to jostle himself into the throne with the King and talks of *our subjects in the colonies.*" In America the response was not as volatile as Franklin and others feared. The new taxes fell mostly on merchants and shopkeepers. Unlike the Stamp Act, they did not put a hand directly into the pocket of almost every citizen. But they were still a troubling symptom of Parliament's determination to assert its authority over the Americans.

Before Townshend could exploit his popularity, he succumbed to influenza. He was interred in one of his brighter waistcoats, and the Duke of Grafton, the acting prime minister, offered the job of chancellor of the exchequer to one of the King's friends, Frederick, Lord North. He received George III's enthusiastic approval; they had played together as boys and had once jointly performed in that paean to liberty, Joseph Addison's play, *Cato*. A fat, amiable man, the new chancellor was considered neutral on American matters. But the anti-Americans countered by bringing into the cabinet Wills Hill, Earl of Hillsborough, an Anglo-Irish peer who made no secret of his dislike of obstreperous colonists. Hill was made secretary of state for the American colonies just in time to encounter Massachusetts's reaction to the Townshend Acts.

Samuel Adams had drafted an open letter that Massachusetts circulated to the rest of the colonies, urging them to resist the Townshend duties. A comparatively moderate document, the letter suggested Americans should attempt to work out an arrangement that would preserve their liberties within the British empire. To apply pressure, the letter called for a continental association that would boycott English goods until the duties were repealed.

In London the cabinet voted to make a "kind and lenient response" to Adams's letter. Lord Hillsborough ignored them. He ordered Massachusetts to rescind the letter and fired off a circular letter of his own, ordering all the colonial governors to treat the Bay Colony's appeal "with the contempt it deserves."

Wilkes and Liberty Again

Running low on money, John Wilkes returned from France and won one of the eight parliamentary seats allotted to the county of Middlesex and the city of London. George III had no intention of letting him get away with this bold move. The King told Lord North, who was acting as the government's spokesman in the House of Commons, that "the expulsion of Mr. Wilkes appears to be very essential and must be effected." North saw nothing wrong with this directive, which William Pitt would have thrown back in the King's face as an insult to Parliament's independence.

Arrested, Wilkes was freed by the London mob. He took his case to a favorable court, which voided his four-year-old conviction for seditious libel. Ten days later the government seized him again and dragged him before a different judge, who sent him to jail. Mobs shouting, "Wilkes and Liberty" rampaged through London once more. On May 10, 1768, a huge crowd, perhaps

ABOVE *Charles Townshend, member of a distinguished English family, was a playboy who often made witty speeches in Parliament while drunk. As chancellor of the exchequer, he surprised everyone, including George III, by proposing new taxes on the Americans.*

as many as 40,000 people, rioted in St. George's Fields, near the King's Bench prison where Wilkes was being held. The magistrates called out the army; the soldiers fired into the crowd, killing six and wounding twenty.

None of this uproar was lost on the Americans. They were all too ready to believe that Wilkes and his supporters were exposing a British government that was flirting with arbitrary power. In Boston, the Sons of Liberty threatened to demolish the homes of the new customs commissioners appointed to collect the Townshend duties. The King's men panicked and asked the Royal Navy for assistance. The man-of-war *Romney* soon plowed into Boston Harbor to threaten the town with her fifty cannon. Unfazed, the Massachusetts assembly voted 92 to 17 to defy Lord Hillsborough's order to rescind their circular letter.

Elsewhere in America, Lord Hillsborough's circular stirred similar outrage and defiance. One colony after another refused to obey the American secretary's order to ignore the Massachusetts letter, and their royal governors dissolved their assemblies. In Pennsylvania, where the preponderance of Quakers tended to mute resistance, Governor John Penn glumly reported Hillsborough's circular had prompted even the most moderate men to join "the general cry for liberty."

Down in Virginia, that moderate man, Colonel George Washington, paused in his efforts to wring a profit from Mount Vernon's mediocre soil to consult his thoughtful neighbor, George Mason, a man with the brain of a scholar and the instincts of a recluse. The colonel shared with Mason his thoughts on the present turmoil.

"At a time when our lordly Masters in Great Britain will be satisfied with nothing less than the deprecation [sic] of American freedom," Washington said it was necessary to "maintain the liberty which we have derived from our ancestors." The question was how to do this. "That no man should scruple, or hesitate a moment to use a-ms in defence of so valuable a blessing...is clearly of my opinion," he declared. But he hastened to add that "a-ms" should be the last resort. For the moment, he was strongly in favor of an ironclad boycott of British goods that would awaken "their attention to our rights."

Under the leadership of Massachusetts and Virginia, a nonimportation agreement soon united the thirteen colonies in stubborn resistance. They were encouraged by the ongoing brawl between John Wilkes and George III. In January 1769 Lord North persuaded Parliament to expel the agitator. In the by-election for his seat, Wilkes ran from jail and was reelected without opposition. Once more the King insisted on expulsion, and Lord North rounded up the votes to back a motion that John Wilkes was "incapable of being elected."

Wilkes ran without opposition in the next by-election and won again. Once more North persuaded Parliament to declare him a nonmember. The King's friends persuaded a man named Henry Luttrell to oppose Wilkes in still another election. Wilkes won by a margin of 5 to 1. But Parliament, once more at the King's insistence, declared Luttrell elected.

ABOVE *This attack on British taxation was published in New Haven, Connecticut, by Benjamin Mecom, Benjamin Franklin's nephew.*

BOTTOM LEFT *Paul Revere's silver bowl salutes "No. 45"—the edition of John Wilkes's* North Briton *that caused George III to suppress the newspaper.*

By this time Wilkes was a hero in America. Virginia shipped him enough tobacco to keep him puffing contentedly for the rest of his life. Massachusetts sent him two turtles, one weighing forty-five pounds, the other forty-seven. This added up to ninety-two, in memory of the "immortal ninety-two" assemblymen who had refused to rescind their circular letter. Silversmith Paul Revere made an elegant bowl dedicated to these immortals, with "Wilkes and Liberty," "No General Warrants," "No 45" and other slogans engraved on its gleaming sides. South Carolina voted £1,500 to the Middlesex Society for Supporting the Bill of Rights, one of Wilkes's chief backers. The royal governor vetoed the grant, but many Americans read about it in their newspapers.

Wilkes reinforced the American determination to import no British goods as long as the Townshend duties remained in effect. But in Boston the Sons of

RIGHT *John Wilkes returned from exile in France and was elected to Parliament, but George III ordered him expelled. London exploded into riots. Americans admired Wilkes as a defender of liberty. Many British saw him as the incarnation of evil.*

Liberty overplayed their hand. Their repeated threats to the houses and persons of the customs commissioners goaded Governor Francis Bernard into asking for two regiments of troops to keep order. This was a recipe for far worse trouble. The soldiers, camped on Boston Common, became a visible symbol of the colony's clash with the Crown. The stench from their latrines wafted through the little city on every breeze. In the streets the "lobsterbacks" were insulted by men and hooted at by boys.

Time for a Truce

George III opened Parliament in 1769 with a resounding declaration that the government would defeat "the mischievous designs of those turbulent and seditious persons" who had "deluded numbers of my subjects in America." Behind the scenes, however, even the most bellicose ministers, such as Lord Hillsborough, knew the Townshend duties had to be jettisoned. The American boycott was beginning to hurt, even though it was porous in many colonies, notably Virginia.

The British government was on the defensive over a whole range of issues. The East India Company, the privately owned corporation that ruled India, was reeling toward bankruptcy. William Pitt, disgusted by the Wilkes fiasco, resigned as president of the Privy Council and came to Parliament for the first time in three years. In a blazing speech he denounced barring Wilkes from Parliament as grossly illegal. It invalidated the entire House of Commons, which should be dissolved and undergo new elections, Pitt declared.

Pitt freely admitted Wilkes was a scoundrel but said that was not the point. What concerned him was the possibility that there was "a power in this country" that undertook to "measure the civil rights of a subject by his moral character or by any other rule but the fixed laws of the land." Charles Pratt, Earl Camden, the lord chancellor of England, rose to second Pitt's denunciation. Within days, at George III's insistence, Camden was booted out of the cabinet.

This highhanded royal reaction inspired the Lord Mayor of London to lead a procession to the government's offices at Whitehall with a petition declaring that Parliament no longer represented the people. It was under the control of the King's friends and should be dismissed. Similar protests poured in from Bristol, Leeds, Newcastle and a dozen other towns and counties. George III did not so much as blink. He informed the petitioners that he considered their calls for reform an insult to Parliament, an affront to him personally and a violation of the British Constitution. An aghast Pitt cried out in the House of Lords that the King's reply was unconstitutional. If Englishmen could not petition their King, what did British liberty mean?

These electrifying words also crossed the Atlantic in British newspapers and swept through the colonies. Americans could only conclude that an epic struggle for liberty was being waged on both sides of the ocean.

That was not how George III saw Pitt's challenge. The Great Commoner had broken with the patriot King's program to restore "subordination" to the government. The King dismissed the man whom Pitt had installed as acting prime minister, the hapless Duke of Grafton, and chose Frederick, Lord North as his successor. North was the perfect prime minister for a patriot King—a friend who would not dream of talking back to him.

RIGHT *In this satiric British cartoon, the King's ministers and members of Parliament are about to kill America, the goose that lays the golden eggs. British firms in the colonial trade extended £5 million in credit annually to Americans—well over a billion dollars in today's money.*

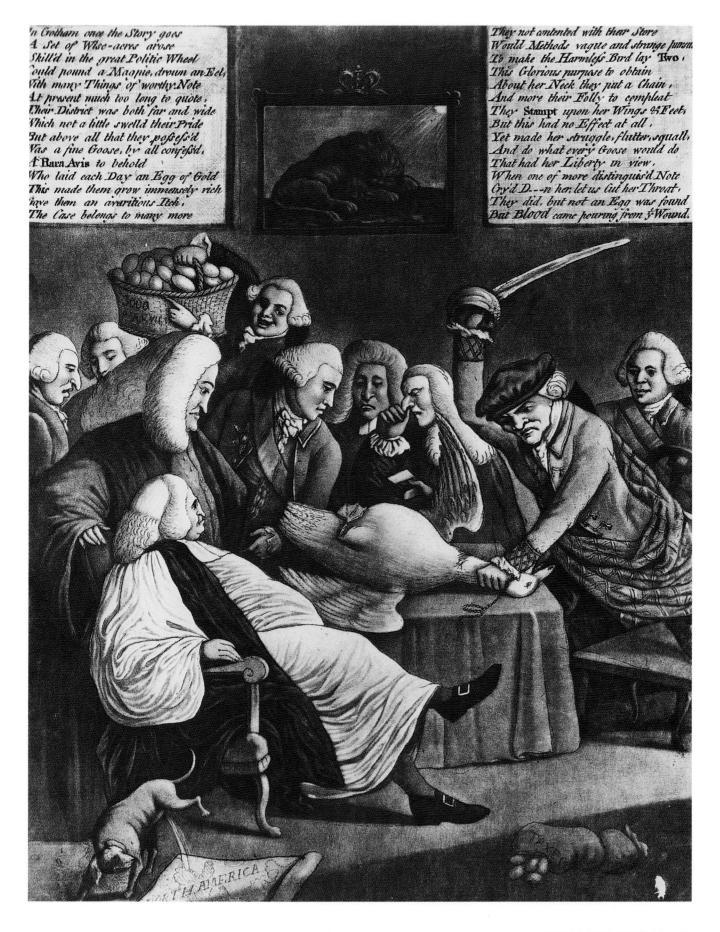

The Blind Trumpeter

At first glance North seemed an unlikely choice to head the government. Horace Walpole remarked on his unprepossessing appearance: "Two large prominent eyes that rolled about to no purpose…a wide mouth, thick lips and inflated visage…gives him the air of a blind trumpeter." His speaking voice was "untunable," and his clothes ranged from sloppy to unkempt. But he was a very likable man and by no means stupid. He had been in the House of Commons since 1754 and had a keen awareness of how things worked. He began his administration with two wise moves. He let John Wilkes out of jail—and he proposed the repeal of the Townshend duties.

But North showed he was the King's man by stoutly resisting any attempt to seat Wilkes in Parliament. He also acquiesced in keeping all the ministers from the previous administration, although many were anti-American. This made him a peculiar prime minister; instead of creating a cabinet, he inherited one. But North was unbothered as long as George III was satisfied with his performance. He would gradually learn that subservience to the King was not the royal road to happiness.

LEFT *A skilled parliamentarian, Lord North served George III as prime minister for more than a decade. Once, during an opposition tirade, he seemed to doze off. The orator complained that the prime minister was asleep. "I wish to God I were," North said in a stage whisper.*

His first step to this discovery came early in 1770, when the cabinet debated the repeal of the Townshend duties. Several members, notably Lord Hillsborough, strongly resisted removing the tiny tax on tea. Something should be retained to affirm Parliament's right to tax, they argued. Others thought this was only asking for future trouble. North, as prime minister, had the deciding vote—and his mind was made up for him by George III. "I am clear that there must always be one tax to keep up the right," the King informed him. "And as such I approve of the tea duty."

Not even Benjamin Franklin, with all his contacts inside and outside Parliament, realized that it was George III who cast this fateful vote. In a letter to a friend, Franklin blamed the refusal to drop the tax on tea to "the idle notion of the dignity and sovereignty of Parliament which they are so fond of." He correctly opined that Lord North was "inclined to satisfy us" and thought the anti-Americans in the cabinet were responsible for Parliament's hard line.

Blood in the Streets

On the same March day in 1770 that Parliament repealed most of the Townshend Acts, a riot exploded in snowy Boston. It started when a young apprentice shouted an insult at a British officer. A soldier on sentry duty in front of that symbol of royal authority, the customs house, gave the apprentice a knock on the ear with the butt of his rifle. The boy howled for help, and an unruly crowd gathered. Someone rang the bells in a nearby church. This drew more people into the street. The sentry found himself confronting an angry mob. A brave man, he stood his ground and called for the main guard. Six men, led by a corporal, responded. They were joined by the officer on duty, Captain Thomas Preston.

Tension between the King's men and the Bostonians had been building toward an explosion for months. Early in September James Otis had been badly beaten in a barroom brawl with supporters of the customs men. A few weeks later, an eleven-year-old boy had been killed in a melee with an outspoken defender of the Hutchinson and Crown policy. Another brawl pitted off-duty soldiers looking for work with Bostonians who insulted and threatened them.

The crowd in front of the customs house soon swelled to almost 400 men. The rioters began pelting the soldiers with snowballs and chunks of ice. Led by a huge mulatto, Crispus Attucks, they surged to within inches of the fixed bayonets and dared the soldiers to fire. Their courage, considerably reinforced by liquor, was based on the assumption that a British soldier could not fire on rioters before a magistrate had read the Riot Act, which authorized the army to restore the King's peace. Since there was not a magistrate in Boston who would risk his house and personal safety by doing such a thing, the rioters thought they had the upper hand. Any soldier who killed one of them would be tried for murder.

General Thomas Gage, the commander-in-chief in America, had admitted this dilemma to Lord Hillsborough a year before. He told the American secretary that the troops were in constant danger of assault and could not retaliate without "suffering by law." Hillsborough stubbornly refused to withdraw them. A year later relations between the army and the townspeople had deteriorated so badly that the soldiers no longer considered themselves bound by British law and customs. They regarded the Bostonians as aliens, as different and hostile as the Irish.

Someone in the crowd struck a soldier with a club, knocking him to the ground. The man sprang to his feet and was struck by another club, thrown from a distance. He leveled his musket and pulled the trigger. Seconds later, the other members of the guard imitated him. The mob fled. As the gunsmoke cleared, Crispus Attucks and four others lay dead or dying. Six more men were wounded.

For a few hours, Boston was close to a bloodbath. The city's well-armed Sons of Liberty outnumbered the 600 soldiers in the two British regiments 5 to 1. Only a desperate speech by Lieutenant Governor Thomas Hutchinson, in which he promised to arrest the soldiers and charge them with murder, restored an uneasy semblance of peace. But it did not look as if it would last. The frantic Hutchinson could not find a lawyer in Boston to defend Captain Preston and his men.

On the morning after the bloodshed, John Adams was in his law office when a distraught Irishman, a friend of Preston's, burst in and begged him to take the case. Two other lawyers had promised to join the defense—if Adams agreed to be the leader. The challenge aroused the idealism in John Adams's combative soul. For a decade he had watched his cousin Samuel Adams construct "a political engine" in Boston, discovering under his tutelage "the wheels...cogs or pins, some of them dirty ones, which composed the machine and made it go." John took a dim view of the violent tendencies of some Sons of Liberty. All these feelings coalesced in his answer to Preston's friend. "Counsel," Adams said, "ought to be the very last thing that an accused men should want [lack] in a free country." He would take the case.

From a popular leader of the Sons of Liberty, Adams became a scorned man. Rocks were flung through his windows and boys jeered him in the streets. He was not helped by his cousin Samuel's tactics. At a Boston town meeting, 3,000 roaring Sons of Liberty demanded the immediate removal of the troops from Boston. A mortified Lieutenant Governor Hutchinson withdrew them to Castle William, in the harbor. Samuel Adams next gathered ninety-six depositions from suddenly proper Bostonians who swore that on March 5 not a citizen in the city was on the streets with anything but peace and friendship in his heart when they were attacked by soldiers wielding bayonets and cutlasses.

John Adams stubbornly persevered in the soldiers' defense. First he made a motion to try Preston and the enlisted men separately, which the court granted. Then he laboriously gathered depositions from dozens of people who portrayed a very different Boston from the one depicted by the Sons of Liberty. John Adams's witnesses reported scores of men roaming the streets with "cudgels" in their hands, looking for soldiers to beat up. A tall man in a red cloak and a short man in a darker cloak seemed to be urging them on. The descriptions fit Samuel Adams and one of his right-hand men, William Molineux.

Next, with the sheriff's help, John Adams selected juries made up entirely of country people, who were unsympathetic to Boston's brawlers. Deploying his witnesses with a nice combination of bluntness and finesse, Adams

ABOVE *This painting comes close to portraying the Boston Massacre as it really happened. The British soldiers fired in self-defense as a furious mob attacked them with clubs and chunks of ice. John Adams won the soldiers' acquittal in the subsequent trial.*

convincingly demonstrated that the soldiers had acted in self-defense against a riotous mob and won acquittals for Preston and his men. He accomplished this feat without using any evidence that might have embarrassed individual Sons of Liberty, in particular Samuel Adams.

For the rest of his long life, John Adams maintained that his "disinterested action" in defending the soldiers was "one of the best pieces of service I ever rendered my country." Unquestionably he won friends in England and in other colonies by demonstrating that Massachusetts upheld the rule of law. In Boston Samuel Adams did not seem to agree. Under the name Vindex he denounced the juries' verdicts and the defense argument in a series of scathing articles in *The Boston Gazette.* But Samuel Adams was a subtle man. Privately, his friendship with John Adams became even more intimate.

It would seem more than likely that Samuel Adams realized that without John Adams at the defense table, the evidence gathered on behalf of the British soldiers might have sent him and other members of the Liberty party to London under arrest for treason. The trials helped John convince Samuel

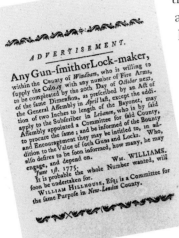

that the Sons of Liberty's policy of violence was almost out of control and must be tempered henceforth.

Elsewhere in America, many people seemed to share John Adams's sentiments. In spite of repeated efforts by the Sons of Liberty to make the "Boston Massacre" a continental griev- ance, it never achieved more than local prominence. If anything it seemed to act as a damper on American passions. *The New York Gazette* editorialized that it was "high time a stop was put to mobbing." In Lon- don William Pitt urged the Americans not to "carry their notions of liberty too far."

The blood of Boston's martyrs also seemed to have a con- trary effect on the boycott against English imports inspired by the Townshend Acts. Nowhere was the ban more flouted than in Boston, where merchants uni- laterally abandoned it without informing the other colonies. This did little to raise their already low opinion of grasping Yankees.

One American reacted very differently to the bloodshed in Boston. Ben- jamin Franklin never forgot his Massachusetts origins; he was deeply distressed by the incident. From London he wrote to the Reverend Samuel Cooper, telling him that the British policy of maintaining a "standing army…among us in time of peace, without the consent of our assemblies" was a grievance almost as serious as Parliament's claim that it had the right to tax Americans. Stationing those regiments in Boston without the consent of the Massachu- setts assembly was unconstitutional, Franklin maintained. The King could not keep troops in England without the specific consent of Parliament.

In Boston the Massachusetts assembly plunged into an acrimonious dis- pute with Acting Governor Thomas Hutchinson over replacing the colony's London agent, who had recently died. Unable to reach agreement with the governor, the assembly decided to hire its own representative. Several people proposed Franklin. Samuel Adams and numerous others opposed him because he was drawing a Crown salary as deputy postmaster general for America. But when the Reverend Samuel Cooper produced Franklin's letter, a majority swung behind him as the right choice.

For Franklin the offer could not have come at a worse time. He was still deep in negotiations with the British government to found a western colony. Lord Hillsborough had done his utmost to block the project. By this time Franklin had invited into the venture a host of prominent Englishmen, includ- ing banker Thomas Walpole, nephew of the former prime minister, who far outweighed Hillsborough politically. The Privy Council voted its approval of the colony, which was applying for 20 million acres in Illinois, and the morti- fied Hillsborough resigned as American secretary.

Should Franklin risk this chance to make a fortune for himself and his son, William? Becoming the agent for the Massachusetts assembly would make him powerful enemies. But Franklin thought about those dead and wounded Bostonians in the snow—shot down because arrogant men such as Lord

TOP LEFT *This urgent call for gunsmiths showed the Americans were serious about resisting the British. Ships scoured the West Indies and Europe trying to buy gunpowder.*

BELOW *Fifty-one-year-old Crispus Attucks, a six-foot-two-inch mulatto, was one of the five men killed in the Boston Massacre. He was part Natick Indian: Attucks means "deer" in the Natick language. A runaway slave from Framingham, he had worked as a sailor for more than twenty years, using the name Michael Johnson.*

Hillsborough believed they could suppress American liberty with gunfire—and took the job. The decision would have a momentous impact on the quarrel between England and America.

Tea and Antipathy

For almost three years, this portentous future was visible to no one. The acrimony between the colonies and the Mother Country receded to the vanishing point. A surge in prosperity on both sides of the Atlantic swept away attempts by activists such as Samuel Adams to agitate about the lingering tax on tea. In 1771 Boston imported 265,000 pounds of the brew, with one of Adams's chief supporters, merchant prince John Hancock, paying duties on 45,000 pounds. "In New York," John Adams reported glumly in 1772, "they laugh at us." Thomas Jefferson lamented that Virginia had fallen into a "state of insensibility."

Americans spent an average of £3.4 million a year on British imports and gulped down ever-larger quantities of tea, some of it imported from England, more of it smuggled from Holland and sold at cheaper prices. In New York smuggling tea from the Dutch and Danish West Indies became a way of life. Tea imports from Britain tea sank from 320,000 pounds in 1769 to 530 in 1772.

In London Benjamin Franklin jousted with anti-Americans in the press, but his wit seemed to make the dispute almost good-natured. "Rules By Which A Great Empire May Be Reduced To A Small One" skewered the government's American policies. "An Edict By The King of Prussia" declared England to be a Prussian colony, because the first settlers had been Germans. In Franklin's satiric scenario, the King of Prussia proceeded to announce taxes and duties similar to the ones England had imposed on America, warning that anyone who protested them would be guilty of high treason.

Meanwhile, with the help of the grim reaper, George III and Lord North gathered strength in Parliament. George Grenville and several other political leaders died, and their followers drifted into the camp of the King's friends. This infusion of support inclined North to grapple with the thorny problem of the East India Company, which was continuing its spiral into bankruptcy. With a monopoly of the trade around the Cape of Good Hope and military and commercial domination of India, the company should have been making a fortune. But a policy of declaring dividends as high as 12.5 percent plus gross corruption among its employees in India had led to a financial decline that

soon became a nosedive. The American boycott of British products during the Stamp Act and Townshend crises had worsened matters. By 1772, the company owed £1.3 million, much of it to the British government, and the Bank of England had stonily refused further credit. Worse, it had a staggering 18 million pounds of unsold tea in its London warehouses.

After conferring with merchants and the company's proprietors, Lord North produced the Tea Act of 1773. To the disapproval of many people who saw it as an

Paul Revere's famous engraving of the Boston Massacre has many details wrong. The sign, Butcher's Hall, is Revere's name for The British Coffeehouse favored by English officers. There were eight soldiers in line, not seven. It portrays the soldiers firing simultaneously; witnesses agree they fired singly, at random. It shows Captain Thomas Preston with his sword raised, ordering the soldiers to fire. Witnesses said Preston never gave the order. It omits the most famous victim, Crispus Attucks. But it was a work of powerful propaganda.

ABOVE *This grenadier wears the uniform of the 29th Regiment, the soldiers involved in the Boston Massacre. The motto on his bearskin cap reads: nec aspera terrent (they fear no difficulty). Most were Irish.*

BOTTOM RIGHT *This broadside commemorated the men killed in the Boston Massacre. The other colonies failed to respond to Massachusetts's outrage.*

invasion of corporate rights, the law virtually made the government the East India Company's permanent partner. It also undertook to help reduce the tea surplus by proposing to repeal the three-pence-per-pound duty that the company paid to import tea to England. This would enable it to undersell competitors in Europe and America.

A member of the opposition asked North if it might be a good idea to remove the American duty too. North, knowing what George III would say to this, resisted the suggestion. He maintained the Crown needed the money to pay for the troops in America. The opposition member wryly noted that the year before, the tea duty had earned £400 after the expenses of collecting it were deducted. That was hardly enough to keep one regiment of infantry eating for a month. North primly insisted that the duty would not be repealed. Someone else suggested keeping the British duty, to which no one objected, and dropping the American duty. More than a little agitated, North admitted there were "political reasons" for retaining the American duty.

The East India Company began chartering ships and giving certain merchants in each colony the exclusive right to sell its bargain-priced tea. Revealing none too subtly the government's influence, the company selected people who had avoided the protests of the previous years. No doubt Lord North and the King thought this would be a neat way to reward loyalty to the Crown. In Boston they compounded this egregious policy by selecting the sons of Thomas Hutchinson to be their agents. The King had already affirmed his fondness for the father by appointing him royal governor in 1771.

As the machinery of the Tea Act creaked into gear, Benjamin Franklin supplied Boston's Sons of Liberty with an argument far more incendiary than the duty on tea. Through one of his more clandestine contacts in London, Franklin acquired a series of letters that Thomas Hutchinson had written to Thomas Whately, a British treasury bureaucrat, during the Townshend Act riots of 1768-69. In the letters, Hutchinson urged the government to send troops to cow the Boston mob. "There must be some abridgement of what is called British liberty," he wrote.

Franklin maintained that he sent the Hutchinson letters to Boston to show the Sons of Liberty that the British were not solely responsible for the policies that were estranging England and America. They were acting on advice they had received from American officials. He may also have been spurred to this dangerous move by the suspicion that the British were opening and reading his mail. In 1771 he told his Boston friend Thomas Cushing that several letters had arrived "badly sealed…appearing as if they had been opened and in a very bungling way sealed again." As a deputy postmaster general, Franklin knew that the British post office could open anyone's mail with an order from a secretary of state.

Franklin cautioned Thomas Cushing to show the Whately letters to only a small group of insiders. One of these, of necessity, was Samuel Adams, who promptly had

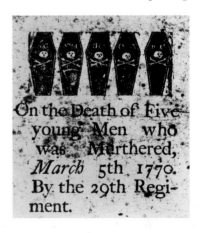

On the Death of Five young Men who was Murthered, *March* 5th 1770. By the 29th Regiment.

copies made and circulated to every town in Massachusetts. From Worcester to Boston indignant citizens demanded Hutchinson's ouster as governor. As the story spread to other colonies, Hutchinson was burned in effigy in several cities and compared to Judas Iscariot, Nero and other villains of history. Soon a petition requesting Hutchinson's removal was on its way to Franklin. As Massachusetts's agent, he was supposed to submit it to William Legge, Earl of Dartmouth, who had replaced Hillsborough as American secretary. Dartmouth, a mild-mannered man who professed to like Americans, would decide whether to show it to the King.

Meanwhile, the tea ships began departing from London to American ports. As Sons of Liberty in the various colonies grasped the dimensions of the British agenda, opposition spread rapidly up and down the continent. At first New York seemed to be the center of the resistance, partly because it was a veritable headquarters for smuggling Dutch tea. The merchants selected to sell East India tea were soon persuaded to resign by truculent Sons of Liberty, led by a pugnacious Scotsman, Alexander McDougall. In Philadelphia, Annapolis, Charleston and other ports, similar tactics produced even hastier resignations.

Only in Boston did the East India concessionaires ignore urgent invitations to resign. Although the animus against the Hutchinsons had been inflamed by the Whately letters, Thomas Hutchinson's sons, encouraged by their father, stood firm. Not even the unanimous vote of a 5,000-man town meeting changed their minds. On October 23, 1773, the North End Caucus, an organization led by silversmith Paul Revere, voted to oppose the sale of the tea with "their lives and fortunes."

A month later, when three ships sailed into Boston Harbor loaded with East India tea, Samuel Adams and the Sons of Liberty were ready for them. So was Governor Thomas Hutchinson, who thought this time he had some trump cards to play. The governor ordered the ships' captains to register their cargoes at the customs house, as required by law, and tie up at Griffin's Wharf. The Sons of Liberty stationed guards aboard the ships to make sure none of the tea was unloaded. The customs commissioners stationed their own guards to make sure none was stolen.

Hutchinson did nothing to intrude on this vigilance. After a day or two, the Sons of Liberty realized the governor had them in a trap. A clause in the customs law stated that if duty was not paid on a cargo within twenty days of its arrival, the customs commissioners could seize it, take it to their warehouses, and dispose of it as they saw fit. As royal officials, they could call on the King's army and navy for support. Camped around Castle William in Boston Harbor was a regiment of regulars. Anchored nearby were a ship of the line and several frigates commanded by an admiral.

As the days ticked by, the Sons of Liberty pressured the ships' captains to ask the collector of the port for a clearance to return to England with the tea. The collector refused to issue this document. It was illegal to import products shipped to America back into England. Without a clearance, the naval officer in command of the port refused to permit the ships to sail. On Thursday morning, December 16, another meeting of more than 5,000 Bostonians gathered in Old South Church and asked one of the tea-ship captains, whose twenty-day limit would expire at midnight, to obtain a clearance from Governor Hutchinson. The captain traveled seven miles to Hutchinson's country house in Milton and made the request. The governor turned him down.

By the time the captain returned to Boston, it was almost dark. He reported the governor's refusal to the reconvened meeting at Old South. Samuel Adams threw up his hands and cried: "I do not see what more Bostonians can do to save their country." Instantly from the gallery of the church a war whoop split the air. It was answered from the doorway, where several dozen men, their faces stained with paint, old blankets around their shoulders, were pretending to be Indians. "The Mohawks are come!" shouted one. "Boston Harbor a teapot tonight!" shouted another.

About fifty in number, the "Mohawks" rushed to Griffin's Wharf, followed by a huge crowd. Quickly splitting into groups, they boarded the three ships and ordered ashore the customs officers guarding them. Some Mohawks dropped into the holds and attached block and tackle to the tea chests. Others hauled them on deck, broke them open with axes, and shoveled the tea into moonlit Boston Harbor. The crowd stood at the foot of the wharf, silently watching the proceedings. In three hours of furious work, 342 chests of blended Ceylon and Darjeeling tea worth £9,659 and six shillings were methodically destroyed. Nothing else aboard the ships was touched.

The next day John Adams informed his diary that there was a "Dignity, a Majesty, a Sublimity" in Boston's Tea Party that stirred his deepest admiration.

FAR LEFT *The British company that lost £9,659 and six shillings worth of tea in Boston Harbor in 1773 is selling the same blend to modern Bostonians and tourists. Sales are reported to be "very satisfactory."*

BELOW *British troops disembark from transports and land in Boston to close the port in punishment for the Tea Party. Benjamin Franklin had recommended paying for the dumped tea, but Samuel Adams had suppressed his letter. Defiant Sons of Liberty staged a second tea party on March 7, 1774.*

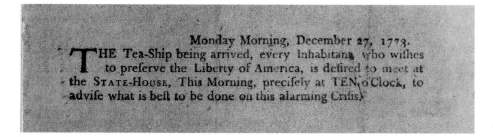

"This destruction of the tea is so bold, so daring, so firm, so intrepid and inflexible, it must have…important consequences."

A Franklin Roast

The first of these consequences occurred in London. Even before the news of the Tea Party arrived, the Whately letters were stirring their own tempest. Thomas Whately was dead and could say or do nothing about his purloined mail. But his brother, William, accused another American, John Temple, of stealing the letters. The accusation was probably untrue. Most historians now think Franklin obtained the letters from a former governor of Massachusetts, Thomas Pownall.

The hotheaded Temple challenged Whately to a duel, in which he inflicted minor wounds. Whately staggered home vowing to issue another challenge. An appalled Franklin decided to prevent further bloodshed and inserted a notice in the *Public Advertiser* stating that "I alone am the person who obtained and transmitted to Boston the letters in question."

Franklin added a brief defense, claiming that the letters were "not of the nature of private letters between friends. They were written by public officers to persons in public stations" and had been passed from hand to hand among many government officials in England.

Fourteen days later Franklin was astonished to learn that the Massachusetts assembly petition to remove Hutchinson as governor of the colony would receive a formal hearing before the King's Privy Council. Something larger than the rejection of the petition, which Franklin considered a foregone conclusion, was afoot. After a preliminary hearing revealed a menacing hostility to the assembly in general and its agent in particular, Franklin decided he had better hire a lawyer.

A few days later the *General Evening-Post* ran the following ditty, aimed at "Doctor Franklin":

> TO D—R F—N
> Thou base ungrateful cunning upstart thing!
> False to thy country first, then to thy King
> To gain thy selfish and ambitious ends
> Betraying secret letters writ to friends
> May no more letters through thy hands be past,
> But may thy last year's office be thy last!

Franklin decided to hire two lawyers. The hearing was scheduled for January 29, 1774. London swirled with rumors that the government planned to unleash one of its most vicious verbal attack dogs, Alexander Wedderburn. This scaly Scot had recently sold his services to the King's friends. A week after he had made a ferocious attack on the administration on behalf of Wilkes and liberty, Lord North and George III had purchased him as casually as they might have acquired a piece of minor statuary for St. James's Palace. They offered him the job of solicitor general, and Wedderburn instantly became the King's most vociferous supporter in Parliament. He had, Lord North remarked, "the gift of an accommodating conscience."

Franklin tried to protect his colleagues in the projected Illinois colony from his sudden descent into public obloquy. A few hours after the preliminary hearing at the Privy Council, he wrote a public letter to Thomas Walpole, resigning from the company that had been organized to finance the settlement. Franklin's troubles were only beginning. On January 19, 1774, the American ship *Hayley*, owned by John Hancock, reached Dover with the news of the Boston Tea Party. On January 22 the *St. James Chronicle* printed a complete description of the affair, taken from Boston newspapers carried aboard the *Hayley*.

FAR LEFT *This broadside began the Boston Tea Party.*

BELOW *The Boston Tea Party triggered what radicals called "the perfect crisis" in the quarrel between America and England. Americans consumed 1.2 million pounds of tea a year: 275,000 came from England, 925,000 pounds were smuggled, mostly from Holland. Tea ranked fourth among the British exports to America.*

On January 25 the ship *Polly* docked at Gravesend with the doleful news that the East India Company's tea—which the ship was supposed to deliver to Philadelphia—was still in her hold. Franklin's adopted city had refused to allow either the tea or the company's agent to land. Nevertheless, as January 29 approached, Franklin remained optimistic. The Boston Tea Party had finally brought the argument with America to a brutally simple point of confrontation. The King's ministers, face to face with the one American in London who could speak for all the colonies, could prove they wanted to settle the quarrel peacefully by letting Benjamin Franklin explain why Thomas Hutchinson's talk of abridging British liberty was at the heart of America's grievance against England.

The Privy Council met at the Cockpit, a section of Whitehall where the prime minister conferred with his cabinet. In the days of Henry VIII it had been an arena for fighting cocks. When Franklin arrived on the twenty-ninth, he realized his optimism was wishful thinking. Never before in the memory of any living Londoner had so many noble lords attended a Privy Council meeting—thirty-six, all in their most gorgeous finery. They sat at a long table in the center of the spacious chamber, built in drawing-room style with a fireplace at one end. Through the windows at that end loomed St. James's Palace, the King's residence.

Around the table swarmed courtiers and politicians, most of them with greedily excited expressions. Near the chair of the council president, Franklin saw two friends, the scientist Joseph Priestley and the Irish orator Edmund Burke. A wealthy newcomer from America, Ralph Izard of South Carolina, managed to squeeze into the room at the last minute. Prime Minister Lord North arrived late, and no seat could be found for him. He stood beside the council president's chair, lending his somnolent authority to the proceedings.

Franklin was wearing one of his best suits, a dark-brown outfit made of Manchester velvet. An eyewitness described him as standing with his elbow on the mantel of the fireplace, "conspicuously erect...the muscles of his face perfectly composed, so as to afford a placid tranquil expression." He was going to need all the tranquillity he could muster. His two lawyers, one of them hampered by a bad cold, spoke on behalf of the petition to remove Governor Thomas Hutchinson. As they retired, Solicitor General Wedderburn stepped forward until he could place his hand on the Privy Council table, then began the government's reply.

This was no simple petition under consideration here, no request for a minor favor from the King, the solicitor general intoned. The question went to the heart of Britain's imperial policy. Could the King now or in the future hope to employ men of proven loyalty to administer his colonies? The answer was NO!, Wedderburn thundered, if the Privy Council seriously entertained this petition from the Massachusetts assembly. Thomas Hutchinson had written *nothing* in his letters to Thomas Whately that any loyal servant of the Crown could not admit with pride. There was also nothing in his official conduct on which grounds for dismissal could be argued. Yet the Massachusetts assembly was asking the King to dismiss him because he had "lost the confidence of the *people*."

Wedderburn, like many ambitious Scots, had long since cleansed his speech

WE HAVE AN OLD MOTHER

We have an old mother that
peevish is grown

She snubs us like children that
scarce walk alone

She forgets we're grown up and
have sense of our own

Which nobody can deny, deny
Which nobody can deny.

If we don't obey orders,
whatever the case;

She frowns, and she chides
and she loses all patience

and sometimes she hits us
a slap in the face,

Which nobody can deny, etc.

Her orders so odd are,
we often suspect

That age has impaired
her sound intellect

But still an old mother
should have some respect

Which nobody can deny, etc.

We'll join in her lawsuits
to baffle all those

Who, to get what she has,
will be often her foes;

But we know it must all be
our own, when she goes.

Which nobody can deny, deny
Which nobody can deny.

Benjamin Franklin

RIGHT **Without Boston's Samuel
Adams, there might never have
been an American Revolution.
His skill at combining agitation
and propaganda put the British
constantly on the defensive.
He created committees of
correspondence to link the colonies
and was the chief organizer of
the Boston Tea Party.**

of a telltale burr. But the way he pronounced "people" covered the word with prickly contempt. He now turned on Franklin the full force of his savage, mercenary rhetoric. The sole reason for this loss of confidence was the private letters Franklin had stolen and sent to Boston. "Dr. Franklin," he roared was the *prime conductor* of this conspiracy against His Majesty's governor.

On behalf of a government that had been rifling Franklin's mail for years, along with the mail of anyone else deemed suspicious, Wedderburn denounced the man from Philadelphia as a thief. "I hope, My Lords, you will mark and *brand* that man, for the honor of this country, of Europe, of mankind," the Scot shrilled. Descending into total hypocrisy, he claimed that private correspondence had been held "sacred" even "in times of greatest party rage."

Wedderburn next assailed Franklin's motives. His ego had become so inflated by the way newspapers mentioned his arrivals and departures and his cordial reception in the best houses of England that he had become drunk with absurd notions of power. He thought of himself as the minister for "the great

American Republic," an independent power for whom he alone was qualified to speak. This delusion had inspired him to act like a foreign ambassador, who could get away with "bribing villains" to steal state papers, because he was not amenable to England's laws.

"But Dr. Franklin, whatever he may teach the people at Boston, while he is here at least is a *subject*," Wedderburn roared. "And the Court of Chancery [where Franklin was being sued by William Whately] will not much attend to his...self created importance!"

Along with Franklin's swollen ego, there was another, more vicious motive for sending the letters to Boston, Wedderburn thundered. He wanted the governorship of Massachusetts for himself. And what kind of government would Franklin and his tools create? "A tyranny greater than the Roman!" Had they not heard in the past few days the latest news from the "good men of Boston?" He meant the Tea Party.

For almost an hour Franklin stood there, enduring this abuse, while the Cockpit rocked with laughter at Wedderburn's sallies and the lords of the Privy Council studied him with mocking, haughty eyes. Ralph Izard, with his hot South Carolina blood, later remarked: "Had it been me that was so grossly insulted, I should instantly have repelled the attack, in defiance of every consequence." Yet Franklin, in the words of another eyewitness, remained "the whole time like a rock, in the same posture, his head resting on his left hand, and in that attitude abiding the pelting of the pitiless storm."

For Franklin it was more than a storm, it was a political and emotional

BELOW *Prime Minister Lord North pours tea down the throat of a prostrate America while Brittania weeps. On the left, a Frenchman and a Spaniard relish the rupture of the British empire.*

catastrophe, the death of his hopes for reconciliation between England and America. The deep affection he had acquired for England and Englishmen had been demolished in front of his eyes. That these great lords, most of whom he knew personally, could allow him to become the target of a man as despicable as Alexander Wedderburn was almost beyond belief. A profound, even immense personal resentment multiplied his rage.

As the meeting broke up and the crowd flowed out of the council chamber into an anteroom, Franklin found himself walking beside Wedderburn. He reportedly took the Scot by the arm and whispered: "I will make your master a little king for this." The story may be apocryphal—but it unquestionably dramatizes what Franklin was thinking.

Acts of War

Having alienated the one man who might have been able to mediate the quarrel—and displayed their contempt for the most famous and admired American of the era—George III and Lord North rammed through Parliament a series of laws designed to punish Boston for the Tea Party. The Boston Port Act closed the harbor to all shipping until the ruined tea, plus the duty on it, was paid for in pounds sterling. Next came an act "for regulating the government in the Province of Massachusetts Bay." The charter granted by the Crown in 1691 was drastically overhauled. The governor's council, which functioned as a sort of senate, would henceforth be appointed by the royal governor. Town meetings could be held only with the governor's permission. All local officials and judges would be appointed by the governor, and their salaries would be paid by the Crown from customs duties. "I propose in this bill to take the executive power from the democratic part of the government," Lord North candidly explained.

Next came the Administration of Justice Act. This bill stipulated that any British soldier or official charged with a capital crime in America would be sent to England or to another colony for trial. So much for John Adams's agonizing struggle to acquit Captain Preston and his men in the aftermath of the Boston Massacre.

The Coercive Acts, as they were called, also dispatched four regiments to Boston and authorized Royal Army officers to quarter troops in the homes of private citizens. To make sure the colonists got the message, the King appointed a new governor, General Thomas Gage, the commander-in-chief of the British army in America.

Gage got the job as the result of an interview with George III not long after the news of the Tea Party arrived. The general happened to be on leave in England with his pretty American wife. An admirer of Lord Hillsborough, Gage assured the King that "the Americans would be lions whilst we are lambs but if we take the resolute part they undoubtedly will prove very meek." George III promptly reported this advice to Lord North, making it plain that it was exactly what he wanted to hear. Now was the time, the King lectured North, to correct that "fatal compliance," the repeal of the Stamp Act. It had only encouraged the Americans "to increase their pretensions to…independency."

For a final fillip, Lord North passed the Quebec Act, which set up a government for that province more than a decade after it had been conquered. The first part of the act had an aura of statesmanship. French-Canadians were given the right to live under French civil laws and practice the Roman Catholic religion. They would be ruled by an appointed governor and council, as they had been under the French colonial regime.

Then came the anti-American part of the act. The boundary of the province of Quebec was extended south to the Ohio River and west to the Mississippi. This annihilated the claims of a half-dozen colonies to parts of this territory. Alexander Wedderburn frankly admitted in Parliament that its chief purpose was to keep the Americans close to the seaboard, where it would be easier to control them. The redrawn boundary incidentally demolished Franklin's proposed colony in Illinois, demonstrating how neatly the King and his friends could kill several American birds with a single stone.

These Coercive Acts passed Parliament by huge majorities—more than 4 to 1 in most cases. A few members warned that they would arouse all the colonies to massive resistance. Edmund Burke urged Parliament to "reflect on how you are to govern a people who think they ought to be free and think they are not." He warned the members that they might soon be "wading up to your eyes in blood." In the House of Lords, William Pitt condemned closing the port of Boston, because it would punish the innocent as well as the guilty. He vowed he would go to his grave declaring "this country has no right under heaven" to tax America.

The King's friends, in firm charge of both houses of Parliament, sneered at these warnings. Lord North assured all and sundry that the other colonies would do nothing to support Massachusetts. " 'Tis said America will be exasperated," scoffed one administration supporter. "Will she then take arms?…She has neither army, navy, money or men." "I say stand and deliver to the Americans!" roared another member, who was soon rewarded by being named paymaster of the forces. Lord North summed up the debate with all-or-nothing brinkmanship: "We must control them or submit to them."

Once more these explosive words, or the gist of them, traveled across the Atlantic in British newspapers. In April 1774 General Gage sailed to Boston to take up his post as governor general of Massachusetts. In June ex-Governor Thomas Hutchinson decided a sojourn in England might provide him with some temporary peace of mind. The day he arrived in London, he was rushed to an audience with the King. Hutchinson came away amazed by George III's grasp of the situation in Boston. His Majesty knew the names of all the principal actors on both sides. Hutchinson commented that the King was "more his own [prime] minister than is generally imagined."

George III gleefully reported to Lord North that Hutchinson had told him Boston was "much dispirited" by the Port Act. The King was "now well convinced that they would soon submit." By this time Parliament had recessed and the members scattered to their country estates. In more than one of these

ABOVE *Although Alexander Wedderburn was George III's solicitor general, even the King commented on "the duplicity that often appears in his political deportment." Another MP remarked: "His character as a man is by no means high." He was "a lawyer on the make," concluded an historian of Parliament.*

RIGHT *The Sons of Liberty listed these Bostonians as traitors to their country because they signed a tribute to Thomas Hutchinson when he resigned as royal governor and went to England.*

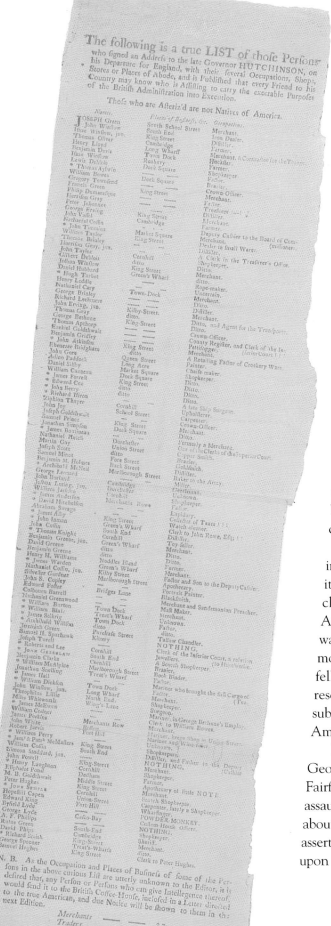

mansions, newspapers were soon reporting news from America that made for restless nights. Not only were the other colonies supporting Massachusetts, but they had also convened something called a Continental Congress, which was scheduled to meet in Philadelphia in the fall.

An Innate Spirit of Liberty

Far from being dispirited, Samuel Adams and the Sons of Liberty in Boston exulted that "the perfect crisis" in the struggle against England's attempts to tax America had arrived. A committee of correspondence rushed letters asking all the towns in Massachusetts to support Boston. Horsemen pounded south with similar pleas to Sons of Liberty and their allies in other colonies. The Bostonians called for a "Solemn League and Covenant" that would vow to cease all exports to and imports from England immediately and ban the consumption of British goods everywhere.

New York, where Yankees were almost as unpopular as Englishmen, insisted that the details of such a boycott and a unified American response to the Coercive Acts should be worked out by a Continental Congress. The Bostonians cried that Boston would starve waiting for thirteen colonies to put together such a cumbersome conclave. They were soon reassured on that point, at least. South Carolina sent the embattled port city £2,700 worth of food. Virginia sent 8,600 bushels of corn and wheat and hundreds of barrels of flour. Connecticut drove hundreds of sheep to the city's rescue.

In Virginia the House of Burgesses, with George Washington in attendance, called the occupation of Boston a "military invasion" and voted that June 1, the day the port was closed, would be a day of fasting and prayer to ask God to help Americans preserve their liberty and avoid "the evils of civil war." The new royal governor, John Murray, the Earl of Dunmore, promptly dissolved the assembly. Washington and his fellow burgesses marched to nearby Raleigh Tavern, where they resolved that "an attack on one of our sister colonies, to compel submission to arbitrary taxes, is an attack made on all British America." They also issued a call for a Continental Congress.

Back in Mount Vernon, Washington joined his neighbor George Mason in drawing up a set of resolutions for the citizens of Fairfax County. They called on all Americans to resist Parliament's assault on Massachusetts. Washington no longer had any doubt about British intentions. In a letter to a friend, he wrote: "We must assert our rights or submit to every imposition that can be heaped upon us, till custom and use shall make us [as] tame and abject slaves as the blacks we rule over with such arbitrary sway." The conduct of the British in Boston "exhibited an unexampled testimony of the most despotic system of tyranny that was ever practiced by a free government." Underscoring how closely he and others followed events in London, Washington wrote to another friend, "If we want further proofs [of British intentions] do not all the debates in the House of Commons confirm" the worst fears?

On August 1 Washington returned to Williamsburg, where another meeting of the House of Burgesses selected him as one of seven delegates to the Continental Congress that was to meet in Philadelphia on September 5, 1774. Only the speaker of the house, Peyton Randolph, and Richard Henry Lee, a brilliant orator and scion of a famous family, outpolled him. Young Thomas Jefferson did not make the list, but he stirred everyone with a fiery pamphlet, *A Summary View of the Rights of British America*, which the burgesses immediately ordered to be printed.

Back in Mount Vernon once more, preparing to leave for Philadelphia, Washington replied to a letter from Bryan Fairfax, brother of George Fairfax, the master of neighboring Belvoir. Bryan wanted a more respectful approach to Parliament and the King. He maintained there was right and wrong on both sides and spent 2,500 words trying to prove it.

Washington's answer was sympathetic but brief. He had "no new lights" to throw on the subject. All he could offer was his personal reaction. "An innate spirit of freedom" had persuaded him that Britain's policies were "repugnant to every principle of natural justice." Further thought had only convinced him that they were also "subversive of the law and constitution of Great Britain itself…"

Blows Must Decide
In London George III told Lord North of his reaction to the news of the fierce spirit of resistance in Boston and the convening of the Continental Congress: "The dye [die] is now cast, the colonies must either submit or triumph." Several weeks later, before any of the Congress's resolutions had reached England, he wrote: "I am not sorry to see that the line of conduct now seems chalked out…Blows must decide whether they [the colonies] are to be subject to this country or independent."

The patriot King could hardly wait for the war to begin. He thought it would be the vindication of the style of government he had launched. With Parliament as his acquiescent partner, he would show the world that Great Britain tolerated no insubordination anywhere within her empire. He easily managed to convince himself that there was no alternative to his authoritarian course. If the Americans became semi-independent, what was to stop other colonies—above all, Ireland, where rebellion constantly simmered just below the surface of mute obedience—from doing likewise?

Ironically, in one of his letters to Lord North, the King added that once the Americans submitted, he would be more than willing to tell them "that there is no inclination for the present to lay fresh taxes upon them." Somehow, in spite of his readiness to strike blows, George III wanted to be a kindly father of his country.

RIGHT *A committee of correspondence confers on what to say to the latest letter from Boston, describing British plans to punish the city for the Boston Tea Party. Benjamin Franklin, the deputy postmaster general for America, did not realize he was creating a revolutionary engine when he overhauled the colonial postal system, vastly increasing the speed at which letters traveled.*

After the British came over the walls of the American fort, the battle of Bunker Hill became a melee. Killed by a bullet in the head was Joseph Warren, the charismatic Boston physician who was second only to Samuel Adams as a revolutionary spokesman.

Over the Edge

"I am not a Virginian but an American!"

—Patrick Henry

Can thirteen very different, deeply divided colonies unite and win a war against the most powerful nation on earth? The British are confident they won't dare try. Concord Bridge and Bunker Hill administer rude shocks to this assumption. After a year of agonizing hesitation, the Continental Congress approves the Declaration of Independence.

I am not a Virginian but an American!" On September 6, 1774, Patrick Henry's words rang out across the crowded rows of the first Continental Congress in Philadelphia's brand-new Carpenters' Hall. There was a lot of wishful thinking in this declaration. The forty-five delegates from twelve colonies (Georgia was unrepresented) were almost all total strangers to one another. At their opening session on the previous day, they had cheered when they realized their number coincided with John Wilkes's famous forty-fifth edition of *The North Briton*. But this common commitment to liberty would have to overcome vast differences in accents and life-styles between sober Quakers from Pennsylvania and elegant grandees from South Carolina, between spare, pious Yankees and worldly New Yorkers, between expansive Virginians, who talked as big as their enormous colony, and men from tiny Delaware and Rhode Island, who were all too aware that the British fleet could devastate them.

More important, the Congress swiftly divided into two political groups. One, led by Patrick Henry and other firebrands, was inclined to declare the connection with England annihilated. The presence of a British fleet and army in Massachusetts meant "government is dissolved," Henry thundered. "We are in a state of nature." The colonies should form a government and go to war to defend their liberty.

Numerous delegates, such as John Jay, an argumentative young lawyer from New York, disagreed strongly with Henry. These moderates and conservatives felt he was being premature. Americans should defend their rights by relying on that powerful but unwritten bulwark of liberty, the British Constitution. Relapsing into a state of nature could be an invitation to anarchy. Speaker after speaker rose to hurl abstract arguments into the humid air. With a large proportion of lawyers on hand, it looked as if the Congress would do little but debate legal theory.

The Massachusetts delegates sat in mute misery, saying little. Samuel Adams was in complete agreement with Patrick Henry, but his more astute cousin John saw that a great many delegates were hostile to anything that

ABOVE **This is one of the two lanterns displayed in the steeple of Old North Church on April 18, 1775, that told Paul Revere the route the British were taking to Lexington and Concord.**

LEFT **Patrick Henry's fiery words failed to impress many members of the Continental Congress. He soon left to become governor of Virginia. The thirty-eight-year-old lawyer had worked his way up from poverty, trying more than 1,000 cases in a three-year period and winning most of them.**

smacked of "independency." John also sensed a majority "shuddered at the prospect of blood." He persuaded Samuel Adams to conceal what he later confessed in a less discreet moment—that the independence of America had been "the first wish" of his heart for the previous seven years.

Before the Congress opened, John Adams had filled his diary with dismayed comments on the pervasive suspicion of New Englanders. A group of Philadelphia Quakers reminded the Massachusetts delegation that their ancestors had hanged several Quakers in the previous century and laws still barred the sect from the province. "We have numberless prejudices to remove here," Adams wrote to one friend back home. "We have been obliged to act with great delicacy and caution."

Patrick Henry lost points with many delegates when he went from arguing that they were in a state of nature to proposing that votes in the Congress should be in proportion to a colony's population. This idea would have enabled Virginia and Massachusetts to dominate the Congress. Men from smaller colonies angrily asked why they should entrust their liberty to people they barely knew. Henry's proposal was rejected in favor of giving each colony one vote. It was the first but by no means the last time that the fear of giving anyone too much power would have fateful consequences for the survival of American liberty.

Before he left Boston, Samuel Adams had arranged for express riders to deliver news from the embattled city as rapidly as possible. Among the first bulletins to arrive was a report that war had broken out. Regulars were murdering citizens in the streets, and the British fleet was bombarding the city. The dispatch threw Philadelphia into a frenzy. "All is confusion...every tongue pronounces revenge," wrote a Connecticut delegate. John Adams told his wife, Abigail, that he was deeply moved by the way every man was as upset as if the capital of his own province had been attacked.

A few days later the report was corrected. There had been a tense standoff between militiamen and regulars in Massachusetts over General Gage's seizure of some gunpowder, but no blood had been shed. Undeterred, Sam Adams continued his program to prevent the Congress from becoming a constitutional debating society. Into Philadelphia pounded another dust-covered horseman from Boston—the burly silversmith Paul Revere. In his saddlebags was a set of resolves recently issued by the leaders of Suffolk County, which included Boston, under the guidance of another Adams lieutenant, Dr. Joseph Warren.

The Suffolk Resolves were fireworks from start to finish. They denounced England as "the parricide which points the dagger to our bosoms" and declared the streets of Boston were "thronged with military executioners." The compact between George III and the people of Massachusetts was "totally wrecked, annulled and vacated." The Coercive Acts were denounced, and

ABOVE *New Yorker John Jay was one of the leaders of the moderate-conservative party that tried to work out a compromise with the British. He soon became an independence man and served with distinction in the Continental Congress and abroad as a diplomat.*

RIGHT **This 1780 British print portrays Samuel Adams as a nobleman in his dressing room, with a vast estate behind him. Actually he was so poor his friends had to buy him a decent suit to wear to the Continental Congress.**

"no obedience" was "due from this province to either or any part" of them. The resolves closed with a call for an immediate stoppage of all trade with England, Ireland and the West Indies and urged Americans to organize the militia for defense, giving commissions only to those men who had proved themselves "the inflexible friends of the rights of the people."

Sam Adams's timing proved superb. Moderates such as George Washington were bored with the legalistic debates, and they joined the firebrands in approving the Suffolk Resolves and ordering them printed in the newspapers. John Adams gleefully informed his diary that he was now convinced "America will support…Massachusetts or perish with her."

Thereafter, the firebrands, or "popular men" as they were sometimes called, were in control of the Congress—a mastery they maintained by carefully muting their defiant rhetoric and decorating it with respectful apostrophes to the King. The Congress issued a declaration of American rights that denied Parliament's authority to tax America, to interfere with the right of trial by jury or to alter the charter of a colony. But the delegates revealed they were badly split on the question of whether Parliament had the right to regulate American trade within the empire. The disagreement implied that many delegates wanted to work out some kind of reconciliation with England.

Next, the Congress compiled a list of grievances, which included all the American legislation passed by Parliament since 1763. Finally and most important, the Congress voted to create a Continental Association, which would prohibit all imports from England after December 1774 and all exports starting in the fall of 1775. That rather distant date was adopted so that Virginia could sell her already planted tobacco crop. To enforce the association, the Congress urged that a committee be chosen in every county, city and town. Almost inadvertently, with this recommendation, the delegates created thousands of small revolutionary engines.

At this point the conservatives, zeroing in on the disagreement about Par-

liament's right to regulate trade, launched a counterattack. They coalesced around Joseph Galloway, a brainy Philadelphia lawyer who was an old friend and colleague of Benjamin Franklin's and for many years the most powerful politician in Pennsylvania. Galloway declared he was "as much a friend to liberty as [any man who] exists." He agreed that England had no right to tax America. But in a dangerous world, America needed the protection of the English fleet and army. Whereupon Galloway proposed a Plan of Union—a written constitution that would unite Britain and America. It would

create an American legislature, called a Grand Council, whose members would be chosen by colonial assemblies. The council would have the power to approve or disapprove laws passed by Parliament but would concede to the British the right to regulate imperial trade. The individual colonies would retain control of their internal affairs.

A surprising number of delegates liked Galloway's plan. Edward Rutledge of South Carolina called it "almost perfect." John Dickinson of Pennsylvania found merit in it. So did John Jay and several other members of the New York delegation. Even Stephen Hopkins of Rhode Island, a Yankee to his bones, favored it.

In response, the firebrands were forced to reveal that they already believed no compromise with Great Britain was possible. Closest to a serious reply to Galloway was Patrick Henry's claim that the Grand Council would be corrupted by the British. John Jay asked Richard Henry Lee of Virginia, who supported Henry, to point out one American liberty that Galloway's plan did not protect. Lee did not even try to answer him.

At the end of a day of inconclusive argument, someone (there are no complete records of the debates) made a motion to table Galloway's plan for consideration at some later date. The conservatives vigorously opposed the motion, aware that it was tantamount to killing the plan. By a hair's breadth, six colonies to five, with Rhode Island's two-man delegation divided, the Congress edged Galloway's brainchild toward oblivion. It was the high-water mark

ABOVE *The Reverend Jacob Duché opened the September 7, 1774, session of the Continental Congress by reading from the Thirty-fifth Psalm and added ten minutes of spontaneous prayer asking God to support the American cause. One member said he was "worth riding 100 miles to hear." In October 1777, a discouraged Duché wrote George Washington, urging him to surrender to the British.*

of those Americans who wanted to stay in the empire by working out a new arrangement with England. In the Congress's final days, the delegates reconsidered Galloway's plan and rejected it by a wide but unrecorded margin—and then voted to expunge all mention of it from the record.

George Washington said little at this first Congress, but his reputation as Virginia's outstanding soldier kept many delegates' eyes on him. Silas Deane of Connecticut was amazed by his height and surprised by how young the forty-two-year-old ex-colonel looked. Deane found his countenance "hard" but liked his "easy soldier-like air." Dr. Solomon Drowne of Rhode Island called Washington "Virginia's hero" and in a musing letter wondered if he could rescue American liberty in single combat with George III. Several delegates, including John Adams, reported that Washington had offered to raise a thousand men at his own expense and march them to Boston. Washington never said this, but it was another indication of the impact that his appearance and reputation made on everyone.

When Washington returned to Mount Vernon, he found an even stronger indication of his growing importance. Militia companies in almost every county in Virginia had elected him their commander-in-chief. Unquestionably, he would be in charge of Virginia's battalions if violence erupted in Boston.

Whether there would be any violence was a large question. In one of its last acts before adjourning, the Congress had issued a stern warning to Massachusetts not to attack the British. But if the British were the aggressors, the delegates promised that the rest of America would stand or fall with the Bay Colony.

The moderates and conservatives were now aware that the popular leaders constituted a party, and they began organizing against them. They recognized Samuel Adams as the dominant figure—a man who, Joseph Galloway said, "eats little, drinks little, sleeps little, thinks much and is most decisive and indefatigable in the pursuit of his object." Galloway also had no trouble connecting the Adams "faction" in the Congress to the confrontation in Massachusetts. The Pennsylvanian and his followers began reminding the rest of America how much they disliked New Englanders. By the time the Congress reconvened in the spring of 1775, the Galloway faction hoped to have a solid majority that would make his Plan of Union a political reality.

A United Province

A great deal—it would be no exaggeration to say everything—now depended on what happened in Massachusetts. One man who feared the worst was Governor-General Thomas Gage. He had long since eaten the blithe words about settling the dispute with four regiments that he had burbled to George III in February 1774. Gage had based his optimism on the assumption that Boston was the only place that needed a glimpse of the royal fist. Instead, thanks to the Coercive Acts, he found an entire province in revolt.

The citizens of towns such as Lexington were outraged and insulted when they learned that under the revised charter they could hold town meetings only with Gage's permission, their elected representatives would no longer have a voice in the appointments of judges, justices of the peace or sheriffs and they could not even nominate people for jury duty. Their long-standing disapproval of the riotous city folk of Boston vanished. George III and Lord

North had handed Samuel Adams what he had vainly labored to achieve for a decade—a coalition between the city and the country.

At Samuel Adams's suggestion, the people of Massachusetts held a series of county conventions that breathed defiance to Gage and the Coercive Acts. The town and county of Worcester declared that they would not allow judges paid by the King and appointed by Gage to hear cases. When some of these judges tried to enter the county courthouse on September 6, 1774, 6,000 armed men were there to stop them. The judges were forced to parade in front of the militia companies and publicly accept the authority of the assembled people.

The Continental Congress did nothing to assuage the governor-general's fears for the future. He told London that the Congress's proceedings would have the virtual force of law in America because there "does not appear to be resolution and strength enough among the most sensible and moderate people to reject them." Gage had long since given up looking for sensible and moderate people in Massachusetts. He had yet to recover from the shock of the province's reaction to his seizure of 125 barrels of gunpowder in Cambridge on September 1, 1774. An astonishing number of armed men—some say as many as 20,000—converged on Boston. Dr. Joseph Warren and the other popular leaders persuaded them to go home peacefully. But Gage realized that he and his small army of 3,000 men could easily be annihilated. He began building fortifications across the narrow neck of land that then connected Boston to the mainland.

Gage's fears of military defeat multiplied as he learned more about what was happening in the interior of Massachusetts. In the spirit of the Suffolk Resolves, the Worcester County Convention persuaded all the towns in the province to elect new officers for the militia—sweeping out everyone suspected of loyalty to the Crown. One-third of each militia company, Worcester urged, should be "ready to act at a minute's warning." This was not a new idea. The term "minutemen" went back to 1750. But the program of drilling and training the minutemen undertook was new. Unlike the old militia, which met only once a year, the minutemen were to meet three times a week. It would not take long for these men—Gage estimated their numbers at 15,000—to become an embryo army. One-third of them were veterans of the war with France. Most of Gage's soldiers, on the other hand, had never fired a shot. England had been at peace for fifteen years.

Gage's only glimmer of hope came from the reports that he received from one of his spies, Dr. Benjamin Church, who doubled as a King's man and a highly respected Son of Liberty. Church told the governor-general that the extra-legal Massachusetts Provincial Congress, which Samuel Adams convened in Concord on October 11, 1774, had rejected the firebrand's call for an immediate assault on the British in Boston. Adams and his group were soundly defeated when he moved on December 10 that "arms be immediately taken up against the King's troops." Thomas Cushing, Benjamin Franklin's favorite Boston correspondent, who had been a delegate to the Continental Congress, denounced the idea as "infamous." He told the Provincial Congressmen that "the southern colonies would not stand by you."

When Adams disagreed, Cushing shouted: "That is a lie, Mr. Adams, and I know it and you know it."

Back in Boston Gage had no illusions that this precarious truce would

RIGHT *General Thomas Gage was British commander-in-chief in America. In 1754 he served in the British army with George Washington. Gage married beautiful Margaret Kemble of New Jersey. She sided with her fellow Americans.*

GENERAL the HONble. Thos. GAGE

hold. He told London that the British could not get their way in America except by "conquering and to do that effectually…you should have an army near 20,000 strong composed of regulars, a large body of good irregulars…and three or four regiments of light horse" plus "good and sufficient artillery."

In another letter the governor-general gave an even more cogent reason why a formidable British army was needed immediately. "A check anywhere would be fatal, and the first stroke will decide a great deal." Gage was in touch with the numerous moderates and conservatives like Galloway who were telling Americans it was madness to challenge the British to war. Break the rebels in Massachusetts with one decisive blow, Gage reasoned, and the spirit of resistance would vanish elsewhere. A defeat, on the other hand, would encourage defiance in the other colonies.

A Royal Surprise

In London George III had decided to make sure there would be no concessions to the Continental Congress. He informed Lord North that it was time for new elections. North was so surprised he almost disagreed with the King, calling the dissolution of Parliament before the statutory seventh year "premature." George III assured his prime minister that with "temper, firmness and due activity" the government would emerge a solid winner. George wanted to make sure an expiring Parliament was not grappling with "American business," making it a major election issue. He also wanted to surprise William Pitt and the rest of the opposition.

North swallowed hard and went to work. What the King meant by "due activity" was soon apparent in North's correspondence with Secretary to the Treasury John Robinson, who had taken over the Duke of Newcastle's role as election fixer. On October 6, 1774, while the Continental Congress was still in session, North was writing to Robinson: "You know that the seat at Plympton is at £3[000]. Lord H[ood] should be informed of that as he said his son should pay £24[00] for it…Mr. Legge can afford only 400£. If he comes in for Lostwithiel he will cost the public 2000 guineas…" He meant the King would have to pay the difference to buy a seat for Legge, who was Lord Dartmouth's son.

Robinson kept lists of peers and members of the House of Commons who held "offices, commands, contracts, lieutenancies or governments." George Selwyn, for instance, was paymaster of the works and surveyor of the mint, two jobs at which he never worked for a day. Richard Vernon was clerk of the

BELOW *Edmund Burke, right, Irish-born defender of America in Parliament, was often frustrated by his backer, wealthy Charles Watson-Wentworth, Marquess of Rockingham. His Lordship was more interested in his racehorses than in politics and complained that the British public was "a silly echo" of the government's hard line.*

jewel office, Charles Scudamore was deputy ranger of Whittlebury. Neither showed up to perform these nonexistent tasks. Their salaries were dutifully paid from the King's £800,000 civil list.

The patriot King had mastered the fine art of corrupting Parliament. He also caught the opposition flatfooted. Lord Rockingham complained of being taken "very much unaware." Edmund Burke could only lament that the disorder and discontent in America seemed to affect most voters "as little as the division of Poland." (That unfortunate country had recently been partitioned among Russia, Austria and Prussia.) The King's supporters exulted. One predicted the surprise would "confound the schemes of a vast number of those...on the popular line."

The election was an administration triumph. On November 14, 1774, an ecstatic Lord North reported to George III that the new Parliament would contain at least 321 members who would support the government no matter what happened in America or elsewhere. That left 237 members, divided into two lists: confirmed members of the opposition and doubtfuls. The latter would probably support the government most of the time. George III had a comfortable majority that would back his hard-line policy toward America.

By this time General Gage's reports on the situation in Boston had begun arriving in London. They were greeted with disbelief and dismay. The King and the cabinet scoffed at Gage's warning that between 20,000 and 30,000 men were needed to pacify Massachusetts. The entire British army, scattered from Ireland to India to Africa to the West Indies, totaled only 48,000 men. George III's previously high opinion of Gage sank to subterranean levels.

On December 13 the mail packet from New York brought the Continental Congress's declarations and decisions to London. They did nothing to soften the King's attitude. When the American secretary, Lord Dartmouth, suggested sending a parliamentary commission "to discuss and settle all claims" with the Congress, the King doused the idea with icy disapproval. He said such a gesture would make it look as if "the Mother Country" was "afraid" of her rebellious children. Dartmouth's days as a cabinet member became numbered.

An Ambassador's Tears

During these tension-filled weeks, Lord Dartmouth attempted to negotiate with Benjamin Franklin, who was still in London watching events with profound disenchantment. He told Thomas Cushing to expect nothing from the new Parliament. "Most of the members are bribing or purchasing to get in," he wrote. This meant "there was little doubt of selling their votes to the [prime] minister for the time being, to reimburse themselves." Even Franklin's closest British friend, William Strahan, who was the King's printer, ran for Parliament as a ministry man to protect his £3,000-a-year contract.

Dartmouth negotiated with Franklin through some prominent English Quakers, and then through Admiral Richard, Lord Howe, whose family had a tradition of friendship with America. Both parleys went nowhere. Basically, Franklin presented the same set of demands the Continental Congress had made, although he couched them in more persuasive language. Dartmouth finally rejected Franklin's proposals as "inadmissible and impractical."

Simultaneously, Franklin was working closely with William Pitt. He had sent the ailing statesman a copy of the petition of the Continental Congress as soon as it arrived in England. On January 20, 1775, he came to the House of Lords at Pitt's request. As soon as Franklin was admitted, Pitt introduced a resolution calling on the King to withdraw the troops from Boston before "any sudden and fatal catastrophe" occurred. In one of his most eloquent speeches, Pitt told Parliament: "It is not repealing a piece of parchment that can restore America to our bosom; you must repeal her fears and her resentments."

Members of the cabinet brutally attacked the resolution, and it was voted down by a large majority. An equally large majority of the House of Commons refused to consider the petition of the Continental Congress, because it was not a legally constituted body. Pitt continued his one-man crusade for reconciliation. He began consulting with Franklin on a comprehensive plan to restore peace to the empire. On Sunday, January 29, the two men spent several hours in Franklin's Craven Street rooms, going over the details of the plan to make sure it would be acceptable to Americans. Franklin could not resist noting it was a year to the day since his humiliation before the Privy Council.

On February 1, 1775, Pitt laid his plan before the House of Lords, once more with Franklin as his special guest. Dozens of members of the House of Commons also crowded into the upper house to watch this climactic moment. Pitt proposed that Parliament, while retaining its role as the supreme lawmaking body of the empire, renounce the right to tax America. He called on the King to recognize the Continental Congress and on Parliament to repeal the Coercive Acts and resolve the other grievances that were alienating the Americans.

Lord Dartmouth, the American secretary, said the plan required "much consideration" and hoped Pitt did not expect an immediate vote. Up sprang John Montagu, the Earl of Sandwich, first lord of the admiralty. He called for the plan's immediate rejection, declaring he could not believe it was "the production of any British peer." It appeared to him "rather the work of some *American*." As he said this, he turned his sallow, haughty face toward Franklin, who was leaning on the bar of the House.

Yes, Sandwich shrilled, he was sure he had in his eye the very person who had drawn up the plan, "one of the bitterest and most mischievous enemies this country has ever known." William Pitt replied that the plan was entirely his own. In the past people had said that his greatest fault was his unwillingness to take advice. But if he were the King's first minister at this moment, he would not hesitate to ask the assistance of the gentleman whom Lord Sandwich had "so injuriously reflected on." He was a man whom "all Europe held in high estimation for his knowledge and wisdom." He was an honor not only to the English nation but to human nature.

Sandwich called for an immediate vote to reject Pitt's plan. The House of Lords complied 61 to 32, with the weak-kneed Dartmouth joining the crushing majority. In a letter to his Philadelphia friend Charles Thomson, Franklin said the bill, "tho' on so important a subject and offered by so great a character…was treated with as much contempt as they could have shown to a ballad offered by a drunken porter."

After that demonstration of the ministry's determination, Franklin's hopes of compromise plummeted. He decided to return to America. As he began

ABOVE *Elevated to the peerage as Lord Chatham, William Pitt lost much of his influence among Londoners. John Wilkes became their hero. A loner who found it hard to work with others, Pitt was frequently ignored by the new generation in Parliament. Americans continued to admire him. Pittsburgh, Pennsylvania, and Pittsfield, Massachusetts, were named after him.*

packing, he received a letter from his old friend Joseph Galloway, enclosing his Plan of Union. Although it was essentially an elaboration of a similar plan Franklin had proposed in 1754, during the French and Indian War, his reply to Galloway revealed the depths of his disillusion with England. "When I consider the extream corruption prevalent among all orders of men in this old rotten state, and the glorious publick virtue so predominant in our rising country, I cannot but apprehend more mischief than benefit from a closer union...."

Then came words that revealed the anguished tug of old affection. "However I would try anything and bear anything that can be borne with safety to our just liberties, rather than engage in a war with such near relations, unless compelled to it by dire necessity in our own defense."

On his last day in London, Franklin spent some time with the scientist Joseph Priestley, going over a bundle of newspapers recently arrived from America. Franklin pointed out articles that might do some good if they were reprinted in London papers. "He was frequently not able to proceed for the tears literally running down his cheeks," Priestley said.

Liberty or Death

In America ordinary people seemed more inclined to prepare for war while their leaders talked peace. Connecticut's Sons of Liberty began a series of "Tory hunts" that forced supporters of the Crown to recant their views or leave the colony. The Rhode Island assembly was bombarded with petitions to establish independent military companies. In New Hampshire about 400 men invaded Fort William and Mary at the entrance to Portsmouth Harbor and carried away a hundred barrels of gunpowder and sixteen cannon. Maryland imitated Virginia and began forming companies of soldiers outside the structure of the old militia. South Carolina imitated New Hampshire and, in the

RIGHT *Supposedly visiting Lady Caroline Howe to play chess, Benjamin Franklin discussed possible solutions to the American crisis with her brother, Admiral Lord Richard Howe. The Howes' mother was an illegitimate daughter of George I.*

words of their distressed royal governor, "persons unknown" stole large amounts of gunpowder and numerous guns from the royal arsenal.

In Virginia Patrick Henry, Richard Henry Lee and other popular leaders were delighted when they learned that Fincastle County in the western mountains was mustering a thousand riflemen, "the most formidable light infantry in the world." But the liberty men were distressed by the attitude of the Old Dominion's leaders. Plump, complacent Peyton Randolph and his circle of conservatives were far more worried about a possible slave insurrection, should war break out. They waited patiently for the royal governor, John Murray, the Earl of Dunmore, to call a meeting of the House of Burgesses, which he coolly refused to do, prompting Lee to compare him to the "tyrant" Stuart Kings who went for years without summoning Parliament.

When Randolph finally succumbed to popular pressure and convened a meeting of the extralegal Virginia assembly, the conservative majority eagerly endorsed a resolution for a "speedy return of those halcyon days when we lived a free and happy people." Patrick Henry riposted by resolving that "this colony be immediately put into a state of defense." The conservatives all but denounced the idea. Henry replied with sentiments that his first biographer converted into immortal phrases: "Gentlemen may cry peace peace—but there is no peace…I know not what course others may take, but as for me, give me liberty or give me death!"

Contemporary accounts have Henry calling George III a tyrant, a fool, a puppet and a tool of a Parliament and of a nation composed of "a set of wretches sunk in luxury." Whatever he actually said, George Washington and Thomas Jefferson were among the delegates who helped his motion to arm Virginia win a narrow majority, 65 to 60. But not much came of the ensuing preparations. When the majority realized it would cost money to raise and equip soldiers, they lapsed back into letting individual counties undertake the task. This unwillingness of the largest and richest colony to pay taxes for its own defense was not a good omen.

The First Stroke

In London George III and his cabinet, their confidence bolstered by their huge majority in Parliament, moved toward a confrontation with the Americans. On February 2, 1775, North introduced a motion to declare the province of Massachusetts in a state of rebellion and asked the King to take steps to support the sovereignty of England. The opposition, led by Edmund Burke, decried this move as a declaration of war. But the measure passed by a majority of three to one. George III was immensely pleased and instructed North to make sure a maximum number of MPs and peers appeared at St. James's Palace to present the measure to him for his approval.

Meanwhile, the King attempted to find a replacement for Governor-General Gage. The soldier with the most prestige, Jeffery Amherst, the general who had won the French and Indian War, declined to take the job. His Majesty decided to send three younger major generals—Henry Clinton, John Burgoyne and William Howe—to America to bolster Gage. He also ordered some reinforcements, little more than 1,000 men—far short of the large army Gage wanted.

The King and his ministers still refused to believe Gage's assessment of the odds he faced. They agreed wholeheartedly with Lord Sandwich's opinion of Americans as soldiers. "Suppose the colonies do abound in men," he sneered in Parliament. "They are raw, undisciplined, cowardly men. I wish instead of 40 or 50,000 of these brave fellows, they would produce in the field at least 200,000, the more the better, the easier would be the conquest."

In the House of Commons, Colonel James Grant—who had served in America, at one point in the same army with George Washington—declared he was certain the Americans "would never dare to face an English army." They were hopeless soldiers, useful only as beasts of burden. Colonel Thomas Clarke, aide-de-camp to George III, declared that with a thousand British grenadiers, he could march through America, gelding all the males, "partly by force and partly with a little coaxing."

In this spirit the King and his cabinet ordered Lord Dartmouth to draft a letter telling Gage that it was time to act. He was to seize the leaders of the rebellion and if necessary meet the rebel Americans in battle and rout them. "A smaller force now, if put to the test, would be able to encounter them with greater probability of success," Dartmouth wrote. If Gage waited for his large army, the Americans would have time to build up their resources. Now, Dartmouth argued, the rebels would be forced to "put every thing to the issue...of a single action." In the comfortable security of his Whitehall office, the American secretary was standing Gage's warning of the importance of the first stroke on its head.

Dartmouth's letter reached Gage in Boston on April 14, 1775. The governor-general immediately began planning the "decisive" action that the American secretary demanded. Thanks to his spies, Gage knew that Massachusetts' reserve of gunpowder consisted of "between ninety and a hundred barrels...at Concord." A hundred barrels was a pathetically small amount of powder for an army of 15,000 men. The Massachusetts Provincial Congress had set 1,000 barrels as a minimum figure.

Gage decided that a swift march on Concord to seize the powder, as well as the fourteen cannon said to be in the town, would have a crippling, even demoralizing impact on the Provincial Congress's plans to form an Army of Observation to pen the British inside Boston. Since early 1775 Gage had been sending detachments of his troops into the countryside to test the provincials' warning system. Each time, the Americans had appeared in force, and the British had returned to Boston.

The Americans saw these encounters as proof that the British did not dare to attack them. This impression had been confirmed by what happened at Salem toward the end of February 1775. Gage had learned that carriages for twenty cannon were being built at Salem forge. He ordered Lieutenant Colonel Alexander Leslie to march his Sixty-fourth regiment aboard a transport and sail to the port city by night to seize them. Landing near Marblehead, Leslie found the good men and women of Salem hoisting the draw on the bridge across the North River between him and the forge.

Leslie ordered them to lower the bridge and told one of his companies to aim its guns at them. Outraged, the people warned him he had "no right to fire without orders." Others told him if a single man pulled a trigger, they would all end up corpses. Minutemen were assembling from all directions. Leslie and the citizens of Salem worked out a compromise. He was allowed to march across the bridge, advance thirty rods (165 yards) into Salem, and return to his ship, so he could say he fulfilled his orders. The story swept through Massachusetts, leaving everyone with the impression that the British were not permitted to fire at the minutemen or anyone else who defied them.

On March 30, 1775, Gage sent a full brigade of his army—1,200 men—into the countryside under the command of Brigadier Hugh, Lord Percy. Again minuteman companies swarmed from all directions and kept the British under close observation. Gage saw these expeditions as a way of familiarizing his troops with the terrain over which they might have to fight. He also hoped to intimidate the minutemen—or at least make them tired of responding to false alarms. Instead he gave them the feeling that they could muster huge numbers of their fellow minutemen and thus increased their self-confidence.

On April 15, the day after Gage received Lord Dartmouth's letter, his industrious spy, Dr. Benjamin Church, reported that the Massachusetts Provincial Congress had voted to send delegates to the other New England provinces to discuss the creation of an army. "A sudden blow struck now," Church added, "would overset all their plans."

These words coalesced with Gage's thoughts about seizing the gunpowder at Concord. The British commander did not see this operation as the first battle of the war. He hoped to accomplish it without firing a shot. With the New England army crippled by lack of ammunition and reinforcements for his army en route, Gage might then be in a position to arrest Samuel Adams and the other rebel leaders and smash any attempt to stop him.

To guarantee success, Gage chose his best troops, the light infantry and grenadier companies from each regiment and from the 400-man Royal Marine battalion he had brought ashore from the navy's ships. The light infantry were the most agile and aggressive soldiers in the army. The grenadiers were the biggest men and supposedly the most fearsome. To command these 700 troops Gage chose fifty-two-year-old Lieutenant Colonel Francis Smith of the Tenth Regiment, one of his most experienced officers. As Smith's second in command he selected fifty-three-year-old Major John Pitcairn of the marines, a stout, likable Scot with nineteen years' service afloat and ashore.

Within twenty-four hours, the expedition was the poorest-kept military secret in history. Dozens, possibly hundreds, of Bostonians noticed that the light infantrymen and grenadiers had been relieved from routine duty. They also noted that the British had collected numerous longboats from the fleet and tied them up to a man-of-war near the shore. This move strongly suggested Gage was planning to send his men across Back Bay to Cambridge rather than wasting time and shoe leather marching them across Boston Neck. [See map, page 126] The governor-general probably knew there was no chance of concealing these facts. What he held in tight secrecy was the goal of the expedition and the time: It was to be a night march.

Alas for Gage, the rebels penetrated this secret too. Some historians think Dr. Joseph Warren had a secret ally inside Gage's headquarters: the governor-general's beautiful American wife, Margaret Kemble Gage. She had already told one friend that she hoped her husband "would never be the instrument of

MINUTEMEN TO THE RESCUE

In the fifteen years of peace between the fall of Quebec in 1759 and the crisis in American-British relations in 1774, the militia of Massachusetts had deteriorated from a military organization to a social club. Annual training days were largely an excuse to get drunk and play jokes, such as firing blanks at an officer's feet.

The minutemen changed this casual style. They took seriously the injunction to train regularly. Not even the brutal cold of the Massachusetts winter lessened their dedication. "I have spent many an evening going through the exercise [drill] on the barn floor with my mittens on," wrote one Framingham minuteman.

At Marblehead companies drilled as many as four times a week. Lincoln called for four hours of drill twice a week. Concord drilled its minutemen two and a half days a week and required them to enlist for ten months, paying them one shilling four pence a week—the equivalent in modern money of about $2.50.

"Express riders" spread the alarm from house to house in widely scattered farm townships.

Drill consisted of a company's learning to obey fifty separate orders to maneuver as a unit on a battlefield. The men also practiced volleying in three ranks, the front rank kneeling and the next two standing, reloading and firing as rapidly as possible until a drum beat a stop. Although they did not use any of these tactics on the battlefield on April 19, 1775, performing them gave the men confidence and got them used to obeying orders—and officers acquired a habit of command.

Each minuteman was supposed to be equipped with a musket, bayonet, cartridge box and thirty-six rounds of ammunition. On April 14, 1775, records show that approximately half of them had bayonets. But many of them carried hatchets, a weapon they had discovered fighting the Indians. About one-third of the minutemen were veterans of the French and Indian War.

The Massachusetts Provincial Congress also directed the minutemen and the rest of the militia to elect their own officers. This order toppled from high ranks a great many prominent citizens who were suspected of Toryism—too much readiness to obey the King and his representatives. Into their places stepped men who had been agitating against British policies, guaranteeing the minutemen a top-to-bottom cohesion. The minutemen became, in the words of one Concord man, "a united family of Sons of Liberty."

Minutemen took seriously their promise to be ready to fight in sixty seconds. In six months they became a well trained embryo army.

sacrificing the lives of her countrymen." Others opine that there was no need for her to betray her husband. Several thousand sets of eyes were watching every move the British made.

At 9:30 P.M. on April 18, 1775, the light infantry and grenadiers assembled at the foot of Boston Common for the boat trip across Back Bay. Sons of Liberty rushed word to Dr. Joseph Warren, who ordered Paul Revere and an adventurous tanner named William Dawes to carry a warning to Lexington, where John Hancock and Samuel Adams were staying in the parsonage, preparing to depart for the meeting of the Second Continental Congress. Knowing Gage had been ordered to arrest the Massachusetts leaders, Warren thought they were the object of Smith's march.

Revere had made his own preparations. He asked a friend to display two lanterns in the tower of Old North Church if the British went by water, and one if the longboats were a feint and they were marching over Boston Neck. The lanterns were for the benefit of confederates in Charlestown, just across the Charles River from Boston, in case Revere was seized by sailors from the man-of-war HMS *Somerset*, which was guarding the ferryway. But Revere made it across the river by staying well downstream of the looming *Somerset*. In Charlestown he mounted a swift mare supplied by Deacon John Larkin and began his famous ride. The largely forgotten Dawes had no trouble talking his

LEFT *Burly silversmith Paul Revere was a forgotten man until 1863, when Henry Wadsworth Longfellow wrote a poem about his midnight ride. One of Boston's foremost Sons of Liberty, he printed the first issue of continental currency, made the nation's first official seal and learned to manufacture gunpowder. He also found time to father sixteen children.*

way past the British sentries on Boston Neck. He too was soon pounding through the moonlit night toward Lexington.

Both men reached the parsonage in Lexington before the British even began their march from the west shore of Back Bay. The Royal Navy failed to supply enough longboats to take all 700 men in one trip. Colonel Smith neglected to put anyone in charge of the embarkation, and men scrambled into the boats haphazardly. Much time was lost on the other side sorting out the scattered companies in the darkness. Not until 1:30 A.M. did the reassembled force get on the road that would take them through Lexington to Concord.

The news brought by Dawes and Revere caused great excitement among the 750 citizens of Lexington. The meetinghouse bell tolled, and by 1 A.M. the 130 members of the Lexington militia company had formed a line on the two-acre common. One-third were minutemen. After conferring about what to do, they resolved not "to make or meddle with the...regulars." Their captain, tall, husky John Parker, dismissed them.

Meanwhile, Dawes and Revere remounted and rode for Concord. About two miles from the town, they collided with a mounted patrol of British officers whom Gage had sent out to cut off messengers intent on sounding the alarm. The British seized the two men, along with a third night rider, Dr. Samuel Prescott, who was returning from a visit to his Lexington fiancée, Lydia Mulliken. The officers forced the Americans into a pasture and began questioning them.

Dr. Prescott was a dedicated Son of Liberty. "Put on," he whispered to Revere, and they broke away in opposite directions. Dawes whirled his horse and raced back toward Lexington to warn Adams and Hancock of this new threat. The British overtook Revere and put a gun to his head, ordering him to tell the truth or they would blow out his brains. He proceeded to tell a series of whoppers. There were 500 minutemen gathering between the British and Boston, and Smith's expedition had gone aground crossing Back Bay and was unlikely to appear. The unnerved British let Revere go, after forcing him to exchange horses with a sergeant of the grenadiers who was riding a small horse that was growing tired.

Revere went straight to Samuel Adams and John Hancock and told them there was little doubt that the British were planning a strike at the gunpowder in Concord. Hancock seized a musket and swore he would join the militiamen on Lexington Common. "That is not our business; we belong to the cabinet," Samuel Adams said. After a great deal of argument, the headstrong Hancock was finally persuaded to join Adams in safer quarters in nearby Woburn.

Meanwhile, Lieutenant Colonel Smith, Major Pitcairn and their men were plodding the eleven miles through Cambridge to Lexington. They soon encountered the patrolling British officers, who told them in excited tones Revere's story of 500 minutemen in the vicinity. The officers gave the impression that they had barely escaped with their lives. Alarmed, Smith sent a messenger back to Boston to warn Gage that he might need reinforcements. He ordered Pitcairn to take six light-infantry companies and march at top speed to seize the bridges at Concord.

Pitcairn's column soon met a well-dressed man in a sulky who told them 600 men were waiting to fight them on Lexington Green. Another man bringing a

load of wood to Boston told them 1,000 minutemen were waiting in Concord. Two British lieutenants spurred their horses ahead of the column and in the gray half-light of approaching dawn saw a number of armed men hurrying toward Lexington along a ridge line on either side of the road. Next they saw a man in a field, aiming a musket at them. He pulled the trigger, and there was a small spurt of flame and a tiny puff of smoke. The musket had flashed in the pan—the powder in the firing pan had not ignited the charge in the gun barrel. The man may not have had a charge in his barrel; it may have been a gesture of defiance. The lieutenants galloped back to Pitcairn to report their narrow escape.

Pitcairn ordered his light infantrymen to halt in the road and load their guns. In the distance they could hear the Lexington church bell tolling an alarm. To the north and south, other town bells were ringing. Pitcairn later claimed he told the troops not to fire without an order. But the alarms and threats they had encountered on the road made this warning an empty formality to men who had spent most of the previous year cooped up in Boston being baited by sharp-tongued Sons of Liberty.

In Lexington a rider sent out by Captain John Parker reported the British column was only fifteen minutes away and marching fast. Sixteen-year-old William Diamond pounded a rolling beat on his brightly painted drum. Some thirty-eight militiamen responded. They had been waiting all night for the British to show up.

Parker mustered his men on the north end of the common, close to the road that led to Bedford. On the opposite side of the common, another branch of the road from Boston bent left toward Concord. The bulky Congregational church, where the militant Reverend Jonas Clark had repeatedly told his flock that the British were plotting to deprive Americans of their liberty, blocked the militiamen's view of the fork in the Boston road.

The militiamen stood in two rows, their numbers growing as more men responded to William Diamond's drum. They included grandfathers like Jonas Parker, the captain's cousin, and teenagers like Isaac Muzzy. They came from families that had been living in Lexington for generations, and most were related to each other. Many fathers stood beside sons. Incongruous among the rows of white faces was the glistening black skin of a slave, Prince Estabrook. He had volunteered to fight and had been admitted to the company by a majority vote.

If Captain Parker and his men had any plan, it was to keep as far as possible from the road to Concord. They had been told that the British numbered between 1,200 and 1,500 men. The militiamen had no orders to fire on British soldiers the moment they saw them. On the contrary, they all believed the rules that had governed previous encounters with Gage's marches into the country still applied—the British were under strict orders not to fire unless the Americans fired first.

As captain, Parker was responsible for his men's safety. No power on earth, not even Samuel Adams or the Reverend Jonas Clark at their most eloquent, could have persuaded Parker to block the British line of march, as he is often pictured doing in popular prints. This would have been an unforgivably reckless invitation to gunfire. A sensible man, Parker saw no reason to begin a war by having himself and his men commit suicide.

RIGHT *Paul Revere, briefly captured by the British, told them some scary lies and escaped. Mounted on Brown Beauty, one of the fastest horses in Massachusetts, Revere alarmed the countryside. But he never said: "The British are coming!" Instead, he shouted: "The regulars are coming out!"*

Soon Parker's men heard the thud of hundreds of feet striking the ground simultaneously. Their eyes focused on the Concord road side of the church, expecting a column of marching men. Instead only a single British officer on horseback appeared, gesturing with a sword. It was Major John Pitcairn. Behind him were three other officers on horseback. Around the Bedford road side of the church came Pitcairn's six companies of red-coated light infantry.

There was a split-second pause. Then the light infantry raced toward the Americans, shouting furiously. Major Pitcairn bellowed: "Lay down your arms!" Another officer roared: "Disperse, you rebels!" A third shrilled: "Surrender!" The appalled Captain Parker told his men to disperse without firing. Almost certainly, he never told them to "stand your ground…If they mean to have a war let it begin here." These unlikely words were put in his mouth fifty years later.

Most of the Lexington men began to scatter, some at a grudging pace, others more quickly. "Surround them!" Pitcairn shouted to the oncoming light infantrymen. They were not listening to him or to anyone else. Pitcairn later claimed that a gun held by a man behind a stone wall on the edge of the green flashed in the pan. American witnesses said one of the British officers on horseback fired a pistol. Within a few seconds, the soldiers of the two lead companies fired a full volley at the Lexington men.

Murderous one-ounce musket balls tore into Captain Parker's men. Ensign Robert Munroe was dead when he hit the ground. Young Isaac Muzzy died at his father's feet. Jonathan Harrington, hit in the chest, crawled to the doorstep of his house and died there before the eyes of his horrified wife and son. A wild

TOP LEFT **This German engraving of the Battle of Lexington indicates the intense interest the American Revolution stirred in Europe.**

LEFT **Who fired the first shot on Lexington Green is a matter of dispute. But the British light infantry unquestionably fired the first volleys, killing eight men and wounding ten. The British outnumbered the Americans 7 to 1.**

ABOVE *Horsemen swiftly carried the news of the bloodshed at Lexington to nearby Massachusetts towns. Minutemen turned out by the thousands. Soon the Americans outnumbered the British 4 to 1.*

melee erupted as Parker's men began firing back. Men who had lingered at nearby Buckman's Tavern began firing from its windows. The rear companies of light infantry stormed into the fight, some returning this fire, others charging Parker's men with lowered bayonets.

"Cease firing. Cease firing!" shouted Pitcairn, riding among the infantrymen, striking up their guns with his sword. Many continued to fire. "The men were so wild, they could hear no orders," Lieutenant John Barker of the King's Own light infantry company said later.

Into this chaos of swirling gunsmoke, shrieking women and children, roaring light infantrymen and cursing officers rode Lieutenant Colonel Francis Smith. He found a drummer and ordered him to beat "to arms"—cease fire. The familiar sound restored some discipline to the light infantrymen. They shouldered their guns and re-formed their ranks.

Near them four Lexington men lay dead or dying on the green. Four others were in the same condition just off the green. Another ten were staggering or limping to safety with painful wounds. One British soldier had been wounded in the leg. Major Pitcairn's horse had two bullets in him.

With order more or less restored, several officers urged Smith to return to Boston. The entire countryside was alarmed, and thousands of minutemen were certain to be assembling. Smith, a fat, stubborn man, said he saw no reason

to deviate from his orders. He told the light infantrymen to give three cheers and fire a volley—a British tradition after a victory. They joined the rest of the column waiting on the road. With drums beating and fifes skirling, they resumed their march to Concord, five miles away.

Firing Ball

In Concord as the sun rose, people knew nothing about the slaughter on Lexington Common. Since 1 A.M., when Dr. Samuel Prescott gave the alarm, almost every man, woman and child of reasonable age had spent the night frantically trying to hide the food, gunpowder, cannon and other stores that had been streaming into the town. They had a lot to hide. The notebooks of Colonel James Barrett, commander of the town's militia, record the receipt of 20,000 pounds of musket balls and cartridges, 50 reams of cartridge paper, 318 barrels of flour, 17,000 pounds of salt fish and 35,000 pounds of rice. There is not much doubt that Massachusetts was getting ready to wage war.

Near dawn Colonel Barrett mustered Concord's two minuteman companies and two militia companies in front of Wright's Tavern. They were joined by a company of minutemen from nearby Lincoln, who brought a rumor of gunfire at Lexington. A moment later a horseman whom Barrett had sent to

ABOVE *"Lay down your arms!" shouted Marine Major John Pitcairn, on horseback, to the Lexington militiamen. A moment later the British light infantry opened fire. The Americans were shocked and angry. They had not expected the British to have loaded guns.*

Lexington returned with an eyewitness account of the first British volley, which had sent him galloping back to Concord.

"Were they firing ball?" Barrett asked, in evident disbelief. Like everyone else in Massachusetts, he still thought the British were forbidden to shoot bullets (ball) unless the Americans fired first.

"I don't know," the scout said. "But I think it probable."

Another veteran of the French and Indian War, the sixty-five-year-old Barrett decided not to imitate Captain Parker. He ordered most of his men onto a long ridge that commanded the road to Concord, seizing control of the high ground—a first principle of combat. He sent another company down the road toward Lexington, hoping this show of force would persuade the British to turn back. But Colonel Smith and his men were in no mood to be intimidated. Smith sent his light infantry swarming up the ridge toward the Americans on the crest. The rest of the column, the grenadiers, came at the company in the road like a compact juggernaut. Following Barrett's orders, both groups of Americans retreated, the men in the road marching smartly in step to the grenadiers' fifers and drummers, and then joining their comrades on the ridge.

By 8 A.M. the British were in the center of Concord. Smith, presuming the militia on the ridge were cowed, ordered his grenadiers to begin searching houses and barns for gunpowder and other war materiel. He hustled one company of light infantry to guard the South Bridge over the Concord River and seven other companies to the North Bridge. Four of these companies headed down the road on the other side of the river to search Colonel Barrett's house and barns, two miles away.

Barrett saw no reason to attack the British. The gunpowder had been moved out of town, and most of the other materiel was well hidden. For the moment, the British outnumbered his men. In a five-mile circle that included Concord and Lexington were 6,000 minutemen and militia who were undoubtedly hurrying to their assistance. Why not wait until American and British numbers were at least equal? Barrett brushed off demands by William Emerson, the town's young pastor, and others that they launch an immediate attack.

RIGHT *At Concord Bridge, 400 American minutemen and militiamen routed three companies of British light infantry. The British ran away, abandoning their wounded. The word "aim" was not in their manual of arms.*

In Concord the grenadiers were getting nowhere in their search for contraband. Wily townsfolk repeatedly talked them out of looking in attics or locked rooms where supplies or weapons were hidden. Others claimed that flour or similar provisions were their private property. The soldiers and even a few officers seemed more interested in getting a decent meal, which they paid for in hard money.

In the courthouse the grenadiers made one of their few finds—wooden entrenching tools, gun carriages, tents and cartridge paper. They piled these items in the street and started a bonfire. Soon smoke was spiraling over the roofs of Concord. Up on the ridge, this sight disturbed many militiamen. Lieutenant Joseph Hosmer, the adjutant of the Concord regiment, rushed to Colonel Barrett. "The British have boasted that they could…lay waste our hamlets and villages and we would never oppose them," Hosmer said. Pointing to the smoke, he asked, "Are you going to let them burn the town down?"

Hosmer was a gadfly who had long opposed Barrett's political leadership in Concord. Barrett, seeing the same question on other faces, decided his men should march into town and make sure the British were not burning any houses. This move would require them to cross the North Bridge, guarded by three British companies totaling about 120 men. By this time, the American ranks had swelled to over 400. Barrett apparently thought an advance by such an overwhelming force would persuade the British to fall back and permit the Americans to march into Concord under the presumed rules of engagement— the British would not fire unless the Americans fired first.

ABOVE *The British column retreated to Boston under fire from the minutemen.*

At the same time, Barrett feared the rules no longer applied. At the head of the column, he placed Captain Isaac Davis and his Acton company of minutemen. Two days a week, the thirty-year-old Davis, a gunsmith, had led his men to a firing range behind his house, where they practiced their marksmanship. Barrett asked Davis if he was willing to lead the march. "I haven't a man that's afraid to go," Davis replied.

Down the slope of the ridge the minutemen began advancing toward the British in a long, snaking column, two men abreast. As they passed Barrett on the crest, he cautioned them not to fire first. The only sound was the shrill notes of the Acton fifer playing a marching song, "The White Cockade." At first the stunned British at the bridge did nothing. Finally they retreated to the opposite side of the river, and their commander, Captain Walter Laurie, massed them around the narrow span. As he saw it, they had to hold the bridge or the four companies that had marched to Barrett's farm would be cut off.

On came the Americans, while the British leveled their guns. Some British officers ran out and started pulling up the planks of the bridge. Major John Buttrick, marching beside Captain Isaac Davis, shouted for them to stop. By this time the Americans were almost on top of them, and the officers scuttled back to their side of the bridge. Several British soldiers fired warning shots into the river. But the Americans kept coming. An instant later, the light infantrymen of the King's Own company fired a full volley at the head of the American column. The other companies imitated their deadly example.

Captain Isaac Davis leaped in the air with a bullet in his heart. Near him, one of his privates, Abner Hosmer, dropped with a bullet in his head. Four other men were wounded. For a moment, the Americans could not believe the truth. "Goddamm it," one man shouted, "They are firing ball!"

Major Buttrick whirled and shouted. "Fire fellow soldiers, for God's sake fire."

The Acton men at the head of the column and many others strung out behind them along the river bank poured a deadly volley into the regulars, who were a perfect target, massed on the other side of the river in their red coats. Two privates were killed and a sergeant, four privates and four officers were wounded. The officers' bright red coats stood out against the faded red of their men's uniforms, making them obvious marks.

The British had expected the Americans to break and run at the first volley like the raw troops Lord Sandwich had claimed they were. But the regulars' 100-plus bullets had hit only six men. "They fired too high," a minuteman said, years later. One of the crucial differences between British and American soldiers was making its first but by no means last appearance. The Americans were trained to aim. The word was not even in the British manual of arms. The bayonet was their weapon of choice.

Unchecked and undaunted, the Americans continued to pour bullets at the easy British targets. In little more than two minutes, the regulars broke and ran down the road in mindless panic, abandoning their wounded. "The whole went to the right about in spite of all that could be done to prevent them," the disgusted Captain Laurie said. Thus ended the battle of Concord Bridge, which Ralph Waldo Emerson, the Reverend William Emerson's grandson, would call "the shot heard 'round the world."

On the road the stampeding light infantry met perspiring Colonel Francis Smith leading a company of grenadiers to reinforce the bridge. His roars of rage swiftly restored discipline to the runaways. The Americans took cover behind a handy stone wall, expecting a counterattack. But Colonel Smith was far more concerned about getting himself and his men back to Boston alive. Retreating to the center of Concord, he called off the search for war materiel and summoned the company that was guarding the South Bridge to join him. He expected to need every man in his ranks to help the four companies he had sent to Barrett's farm get across the North Bridge. To his amazement, the Americans permitted the companies to rejoin their comrades without firing a shot. Most of Barrett's men had drifted away to look for breakfast or go home to their farms.

After waiting two more hours hoping reinforcements would appear, Smith finally began the march back to Boston. He was under no illusions that his column was going to escape without a fight. From the hill above the Concord burying ground, the colonel and Major Pitcairn had seen swarms of minutemen from nearby towns heading for the road to Lexington. As the column left Concord, flanking parties of light infantrymen swept the open fields on the left and the ridge on the right. The British were well aware of the Americans' inclination to fight Indian style.

The Massachusetts men decided Meriam's Corner, a crossroads named after the farm that had stood in the nearby meadows for 112 years, was the place to fight. Here the long ridge ended and a brook forced the light infantrymen back

ABOVE *Light-infantry skirmishers defended the flanks of the British column as the tired soldiers trudged toward Boston. The burning house was set afire because snipers had shot from its windows. In every house, the British killed anyone they caught with a gun in his hand.*

on the road to cross a bridge. At least 600 men from Concord and nearby towns turned the stone walls and farm buildings into a fortress.

As the British approached, both sides opened fire. Once more the British fired high and the American shots struck home. By the time one Concord minuteman joined the fight, he saw "a grait many [British] lay dead and the road was bloody." The light infantrymen charged the Americans behind their barricades. The minutemen fell back and raced ahead of the regulars through the open fields to find another place to ambush them.

The half-mile-long British column resumed its march down the narrow road, which had no resemblance to the modern highway, with its few curves and easy grades. Again and again, the road dropped into small ravines that gave the pursuing Americans high ground from which to fire on the British. Soon there were more than 1,500 minutemen and militia swarming in the fields on the left. On the right, a lesser number scrambled through the thick woods that crowded down to the edge of the road.

At Hardy's Hill five companies of minutemen led by Lieutenant Colonel

Thomas Nixon, another veteran of the French wars, opened a ferocious fire on the British column. More grenadiers and light infantrymen dropped into the dust or staggered out of the formation to bleed on the side of the road. Beyond Hardy's Hill 197 minutemen from Woburn were crouched behind stone walls and rocks close to a sharp turn in the road. They poured point-blank fire into the head of the column, killing eight light infantrymen and wounding another twenty-three with the first volley.

It took the British a half-hour to clear the road at this point, which became known as "the Bloody Angle." Meanwhile, the men from Meriam's Corner swarmed around the rear and left flank of the column, and Nixon's men blasted the regulars from the right flank. For the first time, the British began to think they might be annihilated. "It seemed as if men came down from the clouds," one soldier said.

By now the front of the column was moving at a trot. The Americans who had fought at the Bloody Angle fell behind, blocked by numerous swamps and brooks near the road. As the British crossed the Lexington town line, Colonel Smith, riding at the head of the column, thought the worst might be over. He was wrong. In the woods were the men of the Lexington company, hungry for revenge.

Captain John Parker waited until every man had a target. "Fire!" he shouted as the British crossed a small bridge. Colonel Smith toppled from his horse, clutching his thigh. Major Pitcairn ordered grenadiers and light infantry to charge Parker's men. After some savage fighting, they retreated. The halt gave the pursuers from Meriam's Corner and the Bloody Angle time to catch up and begin wreaking havoc on the rear and center of the column once more.

Major Pitcairn realized the situation was close to disaster. Wounded men were abandoning their companies and fleeing to the front of the column, whimpering hysterically. Others dropped out and hunched by the side of the road in abject surrender. Pitcairn ordered his two marine companies to move ahead and seize a small hill called the Bluff. Riding down the column, he urged the men to hang on until they got past the Bluff, where his marines would hold off the pursuers.

The maneuver got the column moving again. The fugitives staggered past the Bluff and the marines managed to stop the hundreds of pursuing Americans for several minutes, taking heavy casualties. Pitcairn rode to the head of the column, replacing Smith, who had decided he was safer limping in the ranks. Within minutes the marine major and the lead companies met another blast of musketry from fresh American minutemen on Fiske Hill, the next rise in the road. Pitcairn's horse threw him and raced across the fields to be captured by Americans, along with a set of handsome pistols in the saddle holsters.

The woods on Fiske Hill came down to the edge of the road, and every tree seemed to conceal an American musket. Other guns blazed from houses and barns. Five more of the exhausted light infantrymen died, and many more were wounded in desperate fighting to clear the road. As the regulars stumbled up Concord Hill, the last rise between them and Lexington, one of the British officers recalled: "We began to run rather than retreat in order." The men made no attempt to return the American fire. Most were out of ammunition. They had marched all night and most of this warm April day. They were on the brink of disintegrating into a mob of demoralized fugitives.

Suddenly the men in the front ranks began to cheer. Had they gone berserk? Officers who were trying to restore some order in the center of the column turned and saw them pointing toward Boston. Along the hill on the east side of Lexington Common was a line of red-coated regiments—a full brigade of reinforcements. Officers and men alike broke into a headlong dash across the green, dragging their wounded. On the hill two cannon boomed, stopping the pursuing minutemen and militia.

Smith's men fell to the ground in front of the rescuers, begging for food, water and surgeons for the wounded. The commander of the reinforcements, Brigadier Hugh, Lord Percy, looked with amazement on the shattered remnants of Governor-General Gage's elite troops. He summed up their condition in a letter he wrote to his father, the Duke of Northumberland, a few days later. "I had the happiness of saving them from complete destruction."

Lord Percy gave Smith and his men a half-hour to rest and regain their composure while he conferred with his officers about the best way to return to Boston. The Americans too were regrouping. They finally had a general, the only one who reached the field on April 19, a bald, portly farmer named William Heath. With him was Dr. Joseph Warren, author of the Suffolk Resolves and a magnetic leader. He and Heath conferred with the Massachusetts Committee of Safety in Menotomy (present-day Arlington). The

BELOW *Fighting on the British retreat from Concord often took place on the doorsteps of houses. This nineteenth-century painting puts women and children into the battle.*

committee was the ruling body of the colony when the Provincial Congress was not in session. They jointly decided to send express riders to report the fighting throughout New England. They also agreed that war had begun and they should try to destroy the reinforced British column before it reached Boston.

The Battle of Menotomy

At Lexington, Heath and Warren found four full militia regiments and four others at half strength. They ordered them to replenish their ammunition pouches and resume the attack. "They have begun it," Dr. Warren said. "We will end it." General Heath had acquired his military know-how from books, but he was a shrewd student. He had concentrated on the tactics of the skirmish, the

ABOVE *When the 700-man British column began retreating from Concord, more than 4,000 American militiamen and minutemen attacked it. The crude muskets made marksmanship difficult. One historian has estimated that only one out of 300 bullets hit anyone.*

kind of battle he foresaw Americans would fight if the British came out of Boston in strength. Drawing his examples from European use of irregular troops, he conceived the idea of creating a moving circle of fire around a less mobile regular force. He proceeded to put his theory to work, rapping out orders to the various regiments to take up positions along the British line of march. Express riders were rushed down side roads to tell regiments coming from other parts of the province to veer east and take up positions so the British would have not one but several fiery circles to confront. A key site, Heath foresaw, would be the village of Menotomy.

This crossroads town was a logical place for minutemen marching from eastern Middlesex County and neighboring Essex County to gather. Most of the inhabitants had fled, leaving a mile-long stretch of deserted houses and barns and stone walls. Typical of these new arrivals was a minuteman company from Danvers, led by twenty-six-year-old Gideon Foster. He positioned his men along a stone wall that flanked a hillside orchard. Nearby were companies from Lynn, Needham and Dedham. They were joined by fifty-eight-year-old Jason Russell, who owned the stone walls and neat gray clapboard house behind them.

A friend tried to persuade Russell to let the younger men do the fighting. Russell shook his head. "A man's home is his castle," he said.

None of these men had fought the British earlier in the day. They were not familiar with the British response to American Indian-style tactics—flanking parties. One veteran of the French and Indian War warned Foster of their likelihood. The Danvers captain brushed him off, determined to get a decent shot at the retreating column. The clumsy muskets and poorly shaped bullets rarely hit anything beyond 100 yards.

Lord Percy ordered the Royal Welch Fusiliers, one of the best regiments in the British army, to serve as the column's rear guard. As the column departed from Lexington, fifers struck up "Yankee Doodle"—a calculated insult to the Americans. A British army doctor had written the satiric song in 1758, after watching American militia muster in a country town.

Heath's men attacked the Royal Welch ferociously as the column left Lexington. Dr. Joseph Warren was in the forefront of the minutemen, shouting encouragement, ignoring British bullets. "We were fired on from all quarters," Lieutenant Frederick McKenzie wrote in his journal, testifying to the effectiveness of General Heath's circular tactics. The 218 fusiliers, outnumbered 10 to 1, were soon fighting for their lives.

In Menotomy the head of the column collided with hundreds more men awaiting them with loaded muskets. A huge melee, involving perhaps 5,500 men, one of the biggest battles of the Revolution, engulfed the once peaceful village. It was a brawl that spilled out of the road into the fields and orchards and barns—and into the houses. Guns barked from almost every window. Lord Percy grimly ordered Colonel Smith's men, who were at the head of the column, to split into squads and attack every fortified building with the bayonet. "All that we found in the houses were put to death," wrote one British lieutenant.

Others died when they were surprised by the British flanking parties. Lord Percy had five companies of the King's Own regiment sweeping his right flank.

These angry soldiers caught Captain Gideon Foster and his Danvers men. Those who did not die behind the stone walls from a bullet or a bayonet ran for the Russell house. Jason Russell was killed trying to defend his doorway. Inside the house, eleven Americans, including seven from Danvers, died in brutal hand-to-hand fighting that raged from the cellar to the attic.

Outside the houses, sheets of bullets hurtled in all directions as the companies in the road fired full volleys at dodging, twisting minutemen. The whine of Yankee shots mingled with the massed thunder. Clouds of acrid gunpowder swirled down Menotomy's main street. At the rear of the column, the colonel of the Welch Fusiliers went down with a bullet in his thigh. More than thirty of his men were dead or wounded. They were running low on ammunition while the pursuing minutemen replenished their pouches from horsemen who followed them into battle with saddlebags full of bullets.

As the column emerged from Menotomy, Lord Percy ordered the 400-man Royal Marine regiment to replace the fusiliers as the rear guard. Major Pitcairn took charge of them and fought the Americans with skill and ferocity for the rest of the day. Up front, the going became easier for Percy's men. The flanking parties kept most of the minutemen at bay, forcing them to fire from a distance—a waste of ammunition.

As the British entered Cambridge, General Heath made a final attempt to trap the column. He positioned a minuteman regiment from Brookline at a crossroads called Watson's Corner and along the road beyond it, which led to Charlestown. Meanwhile, he ordered a detachment of the Watertown militia to tear up the planks of the bridge across the Charles River. He was hoping the British would swing right on what is now Massachusetts Avenue and return to Boston that way—which would leave them trapped on the bank of the unfordable Charles.

Lord Percy was thinking just as hard as Heath. He realized the Charles River bridge would almost certainly be dismantled. Besides, the route to Charlestown was five miles shorter than a march back through Cambridge to Boston. Once on the Charlestown peninsula, he would have the benefit of high ground on Bunker Hill and the King's ships to help defend his battered troops. Briskly, Percy ordered his two cannon to the head of the column. They opened fire on the Brookline regiment, easily dispersing it.

Percy resumed his march, letting his flanking parties deal with the Americans as they attacked in what he called "a straggling manner." By now it was seven o'clock. Evening shadows stretched across the countryside. The British column swung irresistibly down the Charlestown road (present-day Somerville Avenue and Washington Street). Muskets still flared around the marine rear guard as the head of the column crossed the narrow neck of the Charlestown peninsula and skirted the 300 houses of the village, the oldest settlement in the Bay Colony.

In this last burst of gunfire, the British saw a black man hit by one of their bullets and dragged to safety by white men fighting beside him. It was probably Prince Estabrook of the Lexington company. Many of them were still in the fight. Estabrook recovered from his wound and served in the American army for the rest of the war.

The last casualty of the day was fourteen-year-old Edward Barber of

A SHORT HISTORY OF "YANKEE DOODLE"

The first version of "Yankee Doodle" seems to have been written by a British army physician, Dr. Richard Schuckberg, during the French and Indian War. It was a satiric look at New England's Yankees.

Brother Ephraim sold his cow
And bought him a commission
And then he went to Canada
To fight for the nation;
But when Ephraim,
he came home
He proved an arrant coward,
He wouldn't fight the
Frenchmen there
For fear of being devoured.

Sheep's head and vinegar
Buttermilk and tansy
Boston is a Yankee town,
Sing "Hey, doodle dandy!"

A Continental army drum.

The song continued for many more verses, several of them scatological. With different verses, it soon became popular throughout the colonies. A broadside of the 1770s has a version which became more or less standard. It is a country bumpkin's reaction to his first visit to an army camp.

Father and I went
down to camp
Along with Captain Goodwin
And there we saw the
men and boys
As thick as hasty puddin'.

And there they had a little keg
The heads were made
of leather
They rap't upon't with
little clubs
To call the folks together.

There I saw a swamping gun
As big's a log of maple,
Put upon two little wheels
A load for father's cattle.

I saw a man a'talking there
You might heard to
the barn, sir,
Halooing and scolding too—
The deal of one would answer.

There he kept a riding round
Upon a spanking stallion.
And all the people
standing round,
A thousand or a million.

Another version was published in England in 1775 with the recommendation that it be "sung through the nose," suggesting that it was still a satire on Yankees. Later in 1775, a minuteman named Edward Bangs published a version that might have been sung by a boy visiting the New England army besieging Boston. One verse suggested Yankee wariness of the army's Virginia commander.

And there was Captain
Washington

And gentle folks about him;
They say he's grown so
tarnal proud
He will not ride
without them.

By this time it was obvious that anyone could write verses for "Yankee Doodle." On the march to Lexington and Concord, according to one story, the British troops sang this stanza.

Yankee Doodle's come to town
For to buy a firelock,
We will tar and feather him
And so will we John Hancock.

The verse the American soldiers liked best summed up "Yankee Doodle"'s popularity.

Yankee Doodle is the tune
That we all delight in;
It suits for feasts,
it suits for fun,
And just as well for fightin'.

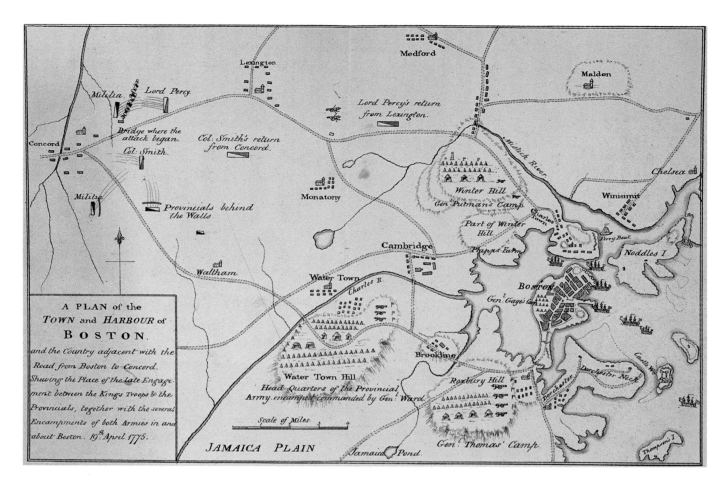

A PLAN of the TOWN and HARBOUR of BOSTON. and the Country adjacent with the Road from Boston to Concord. Shewing the Place of the late Engagement between the Kings Troops & the Provincials, together with the several Encampments of both Armies in and about Boston. 19ᵗʰ April 1775.

ABOVE This map illustrates the march to Lexington and Concord and the British return route. It also gives a good idea of Boston and the surrounding countryside, with its mix of bays and peninsulas and easily fortified hills.

Charlestown, son of a sea captain. He ran to the window of his house to see the regulars pass. By this time, anyone moving inside a house was considered a potential sniper. A regular leveled his musket and killed the boy with a single shot. His twelve brothers and sisters ran screaming into the streets of Charlestown, sowing panic everywhere.

Some of the town's selectmen hurried to Lord Percy to assure him that no one had any intention of fighting the British. Earlier in the day Governor-General Gage had sent them a message from Boston, warning that if anyone was seen with a gun in his hand, there would be "disagreeable consequences." With *HMS Somerset* and its tiers of cannon just offshore, Gage did not have to elaborate. Percy, watching his tired men ascend Bunker Hill, accepted the selectmen's offer of a truce.

Around the same time, General Heath ordered his men "to halt and give over the pursuit." The marines had formed a battle line across the peninsula's narrow neck. Four or five American muskets barked in the darkness. Silence fell. The day that began with sudden death on Lexington Green was over.

British losses totaled 73 killed, 174 wounded and 26 missing; most of the last were wounded left along the road plus a few deserters. American losses are more difficult to compute. There was no organized system of casualty reports. We are fairly certain 49 men were killed, but the semiofficial estimate of only 41 wounded seems unlikely. The ratio of killed to wounded is usually 1 to 3 in land battles. Many of the wounded may have gone home and never reported their injuries.

Spreading the News

As the battle fury died away, men on both sides began assessing the clash. Lord Percy, who had previously scorned American military pretensions, changed his mind. "Whoever looks upon them as an irregular mob will find himself much mistaken," he told one of his friends in England. "They have men amongst them who know very well what they are about." He was now convinced that "the rebels...are determined to go thro with it, nor will the insurrection here turn out so despicable as it is perhaps imagined at home."

Percy was writing as an intelligent soldier, sending home hard truths that his government needed to hear. His letter underscored one of the least-understood realities of April 19. The Americans who responded to the British challenge were a well-led, well-supplied rudimentary army that had been organizing and training for six months. They were much better prepared to fight than were the British regulars. The Americans' training and the knowledge that they heavily outnumbered the King's men added to the confidence with which they went into battle. In short, April 19 was a victory of preparedness. It was not the product of spontaneous enthusiasm.

The political leaders of Massachusetts had no interest in learning military lessons. They concentrated on using the blood spilled on April 19 to win the support of other Americans—especially those living outside New England. In a circular letter written by Dr. Joseph Warren and a longer report by a committee headed, ironically, by Governor-General Gage's spy, Dr. Benjamin Church, the Massachusetts version of the battle denounced "barbarous murders committed on our innocent brethren." It accused the British of "driving into the streets women in child-bed, killing old men in their houses." The Lexington minutemen and militia were described as a "small party of the inhabitants...some with and some without firearms." In Concord Colonel Barrett's menacing 400-man column became "inhabitants...collected at the bridge." At no point was there any mention of minutemen or militia or the slightest hint of military preparations. The Americans who gunned down the regulars along the road were simply "provincials, roused with zeal for the liberties of their country" who "assumed their native valor" and fought so well that the "loss on the part of the British troops far exceeded" that of the Americans.

As political propaganda, the Massachusetts reports were masterpieces. They were backed by ninety-two depositions from eyewitnesses, including three from captured British soldiers. These documents produced an enormous explosion of sympathy and resentment throughout America. Some 20,000 men from western Massachusetts, Connecticut, Rhode Island and New Hampshire rushed to join the minutemen and militia who had pursued Lord Percy to Charlestown neck. They began building fortifications and organizing themselves into an army that effectively blockaded the small British force inside Boston. "In the course of two days," wrote one glum British officer,

ABOVE RIGHT *Brigadier Lord Percy decided the Americans were not "an irregular mob." They had men among them that "knew very well what they are about." He eventually went home, disgusted with the way the British fought the war.*

"from a plentiful town we were reduced to…living on salt provisions."

Underscoring once more the close connection between American and English politics, Warren and the Massachusetts Committee of Safety spent at least as much energy getting their version of Lexington and Concord to London. On April 28, Captain John Derby sailed from Salem in his swift sixty-two-ton sloop *Quero*, with no cargo except a letter to the British people written by Warren, plus copies of stories in Massachusetts newspapers and the depositions taken by Dr. Church's committee. Thanks to their spies, the Americans knew that Governor-General Gage had sent a report of the clash to Lord Dartmouth, the American secretary of state, on April 24 in the slow, cargo-heavy packet *Sukey*. By May 28, Captain Derby was in London, handing his explosive documents to the new Lord Mayor, John Wilkes.

Within twenty-four hours the American version was all over London in extras printed by leading British newspapers. In two more days the story was all over England. Lord North and his cabinet were left floundering, without a shred of information to counter the description of the King's troops as heartless butchers who had been chased back to Boston by aroused farmers. All Lord Dartmouth could do was publish a tepid bulletin calling the news unofficial. Virginian Arthur Lee, who had replaced Benjamin Franklin as the chief American spokesman in London, promptly published a notice announcing that the original affidavits and other documents were available for public examination at the Lord Mayor's mansion.

Lord Dartmouth's undersecretary journeyed to Kew to tell George III that there was "bad news" from America. The King exploded and called the man several uncomplimentary names. When Dartmouth sent clips from the London papers, George stubbornly insisted the news was not bad at all. He declared a victory by claiming the expedition to Concord had destroyed some military stores. In the fighting on the way back, casualties had been roughly equal on both sides. George urged Dartmouth "not to see this in a stronger light than it deserves." Of course it meant war. But His Majesty had already said he was not sorry about that.

After the wild excitement stirred by the American story, Gage's terse, evasive report of the outbreak of hostilities landed in London with a dull thud two weeks later. The newspapers hooted at the government all over again, making fun of bland sentences such as "Lord Percy brought the troops into Charlestown." The Reverend John Horne, founder of the Society for Supporting the Bill of Rights, issued a call for funds to help "our beloved American fellow subjects." He soon found himself in the King's Bench prison. Horne's fate was a clear signal that however much emotion the Americans stirred among some Britons with their appeal to "the united effort of both Englands" to resist military force, George III and Lord North had no doubt that their 3-to-1 majority in Parliament would stand by them.

The Gibraltar of America

In Hartford, Connecticut, en route to the Continental Congress, that tireless man Samuel Adams paused to confer with Governor Jonathan Trumbull. Adams was convinced that the British would try to split New England from the rest of the colonies by sending an army down Lake Champlain, Lake

FREE AMERICA

We led fair freedom hither
And lo, the desert smiled
A paradise of pleasure
Was opened in the wild!
Your harvest bold Americans
No power shall snatch away
Huzza, huzza, huzza, huzza
For free America!

Torn from a world of tyrants
Beneath this western sky
We formed a new dominion
A land of liberty
The world shall own we're
masters here
Then hasten on the day
Oppose, oppose, oppose,
oppose,
For free America

Lift up your hands, ye heroes
And swear with proud disdain
The wretch that would
ensnare you
Shall lay his snares in vain;
Should Europe empty all
her force,
We'll meet her in array,
And fight and shout, and
shout and fight
For North America

Some future day shall
crown us
The masters of the main,
Our fleets shall speak
in thunder
To England, France and Spain
And the nations over the
oceans spread
Shall tremble and obey
The sons, the sons,
the sons, the sons
Of brave America

Dr. Joseph Warren

George, and the Hudson River to New York. Several months earlier he had dispatched an agent to Canada to survey this invasion route and estimate the Canadian attitude toward the Americans' resistance to England. The agent had returned with less-than-optimistic reports of Canadian fondness for "les Bostonnais," but he recommended seizing Fort Ticonderoga "as soon as possible, should hostilities be committed by the King's troops." The huge fort at the junction of Lake Champlain and Lake George was sometimes called the Gibraltar of America.

Adams urged Governor Trumbull to act on this advice as soon as possible. Trumbull's men contacted a former native of Connecticut named Ethan Allen, head of a group of frontiersman called the "Green Mountain Boys," to do the job. For several years they had been exchanging shots and lawsuits with New Yorkers over the ownership of the New Hampshire grants—modern-day Vermont. Simultaneously the Massachusetts Committee of Safety commissioned another Connecticut man, New Haven militia Captain Benedict Arnold, to take the fort and its invaluable cannon and other war

RIGHT *Dr. Joseph Warren was Samuel Adams's right-hand man in Massachusetts. An electrifying speaker and talented writer, he was also a gifted physician. Abigail Adams said that when he died on Breed's Hill, "liberty wept."*

materiel. Arnold had demonstrated an explosive zeal for the Cause from the moment he heard the news about Lexington. He had forced the New Haven town fathers to distribute their supply of gunpowder to his men and had his company on the road to Boston within twenty-four hours. Once there, he disdained the dull siege that had begun, and he sold the idea of capturing Ticonderoga to the Massachusetts politicians.

Men with large egos, Allen and Arnold argued vehemently over who should command the expedition. They finally agreed to do the job jointly. Leading eighty-three men, mostly Green Mountain Boys, in two boats, they landed a half-mile from Ticonderoga at dawn on May 10, 1775. The neglected fort was garrisoned by only forty-eight men, half of them classified as invalids. Quickly overwhelming two sentries, the Americans seized a hapless British lieutenant with his breeches in his hand and demanded the fort's surrender. When the captain in command refused to unlock the door to his room, Allen roared: "Come out, you old rat!" Only much later, when he wrote his version of the event, did Allen claim he demanded the fort's surrender "in the name of the Great Jehovah and the Continental Congress." More important than the details was the booty: seventy-eight serviceable cannon, six mortars, three howitzers, thousands of cannon balls and 30,000 flints.

Still Reluctant Rebels

Unaware of this act of aggression, the forty-eight members of the Continental Congress assembled in Philadelphia on May 10. They were all in a state of shock from the news of Lexington and Concord. No one was more distressed than Benjamin Franklin, who heard about it the moment his ship dropped anchor in the Delaware River opposite Philadelphia. In his trunk was a ninety-seven-page letter he had written on his voyage home, detailing his torturous final year of negotiation with the British. It began with two emotional words: "Dear Son." Even as he wrote this salutation, Franklin knew from numerous recent letters that he and Governor William Franklin did not agree on why America and England were in crisis.

"Has William resigned?" Franklin asked his daughter Sarah and son-in-law

Richard Bache within minutes of reaching his house in what is now Franklin Court, just off Market Street. Faces fell. The answer was no. William felt "obligated" to Lord North and his cabinet for permitting him to retain his post in spite of his father's opposition to the government. The next day Franklin was appointed to the Pennsylvania delegation to the Continental Congress. He was dismayed to learn that his old friend Joseph Galloway, also chosen, had refused to serve. Lexington and Concord had made his plan of union a lost cause.

LEFT *Connecticut Captain Benedict Arnold stepped onto history's stage when he received orders from the Massachusetts Committee of Safety to capture Fort Ticonderoga.*

ABOVE **With less than 100 men, Ethan Allen and Benedict Arnold seized Fort Ticonderoga. Thousands of English soldiers had died assaulting this wilderness citadel in the French and Indian War. Allen launched a premature invasion of Canada a few months later. Captured, he was shipped to England in chains and narrowly escaped being hanged as a traitor.**

A few days later Franklin met with his son and Galloway. He spent hours listening to them denounce both sides in the dispute. With a harsh sigh, Franklin told them where he stood: "I am for independence."

The two younger men could only gasp and shake their heads. They could not believe that the man who had been a symbol of moderation and rational compromise could embrace this radical idea, which thus far only a few extremists dared to whisper in private. In desperation Franklin read them parts of his letter to William. Nothing changed their minds. They were both convinced that the Continental Congress was as wrongheaded as Parliament, with the worse handicap that the Congress had no legal right to exist.

When he took his seat in the Congress, Franklin was dismayed to discover that he was almost as isolated there as he had been in his conversation with his son and Galloway. The Pennsylvania delegation was controlled by John Dickinson, long a foe of Franklin in local politics and a devout believer in solving the dispute short of war. To most of the delegates, Franklin was no more than a name, a voice from a previous generation. William Franklin's refusal to resign as royal governor of New Jersey inclined some people, notably Richard Henry Lee of Virginia, to suspect his father was a British spy.

The mood in the Congress was a peculiar blend of outrage over the bloodshed of April 19 and recoil from its obvious implications. Everyone called the British troops in Boston "the ministerial army" and clung to the notion that George III would be as shocked by the bloodshed as they were and would soon dismiss the bad ministers Parliament had imposed on him and restore peace. Franklin, no longer under any illusions about George III, could only shake his head at this fantasy.

A few men seemed ready to face reality. One of them was Colonel George Washington of Virginia, who attended the meetings in the Pennsylvania State House wearing his old buff-and-blue Virginia militia uniform. But Washington, with no talent as a public speaker, was not the man to change the minds of these shaken politicians. His uniform was merely a silent statement that Virginia was ready to fight. He too went along with denunciations of the "ministerial army."

After pondering the depositions and official account of the clash submitted by the Massachusetts delegation, the Congress sent a stiff rebuke to London, blaming Gage's troops for the bloodshed. But when a message arrived from the Massachusetts Provincial Congress, asking them to appoint a "generalissimo" for the army outside Boston, the Congress collapsed into agitated debate.

The agitation deepened when the news of the capture of Ticonderoga arrived. Worse, Benedict Arnold had captured another British fort on Lake Champlain, Crown Point, and several British ships. Samuel Adams suggested using the forts as staging areas for an invasion of Canada. The idea met with overwhelming disapproval. Instead the Congress voted that the forts would be occupied only until the differences between America and England were resolved.

Listening, a dismayed John Adams wondered if the dead and wounded along the road between Boston and Concord were a bad dream. His cousin Samuel Adams was drifting into isolation and depression, sensing that many of the moderate men secretly blamed him for the crisis. He even tried to resign as a delegate, saying he was not equal to the task of creating a nation. Fortunately for America's future, the cooler, more thoughtful John had the ability to bridge the gap between Samuel's instinctive radicalism and the fears of more cautious men.

Even before the Congress convened, Adams wrote in his diary that they should "declare the Colonies free, sovereign and independent states" and offer to negotiate with Great Britain to restore harmony between the two countries "upon permanent principles." He also thought the Congress should instruct the states to form their own local governments and immediately adopt the militia outside Boston as a "Continental army" and appoint a general.

Adams soon collided with political reality. When he gave a fiery speech denouncing a proposal by John Dickinson to petition George III again to open negotiations for a peaceful settlement, Dickinson coldly warned Adams that he would take Pennsylvania and her neighboring states out of the Congress and leave New England to face the British alone. Only with the greatest reluctance—and much prodding from Adams—did the Congress respond to a request from the Massachusetts Provincial Congress for permission to form a government for the province. The federal delegates gave a wary assent "until a governor of His Majesty's appointment will consent to govern the colony according to its charter."

John Adams quietly exulted because, in spite of the hesitation, the Congress had taken a large step toward becoming a national legislature. His next objective was that request for a generalissimo. Here he had little or no support from anyone. Samuel Adams in his radical way wanted the soldiers to elect their own officers and was inclined to think the army did not need a general, who might turn into an American Cromwell. John Hancock, who had been elected president of the Congress, thought he should be the choice for this daunting job, even though his military experience consisted of leading parades in Boston. Others wanted a New Englander for the currently all-New England army. Only John Adams had the foresight to see that the choice of a non-Yankee could be a major step toward persuading the Congress to adopt the army—and toward uniting the embryonic nation. Moreover, he already had his candidate: Colonel George Washington of Virginia.

On June 14, eight weeks after Lexington, John Adams proposed Washington as a man whose "skill and experience as an officer, whose independent fortune, great talents and excellent universal character would...unite the cordial exertions of all the colonies better than any other person." John Hancock, in the president's chair, did not even try to conceal his chagrin. Samuel Adams redoubled the merchant prince's spleen—and surprised John Adams—by seconding the nomination.

Washington promptly left the room to permit the delegates to debate the proposal. At first the Congress was dubious. The pressure for a New England man was intense. But after a night of politicking by the two Adamses, the vote for Washington was unanimous. John Adams also persuaded the Congress to assume responsibility for the impromptu army around Boston and to promise that they would "maintain him and assist him, and adhere to him, the said George Washington, Esq., with their lives and fortunes." Even at this early date, Washington personified the American cause—which the Congress defined as "the maintenance and preservation of American liberty."

For Washington the nomination stirred profound emotion. Here was honor, an opportunity to serve his country, on a scale beyond the imagination of his brother Lawrence and the Fairfaxes, who had inspired him to become a soldier in his youth. Yet he was starkly aware that this chance for fame was darkened by harsh realities. Looking back years later, Washington wrote: "It was known that the resources of Great Britain were, in a manner, inexhaustible, that her fleets covered the ocean and that her troops had harvested laurels in every quarter of the globe. Not then organized as a nation, or known as a people upon the earth, we had no preparation. Money, the nerve of war, was wanting. The sword was to be forged on the anvil of necessity."

With these grim thoughts in his head, Washington made a brief speech that was anything but a call to arms. After accepting this "momentous and important trust," he added: "Lest some unlucky event should happen, unfavorable to my reputation, I beg it may be remembered, by every gentleman in the room, that I, this day, declare with the utmost sincerity I do not think myself equal to the command I am honored with."

To his wife, Martha, Washington wrote a touching letter a few days later, reiterating this same feeling of incapacity. He went even further with Patrick Henry, telling him: "From the day I enter upon the command of the American armies, I date my fall and the ruin of my reputation."

Tacitly accepting the modesty of the new commander-in-chief, the Congress appointed three subordinate major generals and advised Washington to consult with them before making any decisions. As his second in command the politicians chose Charles Lee, a British colonel who had retired to Virginia on half pay and had become a devotee of the American cause. An elongated eccentric with radical opinions on a host of subjects from women to politics, Lee was an avid self-promoter who loved to flaunt his military expertise. He traveled everywhere with a pack of dogs, whose company he claimed to prefer to humans. He was not one of the Congress's wiser appointments.

Washington, going along with the majority mood in the Congress, saw his defense of American liberty as a "loyal protest" that would make an unreasonable power-hungry Parliament change its ways. Neither he nor anyone else in the Congress realized that the New England army outside Boston was about to transform the family quarrel by fighting a full-scale battle that not even the most reconciliation-hungry delegate could ignore.

The Whites of Their Eyes

Unaware of the Congress's decision to adopt the army and to put Washington in charge of it, the men on the firing line in Massachusetts became more and more concerned about the drift of affairs. The Congress seemed to be ignoring them. The British in Boston had just received significant reinforcements, headed by Major Generals Howe, Clinton and Burgoyne, bringing Gage's army to more than 5,000 men. The 15,000-man American army, commanded by cautious Artemas Ward of Massachusetts, was still a haphazard affair, held together largely by the magnetism of Dr. Joseph Warren, who had persuaded the volunteers to promise to serve until the end of 1775.

The three major generals had come with orders to prod Governor-General Gage into action. They quickly concocted a plan of attack. On June 18, Howe was to land 1,500 men on Dorchester peninsula and seize these heights south of Boston. From there he planned to assault the flimsy American defenses at Roxbury. Simultaneously, Henry Clinton was to launch another attack from boats across Back Bay, landing on the banks of Willis Creek, opposite the American center at Cambridge, where all their supplies and ammunition were stored. Howe was to join Clinton for a combined assault in which the Americans would be forced to commit their raw troops in open fields, where the British were confident their regulars would prevail.

With the rebels' stores and ammunition captured, and their morale shattered by defeat, the siege of Boston would be over. At that point William Howe planned to lay aside the sword and step forward as a peacemaker. His oldest brother, Lord George Howe, had fought beside Americans against the

My Dearest:

I am now set down to write you on a subject which fills me with inexpressible concern, and this concern is greatly aggravated and increased when I reflect upon the uneasiness I know it will cause you. It has been determined in Congress that the whole army raised for the defense of the American cause shall be put under my care, and that it is necessary for me to proceed immediately to Boston to take command of it.

You may believe me, my dear Patcy, when I assure you, in the most solemn manner, that, so far from seeking this appointment, I have used every endeavor in my power to avoid it, not only from my unwillingness to part with you and the family, but from a consciousness of its being a trust too great for my capacity, and that I should enjoy more real happiness in one month with you at home than I have the most distant prospect of finding abroad, if my stay were to be seven times seven years. But as it has been a kind of destiny that has thrown me upon this service, I shall hope that my undertaking it is designed to answer some good purpose....

It was utterly out of my power to refuse this appointment without exposing my character to such censures as would have reflected dishonor on myself and given pain to my friends. This, I am sure, could not and ought not to be pleasing to you and must have lessened me considerably in my own esteem. I shall rely, therefore, confidently on that Providence which has heretofore preserved and been bountiful to me, not doubting but that I shall return safe to you in the fall.

George Washington

French. When he was killed assaulting Fort Ticonderoga during the French and Indian War, Boston had erected a monument in his memory in Westminster Abbey. Playing on his family's long friendship with America, General Howe would offer amnesty to all who lay down their guns and would help negotiate a generous peace.

Unfortunately for this vision of reconciliation, the third major general, John Burgoyne, was a very talkative man. Although patriots were few in Boston since Governor-General Gage had turned half the population out of the city to save food, someone friendly to the American cause overheard Burgoyne discussing the plan of attack and passed the information to Dr. Joseph Warren and his advisers. Chief among these was Colonel Israel Putnam of Connecticut, a blunt, square-jawed man of fifty-three, who had become a living military legend thanks to his exploits as a ranger captain in the French and Indian War.

Putnam convinced Warren it was folly for the Americans to sit passively and let the British decide where to attack them. Better to seize the heights on Dorchester peninsula and on Charlestown peninsula, on the opposite side of the city, fortify them and force the British to pay dearly for this high ground. The general in command of the Dorchester flank of the army refused to consider the idea—a glimpse of how badly the Americans needed a commander more forceful than the temporizing Artemas Ward. Undiscouraged, Putnam pushed for a fort on Charlestown's Bunker Hill, where Lord Percy had sought refuge on April 19.

Some people were dubious. Would the Americans stand their ground against the regulars? On a narrow peninsula there was no room for the kind of pellmell retreats that had enabled most of the minutemen and militia to escape pursuing regulars on April 19. Putnam had a ready answer: "Americans are not afraid of their heads, but they are very much afraid of their legs. Cover them and they will fight until doomsday." In the eighteenth century, a leg wound was more feared than a fatal bullet in the head. Leg wounds frequently led to amputation or infection and slow agonizing death.

In spite of his radical rhetoric, Dr. Joseph Warren still hoped against hope for some sort of peaceful settlement. As a doctor, he recoiled from the blood and suffering of a war. But he gave Putnam his reluctant assent to the expedition. Soon Colonel William Prescott of Pepperell, Massachusetts, received orders from the Committee of Safety to take three regiments, including his own, and fortify Bunker Hill. Another veteran of the French and Indian War, the stern, reserved Prescott had displayed enough military talent to be offered a commission in the British army. He had rejected it to return to his farm.

At 9 P.M. on June 16, Putnam and Prescott filed through deserted Charlestown with the three Massachusetts regiments, supplemented by 200 Connecticut men and a company of New Hampshire men as a show of unity. Terrified by repeated British threats to burn the place, Charlestown's inhabitants had fled into the country. When the Americans reached the heights beyond the town, a fierce argument broke out over which hill to fortify. Putnam preferred a smaller rise, Breed's Hill, because it was closer to Boston. The Americans had no cannon powerful enough to reach the city or the ships in the harbor from the higher but more distant Bunker Hill. The British might decide to ignore a fort up there, leaving the Americans no alternative but a humiliating retreat.

Several men assured Prescott that both hills were often called Bunker Hill—they were connected by a saddle. There was no way to settle the argument; not a man in the expedition was from Boston. Prescott finally yielded to Putnam and agreed to build on Breed's Hill. He and Putnam had become close friends, and both men shared the motive that brought them to this midnight rendezvous: to give the British a crippling blow. The fort was never intended to be a merely defensive structure, as the Massachusetts Committee of Safety would later claim. It was a challenge to battle that the British could not ignore.

In four hours of furious digging on Breed's Hill, Prescott's men built an earthwork bastion 160 feet long and eighty feet wide. Designed by Colonel Richard Gridley, an experienced engineer, the fort's walls were six feet high and a foot thick, reinforced with fascines (bundles of sticks) and hogsheads packed with dirt. It was surrounded by a deep ditch filled with fence rails, bushes and sticks to make life even more difficult for attackers. As the sun rose, the watch aboard the sloop *HMS Lively*, anchored just off Charlestown, goggled in disbelief at this formidable structure and awoke their captain. The *Lively*'s ten guns opened up on the Americans and were soon joined by the heavier cannon of *HMS Somerset* and other ships in the Boston squadron. Not a gun inflicted any serious damage on the solid walls.

While the Royal Navy bombarded, the army held a council of war. According to the mythical version of the battle of Bunker Hill, all the British generals arrogantly agreed that His Majesty's regulars could simply row across the Charles River and chase the rebels off the hill with a few volleys and a bayonet charge. In fact, they argued vehemently over several alternative plans, such as landing troops on Charlestown neck. The plan they finally chose was based on General Howe's expertise in amphibious operations. He pointed out that they lacked the special flat-bottomed attack boats with planked-up sides that they had used against the French in the last war. Rowing across the Charles in open longboats, the troops would be an easy target

LEFT *In four hours of furious digging, the Americans built a formidable earthwork fort on Breed's Hill. The fort put Boston and ships in the harbor within range of American artillery, so the British were forced to attack it. The Americans had been ordered to fortify nearby Bunker Hill, and that name became attached to the battle.*

ABOVE *When a British cannon ball snipped off a man's head, panic rippled through the Americans in the fort on Breed's Hill. Colonel William Prescott steadied his men by leaping up on the parapet to show them there was little danger of anyone else's being hit.*

for an American ambush unless they landed at Morton's (also known as Moulton's) Point, on the open tip of the peninsula, where they could be covered by the navy's guns.

With the site chosen, General Howe persuaded the council of war that the American fort gave them an opportunity to pull off their Dorchester plan in reverse. He pointed to a crossroads behind the Breed's Hill fort. Once he secured his beachhead on Morton's Point, he would send a column of light infantry up the Mystic River shore, out of musket shot of the men in the fort, and seize that crossroads, cutting off any chance of reinforcement or retreat. That would throw the defenders of the fort into a panic. Then he would launch a four-sided attack that would rout them. Simultaneously, Clinton would launch his attack across Back Bay. Howe would pursue the fort's fugitives as they fled across Charlestown neck into the American lines, sowing further panic. The chance to annihilate the American army and end the rebellion looked even better than it had looked through the lens of the Dorchester operation.

If Howe had known what was happening in the American fort, he would have been even more optimistic. Although the Royal Navy's guns did not damage the fort, they severely unnerved Prescott's men. Many if not most of the officers and men of the other two Massachusetts regiments announced they were exhausted and withdrew, leaving Prescott with little more than the 300 men of his own regiment and the 200 Connecticut men. When one man had his head torn off by a cannonball, panic swept the weary garrison. Prescott quelled it by ordering the corpse buried and springing up on the fort's walls, defying the round shot that hissed around him.

In Cambridge Israel Putnam was arguing desperately with the Committee of Safety and General Artemas Ward for reinforcements for Prescott's men. The jittery Ward, fearful of an attack on his center lines around Cambridge and Watertown and the loss of the army's stores, was reluctant to part with a man. Putnam's oratory overwhelmed the Committee of Safety and they ordered more Massachusetts regiments into the fight. Still stubbornly disagreeing, Ward took so long to issue the orders that most of the men never got there. But Ward felt free to send two New Hampshire regiments stationed far out on his left flank to join the imminent battle. It was his best order of the day.

The commander of these New Hampshire men was John Stark, another legendary veteran of the forest war against the French. Tall, lean, laconic, he was Presbyterian Irish, and so were most of his men. As they crossed the thirty-yard-wide Charlestown neck, they came under heavy fire from British ships assigned to cut off reinforcements. When one of his officers suggested they double their pace, Stark replied: "One fresh man in action is worth ten fatigued men" and proceeded at the same steady stride through the flying lead.

By the time Stark reached the fort, Howe had landed 1,500 men on Morton's Point. Israel Putnam had quickly grasped Howe's plan to outflank the fort and ordered the 200 Connecticut troops to man a hastily constructed breastwork along the slope of the hill and a stone wall topped by rails at the base of the hill. Stark added his 800 fresh men to their thin ranks. Surveying the scene, he glimpsed a potentially fatal flaw in the American defense. A twelve-foot-wide beach ran along the Mystic River, at the foot of an eight-foot bluff. Quickly, he ordered 200 of his best men to grab stones from nearby fences and carry them down there. They set up a crude breastwork on the sand, from the bluff to the water's edge. Stark took command of this crucial position.

Vital as were all these preparations, they did little for the drooping morale of the 300 tired men in Prescott's fort. Their mood was transformed by the arrival of a single man: Dr. Joseph Warren. At his request, the Provincial Congress had given him a general's commission, entitling him to share the danger into which he had sent so many of his followers. But he modestly refused to exercise any command, leaving Prescott, Putnam and Stark in charge of the battle.

As portions of other American regiments swelled the numbers along the breastwork and rail fence to 1,500 men, Howe requested two more regiments from Boston. Behind his cool demeanor, the taciturn general must have mentally cursed Admiral Samuel Graves, the indolent commander of the Royal Navy in Boston. Howe had urged Graves to position one of his ships in the Mystic River to make sure the Americans did not fortify their open left flank. Graves refused, claiming he did not know enough about the river's mudflats and shoals, which he had never bothered to chart. Even a sloop such as *HMS Lively* would have cleared Stark's men off the beach and driven most of Putnam's men away from the rail fence.

When the reinforcements arrived, Howe, a gambler by nature, attacked. He was betting that his regulars would have bayonets at the throats of these amateur soldiers before they could get off more than one volley. His men advanced with full packs, including three days' rations—a 100-pound load that more than one historian has ridiculed. The June sun was beating down, sending the temperature soaring into the nineties. But Howe's plan called for a swift rout of the Americans and a pursuit into Cambridge. If all went well,

RIGHT *Bostonians crowded the rooftops to watch the British assault the Americans on Bunker Hill. In the middle distance is a British man-of-war, whose guns set the village of Charlestown on fire to drive out American snipers.*

the British planned to camp that night in Harvard Yard.

As Stark had foreseen, Howe sent his light infantry up the beach to outflank the rail fence. Firing in three alternating ranks, Stark's sharpshooters killed ninety-six of them at point-blank range, and the rest fled. In spite of this stunning setback, Howe personally led an attack by the grenadiers on the men behind the rail fence. He expected artillery support, but the guns bogged down in the swampy ground and never got close enough to do any damage. That ancient battlefield law sometimes attributed to an Irishman named Murphy—if anything can go wrong, it will—was operating at maximum strength for the British on June 17, 1775.

Behind the rail fence, Putnam issued his famous order: "Don't fire until you see the whites of their eyes." It was old soldier's lore, first used by Prince Charles of Prussia in 1745, during a battle with the Austrians. Like Stark's men on the beach, the Americans waited until the grenadiers were within fifty yards and unleashed a devastating blast of bullets. One British officer recalled it as "an incessant stream of fire from the rebel lines…Most of the grenadiers…the moment of presenting themselves lost three-fourths and many nine-tenths of their men." Such losses were more than flesh could endure. The elite troops fled, leaving Howe almost alone on the battlefield.

Two other British regiments, led by diminutive Brigadier Robert Pigot, attacked up the hill toward Prescott's fort. They too were stopped by deadly fire from the fort and from the houses of Charlestown. At Pigot's request, the Royal Navy poured hot shot into Charlestown, and soon all 300 houses were ablaze.

Abandoning his flanking plans, a rattled General Howe ordered Pigot and his men to join him in an assault on the fort while the surviving light infantry attacked the rail fence. Again the Americans cut down the regulars by the dozen with point-blank fire. As on April 19, the officers in their bright scarlet coats were special targets. So many went down that two regiments collapsed and lost all semblance of discipline, retreating to the water's edge. General Clinton leaped into a boat and rushed across the Charles to rally them. Watching his men flee, William Howe later confessed: "There was a moment I never felt before."

In Boston thousands of Americans crowded rooftops and hills to watch the spectacle. The British ships and a battery on Copps Hill continued to fling shot at the Americans as Howe conferred with his officers on the shore of the Charles River. Several officers told him it would be "butchery" to send the men forward again. Howe, his reputation as a general on the line, calmly insisted they would make another attempt. Now, however, all thoughts of grand strategy and ending the war overnight were discarded. There would be only one objective—to take that fort on Breed's Hill.

The men were ordered to throw aside their heavy packs. The artillery received a blistering lecture and were told to concentrate their fire on the

ABOVE *This British cartoon portrays America as a woman with the Battle of Bunker Hill as her latest hairstyle. The British were stunned by their army's heavy casualties.*

breastwork while the light infantry pretended to attack the rail fence to pin down the sharpshooters there. Reinforced by 400 fresh troops, the British began a third advance up Breed's Hill.

In the fort, a new reason for panic was sweeping through Prescott's tired soldiers. They were running out of ammunition. The primitive American supply system had broken down completely in the stress of battle. Outside on the hill, Howe's new tactics were working. His artillery drove the Americans away from the breastwork, and his 150 light infantrymen kept the men at the rail fence busy exchanging shots. That left the fort's 300 men, bolstered by about 100 refugees from the breastwork, exposed to a three-sided assault by 1,500 regulars.

The defenders had enough ammunition to fire a few more deadly volleys. Sharpshooters sprang up on the wall to cut down officers. A black soldier named Peter Salem mortally wounded Major John Pitcairn as he rallied his wavering marines. Then the American fire dwindled, the British plunged over the walls and a hand-to-hand melee erupted inside the fort. Dr. Joseph Warren and a few brave men defended the exit in the rear, enabling many to escape. Warren, his arm bleeding from a bayonet thrust, was one of the last to retreat. Outside, he tried to rally enough men to make a stand. As he turned his head, a bullet struck him behind the ear. He flung his hand to the wound and fell without a sound.

Down Breed's Hill and up Bunker Hill the British pursued the Americans. The men from the rail fence made sure the retreat was no rout. They still had some ammunition, and they put up a running fight from one stone wall to another. They were assisted by some regiments that had arrived late. Nevertheless, the Americans took heavy casualties in the retreat. "My God how the balls flew!" recalled Lieutenant Samuel Webb of Connecticut. "Four men were shot dead within five feet of me." With no general in command and men fleeing in all directions, there was no hope of a sustained defense. By five o'clock, little more than ninety minutes after Howe had begun his advance from Morton's Point, the battle of Bunker Hill, as the clash was soon misnamed, was over.

For the British the aftermath was gruesome. A cascade of bleeding soldiers poured across the Charles River into Boston. A staggering 19 officers and 207 men had been killed, and 70 officers and 828 men

BELOW **This map delineates the geography of the Charleston peninsula.**

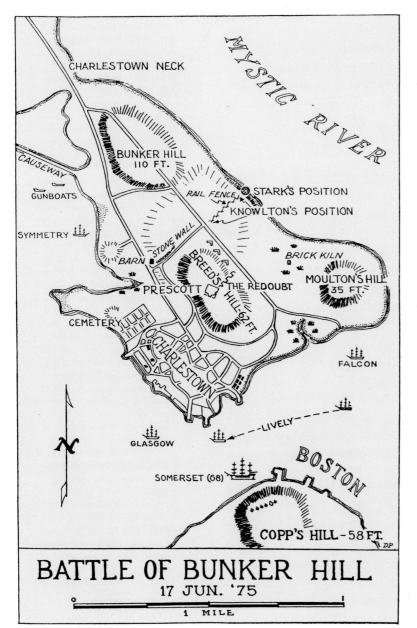

BATTLE OF BUNKER HILL
17 JUN. '75

1 MILE

were wounded—40 percent of the attacking force. Major Pitcairn's son, a lieutenant in his regiment, wept as he helped carry his dying father to a house near the ferry landing.

American casualties were an estimated 441—140 killed and 301 wounded. The actual figure may have been higher, because, as on April 19, many of the Massachusetts wounded may simply have gone home. Inside the American camp, the battle was viewed as a mortifying defeat, and General Artemas Ward was damned for not throwing most of his army into the fight. The criticism considerably eased the touchy problem of replacing Ward with George Washington.

Only gradually did Americans begin to see Bunker Hill as a kind of victory. One of the first to reach this conclusion was a young Rhode Island general, Nathanael Greene. "I wish we could sell them another hill at the same price," he said. Today we know that the battle crippled the British army in America and threw it on the defensive for more than a year.

For many Americans the bitterest result of the battle was the loss of Dr. Joseph Warren. Writing to her husband in Philadelphia, Abigail Adams lamented: "Not all the havoc and devastation they [the British] have made has wounded me like the death of Warren. We want him in the Senate; we want him in his profession; we want him in the field. We mourn for the citizen, the senator, the physician and the warrior. When he fell, liberty wept."

Not Quite as Reluctant Rebels

In the Continental Congress in Philadelphia, Bunker Hill inspired the same contradictory mixture of anger and frantic hope for reconciliation as Lexington and Concord. On June 26 Benjamin Franklin listened to a detailed recitation of the battle's carnage, including the destruction of Charlestown. To his disbelief, John Dickinson, leader of the moderate-conservative coalition, ignored this evidence of all-out war and plowed ahead with his humble plea to George III to restore peace.

On the day the Congress adopted Dickinson's "Olive Branch Petition," Franklin went home and wrote a letter to his old friend William Strahan.

Philadelphia, July 5, 1775

Mr. Strahan: You are a member of Parliament and one of that majority which has doomed my country to destruction. You have begun to burn our towns and murder our people. Look upon your hands! They are stained with the blood of your relations! You and I were long friends. You are now my enemy and I am

Yours,

B Franklin

Franklin never mailed this bitter rebuke, but he made sure it was widely reprinted throughout America and Europe.

On July 21, 1775, Franklin tried to push the Congress a large step further down the road to a decisive break with England. He wrote a declaration of

---

BEN FRANKLIN'S DECLARATION OF INDEPENDENCE

Whereas the British nation, through great corruption of manners and extreme dissipation and profusion, both private and public, have found all honest resources insufficient to supply their excessive luxury and prodigality, and thereby have been driven to the practice of every injustice, which avarice could dictate or rapacity execute: And whereas, not satisfied with the immense plunder of the East, obtained by sacrificing millions of the human species, they have lately turned their eyes to the West, and grudging us the peaceable enjoyment of the fruits of our hard labour and virtuous industry, have for years been endeavouring to extort the same from us, under colour of laws regulating trade, and have thereby actually succeeded in draining us of large sums, to our great loss and detriment; And whereas, impatient to seize the whole, they have at length proceeded to open robbery, declaring by a solemn act of Parliament that all our estates are theirs, and all our property found upon the sea divisible among such of their armed plunderers as shall take the same; And have even dared in the same act to declare, that all the spoilings, thefts, burnings of houses and towns and murders of innocent people, perpetrated by their wicked and inhuman corsairs on our coasts, previous to any war declared against us, were just actions and shall be so deemed, contrary to several of the commandments of God (which by this act they presume to repeal), and to all principles of right, and all the ideas of justice. . .thereby manifesting themselves to be *hostes humani generis* [enemies of mankind]; And whereas it is not possible for the people of America to subsist under such continual ravages without making some reprisals: Therefore, Resolved &c.

Benjamin Franklin

independence and a plan for "Articles of Confederation and Perpetual Union." One delegate, Thomas Jefferson of Virginia, was enthusiastic. But he mournfully noted that many other delegates were "revolted at it." In fact, most of the delegates were so antagonistic, they warned Franklin not to present the proposal from the floor. Nor did they want such a nefarious document in the Congressional journal. Franklin was reduced to presenting his paper as food for future thought.

Simultaneously with this resistance to independence, members of the Congress began making decisions that reflected Bunker Hill's grim reality. They appointed eight brigadier generals to Washington's Continental army to assist the three major generals they had already named. They ordered Washington to leave for Boston immediately and voted to issue $2 million in paper money to support him. They drew up a tough document for Washington to read to the troops, a "Declaration of the Causes and Necessity of Taking up Arms," written in large part by Thomas Jefferson. Most startling, on June 27, the Congress ordered Major General Philip Schuyler to proceed to Fort Ticonderoga and begin raising men for an invasion of Canada.

For John Adams, however, all these warlike gestures could not undo the stupidity (as he saw it) of John Dickinson's Olive Branch Petition to George III. In a letter to his friend James Warren (no relation to Joseph Warren), he wrote: "A certain great fortune and piddling genius, whose fame has been trumpeted so loudly, has given a silly cast to our whole doings." The letter-bearer was captured by the British, who gleefully published these remarks in a Boston newspaper. Relations between Dickinson and his numerous supporters and Adams and his fellow Yankees went from cool to icy.

A Foreign War

In England Bunker Hill had a different but equally momentous impact. The skirmish along the Lexington–Concord road on April 19 was possibly a misunderstanding, an accident in which blame could be distributed on both sides. But a battle fought behind barricades, with cannon and massed musketry, could mean only one thing. On July 26, Prime Minister Lord North wrote to the King that it was now necessary to treat the rebellion as a foreign war and the Americans as an alien foe. The King agreed and ordered his ministers to draw up a proclamation of rebellion.

In the cabinet, only Lord Dartmouth, the American secretary, clung to the cause of peace. Prime Minister Lord North also dreaded war because, he candidly admitted: "Upon military matters I speak ignorantly and therefore without effect." But he was George III's creature, incapable of resisting the King's wishes. Dartmouth's character was not much stronger, but he felt it was his responsibility to urge the King to withhold the proclamation until they heard from the Continental Congress. George III made it so evident that he was tired of Dartmouth's pleas on behalf of the rebels that the American secretary began to absent himself from cabinet meetings. When the Olive Branch Petition reached London, on August 24, it was already a lost cause. The day before, George III had issued the fateful Proclamation of Rebellion.

To no one's surprise, the King decided it was time to replace Lord Dartmouth. George III turned to a man who had recommended the use of force

With grim courage, the British advanced up Breed's Hill a third time, stepping over the bodies of fallen comrades. The Americans, out of ammunition, were forced to flee.

against America from the start of the quarrel—Lord George Germain. Born a Sackville, this saturnine ex-soldier could trace his lineage to William the Conqueror. However, he had a blot on his reputation that made him an unlikely candidate for the cabinet. A general in the Seven Years War, he had been court-martialed for insubordination in battle against the French. Politics had played a major role in the guilty verdict; Germain had been an outspoken critic of sending British troops to fight on the continent. As Prince of Wales, George had shared this opinion and tried to intervene on his behalf. William Pitt had curtly rebuffed the Prince, laying the groundwork for George III's enmity toward the Great Commoner.

In the fifteen years since George III had become King, he had labored to mitigate the disgrace of this strange, embittered man. He had guaranteed Germain a warm reception at his court whenever he chose to appear and had given him a seat on the Privy Council. The King was apparently unbothered by his decision to abandon his famous name when a relative, Lady Betty Germain, offered him £20,000 and a fine country house if he would assume her name—although many people considered it an attempt to escape the aura of shame that surrounded Sackville.

In the 1750s, Lord George Germain had served as his father's chief adviser while the latter was Lord Lieutenant of Ireland. The pair's outrageously arrogant behavior had caused the Irish Parliament, normally the most docile of legislative bodies, to defy them. Germain's aristocratic arrogance was equally visible in his comments on America. He was on record as opposing all forms of representative government in the colonies, even town meetings. He saw no point in "men of a mercantile cast" debating "political matters." After Bunker Hill, he had no doubts about the policy that should be pursued. He favored "exerting the utmost force of this kingdom to finish this rebellion in one campaign."

This was the kind of talk that made George III glow. A man who before his disgrace had been considered one of England's best generals, Germain could infuse the war effort with the energy and decisiveness that the bumbling, doubt-ridden Lord North clearly lacked. Here was a chance to right a wrong that William Pitt had inflicted on one of George's first followers. In early November the King transferred Dartmouth to the harmless post of head of the Privy Council and made the sixty-year-old Germain the American secretary, with far more power than the previous holders of that office had wielded.

Germain swiftly took charge of the war. He moved to a house in London not far from his Whitehall offices and began an all-out push to raise men for an expanded army. When recruiting faltered in England, he received George III's permission to spend millions hiring soldiers in Germany. He was soon telling William Howe, the new commander-in-chief in America, that he could expect reinforcements of 15,000 men in the spring, bringing his total strength to 23,000. Howe was to shift his present army from Boston to New York as soon as ships were available. Another 10,000 men were going to Canada. Germain expected these troops to smash the haphazard American army. He knew nothing about a diffident Virginian who had arrived in Massachusetts and was doing his utmost to change the nature of that army as fast as possible.

PROCLAMATION OF REBELLION

August 23, 1775

Whereas many of our subjects in divers parts of our Colonies and Plantations in North America misled by dangerous and ill designing men and forgetting the allegiance which they owe to the power that has protected and supported them; after various disorderly acts committed in disturbance of the public peace to the obstruction of lawful commerce and to the oppressions of our loyal subjects carrying on same; have at length proceeded to open and avowed rebellion by arraying themselves in a hostile manner to withstand the execution of the law and traitorously preparing, ordering and levying war against us; And whereas there is reason to apprehend that such rebellion has been much promoted by the traitorous correspondence, councils and comfort of divers wicked and desperate persons within this realm: To the end therefore that none of our subjects may neglect or violate their duty through ignorance thereof or through any doubt of the protection which the law will afford to their loyalty and zeal, we have thought fit by and with the advice of our Privy Council, to issue our Royal Proclamation, hereby declaring that not only all our officers, civil and military, are obliged to exert their utmost endeavors to suppress such rebellion and to bring the traitors to justice, that all our subjects of this realm and the dominions thereunto belonging are bound by law to be aiding and assisting in the suppression of such rebellion and to disclose and make known all traitorous conspiracies against us, our crown and our dignity....

George III

ABOVE *Wealthy Pennsylvanian John Dickinson opposed the push for a declaration of independence. He believed the "cause of liberty should not be sullied by turbulence and tumult." But when war came, he was one of the few Continental Congressmen who turned out to fight.*

The Continentals Are Coming

George Washington's early experiences as commander-in-chief only deepened the pessimism that was evident in his acceptance speech. When he took over on July 2, 1775, he was assured that the army had 308 barrels of powder on hand, more than enough for another battle. No one bothered to tell him that the figure dated from before the clash on Bunker Hill, during which most of those barrels had been fired away. On August 2 one of his staff discovered the actual number of barrels in the Cambridge magazine was thirty-six—less than nine rounds per man. For a half-hour, Washington sat motionless behind his desk, unable to speak.

When he recovered the use of his vocal cords, the new general immediately arranged for someone to go into Boston and spread the information that he had so much powder—1,800 barrels—he could not decide what to do with it. The British swallowed this whopper wholesale. He reinforced this first intelligence coup by spreading the same rumor through the American camp. Meanwhile, desperate letters to all points of the compass brought in enough powder to guarantee the army thirty rounds per man—a respectable, though hardly bountiful, reserve.

Not long after the powder crisis was semi-resolved, Washington caught his first spy. Dr. Benjamin Church had recently become surgeon general of the army, giving him an even wider scope for espionage. Now that Boston was enemy territory, however, he had trouble communicating his information. Church tried to send a coded letter with the help of a young woman who also happened to be his mistress. She was caught and talked freely. Church denied everything, confident that the naive Americans could not break his code.

Not to be outwitted, Washington canvassed the army for someone who was good at "ciphering" and soon had the letter decoded. It was a damning document. Church gave Governor-General Gage a rundown of the Americans' manpower, their inadequate artillery, the mood of the Congress and a lot of other information an enemy commander would like to know. Washington wanted to hang the duplicitous doctor but was dismayed to discover that the Congress had restricted the punishment a court-martial could inflict to thirty-nine lashes or a fine of two months' pay. He had to be satisfied with letting Massachusetts deport the ex-surgeon general to a prison in Connecticut.

When Washington took command of the impromptu New England army, he hoped that "all distinctions of Colonies will be laid aside." But he soon found himself up to his ears in local politics. When he appointed Thomas Mifflin of Philadelphia quartermaster general of the army—the man who would buy the soldiers food, ammunition and equipment—John Adams reacted like an outraged Congressman of 1997, fighting to guarantee his constituents a fair share of government pork. Adams fumed that the right to make such a "lucrative" appointment gave Washington too much power and was "a great misfortune for our colony." Washington's opinion of Adams was not enhanced when he discovered that the Congressman's former law clerk, whom Washington had made one of his aides, had been directed to tell Adams everything that went on in army headquarters.

Washington also had to deal with bruised egos in the reorganized army. In the Massachusetts army, John Thomas had been a lieutenant general. Now Washington informed him he was a continental brigadier. When Thomas threatened to resign, Washington urged him to consider his duty to "your country, your posterity, and yourself." Thomas changed his mind and became a brigadier.

Used to officers' being gentlemen in Virginia, Washington was nonplussed to find a Massachusetts captain, a former barber, shaving one of his men. When the new commander began urging officers to separate themselves from their men and start exerting authority and discipline, he ran into a Yankee hornet's nest. He warned fellow Virginian Richard Henry Lee that before long he expected to be "obnoxious" to most New Englanders. He in turn began saying some rather obnoxious things about them in private letters. He told another Virginian that Yankee officers were "the most indifferent" people he ever saw and the enlisted men were "an exceeding dirty and nasty people." Writing to his aide Joseph Reed, who was home on leave in Philadelphia, he opined that "no nation under the sun...pay greater attention to money than they do."

Back came a letter from Reed, warning Washington that Philadelphia was buzzing with stories of his dislike of New Englanders. Washington did not know that Richard Henry Lee had become a devotee of John Adams and was showing the Braintree Congressman his letters. The general thanked Reed for this "proof of his friendship" and vowed to be more circumspect. He admitted the private slurs, but he insisted that he had given no public evidence of his antipathy. Henceforth, Washington scrupulously avoided sectional criticism in his letters and conversation. He ruefully realized that if the army was to become truly continental, the transformation would have to start with him.

Another start in this direction was the arrival of 1,000 big, rambunctious soldiers from the backcountry of Virginia and Pennsylvania. The Virginians were led by thirty-nine-year-old Daniel Morgan, an ex-wagonmaster with a grudge against the British. During the French and Indian War, Morgan had gotten into a fight with a British officer and was sentenced to 500 lashes. Morgan and his fellow sharpshooters were welcome evidence that the rest of the country was supporting New England. Their prowess with their long-barreled, rifled guns astonished everyone; they could hit a target the size of a man's head at 250 yards. But the new troops soon gave Washington major headaches. They were totally immune to discipline. When one of the men was put in the guardhouse, his friends rescued him and, for good measure, burned down the guardhouse.

One day Morgan's men got into a snowball fight with the men from the Marblehead regiment. Soon 1,000 soldiers were punching and kicking each other in the slush. The distraught colonel of the Marblehead regiment rushed to Washington's headquarters for help. Washington leaped on his horse and rode to the scene of the riot. The commander-in-chief sent his mount soaring over a fence and landed in the midst of the brawl. Grabbing two soldiers by

The congress permitted its members and others involved in the Revolutionary War effort to send their mail free of charge. Top, Benjamin Franklin added a typically imaginative touch to his envelopes. He signed them "B. Free Franklin." Above Right, George Washington usually just wrote: "G. Washington." He seldom used the word free. Above Left, Thomas Jefferson's letter was sent during his presidency, which he modestly states as "Pr. U.S." Right, John Hancock ostentatiously wrote: "On Publick Service."

REMEMBER THE LADIES

One could almost write a history of the American Revolution from the hundreds of letters John and Abigail Adams exchanged discussing the great issues and reporting the changes and challenges of the era. Here are two of the most famous. The first, from Abigail, was written soon after Washington drove the British from Boston.

March 31, 1776

I wish you would ever write me a Letter half as long as I write you...What sort of Defence can Virginia make against our common Enemy?... Are not the Gentery Lords and the common people vassals?...I hope their Riffel [rifle] Men who have shewen themselves very savage and even Blood thirsty; are not a specimen of the Generality of the people.

I am willing to allow the Colony great merrit for having produced a Washington but they have been shamefully duped by a Dunmore.

I have sometimes been ready to think that the passion for Liberty cannot be Eaquelly Strong in the breasts of those who have been accustomed to deprive their fellow Creatures of theirs. Of this I am certain that it is not founded upon that generous and christian principle of doing to others we would that others should do to us....

I feel very differently at the approach of spring to what I did a month ago. We knew not then whether we could reap the fruits of our own industry, whether we could rest in our own Cottages, or whether we should not be driven from the sea coasts to seek shelter in the wildnerness, but now we feel as if we might sit under our own vine and eat the good of the land.

I feel a gaieti de Coar to which I was a stranger. I think the Sun looks brighter, the Birds sing more melodiously and Nature puts on a more chearfull countanance. We feel a temporary peace, and the poor fugitives [the people of Boston] are returning to their deserted habitations....

I long to hear that you have declared an independancy—and by the way in the new Code of Laws which I suppose it will be necessary for you to make I desire you would Remember the Ladies, and be more generous and favourable to them than your ancestors. Do not put such unlimited power into the hands of the Husbands. Remember all Men would be tyrants if they could. If perticuliar care and attention is not paid to the Laidies we are determined to foment a Rebelion, and will not hold oursleves bound by any Laws in which we have no voice, or Representation.

That your sex are Naturally Tyrannical is a Truth so thoroughly established as to admit of no dispute, but such of you as wish to be happy willingly give up the harsh title of Master for the more tender and endearing one of Friend. Why then, not put it out of the power of the vicious and Lawless to use us with cruelty and indignity with impunity. Men of Sense in all Ages abhor those customs which treat us only as the vassals of your Sex. Regard us then as Beings placed by providence under your protection and in immitation of the Supreem Being make use of that power only for our happiness.

John's reply follows:

Ap. 14. 1776

You justly complain of my short Letters, but the critical State of Things and the Multiplicity of Avocations must plead my Excuse... You ask what Sort of Defence Virginia can make. I believe they will make an able Defence. Their Militia and minute Men have been some time employed in training them selves, and they have Nine Battallions of regulars as they call them, maintained among them, under good Officers at the Continental Expence.... They are in very good Spirits, and seem determined to make a brave Resistance.—The Gentry are very rich, and the common People very poor. This Inequality of Property, gives an Aristocratical Turn to all their Proceedings, and occasions a strong Aversion in their Patricians to Common Sense. [Thomas Paine's pamphlet]. But the Spirit of these Barons, is coming down, and it must submit.

Your Description of your own Gaiety de Coeur, charms me. Thanks be to God you have just Cause to rejoice—and may the bright Prospect be obscured by no Cloud. As to Declarations of Independency, be patient. Read our Privateering Laws....What signifies a Word.

As to your extraordinary code of laws, I cannot but laugh. We have been told our Struggle has loosened the bands of Government every where. That Children and Apprentices were disobedient—that schools and Colledges were grown turbulent—That Indians slighted their Guardians and Negroes grew insolent to their Masters. But your Letter was the first Intimation that another Tribe more numerous and powerfull than all the rest were grown discontented.—This is rather too coarse a Compliment but you are so saucy, I won't blot it out.

Depend upon it, We know better than to repeal our Masculine systems. Altho they are in full Force, you know they are little more than Theory. We dare not exert our Power in its full Latitude. We are obliged to go fair, and softly, and in Practice you know We are the subjects. We have only the Name of Masters, and rather than give up this, which would compleatly subject Us to the Despotism of the Peticoat, I hope General Washington, and all our brave Heroes would fight....

the shirt, he lifted each off the ground, and roared commands at the rest. In seconds the fight was over.

Major General John Sullivan of New Hampshire, who witnessed the scene, later said: "From the moment I saw Washington leap the bars at Cambridge, I never faltered in the faith that we had the right man to lead the cause of American liberty."

Washington soon had more serious problems. While he struggled to reform the army, the siege of Boston settled into a stalemate. On Boston Neck and along the shore of Back Bay, British defenses were formidable. The Americans lacked the artillery for an assault, even if they had the powder. So the summer and fall trickled away with the British still ensconced in Boston—until it dawned on Washington that his army was about to disappear before his eyes.

The militiamen had agreed to serve only until the end of 1775. Nothing was more sacred to a Yankee than a contract. The Connecticut men announced they would depart first, on December 10, thanks to a clause in their agreement that permitted them to get home by Christmas. As the wintry winds of November began to blow, "the same desire to retire to a chimney corner seized the troops of New Hampshire, Rhode Island and Massachusetts," Washington gloomily reported to Joseph Reed. They announced January 1, 1776, as their day of departure.

A frantic Washington was soon telling Reed, "It is easier to conceive than describe the situation in my mind for some time past." On January 1, he found himself with 5,582 soldiers to man a ring of forts and batteries in an eight-mile semicircle outside Boston. This mass defection underscores one of the forgotten oddities of the Revolution. Contemporary Americans celebrate 1776 as the high tide of patriotic emotion. But the Americans who lived through the revolutionary experience remembered the middle months of 1775 as the crest of patriotism.

Numerous witnesses testify to the frenzy that swept the colonies when Americans heard about the fighting that had broken out at Lexington and escalated to the carnage of Bunker Hill. From Massachusetts to Georgia, militia companies assembled and drilled, and preachers and politicians hurled defiance against the British "butchers." But when the butchers retired timidly inside Boston and dug forts, and the besieging American army did nothing but dig forts on their side of the lines, this patriotic ardor inevitably cooled. By January 1, 1776, the thermometer of patriotism, abetted by the winds of winter, had dropped precipitously.

The crisis prompted Washington to change his mind about enlisting African-Americans in the Continental army. When he took over in July, there were many blacks in the ranks. Their adopted last names often announced why they were fighting. On the muster roll of one Connecticut regiment were Jeffrey Liberty, Pomp Liberty, Sharp Liberty and Dick Freedom.

When Washington took command, he told recruiting officers not to enlist any more Africans. Washington feared that southerners would refuse to serve with them. In September 1775 Congressman Edward Rutledge of South Carolina made a motion to discharge all the blacks in the Continental army. Southerners feared that giving guns and military training to blacks might lead to a slave insurrection.

The Congress rejected Rutledge's motion but left the issue muddled, while the Continental army continued to maintain a policy of exclusion. The blacks in the ranks grew more and more irritated and finally submitted a protest to Washington around the time his army started to disappear. He wrote a letter to the president of the Congress, sympathizing with the black soldiers' complaints, and asking for a clear-cut statement of policy. The Congress voted to permit any African-American who had already served to reenlist. This break in the color line would eventually make the Continental army more integrated than any American force except the armies that fought in the Vietnam and Gulf wars.

Continental privates were being paid $6.50 a month. Washington wanted to offer the men who were still with him a $40 bounty to sign up for another year. But the New Englanders in the Congress could not persuade the men of the Middle States or the South to pay this modest sum. They thought pure patriotism should motivate everyone. When the harassed commander-in-chief requested permission to enlist the new army for the duration of the war, the New Englanders turned on him. John Adams said that only "the meanest, idlest, most intemperate and worthless" men would sign away their liberty under such terms. His cousin Samuel Adams inveighed against the dangers of standing armies. The Congress ordered Washington to limit enlistment to a single year.

The general was discovering perhaps the most unnerving fact of 1776. The Americans had not only become united by the artful propaganda that the Massachusetts men distributed after the battle of Lexington, they believed every word of it. They were convinced that untrained militiamen could stand up to British regulars. Bunker Hill had reinforced this conviction. When Washington urged an army of 40,000 men, he was told 20,000 would be enough. If he needed more men, all he had to do was call out the militia.

Washington, aware that months of inaction outside Boston were causing morale problems, tried to persuade his fellow generals to approve a plan for an all-out assault over Boston Neck and across Back Bay to destroy the British army in one savage stroke. The generals, displaying some of the wishful thinking that was disorienting the Congress, voted against the idea. In spite of George III's proclamation of rebellion, a majority of the high command thought they should delay offensive action until the text of the King's October speech to a new session of Parliament reached America. The colonies were being swept by rumors that George III was going to oust Lord North and his anti-American coalition and restore peace with a wave of his scepter. The Americans were loath to abandon the hope that the brilliant rhetoric Edmund Burke, Isaac Barré and William Pitt deployed on their behalf in Parliament would produce a dramatic change of heart in England.

As 1775 ended, George III's speech reached Boston. Washington's efficient spies—since July he had been paying as much as $333 a clip to secret agents—soon reported that it breathed the same determination to annihilate the Americans as the Proclamation of Rebellion. In fact, so fierce was the speech, some of the British in Boston thought its mere words might frighten the Americans into surrender.

On January 1, 1776, Washington hoisted a new flag over his lines in Boston, a ceremony aimed at concealing the state of his shrunken army. The

THE CONTINENTAL CONGRESS'S OLIVE BRANCH PETITION

The Pennsylvania signers of the Petition.

Most Gracious Sovereign: Attached to your Majesty's person, family and government, with all devotion that principle and affection can inspire, connected with Great Britain by the strongest ties that can unite societies, and deploring every event that tends in any degree to weaken them, we solemnly assure your Majesty, that we not only most ardently desire the former harmony between her and these Colonies may be restored, but that a concord may be established between them upon so firm a basis as to perpetuate its blessings, uninterrupted by any future dissensions to succeeding generations in both countries, and to transmit your Majesty's name to posterity, adorned with that signal and lasting glory that has attended the memory of those illustrious personages, whose virtues and abilities have extricated states from dangerous convulsions, and by securing happiness to others have erected the most novel and durable monuments to their own fame....

banner, called "the Grand Union flag," contained thirteen alternating red and white stripes—and in the upper left corner crosses of St. George and St. Andrew, symbolizing the colonists' continuing loyalty to George III. Many members of the Royal Army thought it was a gesture of submission to the King's speech.

This wildly skewed reaction made Washington wonder how long Americans should continue professing any loyalty to England and her unforgiving monarch. The general had long since made up his mind. After he arrived in Boston on July 2, 1775, and learned the details of the battle of Bunker Hill, he had become convinced that it was time to "shake off all connections with a state so unjust and unnatural."

ABOVE *Six-foot, two-hundred-pound Colonel Daniel Morgan of Virginia led three companies of riflemen in the American army that George Washington ordered to attack British-held Quebec. In the French and Indian War, Morgan received 500 lashes for punching a British officer. Morgan was Daniel Boone's cousin.*

The Fourteenth Colony

Many Americans continued to cling to the relationship that the Grand Union flag proclaimed. One of the most unlikely of these hopers-against-hope was a tall, handsome Irish-born ex-British officer who was doing his utmost, with the help of Americans Daniel Morgan and Benedict Arnold, to convert Canada into the fourteenth stripe in the flag. Discouraged by his lack of promotion in the British army, Richard Montgomery had moved to New York and soon married Janet Livingston, heiress to a hefty chunk of the fortune in lands and cash belonging to her family's Hudson River clan.

Like his American in-laws, Montgomery reacted angrily to Parliament's attempts to tax America. When the Congress ordered General Philip Schuyler to take charge of an invasion of Canada, he turned to Montgomery, quickly wangled him a commission as a brigadier general, and helped raise the men and supplies needed for this gamble. Soon Montgomery was besieging the border fort at St. Johns with a 1,200-man army of Green Mountain Boys, homesick Connecticut Yankees and New Yorkers whom he described in private letters as "the sweepings of the York streets."

The Congress was trying to forestall Sam Adams's prophecy that the British would launch an invasion from the north. Canada also looked like an easy conquest. The British governor, General Guy Carleton, had shipped virtually every man in his command to the embattled army in Boston. Governor Jonathan Trumbull of Connecticut assured George Washington that there were no more than 750 widely scattered British soldiers in Canada. He had the figure almost exactly right—and Montgomery captured most of this force when two regiments capitulated to him at St. Johns on November 2, 1775.

When Washington received dolorous letters from Schuyler, complaining about the way the Connecticut militiamen were going home in droves, the commander-in-chief decided to help. He procured a continental colonel's commission for Benedict Arnold and put him in charge of 1,100 hand-picked men, including three companies of riflemen led by Daniel Morgan. This expeditionary force was ordered to proceed up the Kennebec and Chaudiere Rivers in

present-day Maine and rendezvous with Montgomery in front of Quebec. Along with a supply of hard money, Washington gave Arnold an address to the people of Canada, urging them to join the other colonies in their struggle for liberty. He also issued strict orders to respect the French-Canadians' Catholic religion.

Arnold's route, which numerous Massachusetts men had assured Washington was easy and mostly by water, turned out to be a military nightmare. The rivers were broken by lethal falls and rapids. Most of the boats, built of green wood, fell apart. The marchers waded through oozing swamps up to their hips, tormented by giant "muskeetoes" and black flies, ran out of food, and were reduced to eating their own shoes. Many died, 300 turned back in despair, but the indomitable Arnold refused to quit, and Morgan and 675 others grimly kept pace with him.

Arnold's half-starved men amazed the British when they emerged from the Maine wilderness before Quebec. They quickly learned that Montgomery had captured all the British forts along the invasion route to Canada and had taken Montreal without any resistance. Governor Guy Carleton had labored since 1766 to persuade the Canadian French to accept English rule. He was dismayed to discover that the *habitants*, however submissive to the British flag, had no interest in defending it. The governor was forced to flee downriver from Montreal to Quebec disguised as a civilian.

Carleton reached the city just in time. The French were ready to open the gates to Arnold and his 675 ragged scarecrows. Many of the *habitants* thought only beings with miraculous powers could have survived the privations of their 350-mile march. Washington's call to join "the Great American Congress" in a defense of liberty also had a surprising impact. But Carleton swiftly took charge of Quebec's defenses, exiling everyone suspected of American sympathies and scraping together a makeshift army of about 1,800 men, who compelled Arnold to retreat twenty miles into the country.

Montgomery and Arnold joined forces on December 2, 1775. By this time Montgomery's army had dwindled to about 450 men. Even with Arnold's 675, the Americans were outnumbered by the Quebec garrison. Lacking heavy can-

ABOVE LEFT *This "Grand Union" flag was raised by George Washington's army on January 1, 1776. It was created by running six white stripes through the red field of the British flag, creating thirteen stripes, one for each colony. In the canton are the red cross of St. George, symbolizing England, and the white cross of St. Andrew, signifying Scotland. For the Americans it was a statement that they were still seeking justice within the empire.*

RIGHT *Americans planned to attack Quebec on the first snowy night. Unfortunately the storm became a raging blizzard that blew snow horizontally into the men's faces.*

non, they could not hope to conduct a siege—and they were exposed to the brutal Canadian winter. Mournfully, Montgomery told his brother-in-law Robert Livingston that it would come "to storming the place...at last." He was "very sorry to be reduced to this mode of attack" because he knew "the melancholy consequences." Frontal assaults invariably led to heavy casualties.

Montgomery also confided to his brother-in-law, a member of the New York delegation to the Continental Congress, that he shuddered at the idea of separating from England. He was convinced that if the Americans conquered Canada, the shock would drive Lord North's government from office, and peace and harmony would be restored. Behind his mask of cool, clear-eyed courage, Montgomery was a captive of one of the major political illusions of 1776.

At midnight on December 31, 1775, in a howling blizzard, Montgomery and Arnold assaulted Quebec. They divided their little army into two columns. Montgomery attacked from the south, Arnold from the north. The wind was so fierce, recalled seventeen-year-old rifleman John Joseph Henry of Lancaster, Pennsylvania, who was in Arnold's column, that the snow was driven horizontally into their faces. Carrying scaling ladders to get over the fortress city's immense walls, the men struggled through waist-deep drifts. Not until 5 A.M. were they in position to attack. Then all Quebec seemed to explode.

A sharp-eyed sentry had spotted Arnold's men. Bells rang, cannon boomed. The Americans had to run a three-quarter-mile gauntlet of flying metal before they reached the gate into the lower town, which was guarded by two cannon. "Now lads, all together rush!" roared Arnold. One gun belched a hurricane of grapeshot—the eighteenth-century equivalent of machine-gun fire—over the Americans' heads. It was aimed too high. The other sputtered and did not go off. Snow had wet its powder.

At least thirty men guarding the cannon fired a fusillade of musketry that sent Arnold pitching into the snow with a bullet in his Achilles tendon. He handed command of the column to Daniel Morgan, who mounted a scaling ladder and went over the barricade, ignoring a stupendous volley of point-blank cannon fire and musketry that blackened his face and singed off much of his hair and whiskers. Others followed him and swiftly captured the battery. Charging up the street, they met a Canadian militia company whose captain was drunk. His soldiers threw down their guns and shouted, "Vive la liberté!"

Morgan and his men were soon stopped by a formidable barricade blocking access to the upper town. A British lieutenant stepped through a door in the barrier and called on them to surrender. Morgan shot him through the head. The big Virginian wanted to attack the barricade in the same headlong fashion, but his fellow officers convinced him they should wait for Montgomery's column.

Alas, that force and its gallant leader would never arrive. After struggling for hours along an ice-choked path beside the St. Lawrence River, delayed by barricades that had to be sawed and ripped down, they had neared their point of attack when Quebec's alarm guns boomed. Beyond a final barricade stood a simple frame house. Governor Carleton had converted it into a strongpoint by loopholing the walls for muskets and mounting four small cannon in the windows.

Inside was a motley collection of sailors and French and British civilians.

LEFT *Former British officer Richard Montgomery was only a few hundred yards away from conquering Canada for the Continental Congress when he was cut down by a blast of gunfire from the fortress city of Quebec. His rattled troops fled.*

By the time the alarm guns crashed, they were all drunk, and their first instinct was to flee. They were stopped by a very angry American from Boston, John Coffin, whose family had been driven out of their native city because of their stubborn loyalty to George III. Coffin drew his sword and forced the men back to their posts.

Coffin waited until Montgomery, his aides and a small advance guard started up the narrow road to the house. "Fire!" he snarled. The cannon belched grapeshot and muskets blazed from the loopholes. Montgomery and two aides were killed instantly. The dazed survivors fled.

Coffin's panicky group of defenders also fled. The way was open for the rest of Montgomery's column to advance unopposed into Quebec's lower town and join Morgan. But without Montgomery's charismatic leadership, the New York soldiers lived up to their general's private description of them as the sweepings of the city's streets. They ran away.

For a precious half-hour, Morgan and his 400 men waited for the column to appear. Meanwhile, two feigned attacks by a handful of Americans on other parts of the city had so demoralized the British that Carleton almost surrendered. But when his senior officers reported Montgomery's men had fled and the other attackers had vanished, the British general regained his confidence and threw the full weight of his 1,800-man garrison at Morgan.

Trapped in the narrow street, decimated by bullets pouring from the barricade and nearby houses, the Americans began to surrender in small groups. The last to concede defeat was Daniel Morgan. When a British officer backed by several hundred men demanded his sword, he roared: "Come take it if you dare."

A crowd of French civilians gathered to watch this spectacle of a single man defying an army. Morgan spotted a priest among them. He gave him the sword, declaring: "No scoundrel of these [British] cowards shall take it out of my hands."

Outside Quebec the wounded but still indomitable Benedict Arnold managed to assemble enough men to beat off a British attempt to rout the rest of the American army. Unsure how many men Arnold still had, Carleton decided to hunker down behind Quebec's walls for the rest of the winter. In the city jail were Daniel Morgan and 371 other very discouraged Americans. Captain Simeon Thayer of Rhode Island noted glumly in his diary that it was "a bad method [way] to begin the New Year."

A Dose of Common Sense

In Philadelphia the grim news from Canada contributed to still more ambivalent behavior in the Continental Congress. On one hand, Benjamin Franklin and four other members of a secret committee were meeting regularly with a spy named Archard de Bonvouloir, who had been touring America and sending

ABOVE *This British cartoon saw the struggle between England and America as a boxing match between two angry women. Many Englishmen did not take the Americans seriously at first. Others regarded them as rebellious children. The metaphor of England as the Mother Country was a misleading figure of speech.*

reports on the growing Revolution to the government of the new French King, Louis XVI. Another secret committee, headed by merchant Robert Morris, had a contract to buy $2 million worth of gunpowder, among other war materiel, and was briskly doing business with Dutch and French merchants in the West Indies.

Observing that the King's speech had accused the Americans of plotting independence, James Wilson of Pennsylvania urged the Congress to issue an address to the people of America, denying this outrageous slander. Samuel Adams counterattacked by suggesting that the Congress take up Benjamin Franklin's plan of confederation. The proposal was soundly defeated. But when the Reverend Dr. William Smith gave a funeral oration in praise of General Montgomery, in which he reiterated that the Congress, like Montgomery, recoiled from the idea of independence, a majority voted against printing the speech, because, one delegate noted in his diary, "The Doctor declared sentiments...this Congress can not now approve."

An exasperated Samuel Adams told his friend James Warren that certain members of the Congress had "the vanity of the ape, the tameness of the ox, or the stupid servility of the ass." Many of Adams's fellow delegates returned these compliments by privately calling him "Judas Iscariot." A worried John Adams told Abigail: "There is a deep anxiety, a kind of thoughtful melancholy, and in some a lowness of spirit approaching to despondency" among many delegates, especially those from the southern colonies. But not even the Massachusetts delegation was unanimously for independence. Two of its four members favored reconciliation, and John Hancock, the president of the Congress, sided with them because the Adamses had not backed him for command of the American army.

While the politicians waffled, people were reading an argument for independence far bolder than any yet made in public by an American. In a pamphlet called *Common Sense*, Thomas Paine, an Englishman who had been in America less than two years, assaulted the idea of reconciliation with rhetoric that sent loyalists into shock and anti-independence men like John Dickinson and James Wilson rushing for their pens to scribble agitated replies.

Paine scoffed at the idea that the King should be revered as the symbolic father of the country. "Of more worth is one honest man to society and in the sight of God, than all the crowned ruffians that ever lived," he declared. He sneered at George III's claim to rule England as a descendant of William the Conqueror. Who was he? "A French bastard, landing with an armed banditti and establishing himself...against the consent of the natives." He climaxed this onslaught by calling George "the royal brute of Great Britain"—a treasonable offense that not even John Wilkes at his most irreverent would have dared.

Paine also hacked away at the idea that the Mother Country had nurtured America and enabled her to grow rich within the British Empire. "Nothing can be more fallacious than this kind of argument," he declared. More to the point, Americans had *suffered* because their connection with England had dragged them into endless European wars. The very distance between America and England, and their stark differences in size, were another argument for independence. It might make some sense for a powerful nation to take a small island under its care, "but there is something absurd in supposing a continent

to be perpetually governed by an island."

The ultimate argument in *Common Sense* went beyond negative contentions to a declaration that "a new era in politics is struck." All the plans and proposals for reconciliation had some validity prior to April 19, 1775. Now they were "like the almanacks of the last year." Paine backed this assertion with a vision of America's mission in the world as the champion of liberty: "O ye that love mankind! Ye that dares oppose not only the tyranny but the tyrant, stand forth! Every spot of the old World is overrun with oppression. Freedom hath been hunted round the globe. Europe regards her like a stranger and England hath given her warning to depart. O! receive the fugitive, and prepare in time an asylum for mankind."

A glimpse of *Common Sense*'s impact on the younger generation is visible in a letter that a Connecticut schoolteacher, Nathan Hale, received from a friend on February 19, 1776. He told Hale that after listening to his elders debate independence pro and con, this "little pamphlet" had made up his mind for him. "Upon my word 'tis well done—'tis what would be common sense were not most men so blinded by their prejudices." A stunning 150,000 copies of *Common Sense* poured from the presses—the equivalent of a sale of 15 million in modern America.

Flaming Arguments in Virginia

While Paine was changing minds with his electrifying prose, John Murray, Lord Dunmore, the royal governor of Virginia, was supplying Patrick Henry, Thomas Jefferson and the other pro-independence men of the South with another kind of argument. In April 1775 Dunmore had caused a huge uproar by trying to imitate Governor-General Gage and seize the colony's supply of powder. The imminent arrival of Patrick Henry with several thousand militiamen had persuaded him to restore it. Dunmore soon fled to the man-of-war *HMS Fowey*, off Yorktown, because of "hostile appearances around me." On May 1 he wrote to London, proposing to unglue the revolution in Virginia and the rest of the South by offering freedom to the slaves.

Wangling 150 regulars from the governor of Florida, Dunmore took the offensive. He attacked and dispersed 170 militiamen from coastal Princess Anne County and issued a proclamation declaring martial law and calling on all loyal Virginians to support him. He also urged "all indented servants, Negroes or other [servants] of the rebels" to join His Majesty's troops immediately. Dunmore soon had 500 African-Americans whom he organized into an "Ethiopian Regiment." He used them and his regulars to take over the port of Norfolk and convert it into a loyalist headquarters.

Virginians redoubled patrols on all their rivers and roads and advised slave owners to tell their blacks the British were liars. Instead of giving them liberty,

TOP LEFT *The front page of* Common Sense. *Paine assured the Americans it would be easy to defeat the British.*

RIGHT *American artillery commander Henry Knox solved the shortage of American cannon at the siege of Boston by dragging 59 big guns from Fort Ticonderoga—a 300-mile haul. Three of the large mortars weighed a ton each. The 42 sleds also carried 2,300 pounds of lead for future bullets.*

they were going to sell them to the sugar plantations of the West Indies, a death sentence for a Virginia slave. By early 1776 Dunmore had become one of George Washington's numerous worries. Washington warned Richard Henry Lee that the "fate of America" depended on forcing Dunmore to evacuate Norfolk as soon as possible.

Five hundred Virginians, led by a cautious veteran soldier named William Woodford, marched on Norfolk. They were stopped by a barricade on the Great Bridge, the long causeway that connected the port to the mainland. Woodford decided to build a fort at his end of the Great Bridge and lure the impulsive Dunmore into attacking him. He sent a black man into Dunmore's camp who assured the governor that the Americans barely numbered 300 raw troops who would run away at the first shot.

Dunmore ordered Captain Charles Fordyce and 120 regulars to attack, while the Ethiopian Regiment waited on the causeway with cannon to support them. American sentries, including an African-American named William Flora, slowed the British with several rounds of buck and ball, giving Woodford's men plenty of time to man their breastwork. Howling "The day is ours," Fordyce led his men forward with glorious presumption.

The Americans waited until they could see the whites of the attackers's eyes, and Fordyce died with fourteen bullets in his body. Twelve privates followed him into eternity, and the rest fled. Woodford sent part of his force through the swamps to attack the Ethiopian Regiment's flanks and drove them back in confusion, capturing two cannon. It was, Woodford said, "a second Bunker Hill, with this difference, that we kept our post and had only one man wounded in the hand."

A mortified Dunmore was forced to evacuate Norfolk. The Americans stormed across the Great Bridge and hunted down some 3,000 people in Princess Anne and Norfolk counties who had sworn an oath of allegiance to the King. Many of these loyalists fled to Dunmore's ships. Others stayed in Norfolk and sniped at Woodford's men. When Dunmore threatened to bombard the port unless the rebels supplied his fleet with fresh food, the Virginians, reinforced by 500 North Carolinians, practically begged him to do it. They wanted to destroy the town to make sure it would not be seized by a stronger British force. Dunmore stupidly obliged, pouring hotshot into the waterside warehouses while some of Woodford's men set fire to the houses of leading loyalists. Soon the entire town was aflame; it burned for fifty hours.

Dunmore's "flaming argument" and his call for a slave rebellion radicalized thousands of moderate Virginians. Nicholas Cresswell, a twenty-five-year-old Englishman who had come to America in 1774 and wandered around Virginia for eighteen months, growing more and more appalled by the mounting rebellion, glumly informed his diary: "Nothing but independence

BELOW *John Murray, the Earl of Dunmore, became royal governor of Virginia in 1771. He named his newborn daughter Virginia and was popular until the Revolution began. When he offered freedom to slaves and indentured servants who joined the British cause, he drove even conservatives to "independency."*

will go down. The devil is in the people." Even Colonel Landon Carter, a conservative of the old school who considered *Common Sense* "scandalous," changed his mind about the British government being the best on earth when ten of his slaves looted his silver, stole a new boat from his wharf and joined Dunmore. Carter was, as he put it wrathfully, "compelled to independency."

Mercy in North Carolina

In North Carolina a similar confrontation took place between royal governor Josiah Martin and American revolutionaries. Here the governor built his hopes upon the discontented Scots and Irish of the backcountry. They felt they were unrepresented and overtaxed by the wealthy planters of the seacoast, who ran the colony. In 1771 the westerners had set up their own government, assaulted tax collectors and closed courts to "regulate" taxes and fees. The previous royal governor had led a seacoast army that crushed them and hanged six of their leaders.

Josiah Martin thought these still surly "Regulators" could be galvanized into a loyal phalanx, eager to even old scores against lowland planters such as Cornelius Harnett, who was known as the Sam Adams of North Carolina. Harnett's pugnacious rhetoric soon forced Martin to seek refuge aboard a Royal Navy sloop, *HMS Cruizer*.

Martin's letters proposing North Carolina as a loyalist stronghold persuaded the British that he was on to something. The admiralty all but slavered over the idea of controlling Cape Fear, which would be a magnificent deep-water base for the British fleet. Early in January 1776, word arrived from London that 2,000 troops under the command of Major General Henry Clinton were on their way to support the royal governor.

Martin lost his head. He began appointing ex-Regulators and some recently arrived Scottish highlanders to commands in a loyal militia. But the Regulators, having lost one fight, had no stomach for another. Only the highlanders—who felt bound by an oath of loyalty they had taken to George III—responded, prodded by two Scottish officers who had come to North Carolina supposedly to recuperate from wounds received at Bunker Hill. They turned out 1,400 men—but only 520 had guns.

Meanwhile, Cornelius Harnett was ordering every patriot with a gun into action. When the highlanders began a march to the coast to rendezvous with Clinton and his 2,000 regulars, they found their path blocked by 1,100 men. After several days of marching and countermarching, the Scots attacked across a bridge over Moore's Creek, howling "King George and broadswords." A picked force whirled these formidable weapons, which had almost demolished the British army at Culloden in 1745.

During the night the Americans had removed the planks of the bridge. As the highlanders struggled to cross on the runners, they were easy targets. The rest of their paper army collapsed. The North Carolinians wisely decided pacification was more important than vengeance. "Their errors claim our pity, their situation disarms our resentment," Cornelius Harnett said. This spirit of forgiveness, which the Continental Congress warmly approved, curbed loyalism in North Carolina for a long time.

Cornelius Harnett did not extend his benevolence to Governor Josiah

Martin or his royal master, George III. On April 7 Harnett persuaded the North Carolina Provincial Congress to resolve "that the delegates for this colony in the Continental Congress be empowered to concur with the delegates of the other colonies in declaring independency, and forming foreign alliances."

Celebrating an Imaginary Victory

Petty skirmishes such as the clash at Moore's Creek did nothing to alter the fundamental military fact of the first months of 1776. The British army was still in Boston, and the Continental army commanded by George Washington was still outside it. Not a few Congressmen and other assorted know-it-alls had begun to wonder if there was something wrong with the commander-in-chief. They knew nothing of Washington's worries over lack of powder and the regiments that vanished on January 1, 1776.

Washington needed cannon as well as powder. He finally got some in mid-January, when the commander of American artillery, a former bookseller from Boston named Henry Knox, arrived in Cambridge with fifty-nine big guns he and his men had dragged from Fort Ticonderoga. Hauling almost sixty tons of metal across the frozen Hudson River and up and down the hills of western Massachusetts was a magnificent feat of military engineering. It restored the drooping morale of Washington's army, which still numbered only 8,797 men.

In the succeeding weeks, as he analyzed the reams of information his spies supplied him, Washington began to think he had to do something more

BELOW *When Washington seized Dorchester Heights and emplaced the cannon General Knox had dragged from Ticonderoga, William Howe was forced to evacuate Boston. It took eight days to load the ships. Everything he could not carry away was destroyed. Here he orders heavy cannon thrown into the harbor.*

important than use his new cannon to battter British defenses in Boston. All his secret agents agreed that the British were watering and loading the ships in their steadily growing fleet of men-of-war and transports—and their destination was probably New York City. Washington decided he had to attack and destroy the British army before it left Boston. Only a decisive victory here and now would force the British to abandon the war.

On the night of March 4, Washington sent 2,500 men onto Dorchester Heights under the command of Brigadier General John Thomas. Using wooden frames called chandeliers that could be set on the frozen ground and filled with fascines and barrels full of dirt, they put together a series of forts containing most of Knox's cannon. The British would have to attack or evacuate Boston. While a third or even half of the 7,500-man British army was absorbed in this assault, Washington planned to send 4,000 men in forty-five bateaux, supported by twelve-pound cannon on rafts, across Back Bay to seize high ground near Boston Common. They would then wheel and attack the defenses on Boston Neck from behind, opening the city's gates to more reinforcements waiting in Roxbury. It was an incredibly daring plan, revealing a side of Washington that few if any of his contemporaries saw behind the diffident man who claimed his talents were not equal to the task of winning the war.

In the morning the British awoke to stare in disbelief at what the Americans had built: six solid forts running the entire length of the heights of Dorchester. William Howe was said to have exclaimed: "Good God, these fellows have done more work in one night than I could have made my army do in three months." The British army's chief engineer estimated the Americans had used 20,000 men.

In Boston Howe revealed once more that he was a general who thought big. He ordered Brigadier Daniel Jones to assault Dorchester with 3,000 men. Howe planned to lead another 4,000 across Back Bay to attack the American lines and try to trap the men on Dorchester between the two forces. Behind him in Boston he was leaving only 400 men to guard the defenses that Washington planned to assault. The stage was set for a titanic showdown.

As darkness fell on March 5, the mild weather underwent a violent change. Out of the south whistled a cold, biting wind that soon became mixed with snow and hail. One local diary-keeper called it "a hurrycane." In Boston General Howe was listening to his chief engineer, who urged him to abandon the attack on Dorchester. It would be far worse than Bunker Hill. The Americans had heavy cannon up there, more men and more forts. Finally Howe admitted he was only trying to protect the honor of the British army. He announced that "the badness of the weather" had forced him to cancel the attack.

In the same statement Howe called for working parties to begin loading the Royal Navy's ships as fast as possible. Later that day three selectmen emerged

ABOVE RIGHT *This imaginative painting has a triumphant Washington on Dorchester Heights with the cannon that forced the British to evacuate Boston. In fact, he was disappointed with the results of the maneuver, which he had hoped would destroy the British army and end the war.*

from Boston to beg Washington not to fire on the town. Washington refused to promise anything. But he kept his big guns silent while the British toiled day and night to get their stores, ammunition and baggage aboard the ships. More than a thousand loyalists who had sought refuge with the Royal Army begged Howe to take them and their baggage along. He obliged them, but there was little room for their possessions. In one ship, wealthy Benjamin Hallowell shared a cabin with thirty-six other men, women and children.

On Sunday morning, March 17, small boys came bounding across the neck to inform the American army that "the lobsters" were gone at last. Instead of making a triumphal entry into the city, Washington showed how much he had learned about local sensitivity by giving the honor to Artemas Ward, the senior Massachusetts major general in his army. Not until the next day did he canter casually into the city. He was more than a little awed when he saw the strength of the British fortifications. But he persisted in thinking the battle he had planned would have ended in a decisive victory, if it were not for that violent storm. "I can scarce forebear lamenting the disappointment," he told his brother Jack. "Unless the dispute is drawing to an accommodation and the sword is to be sheathed."

Washington did not reveal his disappointment to anyone else. He let his countrymen convert Howe's bloodless withdrawal into a glorious victory. The Continental Congress voted the commander-in-chief a gold medal, and Harvard College made him an honorary doctor of laws. Throughout America, Washington was hailed as a general on a par with Julius Caesar. "I am at a loss to know how Great Britain will reconcile all this to her military glory," chortled Congressman Elbridge Gerry of Massachusetts.

Fiasco in Canada

Buoyed by this nonvictory, the Congress responded aggressively to Benedict Arnold's pleas for reinforcements for his army in Canada. With a combination of legerdemain and Governor Carleton's caution, Arnold had maintained his siege of Quebec with 500 men. The temperature sank to twenty-four degrees below zero, Arnold's wounded tendon kept him bedridden until March, and he ran out of hard money. Still he persevered, and the Congress vowed to support him. They sent another 1,000 men. To romance the Canadians, they dispatched a committee composed of wealthy Charles Carroll of Maryland, a Catholic; his brother John, a Jesuit priest; Maryland politician Samuel Chase; and Benjamin Franklin. The envoys got nowhere. The few priests who met Father Carroll were immediately excommunicated by the bishop of Quebec, who sided wholeheartedly with George III.

This exhausting midwinter trip almost killed the seventy-year-old Franklin. He and his fellow ambassadors advised the Congress to give up on making the Canadians into defenders of liberty. They ruefully agreed with Colonel Moses Hazen, a Canadian who had joined the American army. In their four months in Canada, Hazen maintained the Americans had managed to alienate the French clergy with their outspoken Protestantism, the Indians by neglecting them, and almost everyone else by forcing them to accept the paper dollars the Continental Congress was printing at a breakneck pace.

The Congress ignored this hardheaded advice and persisted in shipping

men to Canada. They ordered George Washington to detach four regiments from his army, a decision he mildly protested. He pointed out that if a strong British army attacked from Canada, four regiments would be too few to stop them. If the British army that had left Boston headed for New York, he would need these trained troops.

Not only was Washington ignored, he was told to send six more regiments. Along with these men, the Congress dispatched John Thomas—promoted to major general thanks to his starring role in the evacuation of Boston—to take charge of the campaign.

Shortly after Thomas reached Canada on May 1, disasters began occurring in rapid sequence. The British navy, converting one of their ships into an ice-breaker, plowed their way up the St. Lawrence River and relieved Quebec. Carleton attacked the minuscule American army outside the city, and they fled in all directions, abandoning two tons of gunpowder and all their cannon. Retreating to Sorel at the junction of the Richelieu and St. Lawrence rivers, Thomas took command of the four regiments from Washington's army. Unfortunately, some of the fugitives he brought with him from Quebec had small-pox, which spread swiftly through the army. Soon Thomas himself had it. Although he had been a doctor before the war, he was opposed to inoculation.

Thomas retreated to Chambly, ten miles south of Sorel, and set up a makeshift hospital, which was soon jammed with smallpox sufferers. They spilled out into neighboring houses and barns. The few doctors on duty had no medicine to give them. On June 1 Washington's six additional regiments arrived under the command of Major General John Sullivan of New Hampshire. The next day Thomas died, and Sullivan took command.

Ignoring advice from Benedict Arnold, still in Montreal, that it was time to retreat from Canada, Sullivan ordered an attack on the river town of Trois Rivières. Without bothering to reconnoiter, Brigadier General William Thompson of Pennsylvania led 2,000 men in boats on this dubious mission. They found themselves face to face with Major General John Burgoyne and 8,000 British regulars and swarms of Indian allies. The Americans, most from Pennsylvania and New Jersey, fled in disorder into nearby swamps. Their faces swollen by mosquito bites, the survivors stumbled into Sorel, unnerving the rest of the army. No fewer than forty officers informed Sullivan they wanted to resign.

BELOW *This poster was put up by officers from the Continental army on recruiting service. Most states offered recruits a bounty for signing up.*

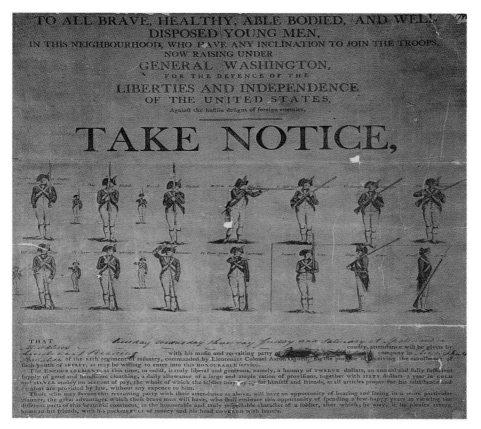

TO ALL BRAVE, HEALTHY, ABLE BODIED, AND WELL DISPOSED YOUNG MEN,
IN THIS NEIGHBOURHOOD, WHO HAVE ANY INCLINATION TO JOIN THE TROOPS,
NOW RAISING UNDER
GENERAL WASHINGTON,
FOR THE DEFENCE OF THE
LIBERTIES AND INDEPENDENCE
OF THE UNITED STATES,
Against the hostile designs of foreign enemies,

TAKE NOTICE,

On June 13, Benedict Arnold told Sullivan that "the junction of the Canadians with the colonies...is at an end. Let us quit them and secure our own country before it is too late." This time Sullivan believed him. He retreated to Ile-aux-Nois, a flat, brush-covered island in the middle of the Richelieu River near its outlet into Lake Champlain. Theoretically, the site blocked the British invasion route south, but in every other respect it was a terrible choice. The mile-long island became a gigantic hospital jammed with men suffering from smallpox, malaria and dysentery. One doctor recorded in his journal a visit to a large barn "full of men...many of which could not see, speak or walk—one nay two had large maggots one inch long, crawl out of their ears." Black flies and mosquitos swarmed over the sick, the dying and the dead.

The last man to leave Canada was Benedict Arnold. He executed a skillful retreat from Montreal to St. Johns with 300 men, made sure they were all safely embarked in boats, then waited until he could hear the skirl of approaching British fifes and the beat of their drums. Arnold stripped the saddle from his horse and threw it into his boat, whipped out a pistol and shot the animal in the head. His aide, nineteen-year-old James Wilkinson, executed his steed in the same scorched-earth style.

By June 25 what was left of the American army straggled back to Crown Point and Fort Ticonderoga. Of the 13,000 men the Congress had invested in Samuel Adams's scheme of invading Canada, 5,000 were dead or wounded, 3,000 were hospital cases, and the remaining 5,000 were so demoralized that the words "fit for duty" in the army's reports were a joke. In Canada were 13,000 fresh British troops poised to invade the rebellious colonies. Only two things were stopping them—the rapids of the Richelieu River, which isolated the Royal Navy in the St. Lawrence River—and the three ships on Lake Champlain that Benedict Arnold had captured after the fall of Fort Ticonderoga a year before. Arnold warned Washington that the British would undoubtedly build ships to challenge this tiny squadron unless "every nerve on our part is strained to exceed them in naval armament." Arnold demanded 300 carpenters to begin building a twenty- or thirty-ship fleet immediately. No one had the slightest idea where this small army of skilled workers would come from, much less where sailors could be found to man this inland navy.

The Great Declaration

In Philadelphia John Adams lamented that Congressmen were continuously wincing at "the dismals from Canada." He willed himself to exude confidence in his by-now-undisguised drive for a declaration of independence. On May 20 he wrote a famous letter to his friend James Warren: "Every post and every day rolls in upon us, independence like a torrent." Surveying the continent, Adams opined that "the four colonies to the Southward" were "perfectly agreed now with the four Northward." He admitted that the five colonies in the middle were "not quite so ripe," but he insisted "they are very near it."

The unripeness of the middle colonies was already starkly apparent. On May 1, 1776, the anti-independence men handily won a special election to fill seventeen seats in the Pennsylvania assembly, guaranteeing John Dickinson continued control of that crucial body. Thanks to his skill in keeping independence at bay, Pennsylvania had felt no need to elect an extralegal Provincial

ABOVE *Royal Governor of New Jersey William Franklin remained loyal to George III, deeply disappointing his father, Benjamin Franklin. William was influenced by his West Indian-born wife, Elizabeth, whom he married in London. After the war the King gave him a pension of £800 a year.*

Congress. In New Jersey Royal Governor William Franklin still sat unmolested and respected in his mansion in Perth Amboy, waiting for the right moment to convene the New Jersey assembly. Late in 1775 the governor had persuaded the colony's legislators to endorse a petition to George III that threatened to unravel the fragile American union. A delegation of Continental Congressmen had rushed to Trenton and barely talked them out of it. In New York John Jay, Robert R. Livingston and other leaders remained stubborn foes of independence. In Maryland the people's elected delegates had resolved on May 15, 1776, "that a reunion with Great Britain on constitutional principles" was the best way to secure their liberty.

John Adams decided on a drastic step to accelerate the pace of independence at the heart of the confederacy. On May 10 his friend and collaborator Richard Henry Lee of Virginia had submitted a resolution urging states to form governments designed to promote "the happiness and safety of their constituents." Adams had already contributed a powerful push to this idea by publishing a pamphlet, *Thoughts on Government*, a how-to guide for constitution makers. Lee's motion passed, Adams gleefully noted, with "remarkable unanimity." Adams suggested the resolution needed a preamble to explain it. The Congress told him to write one.

Adams's preamble began with a ferocious swipe at George III for plotting "the destruction of the good people of these colonies." The King's treachery made it "irreconcilable to reason and good conscience" for any member of an American assembly to take oaths of loyalty to His Majesty. It was time that "any kind of authority" under the crown should be "totally suppressed."

An agitated James Wilson cried that the preamble put the Pennsylvania assembly out of business. It began its sessions by swearing allegiance to the King. A jittery James Duane of New York called the resolution "a machine for the fabrication of independence." With a smile, Adams said he thought it was independence itself. "But we must have it with more formality yet," he added. In a letter to Abigail, John called the preamble "the most important resolution ever taken in America."

He was not far wrong. The resolution inspired the overthrow of the Pennsylvania assembly by a group of pro-independence men led by Thomas Paine. In New Jersey, when William Franklin issued a call for a meeting of the colony's assembly, the revolutionaries of that state ordered him arrested and deported to Connecticut as "an enemy to the liberties of this country."

In Philadelphia, George III provided the independence men with new ammunition. From Washington's headquarters in Massachusetts came copies of treaties that the King had signed with various German princes to hire 18,000 of their troops for service in America. The documents had been smuggled out of England by American sympathizers in London. Here, trumpeted the independence men, was conclusive proof that George III was an enemy of American liberty.

On June 7 Richard Henry Lee rose in the Congress and, obeying instructions from Virginia, resolved "that these United Colonies are, of right ought to be, free and independent states; that they are absolved from all allegiance to the British crown; and that all political connections between them and the state of Great Britain is, and ought to be, totally dissolved."

Conservatives and moderates immediately rose to the attack. John Adams was dismayed to see Edward Rutledge of South Carolina among them—somewhat diminishing his optimism about the southern colonies. For two days the debate raged. On Saturday Rutledge wrote to his fellow moderate John Jay of New York: "No reason could be assigned for pressing into this Measure, but the reason of every madman, a shew of our spirit. The question was postponed; it is to be renewed on Monday, when I mean to move that it should be postponed for three weeks or months."

On Monday Rutledge moved to delay a vote for three weeks. The Congress agreed. This delay would give delegates time to write home for instructions. Meanwhile, both sides agreed it might be a good idea to prepare a declaration of independence. A committee was appointed: "Mr. Jefferson, Mr. J. Adams, Mr. Franklin, Mr. Sherman, Mr. R.R. Livingston."

According to John Adams, Jefferson wanted him to write the declaration. Adams wisely refused, recognizing the unpopularity he had accrued in the bruising debates and maneuvers around the issue of independence. Franklin would almost certainly have been given the job, if he had not had a loyalist son who had just been declared an enemy of liberty. The other two committee members were disqualified for more obvious reasons. Robert R. Livingston deplored the whole idea of a declaration, and Roger Sherman was no writer. Probably the overriding reason for the choice of Jefferson was geography. Canny John Adams recognized how unpopular New England men had become in the Congress and saw the value of a declaration of independence emanating from Virginia.

Later Jefferson said that he had consulted "neither book nor pamphlet." He insisted that he had no desire to find out "new principles or new arguments never before thought of." The declaration was "intended to be an expression of the American mind and to give to that expression the proper tone and spirit called for by that occasion."

Jefferson's modesty blurs the skill with which he made the declaration both a statement of separation from England and a pronouncement of world historical importance. There was no single American mind in 1776 any more than such an entity exists today. If the declaration had expressed the American mind as personified by John Dickinson or John Jay or Edward Rutledge, it would have become a very different document. Jefferson poured into it his experience as an opponent of aristocratic privilege in Virginia. He was in wholehearted agreement with his friend John Adams "that a more equal liberty than had prevailed in other parts of the earth must be established in America." It was this conviction that transformed the declaration into the central document of American history.

Previous declarations of American rights had listed "life, liberty, and property" as the three primary concerns. When Jefferson wrote "life, liberty, and

ABOVE *In this fanciful painting, Thomas Jefferson broods over a candle-lit draft of the Declaration of Independence. Only in this century have historians discovered how often he rewrote it before he was satisfied.*

RIGHT *This early draft shows how heavily Jefferson revised the Declaration. In one version, he changed almost one-third of the words.*

the pursuit of happiness" he was not trying to abolish the right to property. He agreed with John Adams, who had recently advised Massachusetts politicians struggling to write a state constitution that "power always follows property." What Jefferson and Adams were seeking was a containment of the power of property. But only Jefferson, with his more optimistic view of America's future, would have dared to ignore that sacred word "property" and substitute the infinitely more meaningful "happiness."

Almost as interesting, from a psychological point of view, is Jefferson's opening line in his rough draft: "When in the course of human events it becomes necessary for a people to advance from that subordination in which they have hitherto remained..." Here was the central cause of the American Revolution, stated so starkly that Jefferson, after consulting with the rest of the committee, changed it to read: "When in the course of human events it becomes necessary for one people to dissolve the political bands which have connected them with another..."

To reject openly the idea of subordination to the King would have been psychologically disastrous. It would have awakened the very realistic fears in the minds of many moderate Congressmen that Americans might begin rejecting subordination all the way down the line. This could have led to an upheaval, especially in the South, with its explosive mixture of poor whites and black slaves.

At the same time, Jefferson's declaration was a decisive break with British liberty, which was granted by the government within careful limits aimed at maintaining that subordination of which George III was so fond. Jefferson's insistence that all men were created equal and endowed with inalienable rights represented a great leap forward for the idea of liberty. It became more than a right to be debated within the context of the British constitution. In declaring liberty a universal human right, Jefferson moved the argument to a new level of discourse and laid the cornerstone of the American Republic.

In the rest of the document, Jefferson followed the trail blazed by numerous pamphleteers who accused the British of plotting to destroy American liberty. But he added to this formula a touch from Thomas Paine by blaming it all on George III. In twenty fierce indictments, Jefferson did his best to portray the patriot King as the man behind a "long train of abuses and usurpations."

In the final charge Jefferson again revealed his reformer's zeal. He blamed George III for the slave trade. The King had "prostituted" his power by suppressing every American attempt to prohibit or restrain this "execrable commerce." Worse, he was now "exciting these very people to rise in arms among us, and to purchase that liberty of which he has deprived them, by murdering the people upon whom he also obtruded them."

Jefferson closed with an elegiac reference to the hope many Americans had entertained that the opposition's parliamentary oratory would stir sympathy for America in England. He acknowledged the affection that many Americans still felt for England. "We might have been a great people together," he wrote. The Americans had asked the British people for help, but they had not listened. "So we must endeavor to forget our former love for them, and to hold them as we hold the rest of mankind, enemies in war, in peace friends."

Only in this century have we learned how hard Jefferson worked on the declaration. A fragment of one of his early drafts, which Jefferson had ripped up and used to make notes on another matter, was found among his papers in 1943. On this, the earliest existing (though incomplete) draft of the declaration, 43 of the 156 words were additions or substitutions. In the text that for almost two centuries was considered the rough draft, all these changes appear intact.

While Thomas Jefferson toiled through his many drafts on the second floor of a brick house on the corner of Market and Seventh streets, the Congress was getting a steady diet of bad news. The full dimensions of the disaster in Canada became apparent to everyone. The British had committed 2,000 men and a substantial fleet to an attack on Charleston, South Carolina. On June 29, the day after Jefferson laid his final draft on the desk of the Congress's President, John Hancock, excited messengers reported that an estimated 150 ships had been sighted off New York. It was General William Howe and his army, descending from Halifax, Nova Scotia, where they had spent the winter. Within twenty-four hours, they would land on Staten Island without firing a shot.

On July 1, in this aura of imminent military confrontation, the Congress began the final debate on independence. It was noon, and the temperature was soaring into the nineties by the time the delegates disposed of ordinary business and resolved themselves into a committee of the whole, where everything said would be off the record. Benjamin Harrison of Virginia was the chairman of this legislative device, designed to encourage maximum candor.

The first speaker was John Dickinson. Pale and trembling with emotion, he elaborated the last argument of the moderates—independence was premature. To abandon the protection of Great Britain would be "like destroying our house in winter and exposing a growing family before we have got another shelter." They had heard nothing from France. How did they know what that treacherous power had in mind? Dickinson warned of Indian ravages on the frontiers and seaports burned by the British fleet. Finally he predicted that to declare independence without agreeing to a workable confederation would mean the inevitable breakup of the union, even if they won the war with England.

While Dickinson delivered this jeremiad, into the chamber stalked a messenger with a letter for John Adams. It was from Annapolis. Adams tore it open and read: "I

LEFT *John Hancock's name heads the list of signers of the Declaration. Some Congressmen did not add their names for several months. Pennsylvania had the most signatories—nine.*

ABOVE *John Adams, Thomas Jefferson, Benjamin Franklin and the other members of their committee present the Declaration of Independence to the president of the Congress, John Hancock. On the wall are standards of British regiments captured in the American invasion of Canada.*

am this moment from the House with an unan: vote of our convention for independence…Your friend, S. Chase." Maryland had joined the union.

Now it was John Adams's turn. A summer storm mounted above Philadelphia as he began his reply. While thunder rumbled and lightning flashed, Adams refuted Dickinson's scare tactics and insisted a declaration of independence would be the salvation of America. It would force everyone to decide whether to defend American liberty or settle for the subordination and submission of British liberty. No record exists of Adams's words. But Thomas Jefferson later recalled that the Braintree lawyer spoke "with a power of thought and expression that moved us from our seats." Candles were lit in the darkening room, and thunder continued to crash. Adams spoke on, outroaring the storm.

In the doorway appeared three rain-soaked delegates from New Jersey, led by imperious John Witherspoon, president of the College of New Jersey (the future Princeton). They asked Adams to repeat his arguments. Witherspoon said he and his fellow delegates agreed completely that the colonies were ripe for independence. Fixing the recalcitrant New York delegation with a ferocious glare, he added: "Some are rotten for want of it."

Finally bluff Benjamin Harrison of Virginia, chairman of the committee of the whole, called for a trial vote. The results were dismaying. New York's delegates abstained, claiming they had no directions from their constituents; Delaware's two-man delegation divided; Pennsylvania and South Carolina voted no.

With four colonies opting out, independence threatened to become an issue

THE LIBERTY BELL

The Liberty Bell weighs 2,080 pounds.

"Get us a good bell," wrote Isaac Norris, speaker of the Pennsylvania Assembly, to his agent in London in 1751. Little did he think he was acquiring a major headache—and a symbolic piece of American history.

In his letter, Norris directed the agent to inscribe on the bell: "Proclaim Liberty thro' all the Land to all the Inhabitants Thereof—Levit XXV 10." This was not a surprising choice for a resident of Pennsylvania. Isaac Norris's friend Benjamin Franklin had recently published in his newspaper, *The Pennsylvania Gazette*, an essay attributing Pennsylvania's growth to the free society William Penn had established.

The twelve-foot-wide bell arrived a year later and was trundled by wagon to the new state house. There, an amateur bell ringer tested it with a hefty swing of the clapper—and it cracked. The English manufacturers accused the Americans of not knowing the proper way to ring a bell, and showed no enthusiasm for repairing it. The task was handed to two local men, John Pass and John Stow, who hammered it to pieces and cast an entirely new bell. Unfortunately, few people liked its sound.

The mortified Pass and Stow tried again. This time the bell was proclaimed a success and hoisted to the state house tower. But Isaac Norris and many others still did not like its sound, and the speaker ordered a replacement from London, hoping the first bell would be taken for credit. But American pride prevented the old bell's return. It stayed in the state house tower, and the new English bell was attached to the clock.

The "Old One," as Philadelphians began to call the bell, tolled a funereal sound in 1765 to announce the arrival of ships bearing the hated stamps inflicted on Americans by Parliament's Stamp Act. It rang joyously when the act was repealed a year later. It rang in 1771 to summon the assembly to urge George III to repeal the tax on tea. On April 25, 1775, it called the people's representatives to hear the news of the battle of Lexington.

On July 8, 1776, it boomed its mighty clang to summon the citizens of Philadelphia to the state house yard to hear the Declaration of Independence proclaimed to the people. All the other bells in Philadelphia joined in this cascade of sound.

In October 1777, with the British army approaching, Philadelphians lowered the Old One from its tower and carried it into the country, along with the rest of the city's bells. They feared the British would melt them down for bullets. For the next year, the bell lay hidden in the basement of the Zion High German Reformed Church in Allentown. When the British evacuated the city in June 1778, the Old One and the other bells returned. In October 1781 it pealed the glorious news that the British army had surrendered at Yorktown.

The Old One stayed in the service of the state of Pennsylvania until the voters moved the capital to Lancaster in 1799. That same year it tolled the news of George Washington's death. The former state house became a museum run by painter Charles Willson Peale. When he moved out in 1828, the city of Philadelphia sold the bell to a scrap dealer, who balked at the task of taking it down. In the ensuing legal argument, he gave the bell to the city as a gift, and it dawned on people that it was a precious relic that should be preserved.

The Old One rang to welcome the Marquis de Lafayette in 1824, and it tolled his death in 1834. In 1835 its muffled tones announced the death of Chief Justice John Marshall. According to most accounts, in this tribute to one of the last of the Revolutionary generation, the crack that had given Isaac Norris so many headaches reappeared. Bellmen rang the Old One a few more times, but the sound was distressing to the ear. The last distorted bong came in 1846, heralding George Washington's birthday. The Old One now reposes in Philadelphia's Independence Hall, guarded by the National Park Service.

Colonel John Nixon, son of Richard Nixon, an Irish immigrant, read the Declaration of Independence to the public on July 8, 1776.

ABOVE *Boston merchant John Hancock was one of the richest men in America, with a mansion on Beacon Hill and a fleet of ships. Elected president of the Continental Congress, he hoped to become commander of the American army. He went home for an extended vacation in September 1777. When he returned, he discovered the Congress had elected a new president. In 1780, Hancock became governor of Massachusetts.*

that divided and destroyed, rather than united, Americans. Edward Rutledge suggested delaying a formal vote until the next day. A night of frantic negotiations followed. With great reluctance, Rutledge and the South Carolinians agreed to change their vote. John Dickinson and his followers were told they no longer represented the people of Pennsylvania, as the vote for a new state government would unquestionably prove on July 8. Dickinson and Robert Morris agreed to stay home. A post rider dashed to Delaware, and Caesar Rodney, a pro-independence delegate who had gone home to put down a loyalist uprising, rode eighty miles through wind and rain to reach Philadelphia.

The next morning, July 2, the performance for the benefit of the public (and the historians) went smoothly. Twelve colonies voted for independence. Only New York abstained for want of instructions but her delegates declared themselves heartily in favor of independence. An exultant John Adams wrote Abigail that "the second of July...will be celebrated by succeeding generations as the great anniversary festival."

His prophecy turned out to be wrong because the Congress decided to edit Jefferson's declaration. While the hypersensitive Virginian writhed over their "mutilations," whole paragraphs were excised, and phrases added. Out went Jefferson's reproof to the English people. The Congressmen could see no point in alienating what they still fondly believed was substantial support for them in the Mother Country.

Also deleted was Jefferson's indictment of George III for imposing slavery on America. In his later years Jefferson recalled that objections to that passage came from both Southerners, in particular South Carolinians and Georgians, who wanted to continue importing slaves, and New Englanders, whose merchants made a hefty profit shipping them from Africa.

None of the changes was accomplished without vigorous debate, and John Adams was in the forefront of it, "fighting fearlessly for every word," as Jefferson testified later. But Adams got nowhere. Unity was vital in 1776. Let South Carolina and Georgia have their slave trade, the majority decided. After the war, if a nation was formed, then would be the time to do something about slavery. If the colonies decided to go their independent ways—no one was certain what they would do—then slavery was their own dirty business.

Aside from this tough pragmatism about slavery, more than one historian has agreed that the Congress made Jefferson's declaration a leaner, more hard-hitting document. In the closing line, they added one of the more resounding phrases: "with a firm reliance on the protection of Divine Providence." But the declaration remained Jefferson's creation. As one historian summed it up, "His spirit brooded over it, giving light to the whole."

On July 4, the Congress assembled once more, and, with John Hancock presiding, the delegates approved the final version. It was the power of Jefferson's prose that made this day, rather than July 2, the "great anniversary festival."

Historians still debate whether anyone besides President John Hancock signed the Declaration on July 4, 1776. As an old man, Jefferson maintained that a signing took place. A majority of scholars are now inclined to believe no signatures were added until August 2, when, by the Congress's order, it had been "engrossed on parchment." Some members did not get around to signing it until September. One reason for the slow pace may have been Jefferson's final words, which required everyone who signed to "mutually pledge to each other our lives, our fortunes and our sacred honor."

This was not overstatement. Everyone was keenly aware that the Declaration of Independence was treason. When John Hancock placed his large scrawl at the head of the document, he reportedly said: "We must be unanimous; there must be no pulling different ways; we must all hang together."

"Yes," Benjamin Franklin replied. "We must all hang together. Or most assuredly we shall all hang separately."

On July 8, the Declaration was read to the public in the Pennsylvania State House yard. One of the more ardent independence men, Christopher Marshall, told his diary: "There were bonfires, ringing bells and other great demonstrations of joy upon the unanimity of the Declaration." A less enthusiastic eyewitness, aristocratic Nicholas Biddle, saw "very few respectable people" in the crowd and among this minority a number "much opposed to the Declaration."

In New York on July 9, George Washington had the declaration read to his army. The troops returned to their barracks and campgrounds—and the New York mob took charge. A huge crowd rampaged through the city, breaking the windows of prominent loyalists and shouting defiance to the British fleet in the harbor and the Royal Army, whose tents whitened the hills of Staten Island.

Someone pointed to the statue of George III on horseback in the middle of the Bowling Green, at the tip of Manhattan. The Sons of Liberty vaulted the fence around the statue, looped ropes around the horse and the royal rider, and pulled hard. With an enormous crash, the fifteen-foot-high sculpture toppled to the ground. While the crowd watched in awed silence, one man sawed off the King's head. The rest of the statue was dragged away to be melted down for bullets.

There was no longer much doubt that blows would soon decide the future of liberty in America. But thanks to John Adams and Thomas Jefferson, Americans could now make a clear-cut choice between American liberty and British liberty.

ABOVE **Many communities raised Liberty Poles or designated a large tree as a Liberty Tree around which patriots rallied. After independence, these celebrations took place on the Fourth of July.**

Soldiers of Liberty

Washington crosses the Delaware on Christmas night 1776 to attack Trenton.

"Are these the men with which I am to defend America?" —George Washington

The largest fleet and army Britain had ever sent abroad arrive to crush the Revolution. In defeat and retreat George Washington creates a new strategy. Liberty seems to falter as the British invade New Jersey and the Congress flees Philadelphia. Washington's winter victories at Trenton and Princeton revive the expiring cause.

From his tent on Long Island, Lieutenant Joseph Hodgkins of the Twelfth Massachusetts Regiment assured his wife that the American army far outnumbered the British who were accumulating on Staten Island. "We have 42,000 men now and they are coming in every day," he wrote. He devoted several paragraphs to persuading her to forgive him for reenlisting for 1776. Hodgkins had no doubt that the war would be over by the end of the year, and he wanted to be in on the historic victory.

American morale soared even higher with the news of the British repulse at Charleston, South Carolina. Major General Clinton and eight regiments, plus a formidable Royal Navy squadron, had attempted to seize this major seaport on June 28, 1776. A daylong duel with American gunners in Fort Moultrie had left a startling number of His Majesty's ships in deplorable condition. Major General Charles Lee had rallied thousands of militiamen to prevent the regulars from reaching the mainland. Lieutenant Hodgkins and his comrades were confident they could repeat this performance in New York.

At army headquarters, General George Washington was far less sanguine than Lieutenant Hodgkins. The regular or "Continental" American army—soldiers such as Hodgkins's regiment, with some semblance of training and organization—barely exceeded 10,000 men. Obedient to the Congress's military doctrine, Washington had called up some 19,000 militia from Connecticut and other nearby states. But John Adams's torrent for independence had somehow missed half these temporary soldiers, and they had failed to march with their companies. Those who responded to the call trickled into the American camp throughout the summer, giving Washington no time to train them or integrate them into his army.

In early August Washington had only 10,514 men fit for duty, out of a paper strength of 17,225. Hardly enough, he told Governor Jonathan Trumbull of Connecticut, "to oppose an army of 30,000 experienced veterans." On August 19 a head count told Washington he now had 23,000 men. A week later he confessed to John Hancock he did not know how many men he had.

ABOVE **This figure appeared in many American broadsides. The patriots believed their cause was blessed by God.**

LEFT **With ragged uniforms or no uniforms at all, often with guns that lacked bayonets, American soldiers faced a superbly equipped British foe. After the initial outburst of enthusiasm in 1775, recruiting for the army became more difficult every year.**

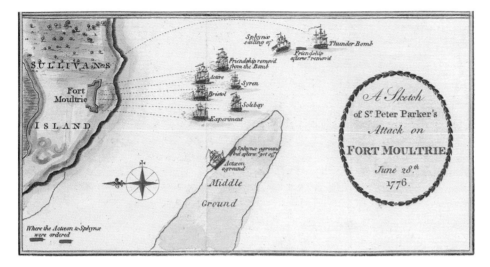

One reason for the confusion was visible in the journal of Second Lieutenant Isaac Bangs of the Second Massachusetts Regiment. On July 14 he wrote: "Almost the whole regiment are sick with the camp distemper." He was referring to dysentery, which rampaged through the American army all summer. Sheer exhaustion may have had something to do with the bad health of some soldiers. In the blazing heat of July and August, Washington and his generals had set them the enormous task of fortifying Manhattan; Governor's Island, off its tip; and, across the East River, Brooklyn Heights.

The men built thirteen forts and batteries within the mile-long limits of New York City, all equipped with cannon. North of the city were a half-dozen more forts, including a formidable work along the East River where the mayor's official residence, Gracie Mansion, now stands. Every street leading from the rivers on either side of the city was barricaded. Each fort involved immense effort. Wells had to be dug in the large ones, along with deep outer ditches and platforms for the cannon. The Americans were intent on repeating Bunker Hill on a grand scale, forcing the British to attack them behind dozens of entrenchments. It did not occur to them that General Howe was unlikely to make this mistake twice.

Another major worry for Washington was the number of New Yorkers who remained loyal to George III. In Massachusetts loyalists were relatively few. In New York they numbered in the thousands. Just across the East River in Queens County, early in 1776 rebel New Yorkers had been forced to ask New Jersey militiamen to help them seize more than 1,000 weapons from known loyalists. Late in June the Americans discovered a loyalist plot to kidnap or kill George Washington, blow up American magazines and destroy Kings Bridge, at the northern end of Manhattan, trapping the American army on the island. One plotter, Thomas Hickey, was a member of Washington's personal guard. According to evidence presented in court, more than 700 men were involved, including David Matthews, the mayor of New York. He was arrested and deported to Connecticut; the rest of the plotters could not be prosecuted because the New York Provincial Congress maintained there was no law against treason in the not-yet-independent United States of America. Only Hickey was tried under the articles of war (revised by the Congress, thanks to Dr. Church) and hanged in a public ceremony.

ABOVE LEFT *On June 28, 1776, a Royal Navy squadron and an army of 2,000 men attacked Charleston, South Carolina. They were beaten off by the guns of Fort Moultrie on Sullivan's Island.*

The Declaration of Independence did little to improve the Provincial Congress's lukewarm patriotism. They stonewalled Washington's request to round up Long Island's 100,000 horned cattle and almost as many sheep and transport them beyond the grasp of the hungry British army on Staten Island. From his intelligence reports during the siege of Boston, Washington knew how much it cost the British to ship Howe's troops wretched salt beef, dried peas and toothcracking ship's bread. If he could force the expanded British army to depend on this diet, it would be a major step toward winning the war. But the New York legislators stubbornly refused to round up the cattle. They had approved the Declaration of Independence only after adding a preamble, regretting the step as a "cruel necessity."

In this ambivalent atmosphere, the new commander of the British navy in American waters, Admiral Richard, Lord Howe, the same nobleman who had tried to parley with Benjamin Franklin in England, announced that he had a commission from George III to negotiate a reconciliation. Posters containing the rosy promises of Howe's proclamation immediately blossomed all over Queens County. It was the start of a peace offensive.

An admirer of William Pitt, Lord Howe was sincere about his hopes for restored harmony. He had insisted on the peace commission as his price for accepting the naval command. This curious document named his brother, General William Howe, as his peacemaking partner. When Admiral Howe arrived in New York on July 12, he was dismayed to learn the Americans had already declared their independence. But he was still determined to pick up the olive branch that had been shot out of William's hand at Bunker Hill. The

BELOW *Sergeant William Jasper became an American hero when he braved British cannonballs to replace the flag that had been knocked off the parapet of the fort on Sullivan's Island. In 1779 Jasper was killed carrying the colors in the American assault on British-held Savannah, Georgia.*

general, having been bombarded and semi-starved by Americans for much of the past thirteen months, was considerably less sanguine. William Howe told his brother there was no point in talking peace until the American army across the harbor in New York City was defeated.

William Howe's pessimism may have been deepened by a look at the terms of the peace commission. Admiral Howe was a first-class fighting sailor, but he was no politician. The commission had been vetted by Lord George Germain, who made sure it gave the brothers very little power. They were forbidden to deal with the Continental Congress. They could not even grant pardons until the Americans were virtually inert beneath the royal standard, manifesting George III's favorite words—submission, subordination and obedience.

Pushing his peace offensive, Admiral Howe sent a lieutenant to New York with a letter addressed "To George Washington Esquire." Under the Germain-dictated terms of his commission, Howe could not recognize Washington as commander of the illegal American army.

Joseph Reed, now Washington's adjutant general, said: "We have no person here in our army with that address."

The British officer asked Reed how Washington should be addressed.

"You are sensible, sir," Reed replied, "of the rank of General Washington in our army?"

"Yes sir, we are," the lieutenant said. "I'm sure Lord Howe will lament exceedingly this affair, as the letter is quite of a civil nature and not a military one."

A few days later, General Howe replied to a letter from Washington complaining about the treatment of American prisoners in Canada. Howe addressed the letter to "George Washington Esq., &ca, &ca." This letter too was refused. The bearer, the adjutant general of the British army, Lieutenant Colonel James Patterson, asked if "General Washington" would be willing to meet with him.

Washington said he would be glad to do so, and hopes for peace momentarily soared. Wearing his full-dress uniform, the American commander received Patterson at the Kennedy mansion, 1 Broadway. Patterson tried mightily to explain away the "Esq. &ca &ca," claiming those terms were often used in diplomatic correspondence when a man's precise rank was in doubt. Washington told him there was no doubt whatsoever about his correct rank and remarked that etcetera etcetera could mean "anything—or nothing."

Patterson gingerly approached the possibility of Lord Howe's talking peace with Washington. The general shook his head. He had no power to negotiate political issues with anyone. He was a soldier serving under the orders of the Continental Congress. Moreover, as far as he knew, the Howes had no real power to make peace. All they could do was grant pardons, when and if the Americans surrendered. The Americans thought they had done nothing wrong in defending

LEFT *Admiral Richard, Lord Howe, was both a peace commissioner and commander of the British navy in America. He once excoriated his cousin, George III, for his "invincible obstinacy" toward America. Howe was popular with his sailors, who called him "Black Dick." This youthful portrait was painted in 1765.*

RIGHT *In his general orders, William Howe warned his troops against abusing and plundering civilians. Many soldiers thought rebels deserved no mercy and ignored him.*

their indisputable right to liberty and therefore "wanted no pardons," Washington said.

Lord Howe had sent similar letters to the Continental Congress and to his friend Benjamin Franklin, asking for negotiations. On July 25 he learned that the Congress had ordered copies of the letters and proclamation to be published in the newspapers so "the good people of these United States" could learn how the British were attempting to "amuse and disarm them."

Franklin published his reply to Lord Howe in the newspapers five days later. In a bravura performance, he shredded Howe's peace commission with devastating sarcasm. He expressed his esteem, even his affection, for Howe and pitied him for allowing the British government to use him in "so fruitless a business." The peace commission was only one more proof that the British considered Americans so stupid they could be tricked into submission after the Royal Army and Navy had spent a year burning their towns and killing their citizens.

While Lord Howe was trying in vain to negotiate, the results of George III's and Lord George Germain's strenuous efforts to make war gathered around him in New York harbor. On August 1 Major General Henry Clinton and eight regiments returned from their failed foray against Charleston, South Carolina. In the next two weeks, the main body of the expeditionary force, some 10,000 men, including 8,000 Germans, arrived. General Howe now had close to 25,000 troops. In New York harbor bobbed some 400 transports and thirty men-of-war. It was the largest fleet and biggest army Great Britain had ever sent from her shores.

On August 20 a worried Washington attempted to scour any hope of peace from the ranks of his army. "A report prevails and is industriously spread far and wide that Lord Howe has made propositions of peace," he wrote in his general orders of the day. "On the contrary, from the best intelligence...the army may expect an attack as soon as the wind and tide are favorable." He urged his men to "shew our enemies, and the whole world, that free men, contending on their own land, are superior to any mercenaries on earth."

The British soon fulfilled Washington's prediction. Lord Howe's warships moved up the harbor,

THE ATTACK OF THE *TURTLE*

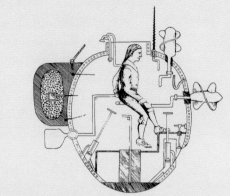

At Yale, David Bushnell had amazed his professors by demonstrating that gunpowder could be detonated underwater. As the quarrel with England escalated into war, he began building the world's first submarine. Bushnell de-scribed it as resembling "two large tortoise shells of equal size, joined together."

The *Turtle*'s hull was made of oak timbers six inches thick, bound with iron bands and coated with tar to make her watertight. She had a hatch that could be screwed down until it too was watertight. The hatch had glass portholes about the size of a half-dollar that enabled the one-man crew to see where he was going underwater.

Like a modern submarine, she submerged by taking water into her ballast tanks and rose by pumping it out. For propulsion, the *Turtle* had a screw propeller attached to an inside crank turned by the crewman. She could make about three knots underwater and stay down for a half-hour.

On the night of September 6, 1776, Bushnell and his assistants lowered the *Turtle* into the water near Manhattan's South Ferry landing and screwed into position a cask of gunpowder, containing a clock and gunlock firing mechanism.

Sergeant Ezra Lee entered the craft and began the first submarine attack. The target was *HMS Eagle*, Lord Howe's flagship. A screw on top of the submarine was supposed to secure the cask to the hull of the *Eagle*. The clock would start ticking. The *Turtle* would have a half-hour to put some distance between herself and the explosion.

Unfortunately, the screw struck the iron bar connecting *Eagle's* rudder hinge to the stern and Lee got nowhere. Rattled, he mismanaged the *Turtle's* ballast, and she shot to the surface as dawn broke. The British spotted her and began hot pursuit. But they changed their minds when Lee cut loose his cask and it exploded. The blast knocked people out of their beds in New York and threw the British fleet into a panic.

A few weeks later, as the Americans' grip on New York grew shaky, the British sank a sloop carrying the submarine up the Hudson, along with numerous other small river craft. Undersea warfare would have to wait another century.

their decks crowded with soldiers. Early on August 22 some seventy-five attack flatboats with planked-up sides, the craft Howe had wanted so badly at Bunker Hill, headed for Gravesend Bay, where frigates and bomb ships had already moved close to shore to cover the landing. By noon 15,000 British troops were on Long Island with scarcely a shot fired at them. A rifle battalion of Pennsylvanians skirmished briefly with the first men ashore and then withdrew.

The British quickly occupied the village of Flatbush and about six miles of Long Island's south shore. There was nothing to oppose them but a few feeble companies of militia in Queens and Suffolk counties. Washington could only grind his teeth at the thought of the enemy enjoying those thousands of cattle and sheep he had begged the New York Provincial Congress to seize.

Most of Washington's trained regulars and a few regiments of militia—about 10,000 men—were entrenched on Brooklyn Heights and its outlying hills, known as the Heights of Guan. The position was formidable. The Heights of Guan were thickly wooded, with steep slopes. The Americans hoped to inflict heavy casualties on the attacking British and fall back to their eight forts and twenty-nine cannon on Brooklyn Heights, where an attacking enemy would take even heavier losses. On August 23, the day after the British landing, Colonel William Douglas of Connecticut exuded confidence in a letter to his wife: "Our troops are...in high sperits and it is a general voice, Let them come on us as soon as they can, or dare!"

For several days various American units skirmished briskly with the British as they moved closer to Washington's army. Finally, on August 27, a day on which the sun rose with "a red and angry glare," the British began their attack. To the Americans, it seemed to go exactly as they had anticipated. On their right flank, commanded by a New Jersey brigadier general, William Alexander, some 5,000 British troops led by Major General James Grant deployed and began exchanging cannon and musket fire with the Americans. Alexander, whom the Americans called Lord Stirling in support of his claim to his family's Scottish title, told his men that he had been in the House of Commons on the day General Grant rose to assert he could march from one end of America to the other with 5,000 men. Alexander urged his men to prove Grant was wrong—although the British outnumbered them three to one.

In the center of the American line, about the same number of German troops skirmished with Massachusetts and Connecticut soldiers under Major General John Sullivan of New Hampshire, who had managed to avoid censure for his awful performance in Canada. On the left flank Colonel Samuel Miles of Pennsylvania was in charge, backed by a huge regiment of riflemen. The overall commander was Israel Putnam, the hero of Bunker Hill. He knew little or nothing about the local geography, having taken command only the day before. For most of the summer, Major General Nathanael Greene had been in charge on "Nassau Island," as Long Island was called in 1776. But he had come down with camp fever and was a very sick man.

On the left flank, Colonel Miles had skirmished with the enemy on previous days and nervously noted that the main body of the British army under General Howe—some 10,000 men—was camped not far away. On the morning of August 27—several hours after sunrise, as the Germans and British blasted away at the American right flank and center—Colonel Miles

ABOVE *Major General Israel Putnam of Connecticut won fame at Bunker Hill. But he soon demonstrated severe limitations as a general. Without a hill to fight from, he was devoid of ideas.*

realized that General Howe and his men were nowhere to be seen.

Not long after Miles made this alarming observation, two cannon boomed somewhere in the rear of the men on the Heights of Guan. The Germans and Grant's British troops abandoned their desultory skirmishing and moved forward in a formal attack, cannon thundering, fifes shrilling, drums beating. Simultaneously, with howls of triumph, 4,000 British light infantry attacked Miles's and Sullivan's men from the rear. General Howe and the cream of the British army were between them and the forts on Brooklyn Heights!

What had happened? In a cruel compound of ironies, the British, thanks to consultation with numerous loyalists in Queens County, knew more about Long Island's geography than the Americans. There were four passes running through or around the Heights of Guan: two in the center; one on the American right, near Gravesend; and one far out on the American left—the Jamaica Pass, almost four miles from the rebel lines in Brooklyn. This pass led to the Jamaica Road, an undefended byway that curved between the Heights of Guan and the forts on Brooklyn Heights. Major General Henry Clinton had persuaded William Howe to march the best troops in the British army through the midnight darkness to reach the Jamaica Pass at dawn. To their amazement and delight, there was not a single American in the pass, a "deep winding cut" that could have been held for hours by a few hundred men with cannon.

Trapped and panicky, the Americans on the left and center had only two choices—they surrendered or fled into the woods, where the British and Germans hunted them down like animals. The Germans were especially merciless because their British employers had told them that the Americans had a special hatred for mercenaries and would give them no quarter if captured. This led to dozens of short, nasty encounters in the woods, as young Americans pleaded for mercy and enraged young Germans bayoneted them with a ferocity that shocked not a few British officers.

General Sullivan and his men fled without bothering to warn William Alexander and the men under his command. They were more than holding their own against General Grant's men. At one point a detachment of Connecticut and Pennsylvania troops charged a British regiment on a flanking hill, knocked them off the crest and killed their commander. But the Americans were not on the hill fifteen minutes before thousands of Germans attacked them from the left and more thousands of British grenadiers assailed them from the rear.

By this time Alexander realized what was happening and tried to retreat. He found a third of the British army between him and the Brooklyn forts. Looking around, Alexander realized that there was only one way out—across the marshes on his right to Gowanus Creek, eighty yards wide at the mouth, with a strong tidal current running. His men would be slaughtered in this watery ditch unless the oncoming British were somehow stopped. With grim-faced Scottish fortitude, Alexander detached 250 Marylanders under their commanding officer, Major Mordecai Gist, put himself at their head, sword in hand, and launched a frontal assault on 10,000 British and Germans surrounding them.

It was the only gallant American moment on this disastrous day. At first the astonished British could not believe their eyes. Then they began blasting away with every available musket and two fieldpieces. The Marylanders, in their first battle, wavered and broke. Alexander and Gist re-formed them and returned to the attack, not once but five times.

In one of the Brooklyn Heights forts beside Israel Putnam, a stunned George Washington had watched the battle unfold. As Alexander's gallant Marylanders advanced for the third or fourth time, he gasped in anguish: "Good God, what brave fellows I must this day lose!"

At last the enemy's firepower became overwhelming. The Marylanders collapsed and fled. By this time most of their comrades had made it safely across Gowanus Creek. Only eight of the heroic 250 reached the American lines. Alexander, miraculously unscathed, surrendered his sword to Lieutenant General Leopold von Heister, the German commander. Around the same time, a regiment of Germans flushed Major General Sullivan out of a corn field.

Sixteen-year-old Joseph Plumb Martin of Connecticut, in his first battle, described the Marylanders who crawled out of muddy Gowanus Creek as "looking like water rats, a truly pitiful sight." With these bedraggled survivors, Martin and his militia regiment fled to the forts on Brooklyn Heights, pursued by British canister and grape "like a shower of hail."

Inside the forts consternation reigned as the fugitives poured into the trenches. Many, if not most, had thrown away their guns. In spite of all the digging they had done, the Americans suddenly saw that the Brooklyn lines were dangerously weak in several places. Washington ordered hundreds of men to pile brush before the open trenches that connected the huge forts. Opposite that fatal thoroughfare, the Jamaica Road, there were practically no defenses. Three New York militia regiments started digging to defend this end of the line.

BELOW *The British navy unnerved the Americans by cruising up the Hudson, ignoring American forts and batteries. But the Americans harassed them with fire ships and aggressively patrolled the shores of the river. Eventually the warships retreated to New York harbor.*

Outmaneuvered and routed by the British in the Battle of Long Island on August 27, 1776, Americans fled across Gowanus Creek to reach their lines on Brooklyn Heights.

THE GERMANS ARE COMING

In late 1775, when it became obvious that George III could not raise enough men in England to send a strong British army to America, he tried to hire 20,000 Russians from Empress Catherine the Great. She rebuffed him with a wise warning: Using foreign troops was a confession of weakness.

The King ignored her and turned to a more certain source of manpower—his fellow German princes. George III was also the ruler of the Duchy of Hanover—and he had no difficulty hiring soldiers from the noblemen who ruled the 300 little sovereignties that composed Germany in 1776. For generations they had been in the business of renting bodies to warring powers to pay for their conspicuous consumption.

The best known of these body merchants were the landgraves of Hesse-Cassel. Their soldiers had been fighting for strangers all over Europe since 1687. The present landgrave, Frederick II, was a relative. His first wife had been George III's aunt. Frederick was delighted to sign a contract for 12,000 soldiers at £7 4s. 4d. per man.

Frederick also persuaded George III to part with an annual subsidy to Hesse-Cassel of £108,181 5s., to be continued for a year after the troops returned. Finally Frederick pressured George to pay him an old claim from the Seven Years War, which amounted to a neat £41,820 14s. 5d. The British also agreed to pay the salaries of the officers and men while they were in America.

George struck similar bargains for smaller numbers of troops with the Duke of Brunswick, who was married to his sister. The Duke's annual subsidy of £11,517 17s. was extended to two years after the troops returned, and would be doubled during that period. Moreover, the Duke would receive the price of a new recruit—£7 4s. 4d. for every man killed and one-third of that for every man wounded.

Other recruits came from specks on the map such as Hesse-Hanau, Anspach-Bayreuth, Anhalt-Zerbst and Waldeck. While the petty princes rubbed their well-greased palms,

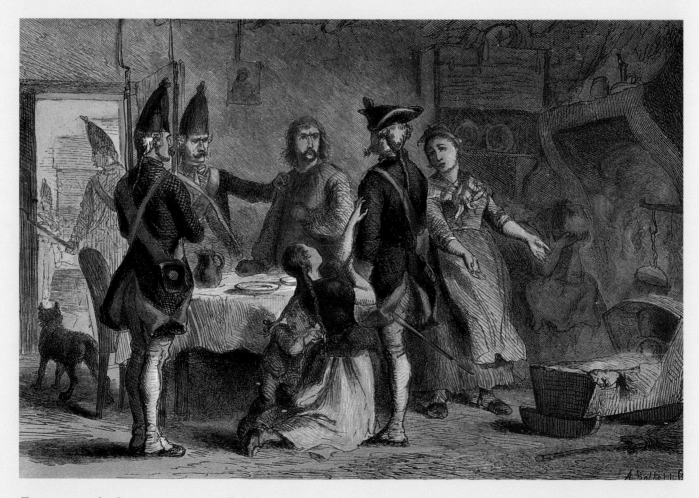

To raise men, the German princes virtually kidnapped some subjects. This man's family is pleading desperately against his conscription.

their recruiting agents swarmed into the German countryside, seizing anything on two legs. Students were waylaid on their way to universities, jails were emptied of bankrupts and deserters from other armies were taken into protective custody.

Johann Gottfried Seume had his university matriculation degree torn to shreds and thus lost "the only instrument of my identity." He found himself in the Hesse-Cassel fortress of Ziegenhain, in company with a dismissed postal clerk from Gotha, a bankrupt haberdasher from Hanover and a runaway monk from Wurzburg.

Many other young men, bored with peasant society in Germany, volunteered. Some were lured by promises that a man might make a fortune conquering such a rich country as America. Others saw a chance to get free passage to a country in which 200,000 Germans were already happy citizens.

All told, 29,867 German soldiers fought for George III in America between 1776 and 1783. Only 17,313 of these men returned to Germany at the end of the war. According to official returns, 548 were killed in action. Another 6,534 died of illnesses endemic in armies of the era. An estimated 5,000 deserted.

The Americans worked hard to promote desertion, smuggling letters in German into the mercenaries' camps, promising as much as 200 acres of land if a man switched sides. The Hessians, the most numerous and best-disciplined troops, had very few desertions in the first two years of the war. But as one of their officers candidly admitted, "Most of the... foreigners (non-Hessian Germans) defect at the first opportunity." As the war dragged on, Hessian desertions mounted, finally totaling 2,949.

The Germans, especially the Hessians, fought courageously in numerous battles. Many were able to convince themselves that they were fighting as allies of England, especially after France joined the war. The corps of Jäger (huntsmen), armed

This German grenadier is completely outfitted, down to his greased pigtail.

with short-barreled rifles, proved notably effective in forest fighting.

Both officers and men were shocked by the American climate, with its extremes of hot and cold and its violent storms. Brunswick surgeon Julius Frederick Wasmus confided to his diary that the winter was "unbearable." In another entry he described a thunderstorm "such as I have never experienced before...One often saw flashes of lightning driven perpendicularly out of the clouds into the ground."

In October 1780 Captain Johann Ewald wrote in his diary: "Since the burning southern wind [in the daytime] and the cold spells are coming again [at night]...the men die like flies and the hospitals are filled."

Used to formal warfare, the Germans were angered by the Americans' unorthodox tactics. Ambushing patrols and sniping at sentries seemed cowardly and dishonorable to them. The officers particularly disliked the American habit of making

them special targets. One wrote in his diary: "Today we cut the aiguillettes from our uniforms and the stripes from our hats...so that we could not be distinguished from common soldiers."

The Germans were especially baffled by the attitude of the German Americans, who opposed them as violently as other Americans. Captain Ewald told of meeting an old woman in Maryland who spoke to him in perfect German and asked: "What harm have we done you? You have come here to ruin us." Another officer complained that Pennsylvania's Germans were "steeped in the American idea of liberty and are...unbearable."

This enthusiasm for liberty perplexed the Germans. Hessian Quartermaster Carl Bauer was awed by the courage with which an American captain, executed as a spy in New Jersey, met his fate shouting: "I die for freedom!" Major Carl Leopold Bauermeister lamented the Americans' "indomitable ideas of liberty, the main springs of which are held and guided by every hand in the Congress!"

Well before the British gave up, the Germans decided the war was unwinnable. As early as November 1777, Hessian Lieutenant General Friedrich Wilhelm von Lossberg wrote: "Personally, I do not see when the rebellion will end. We have to deal with a whole continent and as long as there is one person left, he will be a rebel with all his heart." By July 1781 Major Bauermeister was writing: "Everyone wishes, as much as a soldier has a right to wish, that he may soon return home."

Their commander was shocked to discover that forty yards away was high ground from which the British could fire into their ranks.

Major General Henry Clinton saw the weakness of the Jamaica Road defenses at a glance. He asked Howe for permission to assault the raw New Yorkers. He was confident that he could drive them all the way to the Brooklyn ferry, which would cut off the American retreat. Nearby, Major General John Vaughan was equally confident that he and his exultant grenadiers could carry Fort Putnam, the key to the American left flank, and roll up the whole American line. From other parts of the oncoming British host, regimental officers asked Howe for permission to attack.

General Howe said no—again and again and again. He stopped Clinton and Vaughan, who unleashed a stream of oaths and swore he could take Fort Putnam in five minutes. Still Howe said no, although he had thus far suffered unbelievably few casualties—only 5 officers and 56 men killed, 13 officers and 275 men wounded among the British, 2 men killed, 3 officers wounded and 23 men wounded among the Germans—a total of 377 in an army of 20,000 men. The American killed, wounded and missing already totaled 1,407. Still General Howe said no. He declined to charge the American forts. He told his officers that he preferred "regular approaches"—the eighteenth-century military term for siege techniques. Inside the American lines Washington, Putnam and their fellow generals braced for a climactic assault. Putnam roared his classic advice about the whites of British eyes. Washington brandished two pistols and swore he would shoot the first man who ran. He kept his men on the alert all night, peering into the darkness for an attack that never came. The next morning, still convinced that an assault was only hours away, Washington ferried three more regiments from New York.

Aboard the frigate *HMS Rainbow* in the harbor, Captain George Collier wrote in his diary: "If we become masters of this body of rebels (which I think is inevitable) the war is at an end." He was unquestionably correct. By now Washington, his staff and almost every available general—plus at least 9,000 men, most of them Continentals—were in the Brooklyn lines.

Throughout the day Captain Collier expected orders from Lord Howe to place his ship and four other frigates in the East River between Brooklyn and New York to cut off all possibility of an American retreat. But the order never came. Some historians have suggested Lord Howe's strange passivity—especially strange for him, one of the most aggressive admirals in the Royal Navy—was due to a shift in the wind. But Captain Collier, writing in his journal with you-are-there authenticity, did not seem to think the wind was a problem. He wrote that he and his fellow captains "have been in constant expectation of being ordered" to block the American escape route from Brooklyn.

A bone-chilling rain began falling on the battlefield. In some of the crude American trenches, the water soon rose to the men's waists. The shaken soldiers

TOP LEFT *Thomas Mifflin cast aside his Quaker heritage to become a fierce revolutionary. In 1777 he turned against Washington and conspired to oust him as commander-in-chief.*

struggled to keep their powder dry. One Massachusetts regiment, mostly tough sailors from Marblehead, skirmished with the British along their front. Otherwise the battle line remained quiescent. The gray, rain-whipped day oozed into night without any sign of movement from the enemy. Still the Americans were sure the battle that would settle the fate of the nation was imminent. "It seems the day is come...on which depends the salvation of this country," Lieutenant Joseph Hodgkins wrote to his wife.

At twilight on this dismal day, the British suddenly went into action in front of Fort Putnam. A heavy force of light infantry swarmed forward and quickly drove the outlying American pickets inside the fort. At dawn on August 29, the Americans discovered the reason for this burst of activity. About 600 yards from the fort was a British redoubt. Behind it was a network of trenches. General Howe had begun his "regular approaches."

There was only one sensible thing for the Americans to do—retreat. Washington, however, was too sensitive about his reputation to suggest it. He was rescued from impending catastrophe by Thomas Mifflin, the man who had irked John Adams by becoming the army's quartermaster general. Mifflin, a Quaker who had defied his family's creed by turning soldier, had quit that boring job and become a brigadier general. During the night of August 28, he had patrolled the American lines as the temporary commander while Israel Putnam and other generals managed to get some sleep. As he talked to officers and men, Mifflin grew more and more alarmed by the Americans' plummeting morale. Many militia regiments were talking about surrender.

At 4:30 A.M. on August 29, Mifflin told Washington that another day or two in the lines might produce a mass capitulation. "You must either fight or retreat immediately," he said. "What is your strength?"

"Nine thousand," Washington replied.

Not enough, Mifflin said. "We must retreat."

Washington had been thinking similar thoughts. He called a council of war and found all his generals but one in complete agreement. Washington rushed orders to New York to collect every boat "from Hellgate on the

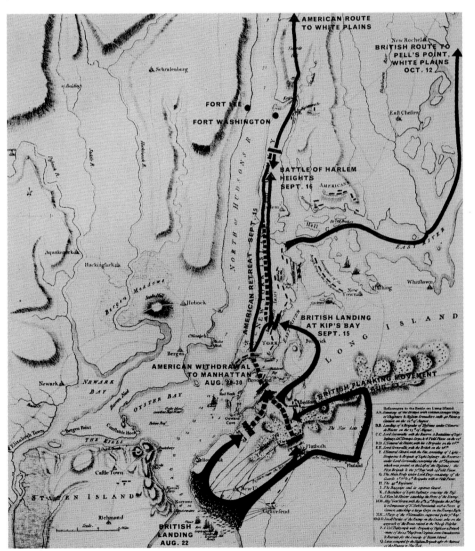

BELOW **This map shows the war of maneuver the British fought in and around New York, using their fleet to outflank the Americans.**

[Long Island] Sound to Spuyten Duyvil Creek [on the Hudson] that could be kept afloat and had either sails or oars." By midnight, in continuing rain and fog, a mosquito fleet had been collected—and the retreat began.

Fearful that a deserter would give away the secret, Washington issued orders explaining the movement as a rearrangement of positions. Not until a regiment marched to the Brooklyn ferry and boarded boats did they know where they were going. The best troops, Continentals from Pennsylvania, Maryland and Delaware, were left in the forts. But no one replaced the men who were withdrawn from the connecting trenches, leaving huge holes in the American lines that an aggressive enemy could have easily exploited.

For the first two hours, the exodus went smoothly. Then a strong northeast wind began to blow. The sailboats could make no headway against it; only rowboats could be used. Brigadier General Alexander McDougall, in command at the Brooklyn ferry landing, was in despair. He told Washington there was no hope of getting all the men and supplies to New York by morning.

At eleven o'clock, the wind suddenly swung around to the southwest—the best possible breeze to speed sailing vessels from Brooklyn to New York. The water became "smooth as glass," encouraging some sailors to pile men and equipment into their boats until there were only three inches of freeboard.

There is not a word in the American accounts of this tense night about any of these overloaded boats carrying defensive weapons. The British navy had dozens of cutters on which small swivel guns—light cannon—were often mounted. Even one of these swift-moving craft manned by expert oarsmen could have wreaked havoc on the American boats.

But Admiral Howe was not interested in preventing an American retreat. On the contrary, he was once more pursuing a negotiated peace. Aboard his flagship, *HMS Eagle*, he had spent much of the previous day in conversation with the two captured American generals, William Alexander and John Sullivan. He got nowhere with Alexander, whose family had seen savage British repression of Scottish revolts. But John Sullivan was more naive and emotional. He eagerly agreed to become his Lordship's emissary to the Continental Congress.

MILITIA AND CONTINENTALS

For contemporary Americans the difference between militia and regular, or "Continental," soldiers is hard to grasp. Both fought in the war. Both suffered casualties. Both have supporters who claim they won the war. For decades after the Revolution, politicians spouted clouds of hot air on the subject, mostly aimed at denigrating the regular army in favor of the militia.

The militia long predated the American Revolution. As early as 1691 the Massachusetts charter empowered the royal governor to organize regiments of militia in every county. All able-bodied men between sixteen and sixty were required to serve. Each had to keep a musket, bullets and powder ready to repel an attack by the French or Indians. The militia was a kind of standing home army that met on training days to stay acquainted with handling guns and performing military maneuvers.

The minutemen were an elite group of militiamen who met and trained hard in the sixteen months between the Boston Tea Party and the battles of Lexington and Concord on April 19, 1775. Many people, including members of the Continental Congress, have confused them with ordinary militiamen. The latter never approached the minutemen's state of battle readiness. As a result the militia performed disastrously in the opening years of the Revolution.

In late 1776 George Washington, discouraged by the way militiamen tended to run away at the sight of a British soldier, wrathfully informed the Congress: "If I were called upon to declare...whether the militia had been most serviceable or hurtful upon the whole, I should subscribe to the latter."

Emergency soldiers, summoned from home on short notice, the militia lacked confidence on the battlefield. But Washington eventually concluded that if they had a regular army to support them, some of these amateurs were willing to fight and could inflict significant damage on the enemy.

Washington and some of his generals, notably Daniel Morgan and Nathanael Greene, learned to use the militia as auxiliary troops around a core of regulars with triumphant effect at battles such as Cowpens. At Saratoga the militia poured in after the Continentals had proved they could fight the British army to a standstill. Their raw numbers convinced General John Burgoyne that he was hopelessly surrounded. When the British invaded New Jersey in 1780, the militia, knowing the Continental army was in nearby Morristown, fought vigorously.

When the war shifted to the South and the southern Continental army was virtually destroyed by successive defeats at Savannah, Charleston and Camden, the militia under the leadership of experienced soldiers such as Thomas Sumter carried the brunt of the resistance for a while. But their lack of discipline and fondness for plunder alienated as many people as their battlefield valor encouraged. It required the revival of the southern army under Nathanael Greene to make a decisive impact on the war.

At Bennington and King's Mountain, the militia, again led by experienced officers, won victories without the help of the Continentals. When Washington marched to Yorktown, he left New Jersey completely in the hands of the militia. The conclusion seems inescapable: The militia could not have won the war alone—but the war probably could not have been won without them.

After the battle of Springfield, two voices summed up the appeal of both types of soldiers. One of Washington's officers, who remembered the starvation and neglect the regulars had endured during the brutal winter of 1780 in Morristown, wrote: "I cherish those dear ragged Continentals, whose patience will be the admiration of future ages, and I glory in bleeding with them."

Yet even a sternly impartial historian must confess the appeal of the militia's simpler, more spontaneous solidarity in a New Jersey colonel's mustering-out message to his regiment. He took "the greatest pleasure" in the way the men under his command had lived "in the greatest harmony."

He hoped they would continue in "the same peace and unity...and convince the enemy's of the United States that we mean to live and dye like brothers and go hand in hand in supporting our country against its aprosors...."

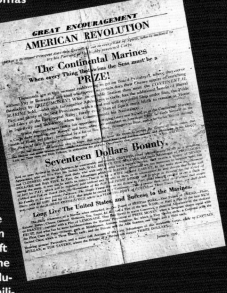

The Continental navy dangled the lure of prize money from captured ships before recruits.

To achieve the kind of peace Admiral Howe envisioned, Washington's army had to survive. If it was battered into mass surrender in Brooklyn or slaughtered on the dark East River, hard-liners such as Lord George Germain would insist on a peace of unconditional surrender, which would make America another Ireland. That was why General Howe was pursuing "regular approaches"—and no Royal Navy cutters knifed through the night belching death and destruction at Washington's men.

As August 30 dawned, the men guarding the forts on Brooklyn Heights were still waiting for orders to depart. In the confusion of the previous night, they had been ordered to march to the ferry landing and then sent back to the forts—so they knew the army was retreating. "We became very anxious for our own safety," Major Benjamin Tallmadge of Connecticut later recalled. The moment the British saw the empty trenches and the boats on the river, both the army and the navy would attack without waiting for orders from anyone.

Then came another change in the weather that many Americans chose to call providential. A dense fog engulfed the British and American lines. "I could scarcely discern a man at six yards distance," Tallmadge recalled. Well after the sun rose, the fog remained so dense that Tallmadge and the rest of the rear guard were able to escape undetected. Stepping into one of the last boats was the tall, cloaked figure of Washington. For forty-eight hours, he had not closed his eyes.

In New York, with the fog persisting, Tallmadge decided to recruit some volunteers and return to Brooklyn to rescue his horse—a mission that Washington, a fellow horse-lover, approved. As they pulled away a second time, frustrated British infantry appeared at the ferry landing and fired a volley of musketry that hit no one. "In the history of warfare, I do not recollect a more fortunate retreat," Major Tallmadge declared.

Talking Peace and Planning Protracted War

The Continental army's troubles were far from over. Civilians such as the pastor of New York's Moravian Church thought Washington's men looked "sickly"—hardly surprising, after three days and nights with little or no sleep in the chill wind and rain. More to the point, many looked "cast down." Numerous militiamen began having second thoughts about defending American liberty to the death. Whole companies talked things over, town-meeting style, and voted to go home. In a matter of days, 6,000 out of 8,000 Connecticut men departed.

The Continentals' morale also plummeted as they began to assess the significance of the British ability to land troops where they pleased. Lieutenant Hodgkins told his wife how "discorredging" it was to realize that all the forts they had spent the summer digging in New York City would probably be abandoned and they would have to meet the British in "the oppen field."

Into this atmosphere of gloom and panic came Major General John Sullivan with a request to go to Philadelphia to discuss Lord Howe's peace mission with the Continental Congress. Washington reluctantly consented—and on Sullivan's heels sent a long letter, telling the Congress it was time to enlist a serious regular army for the duration of the war. He also warned them that he was having second thoughts about obeying their orders to defend New York City.

ABOVE *New Hampshire Major General John Sullivan retained Washington's confidence in spite of his role in several American defeats. He fought well at Trenton and led a devastating retaliatory attack on the Iroquois in 1779. One of his brothers, Daniel, died aboard a British prison ship. Another brother, James, was a powerful politician in Massachusetts.*

In the British camp, no fewer than three generals wrote letters home declaring that the war was all but over. An officer in the Forty-second Scottish Highlanders said the same thing and incidentally revealed what motivated more than one of Howe's officers. "We have given the rebels a d—d crush," he exulted. "I expect the affair will be over this campaign and we shall all...have the cream of American lands allotted to us for our services." Among the standard British punishments for treason was the confiscation of the traitor's property.

But no coup de grace was struck. For two weeks the British army sat in their tents in Brooklyn, and the fleet rocked in New York Harbor while Captain Collier and no doubt many others fumed at giving the enemy "time to breathe." Lord Howe was waiting to hear from General Sullivan and the Continental Congress.

The New Hampshire soldier got a very cold reception in Philadelphia. John Adams said he wished the first bullet fired on Long Island had gone through Sullivan's head. The peace emissary could not have arrived at a worse moment. Ever since the Congress passed the Declaration of Independence, the delegates had been wrangling over the terms of "Articles of Confederation and Perpetual Union." Small states and large states were at each other's throats. Pennsylvania was denouncing Virginia's claim to most of the West. Many delegates opposed giving the Congress the power to tax, fearing it would become as voracious as Parliament.

The politicians decided they could not afford to ignore Lord Howe's request for a meeting with a Congressional committee. They appointed Benjamin Franklin, John Adams and Edward Rutledge, and the three met Howe at the stone mansion of Colonel Christopher Billopp, commander of Staten Island's loyalist militia. The meeting went nowhere. Lord Howe's military mind was too rigid to depart from the letter of his instructions. He insisted that "Great Britain did not require unconditional submission." But he recoiled from Benjamin Franklin's suggestion that he transmit to Parliament a proposal to negotiate with America as an independent state.

Howe talked "altogether in generals [generalities]," Rutledge reported to an anxious Washington on the night of the meeting. "Our reliance continues, therefore, to be, under God, on your wisdom and fortitude, and that of your forces."

The British mood was equally grim. Lord Howe's secretary, Ambrose Serle, a virulent anti-American who had been assigned to the peace mission by Lord George Germain, confided to his journal: "They met, they talked, they parted. Nothing now remains but to fight it out against a set of the most determined hypocrites and demagogues, compiled of the refuse of the colonies, that ever were permitted by Providence to be the scourge of a country."

General Washington reorganized his army, leaving only 5,000 men in New York City. He positioned 9,500 on the heights of Harlem and at Kings Bridge, on the north end of the island, where they could make a rapid retreat to Westchester County. He distributed another 5,000 along the shore of the East River above New York, to prevent a British landing. Noting that the British had not fired a shot at New York from Brooklyn Heights, he realized they were looking forward to making the city their winter quarters. Major General

Nathanael Greene, noticing the same thing, urged Washington to burn the place. Two-thirds of the property belonged to loyalists.

The day after Greene offered this advice, Washington received a letter from the Congress, informing him that they wanted "especial care taken" not to damage New York in any way if he decided to abandon it because they were confident he would be able to "recover the same." Washington replied with a letter that revealed for the first time his growing awareness that the Congress knew nothing about fighting a war. He urged the politicians to reconsider their directive about New York. Then he started revising the Congress's theory of winning the war in one big battle—what the eighteenth century called "a general action." On the contrary, Washington now thought, "we should on all occasions avoid a general action or put anything to the risk, unless compelled by necessity, into which we ought never to be drawn." Instead they should "protract the war" and aim at making the British quit from exhaustion. This meant the Americans would often have to retreat, and he was aware that might subject him to "reproach." But the "fate of America" was at stake, and he hoped the Congress would let him pursue this policy.

American Sprinters Versus British Liberators

On the evening of September 14, Connecticut militiamen guarding the shore of the East River watched five frigates drop anchor in Kips Bay, an indentation in Manhattan Island near present-day Thirty-fourth Street. Our sixteen-year-old friend, Joseph Plumb Martin, and his fellow militiamen exchanged insults with the British sailors for most of the night. When dawn broke, the frigates were close enough for Martin to read the name of one, *HMS Phoenix*, "as distinctly as though I had been under her stern."

Two hours passed while the British briskly loaded their cannon and prepared their ships for action. The sun beat down; it was a hot, humid day. Out of Bushwick Creek, opposite Kips Bay, came dozens of British attack flatboats carrying seven battalions of red-coated British light infantry and three battalions of blue-coated Germans. The East River soon looked to young Martin like "a large clover field in bloom."

The American commander along the East River was an aging major general from Connecticut named William Spencer. He seems to have made no attempt to take charge of his sprawling regiments, letting the colonels position their men as they pleased. Some decided the British were heading for Stuyvesant Cove, near present-day Fifteenth Street; others that their goal was Turtle Bay, near present-day Forty-second Street. Spencer let the militiamen run up and down the shore helter-skelter.

At 11 A.M., when the flatboats were about fifty yards offshore, the eighty-six cannon on the five frigates crashed. Joseph Plumb Martin, who had straggled into a nearby warehouse, thought "his head would go off with the sound." As round shot whistled and the guns crashed again and again, Martin dived into a trench and lay there trying to decide "which part of my carcass was to go first." The frigates concentrated on the militiamen who had dashed to Stuyvesant Cove. With these reinforcements cut off, the flatboats headed for the Kips Bay shore.

Martin and his comrades took one look at these murky, murderous shapes

ABOVE *This medicine chest belonged to Dr. Benjamin Rush, the surgeon general of the Continental army for the Middle States. He advocated drastic bloodletting as a cure.*

looming out of the cloud of gunsmoke shrouding the cove and started running. In minutes only their colonel and a handful of men were in the trenches. Five more regiments of Connecticut militia were stationed near present-day Twenty-third Street. They should have rushed to support Martin's brigade. Instead they joined the stampede north up the Boston Post Road.

Around present-day Forty-second Street, they encountered George Washington and several officers from Connecticut who tried to rally them. "Take the wall! Take the corn field!" Washington shouted, pointing to a nearby farm where corn stood high. But the sight of about seventy British light infantrymen cautiously advancing along the crest of a hill a quarter-mile away was too much for them. The militiamen resumed their flight, and the commander-in-chief went berserk.

Cursing stupendously, Washington flung his hat into the dust and cried: "Are these the men with which I am to defend America?" He lashed the runaways within reach of his riding crop. No one paid the slightest attention to him. In ten minutes the general was left alone in a road littered with abandoned muskets, knapsacks and canteens.

When Washington's volcanic temper went out of control, he lapsed into a near stupor afterward. Slumped in his saddle, he stared dazedly around him while the British infantry, suspecting a trap, hesitated. Eventually one of Washington's aides seized the reins of his horse and led him up the road in the wake of his fleeing troops.

The British, expecting a heavy American counterattack, did not attempt to extend their lines across Manhattan Island. This enabled the 5,000 men still inside New York City, including most of the army's artillerymen, to escape up

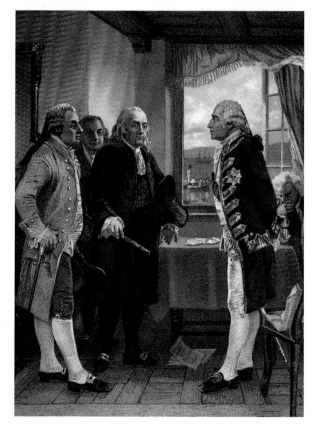

BELOW *Benjamin Franklin led a three-man Congressional delegation to meet with British Admiral Richard, Lord Howe, on Staten Island. All Howe offered was a vague promise that American grievances would be considered after the Americans surrendered.*

the west side of Manhattan. Admiral Howe sent a party of marines into the city to hoist the British flag. A crowd of loyalists swarmed around the seagoing soldiers. They trampled the American Grand Union flag "with the most contemptuous indignation," and greeted the British as liberators, according to Ambrose Serle, who was watching from the deck of *HMS Eagle.*

At dawn the next day, a dispirited Washington wrote to the Congress that he still hoped for a victory if the British attacked his army on Harlem Heights. But that hope depended on his men's acting with "tolerable resolution." As he wrote, a party of 120 scouts led by Colonel Thomas Knowlton of Connecticut collided with advance elements of the Forty-second Highlanders and two light-infantry battalions. Outnumbered, the Americans fell back until they reached a depression known as the Hollow Way, near present-day 125th Street.

Washington joined his adjutant general, Joseph Reed, to watch the skirmish from Harlem Heights. As the light infantry appeared on a rise not far from the present site of Grant's Tomb, there floated up to the ears of the American spectators the sound of bugles blowing the whoo-whoop of a fox hunt. Reed and Washington, already writhing at the sight of more Americans retreating, felt this was the ultimate mortification.

"It seemed to crown our disgrace," Reed told his wife a few days later.

Washington, spurred by Reed, decided he could not ignore this arrogant challenge. He told Knowlton to take his rangers and three rifle companies from Virginia and try to cut off the light infantrymen. Other Americans, many of them volunteers, poured into the Hollow Way and began skirmishing with the British. As Knowlton and his men emerged from some woods along the slopes of Morningside Heights, he was cut down by a British bullet. His men launched a ferocious attack on the stunned light infantrymen. For an hour the fight swayed back and forth on the edge of a buckwheat field between what are now 120th and 119th streets, with both sides pouring in men. The British, low on ammunition, finally broke and ran, the Americans pursuing them with whoops and bullets.

The Americans were heartened by this minor clash. Lieutenant Joseph Hodgkins reported to his wife that two glum British prisoners told him they realized too late "they had not the Milisha to deal with...this time." The Continentals and the militia were on their way to becoming two very different kinds of soldiers. In his letters, Washington labored to get this point across to the Congress. A dependence on militia would lead to "certain and irretrievable ruin," he warned. "Just dragged from the tender scenes of domestic life," militiamen were "ready to fly from their own shadows." Moreover, they were impossible to discipline, and their indifference to orders infected the rest of the army.

A Flaming Response

The Howes chose this moment to try to appeal over the heads of the Continental Congress to the American army and the people. They issued another peace proclamation, urging Americans to "reflect seriously" on the grave situation and confer with them on how to restore public tranquillity and establish a "permanent union" between England and America. Washington's men gave them a decidedly defiant answer. At midnight on September 20, they set New York City ablaze.

The torching was well planned; flames leapt simultaneously from a dozen buildings. Two men were seen setting fires on the roof of Anglican Trinity Church, a symbol of British authority. A brisk south wind carried the flames uptown along the shore of the Hudson River. Lord Howe dispatched hundreds of sailors from the fleet to fight the flames. His brother, fearing an American attack, was loath to commit any of his soldiers as firemen. The sailors caught several Americans in the act of setting more fires and hanged them. Trapped in the conflagration was a young Connecticut captain named Nathan Hale, who had been sent into the British lines as a spy several days earlier. He too was caught and hanged. He was denied the courtesy of a court-martial because he was suspected of being one of the arsonists. By the time the British got the inferno under control the next morning, about 600 houses, a quarter of the city, were in ashes.

Since the Congress had forbidden Washington to burn the city, he denied any knowledge of the plot. It was one of the few times during the war when he deviated from strict obedience to his civilian superiors. In private he left little doubt of his opinion of the conflagration. "Providence," he told one friend, "or some good honest fellow, has done more for us than we were disposed to do for ourselves."

ABOVE *Washington promoted Joseph Reed from aide to adjutant general of the Continental army— and discovered he was a secret critic of the commander-in-chief's supposed "fatal indecision."*

The Howes, their optimism banished by Washington's flaming response to their peace proclamation, resumed the offensive on October 12. Once more General Howe declined to repeat Bunker Hill by attacking Washington's army on Harlem Heights. Instead he put 5,000 men in his assault flatboats and moved them up the East River through the perilous waters of Hell Gate to land them north of New York, first at Throgs Neck, then at Pells Point in present-day Pelham.

Washington's only alternative was an immediate retreat. To comply with the Congress's wishes to bar the British access to the Hudson River, he left 2,000 of his best men in Fort Washington, a stronghold overlooking the river in northern Manhattan. There was a similar bastion on the New Jersey side of the river, named Fort Lee after Washington's eccentric second in command, Major General Charles Lee, who had recently rejoined the army after service in the South. Washington led the rest of his dispirited army on a torturous march north. Short of horses, they had to drag some of their cannon by hand. By late October they had reached comparative safety in the hills around White Plains. There, visions of another Bunker Hill once more danced through some heads. Even Joseph Reed, among the more realistic of Washington's staff officers, told his wife that "the business" would probably be settled in a titanic battle within the week.

On October 28 the British attacked and quickly drove the Americans off Chatterton's Hill, a crucial height that exposed the entire American line to hostile cannon fire. Instead of continuing the attack, Howe ordered his men to camp. Once more some of his senior officers were mystified by the British

BELOW *The Scottish Forty-second Highlanders, the famed "Black Watch," were forced to make an undignified retreat when they collided with Washington's Continentals at Harlem Heights.*

commander's reluctance to go for the American jugular. One colonel wondered whether it was through "incapacity or by design" that Howe let so many "great opportunities" slip out of his hands. "I am inclin'd to adopt the latter," he concluded. The Howes' desire for a moderate peace was not shared by most of their officers.

While Washington shifted his troops to higher ground beyond White Plains, his army began to dissolve again. His secretary, Robert Harrison, reported to the Congress that "large numbers of militia [were] returning home by different roads." Sickness also eroded the ranks. Many of the Continentals, separated from their baggage in the retreat, slept in the woods without blankets while the first snow of the year fell on them.

On the night of November 4, strange sounds began emanating from the British camp. American sentries heard the rumble and clank of wheels, the clop of hooves. When dawn broke they saw with unbelieving eyes that the British were retreating to Manhattan. Watching Howe depart, Washington realized that the British probably planned to "bend their force against Fort Washington."

What to do about the 2,000 Continentals in this fort, who were now marooned in a sea of British and Germans? Major General Nathanael Greene, in command of both that fort and its New Jersey twin, Fort Lee, recommended letting them stay—and even reinforced them. In spite of the disaster on Long Island, the Rhode Islander still hoped to repeat Bunker Hill. He also feared the impact of another retreat on the morale of militia regiments under his command. One New York regiment had mutinied and told their colonel that General Howe had promised them "peace, liberty and safety," and that was all they wanted. The words were an exact quote from the First Continental Congress's petition to the King.

Washington allowed Greene to keep the men in Fort Washington, in spite of urgent advice from General Lee to evacuate them. While the Americans debated, General Howe detached Lord Percy, the savior of the expedition to Concord, and three brigades to assist the German general, Wilhelm von Knyphausen, and his troops in an all-out attack on the fort. Howe gave Percy a detailed plan of the stronghold and its outworks, which had been supplied by a turncoat American officer.

In the meantime, Washington had divided his army, taking 2,500 men with him into New Jersey to block an anticipated enemy thrust into that state and leaving 11,000 under Major General Charles Lee in Westchester to bar a British advance into New England. The American commander urged New Jersey officials to call out all 16,000 men on their militia rolls to assist his Continentals. Not until November 15 did he turn his attention to Fort Washington again. He was alarmed to learn that the British had just demanded the surrender of the fort. Rushing from Hackensack, where he had been conferring with New Jersey politicians, Washington met Generals Greene and Putnam returning from the fort. They assured him all was well. The hero of Bunker Hill said the men were in high spirits, and he was sure they would inflict a terrific defeat if the British attacked.

At dawn the next day, as a still-worried Washington prepared to cross the Hudson to inspect the fort, heavy firing broke out all around it. In a perfectly coordinated assault, British and German troops stormed the stronghold from

ABOVE *Eccentric British-born Major General Charles Lee, the American army's second in command, was captured by British cavalry on December 13. He had become a savage critic of Washington.*

Already expert at building fire ships that exploded into flame to menace the British fleet, the Americans used similar techniques to set New York ablaze. They hoped to deny the British the use of the city as winter quarters. More than 600 buildings along the Hudson River were destroyed.

three sides while artillery poured round shot and grape from nearby heights. A German regiment led by Colonel Johann Rall clawed their way up the almost vertical slopes on the northern side of the fort. Everywhere the men defending the outworks were forced to retreat to the fort itself, which was soon jammed with almost 3,000 panicky soldiers. A German officer approached the American commander, Colonel William Magaw, under a white flag and gave him a half-hour to surrender. If he refused, the officer said the Germans, who had suffered heavy casualties, would storm the fort and massacre its defenders to the last man. Magaw capitulated.

On the other side of the Hudson, a stricken Washington could only lament the loss of 2,811 Continentals, "many of whom have been trained with much more than common attention," tons of gunpowder and supplies, and forty-three cannon. Washington was in danger of becoming a parody of a general, and many people knew it. On the day Fort Washington fell, his acerbic second in command, Charles Lee, began exchanging letters with the army's adjutant general, Joseph Reed, about General Washington's shortcomings. Lee also wrote friends in the Continental Congress, practically urging Washington's dismissal. Revealing his radical streak, Lee suggested he could rescue the situation if the Congress would make him a dictator for a week. He did not mention that, in spite of his fulminations, some 5,000 Massachusetts militia had decided to go home, cutting the size of his army in half. One dismayed Connecticut officer summed up a widespread opinion: "I am...in great fear for our political salvation."

In Hacksensack Washington confessed to his brother Jack: "I am weary almost to death with the retrograde motion of things." Everything had gone wrong and was still heading in the same disastrous direction. The Congress

NATHAN HALE—A WASTED SPY

When the American army was routed on Long Island and retreated in disarray to Manhattan, George Washington sent out an urgent call for men to volunteer as spies. He desperately needed to know where the British would strike next.

Captain Nathan Hale of Connecticut volunteered, in spite of repeated attempts by his friends to talk him out of it. One pointed out that the former schoolmaster's nature "was too frank and open for deceit and disguise." Besides, the friend said, "Who respects the character of a spy?" Hale replied that every kind of service for the public good "becomes honorable by being necessary."

Hale's commanding officer, Colonel Thomas Knowlton, was a good combat soldier but unfortunately knew nothing about intelligence work. His orders to Hale were vague. He gave him neither invisible ink, although it had been invented three years earlier by an American, nor any code that might have enabled him to write letters in cipher.

For a disguise Hale chose the role of Dutch schoolmaster. Armed with nothing but his Yale diploma, he wandered through the British army camps in Brooklyn.

Before Hale found anything important to report, the British attacked across the East River, routing the Americans at Kips Bay and seizing New York City. Hale decided to follow them into the city. No one knows exactly when he arrived, but he spent enough time there to make notes on British troop dispositions and field fortifications.

On September 20 he was trapped inside the city when the Americans sent in teams of soldiers to set New York ablaze and deny the British winter quarters. Hale may have participated in this scorched-earth warfare. At any rate, it was his undoing. The infuriated British began checking the identity of almost every young American they saw. Hale, with his Connecticut accent and soldierly bearing, undoubtedly attracted their attention.

Before he was hanged, Hale chatted with a British engineer, Captain John Montresor, who was moved by his "gentle dignity, the consciousness of rectitude and high intentions." The American gave Montresor some farewell letters to his family and friends.

Asked if he had anything to say as the noose was placed around his neck, Hale may well have uttered the words attributed to him: "I only regret that I have but one life to lose for my country." It is a paraphrase of a line from Joseph Addison's *Cato*, eighteenth-century America's favorite play.

Captain Montresor gave Hale's letters to the British provost marshal, a hardhearted character named William Cunningham, who refused to deliver them. "The rebels should never know they had a man who could die with so much firmness," Cunningham said.

Montresor later told the story of Hale's death to the Americans during a parley over an exchange of prisoners. Hale's friends were ashamed of the way he died and said nothing until fifty years later, when one of them confided the story to his daughter.

Only then did Yale orators and others convert him into a national hero. In 1776 Nathan Hale was closer to being an unknown soldier.

Captain Nathan Hale was hanged after he was caught with documents in his shoes that proved he was a spy. His Yale classmate and close friend, Benjamin Tallmadge, later became Washington's intelligence director.

had refused to let him appoint officers to the regiments of the new army that had to be recruited for 1777, reserving that power to the states. They were nominating men "not fit to be shoeblacks." When he thought of what had happened to his army in the defense of New York, Washington could only conclude that his reputation was forever ruined.

On the evidence, he was not far wrong. The British had captured 329 officers and 4,100 men. Several thousand more Americans—no one knows how many, since most were in the militia, which did not keep good records—had died of disease. Another 600 had been killed or wounded. Gone beyond recall were 218 cannon and thousands of tents and blankets and entrenching tools. Even more damaging were the thousands of militiamen from New England and New York who had picked up their guns and gone home to spread the word that anyone who risked his life in the American army was out of his mind.

Admiral Benedict Arnold

If the future looked bleak for Washington's army, hopeless described the prospects of America's Northern army, the would-be conquerors of Canada. Their numbers down to some 3,500 men, they clung to Fort Ticonderoga, where, in the words of Colonel Anthony Wayne of Pennsylvania, they found themselves "destitute of almost every necessary for a soldier, shoes, stockings, shirts and coats."

From Canada came the dismaying news that the British had just received 3,000 German reinforcements, swelling their ranks to 16,000 men. But a march along the forested, swampy shores of 135-mile-long Lake Champlain was impossible. This enemy host would have to come by water. To stop them, Benedict Arnold had turned admiral and was building a fleet.

Prodded by Arnold, Philip Schuyler, commander of the Northern army, lured carpenters from Rhode Island and found hard money to pay them. They had to build the ships with green timber, which warped and leaked. For sailors, Arnold drafted men from the army who knew nothing about handling a ship and had no enthusiasm for fighting on the water. Arnold not only supervised building and manning this impromptu navy but also designed most of the ships—flat-bottomed gondolas powered by two big, square sails and sixteen oars, as well as larger row galleys with thirty-two oars. All carried cannon.

Arnold's frenzied activity forced the British commander, General Guy Carleton, to spend months building a fleet of his own at the other end of Lake Champlain. It included twenty-four gunboats, two schooners and a full rigged ship—the eighteen-gun HMS *Inflexible*—which alone was capable of annihilating Arnold's entire flotilla.

When Arnold heard about the *Inflexible*, he decided not to challenge the British on the open lake. He anchored his makeshift fleet across the mouth of Valcour Bay, about halfway down the lake. On October 5 the British headed down Champlain, the three-masted *Inflexible* leading the way. Behind her came the rest of the fleet, followed by the army in 640 flatboats.

Five days later, the vanguard of the British armada sailed past Arnold's fleet in the mouth of Valcour Bay without seeing it. When the Americans opened fire on the smaller craft in the British rear, the *Inflexible* and the other large ships found it almost impossible to come about and get within range

against the prevailing north wind. But the British gunboats and a few smaller sailcraft began a furious duel.

From 12:30 P.M. until dusk, the two fleets blazed away at each other. Aboard the flagship *Congress*, Arnold, his hair singed, his face blackened with powder, ran from gun to gun, aiming them for his amateur sailors. The Americans' cannon wreaked havoc on the British and Germans manning the open gunboats. One took a direct hit in its ammunition locker and exploded.

The British concentrated their fire on the *Congress*, which soon had a dozen holes in her hull. Aboard the nearby *Washington*, the captain was the only officer still in action. The battered *Philadelphia* wallowed deep in the water. From the shore, England's Indian allies howled threats and insults and peppered the Americans with musketry and arrows.

Not until twilight did the *Inflexible* get into the fight. She flung dozens of twelve-pound shot and bursts of deadly grape and chain shot across the already bloody American decks. But the indomitable Arnold kept enough guns firing aboard the *Congress* to persuade the big ship to retreat to a longer range, and the battle ended for the night.

The British distributed their ships across the mouth of Valcour Bay, confident that they would finish off Arnold in the morning. But the impromptu admiral led his fleet through the foggy night in a silent retreat around the western end of the enemy blockade. Morning found Arnold far down the lake, his men rowing for their lives. For a day and a night, the British pursuit was frustrated by Champlain's tricky winds.

ABOVE *From Fort Lee on the New Jersey shore, George Washington watched the battle of Fort Washington slide into disaster. Israel Putnam, the hero of Bunker Hill, had persuaded him the Americans could repeat that triumph if the British attacked. Here a messenger tells Washington that the fort is about to surrender.*

When the British finally caught up, the *Congress* and the row galley *Washington* took on their entire fleet while the smaller ships fled. The *Washington* struck her colors, but Arnold fought on. When defeat seemed imminent, he ordered his exhausted men to row through a hole in the enemy cordon to windward, where the British had trouble following him. Five crippled gondolas joined him in a dash to the nearest shore, where the Americans burned the ships and retreated to Fort Ticonderoga.

There the Northern army concealed its weakness by blasting cannon and small arms at British scouting parties. General Carleton decided the fort was too strong to storm—and too much time had been lost dealing with Arnold's fleet to start a siege. His Indian allies warned Carleton that snow would soon begin to fall, and Champlain's waves would be whipped to dangerous heights by winter winds. The British commander decided to retreat to Canada.

"If we could have begun our expedition four weeks earlier," sighed the commander of the German troops. It had taken exactly four weeks to launch the *Inflexible*. Admiral Arnold and his green fleet had bought Americans a precious nine months to solidify their grip on northern New York.

Farewell to Illusions

Early on the morning of November 20, a local farmer rushed into General Greene's headquarters at Fort Lee and informed him that 4,000 or 5,000 British had crossed the Hudson at Dobbs Ferry and were marching south toward the fort. Greene sent a messenger to Washington in Hackensack, asking what he should do. Washington leaped on his horse, galloped to Fort Lee and ordered an immediate retreat.

The British, reinforcing their invading army to 10,000 men, prepared to push across New Jersey and take the American capital, Philadelphia. With this symbolic triumph, they were sure the war would be over. Washington asked General Charles Lee to join him for a stand on the Raritan River in the center of New Jersey. Lee, by now openly contemptuous of Washington, ignored him. Lee was corresponding with Massachusetts politicians, urging them to give him enough men to create an independent army. He would "answer for their success."

In New Brunswick on November 29, Washington was handed a letter from General Lee, addressed to Adjutant General Joseph Reed. He was in western New Jersey, trying to turn out the state's militia, few of whom had yet appeared in spite of urgent calls. Thinking the letter was army business, Washington opened it and discovered Reed and Lee were discussing his "fatal indecision of mind." Another man in Washington's situation

BELOW *At Valcour Bay on Lake Champlain, Benedict Arnold's flat-bottomed row galleys and gondolas fought a British fleet, led by the eighteen-gun* Inflexible. *The impromptu admiral lost the battle and was denounced by numerous critics. But the British retreated to Canada, leaving the Americans in control of northern New York.*

might have exploded. He had promoted Reed from aide to adjutant general, a job that presumed mutual trust. Washington simply forwarded the letter to Reed with an apology for opening it.

A new George Washington was beginning to emerge from this crisis—a man who realized he was alone. He could depend on no one—not the affable Reed, in whom he had thought he could confide. Not Charles Lee with his gilded professional soldier's reputation. Not Israel Putnam, with his compulsion to replay Bunker Hill. Not Nathanael Greene and younger generals like him, who were only beginning to learn the art of war.

A calm tough realism now informed Washington's letters. He told the Congress that within twenty-four hours, on December 1, 1776, when many militiamen were slated to go home, "our force will be reduced to a mere handfull." He ordered an immediate collection of boats to ferry his men across the Delaware. He also wanted the river scoured for any craft that the British might use to pursue him.

When General William Heath, in command in the Hudson Highlands, wrote to him bemoaning the "infamous" failure of the New Jersey militia to turn out, Washington's response again showed him thinking his way to a new strategy. The militia had failed to fight "for want of an army to look the enemy in the face." Only a trained, well-officered army, equipped with bayonets and cannon, could withstand the professional force the British were putting in the field. If America hoped to win the war, they had to maintain such an army and deploy it wherever the British invaded.

ABOVE *The British attack on Fort Washington was a military masterpiece. This view from across the Harlem River shows light infantry and the Scottish Black Watch landing from flatboats. Other units attacked from the north and south. An American defector had given the British a complete description of the fort's defenses. Almost 3,000 men became prisoners of war.*

ABOVE *On November 20, 1776, the British shipped 5,000 men across the Hudson and marched on Fort Lee. Washington ordered an immediate retreat. He left behind more than 100 militiamen who got drunk and refused to obey his orders.*

The British army paused at New Brunswick, New Jersey, until General Howe joined them. Along his route, the general's staff distributed copies of a new proclamation aimed at taking New Jersey out of the war. It offered rebel Americans pardons and guarantees against "forfeitures, attainders and penalties" if they appeared before a British official within the next sixty days and signed a statement promising to "remain in peaceable obedience to His Majesty."

The Howes were betting that there was heavy loyalist and neutralist sentiment in New Jersey. They saw a chance to pacify the colony and use it as an example of British moderation to persuade Pennsylvania and New York to accept similar terms. The business of distributing the proclamation gave Washington time to get his beaten army across the Delaware without harassment.

Charles Lee, fighting the war his way, finally led his depleted army into New Jersey. On December 13 a British cavalry patrol surprised him and his staff in a tavern in Basking Ridge. After brief resistance, Lee surrendered, and the British were sure the war was won. An elated German officer confided to his diary: "We have got our hands on...the only rebel general we had to fear."

Meanwhile, thousands of New Jerseyans were succumbing to General Howe's offer to save their lands by promising to remain in peaceable obedience to His Majesty. The delighted Howe abandoned his plans to fight his way to Philadelphia and decided to support these newfound loyalists with a chain of posts along the Delaware from Burlington to Trenton. He installed similar garrisons in other towns throughout the state.

Washington, observing these developments from the other side of the

The beaten American army, reduced, in Washington's words to "a mere hand-full"
retreated across New Jersey. Washington summoned the state's 16,000 militiamen to
support his regulars. Barely 1,000 responded.

Delaware, began taking charge of the war. He noted that the British garrisons were "a good deal scattered" and were vulnerable to "a stroke"—a surprise attack. He was unperturbed when he learned that a panicky Continental Congress had retreated from Philadelphia to Baltimore on December 13, leaving him with "full power to direct all things relative to…the operations of the war." At this moment, what Washington needed far more than political power was information. He issued orders to all his generals to find "some person who can be engaged to cross the river as a spy." He added that "expense must not be spared" to find a volunteer for this risky business. The search soon turned up a former British soldier named John Honeyman, who was living in nearby Griggstown, New Jersey.

On Washington's orders, Honeyman suddenly rediscovered his loyalty to the King and began selling cattle to several British garrisons. He had no trouble gaining the confidence of Colonel Johann Rall, who was in command of three German regiments in Trenton. Honeyman listened with wide-eyed admiration as Rall described his heroic role in the conquest of Fort Washington, and agreed that the Americans were hopeless soldiers.

On December 22, after spending about a week in Trenton, Honeyman wandered into the countryside, supposedly in search of cattle. He was captured by an American patrol and hustled to Washington's headquarters, where he was denounced by the American commander-in-chief as a "notorious" turncoat. Washington insisted on interrogating Honeyman personally, growling that he would give the traitor a chance to save his skin if he recanted his loyalty to the Crown.

A half-hour later, the general ordered his aides to throw Honeyman into the guardhouse. Tomorrow morning, he thundered, the despicable Tory would be hanged. That night, using a key slipped to him by the American commander-in-chief, Honeyman escaped from the guardhouse and legged it past American sentries as musket balls whistled around him. Sometime on December 24, he turned up in Trenton and told Colonel Rall the story of his narrow escape.

The German naturally wanted to know what Honeyman had seen in Washington's camp. The spy assured Rall that the Americans were falling apart. They were half-naked, freezing, without the food or basic equipment, such as shoes, to make a winter march. Colonel Rall was delighted with this news and prepared to celebrate Christmas with no military worries to interrupt the feasting and drinking that were traditional in his country. He never dreamt that Honeyman had given Washington a detailed, professional soldier's description of the routine of the Trenton garrison, the location of the picket guards, and everything else an assaulting army needed to know.

The following day Washington wrote to Joseph Reed at Bristol, Pennsylvania, where he was mustering local militia: "Christmas Day, at night, one hour before day, is the time fixed for our attempt on Trenton. For heaven's sake keep this to yourself…necessity, dire necessity, will, nay must, justify my attack." He did not have to explain the meaning of those last words to Reed. Better than anyone else in the army, the adjutant general knew that in five days, most of the trained Continentals would go home to New England.

Washington ordered Reed and the Pennsylvanians to assail German garrisons south of Trenton, hoping to spread confusion and panic up and down

THE CRISIS

The *American* CRISIS.

NUMBER I.

By the Author of COMMON SENSE.

THESE are the times that try men's souls: The summer soldier and the sunshine patriot will, in this crisis, shrink from the service of his country; but he that stands it NOW, deserves the love and thanks of man and woman. Tyranny, like hell, is not easily conquered; yet we have this consolation with us, that the harder the conflict, the more glorious the triumph. What we obtain too cheap, we esteem too lightly:——'Tis dearness only that gives every thing its value. Heaven knows how to set a proper price upon its goods; and it would be strange

With Washington's collapsing army as he retreated through New Jersey was Thomas Paine, the English journalist who had helped change American minds with *Common Sense*. Paine saw the stark outlines of oncoming panic and reached for his pen to stem it. On a drumhead beside an army campfire, he wrote words that have become so famous they seem hackneyed to modern ears: "These are the times that try men's souls. The summer soldier and the sunshine patriot will, in this crisis, shrink from the service of his country; but he that stands it now deserves the love and thanks of man and woman. Tyranny, like Hell, is not easily conquered; yet we have this consolation with us, the harder the conflict, the more glorious the triumph. What we obtain too cheap, we esteem too lightly; it is dearness only that gives everything its value."

Paine insisted Americans were far from beaten: "Tis surprising to see how rapidly a panick will sometimes run through a country. All nations and ages have been subject to them….Yet panicks, in some cases, have their uses. They produce as much good as hurt. Their duration is always short; the mind soon grows through them, and acquires a firmer habit than before."

"The Crisis" appeared in *The Pennsylvania Journal* on December 19, 1776. Four days later it was printed as a pamphlet. Washington's victory at Trenton gave the writer a prophet's aura. Paine wrote eighteen stirring essays in the course of the war. He donated them to the American cause, refusing to take a cent of profit from their publication.

ABOVE *This painting shows Washington leading his ragged army to the banks of the Delaware on Christmas night 1776. "Surprize" was one of the favorite words in his military vocabulary. He often used spies and disinformation to befuddle the enemy.*

the Delaware. "No man," he confessed to his brother Jack in another letter, "ever had a greater choice of difficulties and less means to extricate himself from them." But he retained an amazing faith that the American cause would not fail: "Under a full persuasion of the justice of our cause, I cannot entertain an idea that it will finally sink tho it may remain for some time under a cloud."

For this predawn attack, Washington had conceived a plan that was rooted in his experience as a frontier soldier. By nightfall, he had assembled 2,400 men at McKonkey's ferry, nine miles north of Trenton. A swarm of big, ugly Durham boats, used to transport grain on the Delaware, bobbed beside the riverbank. Orders were issued to each brigade, detailing its route of march and point of attack.

If Washington and his men failed, America would never pursue a separate destiny. Never again would the British permit the Americans to mount a revolution. Worse, the success of the Howes' war for hearts and minds in New Jersey suggested that Americans might never want to mount one. They would accept what the Howes offered—British liberty, carefully circumscribed by the King and his nobles. Americans would become meek, humble, second-class citizens of the omnipotent empire.

The big man on his horse by McKonkey's Ferry did not know all this, of course. He was neither a historian nor a philosopher. He was something else, much more remarkable—a leader, fighting for that equally rare thing, a good cause. It was a cause that transcended the failures and imperfections of those who supported it. But the cause would not survive, no matter how good, how noble, if it did not receive the leadership it deserved. This was what George Washington was finally giving it.

London's Hard Line

In London the popular mood was euphoric. On October 10, the city had exploded with joy when a packet boat brought the news of William Howe's victory on Long Island. Bonfires burned on street corners, church bells clanged. In a speech from the throne, George III exuded confidence in the early re-establishment of British authority in America. America's supporters in Parliament were shattered by the news. They were already in disarray, thanks to the Declaration of Independence, which had enabled the anti-Americans in the government to hoot, "I told you so!"

ABOVE *In the march across New Jersey, British and German troops looted the houses of loyalists and rebels indiscriminately. Not a few supporters of George III changed their minds after their homes were stripped of valuables. Even feather beds were stolen.*

Only one man had the courage to defend the Americans—Charles James Fox, the dissolute son of Henry Fox, the corrupt politician whom George III had employed and discarded early in his reign. Fox demanded to know how the government planned to establish British authority in America. By the bayonets of disciplined Germans? He predicted it would take a huge standing army to break the spirit of the Americans. Such a body of men, who lived by trampling on the rights and living on "the spoils cruelly wrung from the sweat and labour of their fellow subjects," would become a menace to the liberties of England. The government pretended Fox did not exist. Parliament approved the King's speech by a huge majority.

The most successful newspaper in England, *The Morning Post*, hitherto one of Prime Minister Lord North's roughest critics, switched sides and began praising everyone in the government. The editor, a dissolute ex-clergyman named Henry Bate, had been purchased from the King's secret-service fund for £200 a year. Bate was soon sneering at the "cowardice of panic-smitten Yankees on Long Island."

Only one piece of news from America met disapproval in London: the Howes' amnesty proclamation of November 30. Lord George Germain called it "a sentimental way of making war" and informed the Howes that they did not have the authority to make such a generous offer of pardon again. The Americans who failed to repent within the sixty-day limit would have to face the kind of punishment Lord George was looking forward to giving them: wholesale confiscation of their lands and a distribution of them to the friends of the government—and to the friends of Lord George Germain. If Washington's desperate gamble on the Delaware failed, Germain would become the most powerful man in the British government, with a passionate loyalty to George III. No wonder men such as Edmund Burke and Charles James Fox and William Pitt feared for British liberty.

Gallant and Spirited Behavior at Last

At first everything seemed to be going wrong. A mixture of sleet and snow slashed out of the black sky on a northeast wind. The Delaware was high, and the current sent chunks of ice smashing against the clumsy Durham boats, making them difficult to handle. Eighteen cannon had to be dragged aboard the boats by hand. It was 4 A.M. before the last guns reached the New Jersey shore and the regiments were placed in order of battle.

Five miles below the ferry crossing, the little army split into two columns. One, led by Major General John Sullivan (recently exchanged for a captured British general), took the river road; the other, under Major General Nathanael Greene, took an inland road. Washington ordered all the officers to synchronize their watches with his and urged them to remind their men of the password: Victory or Death.

The road was a glaze of ice beneath the soldiers' feet. The wind beat the sleet relentlessly onto their backs. One captain in Sullivan's column, checking his musket, discovered the sleet had soaked through a handkerchief he had placed over the priming pan, ruining the powder. A quick check revealed almost every gun in the same condition. Sullivan asked Washington what he should do. "Use the bayonet," Washington replied. "The town must be taken."

Several times Washington rode down Greene's column, calling, "Soldiers, keep by your officers, for God's sake, keep by your officers." During one of these trips, his horse's hind feet lost their traction in the icy road, and it looked for a moment as if the general and his steed would crash down a steep, slippery bank into a gulley. One of his big hands seized the horse's mane, and Washington heaved the animal's head erect with a single motion of his powerful arm. Forty years later a Connecticut artilleryman remembered this as the moment when he knew they were on their way to victory.

Inside Trenton the Germans were sleeping off their Christmas celebration. Colonel Rall had spent the latter part of the night playing cards with a New Jersey loyalist. Around midnight another loyalist from Bucks County, on the Pennsylvania side of the Delaware, came to the house and gave Rall a note, telling him the Americans were crossing the river. Rall stuck the note in his pocket without reading it and went back to his card game.

At about 8 A.M. Washington's two columns came out of the whirling sleet and snow to attack both ends of the little town of 100 houses. The German pickets fell back, firing their muskets, shouting: "*Der Feind! Der Feind! Heraus!*" (The enemy! The enemy! Turn out!).

The three German regiments spilled from their barracks and tried to form a line of battle. But American artillery raked the two principal streets, and the infantrymen, ducking into houses, dried their priming pans and were soon shooting the Germans from windows and doorways.

For about an hour, the Germans fought bravely, at one time attempting a bayonet charge. But blasts of grapeshot from Henry Knox's cannon, two of them commanded by Captain Alexander Hamilton of New York, demoralized them. One regiment fled across nearby Assunpink Creek, followed by twenty British dragoons who had been stationed in Trenton. Sullivan's men seized the bridge, trapping the other two regiments in the town. Colonel Rall, befuddled by a hangover, gave incoherent orders until he was mortally wounded by grapeshot and carried into a nearby church. His soldiers threw down their guns and surrendered. The Americans took 868 officers and men prisoners of war. Another 106 Germans were killed or wounded. Between 300 and 400 of these elite troops escaped only by running for their lives. The Americans had only four men wounded, none killed. George Washington had finally won an unqualified, undebatable victory.

Should he follow up this triumph with an attack on other British outposts along the Delaware? Regretfully, Washington decided against it. The enemy in the vicinity outnumbered his

> "ONE OF THE MOST MISUNDERSTOOD THINGS ABOUT WASHINGTON IS THE IDEA THAT HE WAS A LACONIC, DISTANT MAN WHO DIDN'T KNOW HOW TO COMMUNICATE. HE WROTE STRONG, EFFECTIVE LETTERS. HE WROTE MORE LETTERS DURING THIS WAR TO PUBLIC OFFICIALS THAN HAVE EVER BEEN WRITTEN BY AN AMERICAN COMMANDER-IN-CHIEF IN TIME OF WAR."
>
> *Don Higginbotham*
> *Professor of History,*
> *University of North*
> *Carolina at Chapel Hill*

ABOVE *Wearing the uniform of the New York artillery in which he captained a battery, Alexander Hamilton broods beside an unidentified fortification. The young West Indian was soon invited to join George Washington's staff and swiftly became his most trusted aide.*

LEFT *Washington and his 2,400 men attacked Trenton about 8 A.M. on December 26, 1776. The enemy cannon were captured in a headlong charge led by Captain William Washington, the American commander's second cousin, and Lieutenant James Monroe, future President of the United States.*

troops—and his men were exhausted. It took most of the day to get the captured Germans and the wet, weary Americans back across the ice-choked Delaware. By the time the men returned to their tents on the other side of the river, they had been on their feet for thirty-six hours. One Connecticut captain asked for a dish of pudding. He fell asleep eating it and awoke the next day with the spoon still in his hand.

A Fine Fox Chase

At British headquarters in New Brunswick, all was shock and consternation. Beefy Major General James Grant, who had boasted he could march the length of the continent with 5,000 men, gasped: "I did not think that all the rebels in America would have taken that brigade prisoners." In New York William Howe ordered his most aggressive general, Charles, Lord Cornwallis, to pull his baggage off a homeward-bound ship and take command in New Jersey.

On December 30 Washington decided to recross the Delaware. Several thousand Pennsylvania militia, heartened by the victory at Trenton, had crossed the river south of the town and reported that the Germans at Burlington and nearby posts had fled. At Morristown and Springfield Continental generals had gathered several hundred New Jersey militia. Washington urged them to tell their men that "nothing is wanting but for them to lend a hand" to drive the enemy out of New Jersey.

But his own army posed an alarming question mark. On January 1, forty-eight hours away, most of his men were slated to go home. In Trenton, Washington ordered the regiments paraded and appealed to them personally to reenlist for another six weeks for a bounty of $10 per man. He admitted they had done "all I asked you to do and more than could be reasonably expected." But now their country's future was at stake. Every man who would stay and serve—step forward now.

The regimental drums rolled. Not a man moved. Washington rode down the line, asking, even pleading, for the men to stay. Friends exchanged glances. The total sincerity, the absolute commitment of the man before them reached deep into their souls. The drums beat again. One man stepped forward, then another. "I will stay if you will," said a man to a friend beside him. In a few minutes everyone except the invalids had volunteered.

Washington rushed a messenger to Robert Morris, the wealthiest merchant in Philadelphia, asking him to find $50,000 in Continental dollars to pay the bounty. He begged Morris to "borrow money where it can be done…upon our private credit." Even more urgently, he asked Morris to get him £150 in hard money to pay "a certain set of people who are of particular use to us."

Morris came through with the Continental dollars and with two canvas bags filled with 410 Spanish silver dollars and assorted other coins—totaling £124.7.6. Seven years later, when Washington was settling his accounts with

In this depiction by John Trumbull, the mortally wounded German commander, Colonel Johann Rall, surrenders to Washington at the close of the battle of Trenton. Rall ignored warnings from loyalists that the Americans were about to attack him. Washington smashed three German regiments, capturing 868 officers and men, including two military bands.

the Congress, he remembered the precise amount of this hard cash, "the time and circumstances of [its receipt] being too remarkable ever to be forgotten by me." It was needed to pay a spy or spies who were in the British camp at Princeton. By December 31 Washington had his hands on a map which told him where the British were quartered, the location of their artillery and other vital details.

On the last day of the year, Washington received a letter from the Congress informing him that he had been made a dictator for six months. The Congress was finally admitting they were not an assembly of generals. They gave Washington power to recruit a new army and to displace and appoint all officers below the rank of brigadier general. He could also confiscate supplies if the owners would not sell them and arrest anyone who would not take Continental money or was "disaffected" from the American cause.

Here was Washington's chance to become an American Oliver Cromwell. Instead he assured Robert Morris that he would constantly bear in mind that "the sword was the last resort for the preservation of our liberties, so it ought to be the first thing laid aside when those liberties are firmly established." It would be difficult, perhaps impossible, to choose George Washington's greatest contribution to the American republic. But this response should certainly rank near the top of any list. In his instinctive, pragmatic way, he was creating a workable compromise between the idea of civilian control of an army and the need for an army's leaders to have the autonomy to make command decisions that create victory. The essence of that crucial compromise has been built on Washington's example: mutual trust between citizen and soldier.

The British were planning to eliminate George Washington from any future role in American history. Lord Cornwallis arrived in Princeton on January 1. The next day he led 7,000 men down the road toward Trenton, leaving 1,200 men behind to protect his communications to the main British base in New Brunswick. Washington's Continentals skirmished briskly with the British column on the march. In Trenton the Royal Army found Americans blazing away at them from every window. Not until 4 P.M. did they clear the town—and realize that Washington's main army was on a hill on the other side of Assunpink Creek.

Cornwallis ordered his tired men to pitch their tents. Tomorrow morning would be time enough to "bag the fox," he told his staff. Brigadier William Erskine warned his Lordship that "if Washington is the general I think him to be, he will not be there tomorrow morning." Cornwallis scoffed and told his men to cook their suppers.

Where could Washington go? Cornwallis asked himself. If he tried to retreat across the Delaware, the rear half of his army could be smashed with ease. If he

ABOVE LEFT *Charles James Fox was a fervent supporter of the Americans. Unfortunately, politics was only one of his passions. He pursued two others, women and gambling, with equal energy. His father, Henry Fox, sacrificed much of his estate to raise £140,000 to pay his gambling debts.*

BELOW *This map of Princeton was sent to Washington by an American spy on December 31, 1776. Washington used it to plan his end run around the British army three days later.*

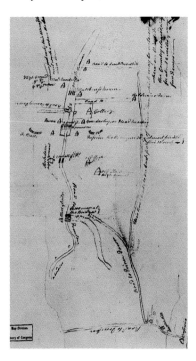

ABOVE *George Washington's stepgrandson, George Washington Parke Custis, painted this version of the American attack on Princeton. In the foreground are the dying General Mercer and Colonel John Haslet of Delaware, both killed in the battle's opening clash. Haslet had only four officers and two privates left in his regiment.*

retreated down the river on the New Jersey side, he was in a hopeless trap. It never occurred to Cornwallis that Washington was planning an attack.

As soon as darkness fell, Washington sent his baggage wagons and supplies south to Burlington. Thanks to spies and scouts, he knew there was a bridge several miles beyond the British left flank that led to a little-used "lower road" to Princeton. Washington was putting his army, an unstable mix of Continentals and Pennsylvania militia, between two British armies. But he would "avoid the appearance of a retreat." That, he later said, "was the one thing I was sure of." As for the danger of the army's being cut off, the new Washington, who lived on risk, coolly declared that was "unavoidable."

In each brigade, staff officers ordered regiments to build their campfires higher until there were several dozen veritable conflagrations blazing on the heights south of Assunpink Creek, convincing the British that the Americans were still there. Meanwhile, one by one, the regiments were ordered to fall in and march. Five hundred men were left behind to feed the fires throughout the night. As an afterthought, Washington told them to keep warm by clanging picks and shovels on the frozen earth. The noise convinced British sentries that the rebels were building earthworks against tomorrow's assault.

At dawn the American advance guard crossed Stony Brook bridge, three miles from Princeton. Buckets of rum were passed to the half-frozen men, and they formed two columns. The advance guard of one column collided with two British regiments marching to reinforce Cornwallis. A brisk battle erupted, with the British having the better of it until the rest of the column came up and Washington deployed them into line of battle.

He led them toward the British, who had taken cover behind a fence. At thirty yards Washington shouted: "Halt and fire." Both sides blasted full volleys. A cloud of gunsmoke enveloped the battlefield. One of Washington's aides put his hat in front of his eyes, certain that the general was dead. As the smoke cleared, the aide saw the big man still erect in the saddle.

The Americans swarmed around the British flanks. With the enemy outnumbered 5 to 1 and men falling fast, "a resolution was taken to retreat, i.e. run away as fast as we could," recalled one junior officer.

All warrior now, Washington joined the pursuit, memories of that insulting bugle call on Harlem Heights adding to his enthusiasm. "It's a fine fox chase, my boys," he roared, as vaunted British regulars littered the road with muskets, knapsacks and canteens in a style recently displayed by Americans. The rest of the British in Princeton swiftly surrendered or fled in the same helter-skelter fashion. Re-forming his men, Washington set fire to enemy magazines and headed east with 300 prisoners, while Cornwallis's red-faced troops huffed and puffed into the other end of the little village, "swearing at being so outwitted."

At New Brunswick was the main British supply depot, crammed with food, guns and ammunition—and a chest with £70,000 in hard money. To seize that money and destroy those stores and magazines might "put an end to the war," Washington thought. He sent horsemen racing off with orders to burn every bridge on the roads to New Brunswick except the ones he would use. But when Washington looked at his exhausted men, most of whom had eaten nothing since the previous morning, he began having second thoughts.

At Kingston the road forked, running on the right to New Brunswick and on the left to Morristown—high ground where his army would be relatively safe from British attack. With a sigh, Washington decided New Brunswick was beyond the strength of his men. He ordered the column to turn left. By the time he got to Morristown, his scouts and spies had assured him there was no need to worry about a British pursuit. Cornwallis had marched his army all night to reach New Brunswick, where he put the weary men in order of battle on the hills around the town. When no American attack materialized, the British realized they had been outfought, outgeneraled and—worst of all— made to look ridiculous.

The British high command decided it could no longer risk isolated garrisons. All troops were withdrawn to a fortified defensive line along the Raritan River. Instead of occupying New Jersey, the British soon barely controlled one-fifth of it. Elsewhere the American government was in charge. Washington, taking advantage of the political power the Congress had given him, issued a proclamation calling on all those who had accepted British pardons to visit the nearest American military post and swear allegiance to the United States. The Howes' dream of making New Jersey the first state to submit to the King's peace soon went glimmering.

Outside of New Jersey, the news of Trenton and Princeton had an electric effect on the morale of the infant United States. Loyalist Nicholas Cresswell, who had wandered from Virginia to New York and back to Virginia trying to avoid the war, wrote gloomily in his diary: "The minds of the people are much altered. A few days ago they had given up their cause for lost. Their late successes have turned the scale and they are all liberty mad again."

ABOVE **This version of the battle of Princeton was painted by William Mercer, the deaf-mute son of slain General Hugh Mercer. About 200 British retreated to Nassau Hall, the main building of the College of New Jersey (later Princeton). They quickly surrendered when American artillery opened fire on them.**

Year of the Hangman

Benedict Arnold's headlong charge at the second battle of Saratoga captured a key redoubt and made a British surrender inevitable. One of his soldiers called Arnold "as brave a man as ever lived."

"A sovereign cordial to the dying."

—Silas Deane

Benjamin Franklin arrives in France in search of guns and money. George III unleashes the Indians to aid General John Burgoyne's invasion from Canada. Benedict Arnold's battlefield heroics force "Gentleman Johnny" to surrender at Saratoga. Franklin signs a Treaty of Alliance with France. The Revolution becomes a world war.

While George Washington led his disintegrating army across New Jersey to his rendezvous with history at Trenton, Benjamin Franklin was taking a much longer journey aboard a ship whose name evoked the personal side of his war with George III. The *USS Reprisal* was carrying the seventy-year-old patriarch across the wintry Atlantic to France. His seemingly impossible mission: to persuade America's former enemy to become her ally in the war for liberty.

The day before he sailed, in words that remarkably echoed George Washington's on the eve of Trenton, Franklin wrote to a friend: "I hope our people will keep up their courage. I have no doubt of their finally succeeding by the blessing of God, nor have I any doubt that so good a cause will fail of that blessing."

Yet Franklin faced the freezing ocean with a heavy heart. His son, William,, the former royal governor of New Jersey, was still a prisoner in Connecticut. Franklin had decided to take William's son, William Temple Franklin, with him to France rather than leave him exposed to the appeals of his loyalist stepmother. This sad, fragile woman had written her father-in-law bitter reproaches for abandoning her to the untender mercies of rebel New Jerseyans. The loving family with whom Franklin had hoped to surround himself in his old age had been destroyed. Moreover, he feared his mission was a mistake. He did not want America to come to France as a supplicant.

In spite of his personal woes, Franklin's fighting spirit was undimmed. When the captain of the *Reprisal* spotted two British merchantmen as they approached the French coast, he asked Franklin for permission to seize them. The captain had strict orders to avoid all encounters with the enemy until he had deposited Franklin safely in France. Franklin all but ordered him to attack, and both ships surrendered without a shot. Prize crews were put aboard them, and Franklin had the satisfaction of arriving in France as a victorious if accidental admiral. It would not be his last performance in this role.

Franklin landed at the little fishing village of Auray, near Nantes, and

ABOVE *This powder horn was carried by a Revolutionary soldier.*

LEFT *Howard Pyle titled this vivid painting "The Nation Makers." It hangs in the Brandywine Battlefield Park Museum at Chadds Ford, Pennsylvania. It may portray a moment in the American defeat at Brandywine or in the equally frustrating battle of Germantown four weeks later.*

immediately fired off a letter to Silas Deane, the Connecticut politician who had been the Congress's representative in Paris for the previous eight months. Almost immediately, the British secret service, which had agents swarming through France, reported Franklin's arrival. Government-paid writers spread the rumor that he had fled the collapsing Revolution. Edmund Burke was among the many friends of America who refused to believe Franklin would "conclude a long life, which has brightened every hour it has continued, with so foul and dishonourable a flight." Burke's mentor, Lord Rockingham, agreed and remarked that getting Franklin to Paris was a bigger victory than the few acres of Manhattan and Long Island that General Howe had conquered.

As a member of the Congress's secret committee of foreign correspondence, Franklin was well aware that France had already funnelled a substantial amount of aid to the Americans. But when the bad news of Washington's defeats on Long Island and at Kips Bay arrived, the French foreign minister, Charles Gravier, the Count de Vergennes, did an abrupt about-face. He canceled the clearance papers of four ships loaded with war materiel and wrote an unctuous letter to the British ambassador, David Murray, Lord Stormont, congratulating him for "the success of British arms" in New York.

Franklin arrived in Paris on December 21, 1776. He was wearing a marten-fur hat he had acquired during his mission to Canada and had worn almost continuously in his freezing cabin aboard the *Reprisal*. His suit was plain brown broadcloth, without a single decoration. His shirt was an equally simple white. Minutes after he disappeared into Silas Deane's residence on the Rue de l'Université, Paris buzzed with news of his strange appearance. To the style-conscious French, it was incredible that the representative of a foreign state would appear in such a casual costume.

Franklin knew precisely what he was doing. His book, *The Way to Wealth*, a compilation of the sayings of Poor Richard, had been translated into French and had sold well among the tightfisted bourgeoisie. In his introduction, the

translator had portrayed Franklin as the supreme example of France's idealized vision of America, compounded from the writings of Voltaire and Rousseau.

Voltaire, the guiding spirit of the French *philosophes*, the apostles of modernization and enlightenment, pictured Pennsylvania as an idyllic world of social equality and religious toleration. At its center was the Good Quaker, whose simplicity of manners and style France, entangled in the rituals of aristocracy, conspicuously lacked. Rousseau extolled the supposed nobility of the savage, the purity of "primitive" Americans.

Franklin saw that these ideas, whether myths or facts, were a superb opportunity for him to dramatize America's cause. He made sure all his clothes were simple and plain—invariably topped by the marten-fur hat.

One excited Frenchman declared, "Everything about him announces the simplicity and innocence of primitive morals....The people clustered around as he passed and asked: 'Who is this old peasant who has such a noble air?' "

Meanwhile, at Silas Deane's residence, Franklin was talking hard facts with Deane and his secretary, Edward Bancroft, a Massachusetts man Franklin had met in London and recommended to Deane. They introduced him to two

ABOVE *Benjamin Franklin's fur hat enchanted the French man in the street—who thought it proved he was a simple American Quaker. Franklin did his best to maintain that illusion while outwitting the French and the British secret services.*

Frenchmen who had done a great deal to procure the secret aid France had already given the Americans. One was the swaggering, flamboyant playwright Caron de Beaumarchais, a former French foreign agent who claimed, with some reason, to have persuaded King Louis XVI to support the American cause to the tune of 2 million livres—about $500,000.

Franklin was more impressed with the second man, stocky, energetic Jacques Donatien Leray de Chaumont. Rich from trade in the East Indies, he had bought himself into the nobility—not hard to do in France—and had advanced Deane 1 million livres on his own credit. It was Chaumont who undertook the job of selling Franklin to the French people. He owned a ceramics factory, and within the week he was turning out thousands of terra-cotta medallions of Franklin wearing a fur hat. It was not Franklin's Canadian chapeau but a more famous (to the French) one worn by Rousseau.

While this publicity campaign unfolded, Franklin blithely assured the French that all this talk of British victories was nonsense. He claimed that, so far, the British had only gained a "footing" on two islands (Manhattan and Long Island). They had made no progress in invading the continent. In several skirmishes, the Americans had driven the British from the field. Unlike provincial Silas Deane, who had gone into frenzies when the French canceled their aid, Franklin had hobnobbed with the rulers of the British empire for twenty years. He had no illusions that statesmen were motivated by anything but national self-interest.

In his first meeting with the French foreign minister, Count de Vergennes, Franklin made it clear that America was not a beggar nation, forlornly hurling herself into the arms of France. She had an immensely profitable foreign trade that she was willing to divert from England to France by signing a commercial treaty. Franklin did not say a word about a military or diplomatic alliance—a tactic that left Vergennes dumbfounded.

Eight days later Franklin followed up this opening dance with a bold letter asking for eight fully manned ships of the line to help deal with Admiral Howe's fleet. He also dangled before Vergennes the promise of American military cooperation to help conquer the British West Indies after the war on the American continent was won. Next he politely inquired why the "private

ANOTHER KING, ANOTHER COUNTRY

Louis XVI had a good grasp of European dynastic diplomacy. But his judgement of men was poor and he knew nothing about military matters.

In 1777 twenty three-year-old Louis XVI was a popular King, largely because he was not his dissolute grandfather, Louis XV.

There were celebrations in the streets of Paris when the old King died in 1775. Not unlike George III, Louis XVI began his reign resolving to free his nation of the previous regime's corruption.

One of his first gestures was a gift of 200,000 livres to the Paris poor. He also renounced the *joyeux avenement* ("joyful accession"), a special grant usually given to the King on his coronation day to help him launch his reign in style. It had cost the French taxpayers 20 million livres for Louis XV. The new monarch's Queen, nineteen-year-old Marie Antoinette, renounced a similar gift. These gestures won cheers from Parisians.

Nonetheless, no ruler in Europe approached the splendor in which Louis XVI lived in his vast palace at Versailles. With its hundreds of servants, its swarms of courtiers, its elaborate rituals, the royal court was

an apotheosis of the absolute power the former King's great-grandfather, Louis XIV, had created in his drive to make France the ruler of Europe. Louis XVI's annual revenues were 500 million livres—the equivalent of $100 million or £20 million.

That was far more than George III's excise men collected for his royal purse, twice as much as the Austrian emperor's income, and three times the incomes of the crowns of Russia, Prussia or Spain. Yet such was the extravagance of Versailles and the ability of the aristocracy to wring gifts and favors from the King, the government ran an annual deficit of at least 37 million livres and owed more than 235 million livres on which it was paying outrageous interest.

France's finances were organized around the Farmers General, a corporate entity that was a state within the state. The Farmers advanced to the King the money he needed to keep Versailles functioning and the army, navy and other organs of government operating. In return for their cash, the King gave the Farmers the right to collect his taxes—at an enormous profit. There were sixty farmers plus hordes of croupiers, parasites who had attached themselves to the operation through various forms of political influence. Marquises and dentists were side by side with the nurse of the Duke of Burgundy, discarded mistresses of Louis XV, and a singer at Marie Antoinette's concerts, each clipping a few thousand livres.

The politics of Versailles were as complicated as the country's finances. Around the King's three royal aunts clustered a circle of cardinals, bishops and true believers (known as the *dévots*) who were convinced that all-out support of the Catholic Church was France's salvation.

Next came the spokesmen for the nobility, who fought to maintain aristocratic rights and privileges—especially the right not to pay taxes—against the rising bourgeoisie and the restless masses. Another circle had formed around Marie Antoinette,

who was determined to emulate her mother, Maria Theresa of Austria, one of the great politicians of the era. Finally there were the savants of the Englightenment, who wanted to break the grip of the Church on the mind of the masses and were convinced that rational thinking would set France on the path to greatness.

Trying to keep all these people happy, Louis XVI put together a government that was perpetually at odds with itself. His one creative gesture, which he seems to have made on his own, was the appointment of Baron Anne Robert Jacques Turgot as his minister of finance. A blunt, fiercely honest savant who was convinced that the future of France lay not in fighting England but in trading with her, Turgot announced plans to equalize the tax structure and eliminate the innumerable exemptions enjoyed by the nobility. He also abolished the trade guilds, which had become closed corporations, rife with nepotism.

Turgot was soon under attack from all quarters. The dévots called him an atheist because he did not go to mass. Marie Antoinette's circle called him a coward because he had cautioned Louis against getting into a war with England over the American Revolution. The aristocracy, hungry for a chance to regain France's tarnished glory, agreed with the Queen. Turgot defied them all. "The first gunshot will bankrupt the state," he warned the King.

Ironically, French Foreign Minister Charles Gravier, Count de Vergennes, was encouraged by the success of Turgot's reforms to give the Americans secret aid and consider forming an alliance with them. Turgot vehemently opposed this policy.

In the opening months of 1776, Vergennes sent Louis XVI a series of "Considerations"—state papers that argued France and Spain should begin rearming and take a more aggressive stance toward England without committing themselves to anything as reckless as a declaration of war. Marie

This idealized painting purports to be Benjamin Franklin's reception by Louis XVI and Marie Antoinette (seated on the sofa) after Franklin signed the treaty of alliance with France. It does show French esteem for Franklin—and the formidable influence of women in French politics.

Antoinette and her circle threw their influence behind this policy.

On May 10, 1776, Turgot journeyed to Versailles to see Louis XVI. "What do you want?" Louis said. "I have not time to see you."

The next day, when the minister of finance returned to Versailles, he was told the King was hunting. He called later in the day and was told the King was dressing. On May 12 a courtier informed Turgot that the King wanted his resignation.

Turgot fought back with one of his bluntest letters. He urged Louis to stop trying to please everyone: "Do not forget, Sire, that it was weakness that placed the head of Charles I [of England] on the block....It was weakness that led to all the unhappiness of the last reign." The King still demanded his resignation.

Mournfully, Turgot wrote a few days later to a friend: "I shall part with the regret of seeing a good dream disappear, of seeing a young King, who deserves a better fate, and a kingdom lost entirely by one who ought to have saved it." Turgot's dismissal made the Count de Vergennes, proponent of intervention in the English family quarrel, the most powerful man in the French government.

purchase made by Mr. Deane" had been canceled. He was referring to the four ships loaded with war materiel that Vergennes had stopped from sailing. If Deane was persona non grata for some reason, Franklin deadpanned, then he would undertake to buy in the name of Congress 20,000 or 30,000 muskets and a matching amount of ammunition and brass cannon, which he trusted Vergennes would send to America "under convoy."

Vergennes was too wary to commit a written response to this sudden advance. He sent his undersecretary to reply in person. The foreign minister sidestepped the wild proposals of eight ships of the line or goods sent by convoy. But he said King Louis XVI wanted to prove his good will to America. Henceforth, French ports would be open to American vessels in distress—an oblique way of saying privateers could seek safety in French waters—and Americans could buy arms and supplies on credit. The government would advance 3 million livres (about $600,000) to the Americans.

The French warnings to keep this aid secret were so severe that Franklin did not even tell the truth in a dispatch he wrote to the secret committee of foreign correspondence a few days later. He explained the loan as "the inclination of the wealthy to assist us." Unfortunately, the British ambassador in Paris, Lord Stormont, knew about the loan and every other detail of France's secret aid long before Congress heard about it. Edward Bancroft, Silas Deane's personal secretary, a man Franklin trusted implicitly, was a double agent, funneling information to London on everything the Americans in Paris were doing and saying—for £500 a year.

Enmeshed in such a web of duplicity, Franklin's mission would seem to have been doomed from the day he landed. But the wily old man was a step ahead of the British secret service. When a Philadelphia woman living in France warned him that the British had spies everywhere, he serenely revealed the tactics that were to frustrate George III and his £80,000-a-year intelligence payroll. His policy, he told the lady, was to be involved in no affairs he would "blush to be made public." If his French valet was a spy, "as he probably is," Franklin said he would not discharge him if he was satisfactory in other respects.

Franklin could afford to ignore George III's spies—and even use them against him. Vergennes might want to keep French aid a secret because he and his King were not yet sure the Americans were worth a war with England. But Franklin saw it was to his country's advantage if the English knew all about the aid. The more George III found out, the more likely would be an English declaration of war on France. Who did the declaring did not matter to Franklin. His mission was to get France into the war on the American side, the quicker the better. Already, with the new gift of 3 million livres, he had moved the French a step closer to this goal. Extracting this gesture of support in spite of the deluge of bad news from America was a tremendous achievement.

George III, Lord North and Lord George Germain read the reports of Edward Bancroft and their other agents and decided to say nothing about France's clandestine aid, which violated their solemn treaty of peace and amity with England. When the news of Trenton and Princeton reached Paris, in February 1777, Foreign Minister Vergennes gave permission for the four delayed ships, crammed with weapons and gunpowder, to sail. It was a blatantly hostile act, but the British ignored it, thereby admitting that a war with France

ABOVE *French Foreign Minister Count de Vergennes had no enthusiasm for backing the Americans as long as they looked like losers. He saw the Revolution as a chance to humble England.*

was the last thing they wanted. The North ministry also carefully avoided telling Parliament about France's secret tilt toward America

Along with the good news about Trenton came a letter from that hard-headed Philadelphia merchant Robert Morris, warning Franklin that from where he sat, the future looked ominous. The Continental dollar was depreciating, trade was at a standstill thanks to a tightening British blockade, Washington's army had all but disappeared, and there was alarming evidence that England was girding for a tremendous effort to end the war in 1777.

The Strategy of Contempt

In British-held New York, people were calling 1777 "the year of the hangman" because the three sevens were shaped like gallows. They saw it as an omen that meant Franklin, Washington, Adams, Jefferson and other rebel leaders would be swinging from a gibbet before the end of the year.

In Morristown General Washington's anxious letters to Congress sounded as if he agreed with the enemy. The Continental army numbered little more than 3,000 men. By now an expert at the disinformation game, Washington had distributed his thin regiments throughout the villages around Morristown to make them look three or four times more numerous. When an officer rushed into headquarters to report he had spotted a loyalist spy, Washington told him to invite the man to dinner and give him a chance to steal an "official" return of the American army, prepared personally by the commander-in-chief, reporting the Continentals at 12,000.

In spite of—even because of—his paltry numbers, Washington put on the boldest, most aggressive face for the benefit of the British army in New Jersey. Sentries in their camp around New Brunswick were constantly sniped at, and foraging parties were met by skirmishers who harassed them with volleys from woods and fences, killing and wounding dozens of officers and men. This aggressive activity—and similar rough tactics against the British camped near Kings Bridge, in northern Manhattan—had much to do with convincing the Howes that the rebellion was very much alive.

Congress, still meeting in distant Baltimore, was woefully out of touch. In February, when Washington was begging the state governors to send him enough men to make a stand against a British army that numbered 27,000 men, John Adams wrote to Major General John Sullivan: "Are we to go on forever this way, maintaining vast armies in idleness and losing completely the fairest opportunity that was ever offered of destroying an enemy completely in our power?"

Ironically, loyalists in New York were soon saying similar things about Sir William Howe (George III had made him and Henry Clinton Knights of the Bath for the victory on Long Island). The general seemed in no hurry to begin the campaign. Howe had acquired a mistress, the attractive blond wife of his commissary of prisoners, Bostonian Joshua Loring Jr. Like their friends the Hutchinsons and Olivers, Loring and his family had enjoyed cushy government jobs. On April 19, 1775, when Joshua Sr. heard of Lexington and Concord, he reportedly said he had "always eat[en] the King's bread and I always intend to." When General Howe retreated from Boston, the Lorings went with him. Whether Mrs. Loring was enthralled with Sir William is open to some doubt. A commissary got a percentage of the money he spent. The man who approved or disapproved his possibly dubious bookkeeping was the army's commander. It was worthwhile for both husband and wife to keep General Howe in a positive frame of mind.

The more critical loyalists were soon singing a sarcastic song:

Awake, awake Sir Billy,
There's forage on the plain
Oh leave your little filly
And open the campaign

It was not Mrs. Loring who was distracting Sir William. It was the galling memories of Trenton—and the knowledge that his role as the conqueror of America had been seized by General John Burgoyne. That handsome, self-assured soldier had gone back to London after the failure of the Canadian army to take Fort Ticonderoga and had persuaded the King and Lord George Germain to give him command of that army, relegating Governor-General Guy Carleton to the status of a spectator. Germain was more than agreeable. The American secretary hated Carleton because he had served on the court-martial

LEFT *"Gentleman Johnny" Burgoyne had distinguished himself as a cavalry leader in Portugal, fighting the Spanish in the 1760s. One English historian summed him up as "vain, boastful and superficial." But he was courageous in battle.*

board that had found Germain guilty in 1759. Lord George was also not averse to making the Howes and their attempts to reconcile the Americans look bad in comparison with Burgoyne's hard-line approach. George III was enchanted by the confidence Burgoyne exuded. It was a refreshing contrast to the gloomy letters the Howes sent home.

Burgoyne's proposal called for a descent from Canada down Lake Champlain with an army of 8,000 regulars, bolstered by 2,000 Canadians and 1,000 Indians. A smaller force under Lieutenant Colonel Barry St. Leger would come down the Mohawk Valley with more Indians to siphon potential American support from that populous region. At Albany the two forces would unite with William Howe's army, cut off New England—the heart of the rebellion—from the rest of the colonies and, if the Yankees continued to resist, lay it waste.

George III participated in the planning of this operation down to the most minute details. He shaved Burgoyne's regular force to 7,000 and recommended adding 400 German *chasseurs* (light infantry) to St. Leger's force. Revealing a usually well-concealed loyalty to his Teutonic ancestors, the King added tartly that Burgoyne seemed to "undervalue" the "German recruits" who would compose half his army. "Indians must be employed," George added, underlining the sentence for emphasis. The patriot King no longer had a shred of compassion for his rebellious American subjects.

While Burgoyne was obtaining George III's blessing, Sir William Howe was evolving a plan to capture Philadelphia and erase the blot of Trenton and Princeton. This victory would encourage the thousands of loyalists that Howe firmly believed still existed in New Jersey and Pennsylvania to flock to the royal standard. As for Burgoyne's campaign, Howe made it clear that it was no more than a speck on his maps. When Burgoyne got to Albany, Howe would decide on subsequent operations, depending "on the state of things at the time."

Lord George Germain, the man in charge of overall planning, approved both campaigns. His ignorance of America—and his contempt for Americans—had been noted by Sir Henry Clinton when that general, also home on leave, had visited the American secretary. Germain thought Howe could capture Philadelphia and then march his army to Albany to meet Burgoyne as if George Washington and his Continentals did not exist. As Sir John Fortescue, the historian of the British army, later put it: "Never was there a finer example of the art of organizing disaster."

A March to Nowhere

Finally abandoning the charms of Mrs. Loring, Sir William Howe led his army into New Jersey on June 17, 1777. Bolstered by reinforcements of nearly 7,000 men, he sent a strong force down the road to Philadelphia, hoping that Washington, in the hills to the north, would come down to the flat country and fight. But Washington's army was still too small—little more than 9,000 men—and he was determined to hew to his strategy of avoiding a general action. Howe was just as determined not to attack Americans on hills, so the two armies did little or nothing for several days.

On June 21, to Washington's amazement, the British began retreating. Howe had decided he could not advance across New Jersey and leave Washington behind him to strike his line of march. A remarkable turnout of the revived New Jersey militia—which created "ambuscades," as one rueful staff officer called them, all around the British camp—and word of thousands of Pennsylvania militiamen guarding the banks of the Delaware may have influenced this decision. To Washington's further amazement, the British soon evacuated all of New Jersey. His spies informed him that Admiral Howe was watering his ships and preparing the entire fleet for a voyage. Where were they going? Up the Hudson? Into the Atlantic to attack Philadelphia via the Delaware? A distressed Washington did not know.

Then came news that momentarily made Howe's destination unimportant. General John Burgoyne and his army had captured Fort Ticonderoga! Washington was filled with "chagrin and surprise." The news filled Congress and thousands of other Americans with panic. Everyone assumed that the Northern army had used the year of grace Benedict Arnold won for them with his Lake Champlain fleet to make the Gibraltar of America impregnable.

Here Comes Gentleman Johnny

The reality of the Northern army was grimly visible in a report on its ten Continental regiments that the army's adjutant general made to Major General Arthur St. Clair on June 17, 1777. Only twenty-three men in Colonel Seth Warner's regiment had bayonets. The regiment commanded by Colonel Nathan Hale (no relation to the hero spy) was minus 264 powder horns and 334 priming wires. All the regiments were pathetically under strength. Warner had only 173 men instead of 640. Another regiment had dwindled to 85. Overall, the regiments were short 3,506 enlisted men and proportionate numbers of officers.

With barely 1,576 Continentals and two regiments of militia—about 900 men—newly arrived for three months' duty, St. Clair was supposed to defend not only Fort Ticonderoga but also an even more extensive unfinished work, Fort Independence, on a height across the narrow neck of water connecting the two parts of Lake Champlain. If St. Clair put every man in his army on the lines, he would have only one soldier per yard of front—and not a musket in reserve. Worse, a number of outlying redoubts covering Ticonderoga's exposed northwest flank would have to be abandoned.

The Scottish-born, forty-year-old St. Clair (pronounced Sinclair), a former British lieutenant who had distinguished himself at Quebec in the French and Indian War, had arrived at the fort on June 12. He replaced Major General Horatio Gates, who had retreated to Philadelphia to continue his quarrel with Philip Schuyler, the commanding general in the northern department. Brigadier General Benedict Arnold, who should have replaced Gates, was sulking in Connecticut. Congress had promoted St. Clair and four other brigadiers to major general but ignored Arnold because Connecticut already had its share of men at this rank.

Descending Lake Champlain as St. Clair nervously read his adjutant's report was General Burgoyne's army of 7,586 fighting men backed by a fleet of gunboats and pinnaces manned by 700 Royal Navy sailors. His men were confident that "Gentleman Johnny" (a term of respect and affection because he treated them well) was going to lead them to the victory that would crush the rebellion. In canoes beside the 260 bateaux carrying His Majesty's rank and file paddled hundreds of war-painted Indians eager to collect a bonanza in American scalps.

Incredibly, no one in the American army—or Congress, for that matter—believed in the existence of this imposing force. American attempts to scout into Canada had been frustrated by the screen of Indians the British spread along the border. The Americans remained convinced that the main British army of 27,000 men under Sir William Howe would soon sally from New York to attack Philadelphia—and Burgoyne, who they knew was in Canada, would assemble every man who could be spared from the defense of that colony and sail south to join him.

Even when Burgoyne's fleet and army appeared in full view from Ticonderoga's ramparts on June 30, St. Clair refused to take them seriously, maintaining that the display of armed might was a feint. Not until his pickets clashed with a British patrol and captured an Irish soldier, who told them in convincing detail the size of the British host, did the Americans realize they were in imminent danger of annihilation.

St. Clair spent the next three days in an agony of indecision. In memoirs written decades later, Assistant Adjutant General James Wilkinson said he "lacked the resolution to give up the place, or in other words to sacrifice his character for the public good." The remark pithily, if heartlessly, summed up St. Clair's dilemma. He was acutely aware his reputation would never recover if he retreated. But he was also aware the Continentals under his command were precious assets that could not be replaced.

As the British began surrounding the fort, St. Clair convinced himself that they planned an immediate assault. He toyed with the possibility of replicating Bunker Hill in the northern woods. But General Burgoyne had no intention of repeating the mistakes made at that by-now-legendary battle. On July 4 his engineering officer, a lieutenant named Twiss, slogged to the top of an outlying hill called Sugar Loaf. Several American engineers had urged previous commanders of Ticonderoga to fortify it, because cannon could fire into the fort from its 750-foot-high crest. But shortages of men and equipment—and the complacent assumption that no one could drag a cannon up its steep, forested slope—left it exposed to an enterprising enemy.

By July 5 the extremely enterprising Twiss had two twelve-pounders on top of Sugar Loaf, firing at vessels in the narrows between Ticonderoga and Fort Independence. St. Clair took one look and said, as reported in the stilted style of Wilkinson's memoirs: "We must away from this because our situation has become desperate." We can be fairly sure this bluff soldier's actual words were a lot more graphic. At a hastily convened council of war, his brigadier generals agreed that retreat was the only option.

The painful decision revealed the generals had learned one of the fundamental lessons Washington derived from the disasters of 1776. They were no longer fighting a "war of posts": forts, even cities, should be sacrificed to the

ABOVE *Unlucky Major General Arthur St. Clair surrendered Fort Ticonderoga to save his Continentals from capture. He was execrated by the Continental Congress and almost everyone else, but he retained Washington's confidence.*

all-important task of preserving an army to look the enemy in the face.

Piling ammunition and stores, along with numerous sick soldiers, into a fleet of 200 bateaux and sloops, 600 Continentals sailed that night for Skenesborough, now Whitehall, at the narrow southern end of Lake Champlain. The 900 militia and the rest of the Continentals retreated with St. Clair down a rough road cut through the forest toward the same destination. In the confusion, they almost left 1,000 men in Fort Independence, because their brigadier got drunk and forgot to pass along the evacuation order.

The Continental rank and file, most of them New Englanders, remained confirmed Bunker Hillists. They wanted to fight it out on Fort Ti's ramparts. "Such a retreat was never heard of since the creation of the world," wrote one fuming New Hampshire soldier. "I could scarcely believe my informant was in earnest," recalled Dr. James Thacher of Massachusetts, who was awakened at midnight with the news that it was time to flee.

In Ticonderoga St. Clair had left four artillerymen manning a battery of guns loaded with grapeshot, trained on the bridge between the two forts. These ambushers had orders to fire the guns and run when a sufficient number of British went to work on repairing the bridge, in which the Americans had hastily chopped some large holes. The British methodically replanked the bridge without a shot being fired. Mounting Ticonderoga's ramparts, they found the four heroic gunners dead drunk beside a case of Madeira.

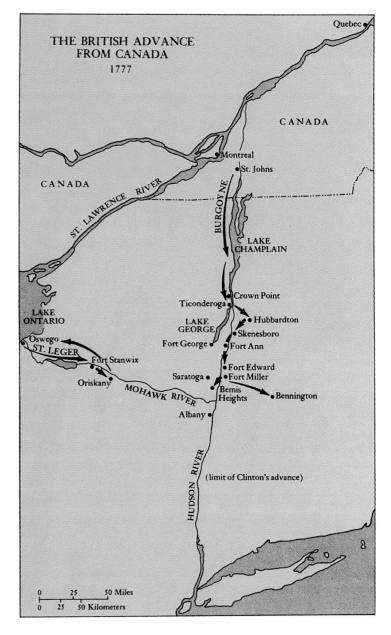

ABOVE *This map underscores the dangerous distance Burgoyne traveled from his Canadian base during his invasion of northern New York.*

Not All Poltroons

No wonder British confidence soared. Burgoyne immediately ordered the 850-man British light-infantry battalion, commanded by another enterprising soldier, Brigadier Simon Fraser, to pursue the retreating Americans. On July 6, in hot, humid weather, they marched at a killing pace from 4 A.M. until 4 P.M. Not far behind them slogged 1,280 German troops under aggressive Major General Baron Friedrich Adolf von Riedesel. The British scooped up another twenty drunkards and assorted other stragglers along the rutted road. From them they got a good idea of the size of the American rear guard, which consisted of Colonel Ebenezer Francis's Eleventh Massachusetts Regiment, reinforced by picked companies from the rest of St. Clair's army.

The Americans retreated at a frantic pace. One man said they "hurled thro' the woods at 35 miles a day...oblidged to kill oxen belonging to the inhabitants wherever we got them; before they were half-skinned every soldier was oblidged to take a bit and roast it over the fire, then before half done oblidged to march...." In Hubbardton, a "town" of exactly two houses, St. Clair paused to let Colonel Francis catch up with him. When Francis did not materialize, the harried general left Colonel Seth Warner and his regiment with orders to reinforce Francis and join the main army at Castleton, six miles down the road. When Francis finally showed up, he had with him more than 500 sick stragglers, guarded by Colonel Nathan Hale's New Hampshire regiment. Recently recovered from the measles, the convalescents were utterly exhausted by the pace of the retreat. As the senior officer, Warner decided to spend the night in Hubbardton.

Although they knew the British were pursuing them, Hale's men, who camped closest to the enemy, posted only one sentry. Arising at 3 A.M. on July 7, Fraser's light infantry reached the American camp at dawn and routed Hale's regiment and the invalids as they were cooking breakfast. But Warner's and Francis's regiments gave Fraser's men a very different reception. A brawny New Hampshireman, Warner had commanded the rear guard on the retreat from Canada in 1776 and knew his business. Posting most of his men behind log barricades on high ground, he cut down twenty-one attackers as they came up the steep slope. Among the victims was a British major who made the mistake of climbing onto a fallen tree to reconnoiter the position.

A ferocious firefight erupted along a half-mile front. Fraser expertly shifted men to the right to envelop the American left flank. Francis promptly demonstrated that the Continentals had learned some tactics in two years of warfare by attacking the British left. For a while the battle seesawed, with muskets crashing and gunsmoke billowing through the woods and men falling fast on both sides.

In Castleton the gunfire made St. Clair wonder if he should march to Warner's rescue. Finding no enthusiasm for the idea among his brigadiers, the general contented himself with dispatching aides to order the two militia regiments, who were camped several miles closer to Hubbardton, to support the embattled rear guard. The aides met the militiamen on the road and barely avoided being trampled by the amateurs' mad rush to put as much distance as possible between themselves and the shooting.

On the battlefield the British were growing panicky in the face of the ferocious American resistance. Suddenly through the booming musketry came the astonishing sound of a military band. Baron von Riedesel had arrived with a 180-man-advance guard; he struck up the band to make the Americans think he was leading a brigade. Some of his men were Jäger (huntsmen) armed with short, accurate rifles and the training to counter the Americans' woodland tactics.

The Germans swiftly enveloped Francis's flanks and, when the Yankee colonel tried to rally his men, they cut him down with a bullet to his heart. His shaken soldiers scattered into the woods, and a chagrined Warner ordered his New Hampshiremen to do likewise. Colonel Hale, still trying to protect his measles victims, surrendered with 270 of them soon after the firing ceased.

The two-hour clash ended British thoughts of hot pursuit by land. Fraser had lost roughly 21 percent of his light infantry; 50 men had been killed and 134 wounded. The small German detachment, in action only a few minutes, had lost 13 percent of its men. American casualties were 41 dead and 91 wounded, plus 324 captured, most of them invalids. One British officer confided to his journal that the light infantry had discovered "neither were they invincible nor the rebels all poltroons."

Is It Time to Shoot a General?

The British check at Hubbardton was soon obscured by a sensational success on the water. The American fleet had cruised down Lake Champlain, enjoying band music and a bit of tippling, secure in the illusion that the entrance to the lower part of the lake was blocked by a sturdy bridge and a massive chain across the narrows. But Royal Navy sailors chopped down the bridge and broke the chain with a few well-placed cannon balls. Descending on the dismayed Americans at Skenesborough, the British captured most of their fleet and forced them to abandon all their cannon and staggering amounts of flour and salted meats. At Fort Edward a mortified St. Clair found a distraught Major General Philip Schuyler with a paltry 700 Continentals and 1,400 jittery militia—the sum total of the Northern army's reserve.

When George III heard the news of Ticonderoga's fall, followed by the apparent rout at Hubbardton and the debacle at Skenesborough, he rushed into Queen Charlotte's bedroom shouting: "I have beat them all, beat all the Americans!" Congressman John Adams, equally overwrought, told Abigail: "I think we shall never defend a post until we shoot a general."

The crisis came close to unraveling the normally steady Schuyler. The enemy, he told Washington, was "flushed with victory, plentifully provided with provisions, cannon and every warlike store" while the Americans were "dispirited, naked...without camp equipage, with little ammunition and not a single cannon." At dilapidated Fort Edward, the disgruntled Ticonderoga fugitives began accusing Generals Schuyler and St. Clair of treason. They claimed the British had fired "silver balls" from their cannon into the fort to bribe them.

In Philadelphia Major General Horatio Gates, warmly supported by New England delegates, trumpeted his detestation of Schuyler, who owned thousands of prime acres along the Hudson and Mohawk rivers and found it hard to practice the crude and often rude democracy favored by the Yankees. Nevertheless, there were few men who made a larger contribution to the American cause. Schuyler's skillful diplomacy kept most of the Iroquois neutral for the first years of the war. Without his talents for organization and supply, the Northern army would have long since collapsed.

Schuyler was soon reporting more bad news to Washington: "A very great proportion of the [local] inhabitants are taking protection from General Burgoyne." Gentleman Johnny, who fancied himself a gifted writer— he had had several plays produced in London—had issued an orotund proclamation, warning the Americans in his path that if their "phrenzy of hostility should remain," he would execute "the Vengeance of the State against the wilful outcast." Many civilians decided to swear allegiance to the King and

ABOVE *English-born General Horatio Gates politicked in Congress to obtain command of the Northern American army. Later he would scheme to depose Washington as commander-in-chief.*

BELOW LEFT *Some historians consider Philip Schuyler the most underrated American general of the Revolution. He was a superb organizer and Indian diplomat.*

accept a certificate guaranteeing their safety. They would soon learn that Burgoyne's Indians were not interested in reading documents.

Even more worrisome to Schuyler were the 1,800 regulars, Indians and loyalists under the leadership of Lieutenant Colonel Barry St. Leger, who had sailed across Lake Ontario and marched on Fort Stanwix, the bastion that guarded the Mohawk River Valley. As the British foresaw, their presence made it impossible to raise any militia from this region to defend the Hudson River Valley from Burgoyne. Thanks to Schuyler's foresight, however, Fort Stanwix had been rebuilt earlier in the year and garrisoned with 650 Continentals. They were commanded by two tough, savvy New Yorkers, Colonel Peter Gansevoort and Lieutenant Colonel Marinus Willet, who defiantly declined St. Leger's invitation to surrender.

What to do? Washington's first instinct was to dispatch the man who had already saved the northern frontier once, Benedict Arnold, to Schuyler's aid. He also sent a newly minted major general, Benjamin Lincoln of Massachusetts, who had wide experience commanding New England's cantankerous militia. Congress added its mite by finally promoting Arnold to major general, though still leaving him junior to those previously elevated, presumably to teach him a lesson in humility. The politicians also fired Schuyler and St. Clair and appointed Horatio Gates the commander of everything north of Albany.

Washington debated marching his army through a Hudson Highlands pass known as the Clove to West Point. He and everyone on his staff assumed the

BELOW *Americans tried to slow Burgoyne's invasion with scorched-earth tactics. Here, the wife of General Philip Schuyler burns the family's wheat. Schuyler also deployed axmen to cut down trees and destroy bridges in Burgoyne's path.*

ABOVE *Fort Stanwix's 650-man garrison guarded the Mohawk Valley. They were besieged by a mixed force of British, Germans and Indians. When the British demanded surrender, the American commander, Colonel Peter Gansevoort, said he was determined to hold the fort "at every hazard, to the last extremity."*

British commander-in-chief, Sir William Howe, planned to fight his way up the Hudson and meet Burgoyne in a pincer movement designed to cut off militant New England from the rest of the colonies. On July 24 Washington had most of his army in the Clove when he received the amazing news that the British fleet, with General Howe and most of the main Royal Army aboard, had put to sea and was last seen heading south. On July 27 they were spotted off Egg Harbor, New Jersey. A bewildered Washington turned his footsore soldiers around and headed for Philadelphia. "Howe's in a manner abandoning Burgoyne," he wrote to Horatio Gates, "is so unaccountable a matter that…I cannot help casting my eyes continually behind me."

Gentleman Johnny vs. Granny Gates

The Americans were only beginning to discern the rivalries dividing the British high command. Horatio Gates was one of the few generals on the American side who understood this tangled psychology. Nothing else explains the eagerness with which he sought the seemingly thankless job of commanding the Northern army. Gray-haired, ruddy-faced, with thick spectacles that often slid down his long, pointed nose to give him an old-womanish look, the fifty-year-old Gates had an odd nickname for a soldier: "Granny." The son of a Duke's housekeeper, he had risen to major in the Royal Army thanks to his talent as a staff officer. Frustrated by his failure to advance beyond that rank, he moved to Virginia and ingratiated himself with George Washington, among others. As the American army's first adjutant general in 1775, he had proved himself an invaluable organizer and administrator.

Gates's combat experience was almost zero—about fifteen minutes in General Braddock's 1755 debacle, before he was struck down by an Indian bullet. In the attack on Trenton on Christmas night 1776, Washington had offered Gates command of the right wing. He had excused himself for reasons of "health" and rushed to Baltimore to lobby Congress for command of the Northern army.

Yankees in the Northern army ignored Gates's shortcomings and attributed to him near miraculous powers. One declared his mere arrival in Albany lifted them from "this miserable state of despondency and terror." Unquestionably, getting rid of Schuyler and St. Clair eliminated the paranoia in the New England Continental regiments. Gates also benefited from Burgoyne's decision to rebuild a twenty-three-mile road through the forest from Skenesborough to Fort Edward, a task that consumed three weeks and gave the rattled Americans time to regroup.

Schuyler skillfully impeded Burgoyne's progress, putting 1,000 axmen to work felling huge pines and hemlocks in his path and destroying some forty bridges over numerous creeks and ravines. Burgoyne dispatched neither his Indians nor his light infantry to deal with this scorched-earth policy. Relaxing in the fine stone house of Philip Skene, the principle citizen of Skenesborough, Gentleman Johnny enjoyed the wife of his commissary à la Sir William Howe and remained euphoric over the easy capture of Ticonderoga.

Still another reason that American morale rebounded was a resupply of cannon. Some had come from Washington's army, others from Portsmouth, where a French ship had slipped through the British blockade with thousands of muskets and other war materiel, including fifty-eight brass cannon. Schuyler had requisitioned a half-dozen. Thanks to his efforts, by mid-September, the Northern army had twenty-two big guns.

Gates was also the beneficiary of the first good news the Northern army had received in a long time. In the Mowhawk Valley 800 militiamen marching to relieve Fort Stanwix had fought a bloody drawn battle with Barry St. Leger's army at Oriskany, inflicting heavy casualties on his Indian allies. On Burgoyne's eastern flank, 1500 Germans he had dispatched to seize stores and horses in Bennington had been virtually destroyed by New Hampshire militia under Colonel John Stark and Continentals led by Seth Warner.

Death in the Forest

To the settlers of the Mohawk Valley, Oriskany was not good news. It demonstrated the things that could go wrong when militia operated on their own. The militia commander, Nicholas Herkimer, sent four messengers ahead of his column, asking the Continentals at Fort Stanwix to fire three cannon and sortie to join his men in attacking St. Leger's army. When two days passed with no cannon shots, Herkimer's subordinates urged him to attack anyway—and accused him of cowardice when he balked. The infuriated Herkimer led them forward—to disaster.

St. Leger dispatched 400 Indians and an assortment of loyalists and Canadians to ambush the militiamen as they entered a deep, thickly wooded ravine that was so swampy it could only be crossed on a narrow road. At the shriek of a loyalist ranger's whistle, the Indians opened up on the mile-long column from the front and flanks. All the field-grade officers were killed or wounded in the first volley, and the 200-man rear guard ran away. But Herkimer, his leg shattered by a bullet, managed to rally the survivors, and for the next six hours one of the most sanguinary battles of the war raged. Finally St. Leger's Indians pulled out, leaving at least 100 dead on the battlefield. Herkimer died of his wound, and the surviving militia, their morale shattered by their losses, retreated to their homes.

At Fort Stanwix Lieutenant Colonel Marinus Willet sortied when he heard the gunfire from Oriskany and plundered the thinly defended enemy camp, returning with twenty-one wagons loaded with food, ammunition and weapons. St. Leger's Indians were dismayed when they returned from Oriskany to find their tepees stripped of everything from their deerskin beds to their sacred medicine bundles, which supposedly protected them in battle. Already disheartened by their losses, they had little enthusiasm for continuing the siege. But St. Leger's oratory and promises of scalps and presents persuaded them to stay with him—which meant the men inside Stanwix could expect no mercy from the final storming party.

John Stark to the Rescue Again

The battle of Bennington showed what militia could accomplish when they were led by an able officer such as John Stark. The hero of Bunker Hill had resigned from the Continental army at the close of 1776 when he was not promoted to brigadier general. This providential fit of pique put him in New Hampshire at exactly the right moment to turn out the militia and fight a brilliant battle against Burgoyne's befuddled Germans—who never should have been sent on the expedition in the first place.

Burgoyne fretted over an acute shortage of horses. Only one-third of those promised him by the Canadians had been delivered, and the result was constant headaches and slowdowns in feeding his men and transporting his heavy cannon over the atrocious roads of northern New York. He decided to remedy matters by sending Colonel Friedrich Baum, commander of the Brunswick dragoons, to find horses, apparently on the theory that he needed them more than anyone else in the army. His 250 dragoons had all been reduced to foot-soldiers by the shortage.

Baum commanded some 374 Germans, 300 loyalists and Canadians, and a sprinkling of Indians. His orders were an amazing hash of instructions to seize hostages; impose taxes; collect cattle, horses, bridles and saddles; and tell everyone he was the advance guard of an army marching on Boston. Burgoyne must have written them while he was drunk. Although Burgoyne's German counterpart, Baron von Riedesel, warned him of the danger, Gentleman Johnny remained blithely unconcerned that he was sending Baum, who could not speak English, twenty-five miles from the main army into a countryside rife with potential enemies.

In Manchester, New Hampshire, meanwhile, Major General Benjamin

BELOW *Militia general Nicholas Herkimer's column was ambushed by Indians and Canadians at Oriskany, in the Mohawk Valley. Fighting from behind trees, his men inflicted heavy casualties on the Indians. Herkimer's leg was amputated ten days later. He died reading aloud the Thirty-ninth Psalm.*

BIRTH OF THE STARS AND STRIPES

This painting commemorates Betsy Ross's mythical presentation of the first flag to George Washington.

On June 14, 1777, there appeared in the *Journal of Congress* the terse entry: "Resolved that the flag of the U.S. be 13 stripes alternate red and white and the union be 13 stars in a blue field, representing a new constellation."

There was no mention of any debate about this choice, or the names of the persons responsible for the design.

A hundred years later, the descendants of Elizabeth Griscom Ross, wife of a Philadelphia upholstery maker, announced that she had designed the national banner at the request of George Washington. Historians have declined to take the story seriously, which has left us with the mystery of who created the flag.

After the war Francis Hopkinson, the witty Philadelphia poet and patriot, asked Congress for "a quarter of a cask of public wine" in payment for his role in the birth of the flag. The legislators declined to take him seriously—and he may in fact have been joking.

The origin of the design is not hard to deduce. Before the Declaration of Independence, Washington's army flew the Grand Union flag—thirteen red and white stripes with the crosses of St. George and St. Andrew in the upper left corner.

Congress replaced the latter symbol of loyalty to George III with the thirteen stars of the newly united states. The flag resolution, which appeared as a sort of parenthesis in the midst of matters pertaining to the Continental navy, was probably intended to create a banner for use on American men-of-war.

But as late as 1779, Richard Peters, secretary of the Board of War, wrote: "It is not yet settled what is the standard of the United States." The flag seems to have progressed from sea to land. In paintings of the British surrender at Yorktown in 1781, the Stars and Stripes flies proudly over the American tents.

Lincoln was trying to turn out all the militia he could find and harass Burgoyne's flank and rear. Lincoln had gathered only 500 militiamen and Seth Warner's regrouped Continental regiment of 140 men when Stark appeared with 1,500 men, many of them veterans who had followed him from Bunker Hill into the Continental army for 1776. At the head of the column they carried their version of the new American flag, with thirteen stripes and a large "76" in the center of an arch of eleven stars, and two more stars in the top corners of the field.

Ex-Colonel Stark declined to take any orders from Major General Lincoln, who urged him to join the Northern army. Refusing to be offended by Stark's crustiness, Lincoln agreed to let him fight his own war, which brought Stark to Bennington in response to cries of alarm about the depredations of the Indians in Baum's force.

The German sent a horseman back to Burgoyne, asking for reinforcements. Gentleman Johnny dispatched a hulking martinet, Lieutenant Colonel Heinrich von Breymann, with 800 men, most of them Germans. Baum meanwhile entrenched on high ground above the Walloomasac River, outside Bennington, scattering his small command all over the landscape. Some men were a half-mile from the main redoubt, where he planted himself and his dragoons. On August 16 Stark attacked Baum from four sides and swiftly overran the isolated outposts of loyalists and Canadians. The Indians fled, but Baum's dragoons stood their ground until they ran out of ammunition. Against odds of 8 to 1, they tried to cut their way to safety with their swords. They were doing fairly well until their leader went down with a mortal wound. At that point, they surrendered.

With half his little army chasing fugitives through the woods, Stark was horrified to discover that Lieutenant Colonel Breymann and his reinforcements were almost on top of him. For a while, the battle seesawed, much like Hubbardton. As the American line wavered, down the road came Seth Warner's Continentals, backed by some 200 Green Mountain Boys. They hit both of Breymann's flanks, and the Germans crumbled. Breymann tried to organize an orderly retreat, but it soon turned into a near rout. Only darkness enabled him to escape with about two-thirds of his command.

Bennington cost Burgoyne more than 1,000 men. But it did not produce a tidal wave of militiamen eager to help the Northern army finish off the staggered foe. Instead Stark and his followers picked up their guns and their flag and went home.

The Murder of Jane McCrea

At this point we encounter the sad, confusing story of Jane McCrea. As Burgoyne advanced on Fort Edward, Schuyler retreated, leaving behind only a small picket guard to report the enemy's movements. On July 27, two days before the British reached the fort, a party of Indians attacked the place. The picket guard fled, and in the cellar of a nearby house the Indians discovered twenty-three-year-old Jane McCrea, who greeted them warmly and made it clear that she was a friend.

The daughter of a New Jersey Presbyterian minister, McCrea was engaged to a loyalist, Lieutenant David Jones, who had joined Burgoyne's army. He and his brother had raised a company of sixty fellow loyalists to support the royal cause. McCrea had journeyed to Fort Edward to meet Jones. Some historians have described her as a beauty with dark hair a yard and a quarter long; others have portrayed her "clustering curls of soft blonde hair." James Wilkinson, the Northern army's assistant adjutant general, said in his memoirs that she was "a country girl…without either beauty or accomplishment."

As the Indians led McCrea away on a captured horse, they began arguing about who should have the privilege of delivering her to Lieutenant Jones and collecting an expected reward. In a fury, one of the Indians, Wyandot Panther, shot McCrea off her horse and scalped her to collect the bounty Burgoyne was paying for American scalps.

In Burgoyne's camp, a distraught David Jones accused Wyandot Panther of murdering his fiancée. Gentleman Johnny demanded that the Indians surrender the killer for trial and possible execution. The Indians threatened to go home en masse, and Burgoyne backed down. Horatio Gates, undeterred by the murdered woman's loyalist leanings, decided to make propaganda out of her death. He wrote a letter to Burgoyne that was designed to get under his skin and arouse American militia to join the Northern army.

Gates asked how "the famous Lieutenant General Burgoyne, in whom the fine gentleman is united with the scholar" could "hire the savages of America to scalp Europeans and the descendants of Europeans." Gates mentioned a number of Americans whom the Indians had slaughtered but he especially descanted on "the miserable fate of Miss McCrea," who was "dressed to receive her promised husband but met her murderer employed by you." Burgoyne indignantly denied any responsibility for McCrea's death. He attempted to explain

BELOW *Colonel John Stark, one of the heroes of Bunker Hill, leads New Hampshire militiamen in a charge at Bennington. He reportedly shouted: "We'll beat them before night or Molly Stark will be a widow!" Stark had quit the Continental army when Congress failed to promote him to brigadier general.*

ABOVE *Victorious Bennington militiamen carry the dying German commander Colonel Frederick Baum and another mortally wounded officer into a nearby house. Baum could not speak a word of English. Why General Burgoyne put him in command of the expedition to Bennington remains a mystery.*

it as an accident committed in a moment of "savage passion." But he could not deny that he and his government had hired the Indians and were paying them for American scalps.

According to some versions of the story, Gates's letter caused the New England militia to turn out by the thousands. But on August 27, a month after Jane McCrea's death, Gates was complaining to Washington that he had yet to see very many of them. Benedict Arnold, whom General Schuyler had sent to relieve besieged Fort Stanwix in late July, also tried to use McCrea's death to arouse the Mohawk Valley militia—with almost total failure. On August 24 he was stranded at Fort Dayton, thirty miles from Stanwix, with 913 Continentals and "a fine militia, not exceeding 100, on whom little dependence can be placed."

Victory by Messenger

Lacking manpower, Benedict Arnold decided to rescue Fort Stanwix with brainpower. He sent a captured loyalist named Hon Yost Schuyler (no relation to the general) to Stanwix along with a shrewd Oneida Indian to spread lies and confusion in St. Leger's army. Hon Yost was supposedly somewhat crazy—which gave him great influence among the Indians, who regarded the insane as holy men.

Wearing a coat that Arnold had shot full of holes to simulate hot pursuit, Hon Yost rushed to Stanwix and told St. Leger's Indians that the fearsome Arnold was on the march with 3,000 men. The Oneida confirmed everything Hon Yost said, and most of St. Leger's Indians vanished into the woods. The British colonel followed them, abandoning his cannon and leaving his tents standing, with some of his men asleep in them.

This news—which Arnold triumphantly announced when he returned from Fort Stanwix in early September with 1,200 men behind him—probably had far more to do with turning out the militia than the murder of Jane McCrea. Another arrival had an equally large impact on their willingness to march. Into the American camp swaggered Colonel Daniel Morgan and his corps of 400 frontier riflemen. No soldier, except perhaps Arnold, was closer to a living legend in the American army.

Exchanged for a captured British officer after his reluctant surrender in Quebec, Morgan had recruited and trained his rifle corps and rejoined Washington's army. Along with Morgan's men, the commander-in-chief sent Horatio Gates two Continental brigades from the Hudson Highlands, totaling some 1,500 rank and file—manpower he badly needed to defend Philadelphia from Sir William Howe. This generosity raised the Northern army's Continental ·strength to about 6,200.

General Gates decided it would be good for morale if they marched north "to meet the enemy." Starting on September 8, the army advanced to a rugged site overlooking the Hudson called Bemis Heights, twenty-eight miles north

of Albany. There a foreign volunteer, the gifted Polish engineering officer Thaddeus Kosciuszko, constructed an elaborate array of field fortifications on 300-foot-high bluffs and a 500-foot-wide strip of level ground along the Hudson. To the west, the ground was thickly forested, broken by occasional clearings and cut by deep east-west ravines—ideal for American woodland tactics.

Some historians say Benedict Arnold was responsible for this move north. If so, it was the last advice Gates took from his fellow major general. An intriguer himself, Gates saw conspiracies everywhere—and Arnold's popularity with several young officers who had been on Schuyler's staff put Horatio's long nose out of joint. When it came to touchiness, Arnold was in a class by himself. As Gates began countermanding his routine orders and excluding him from staff meetings, the hot-tempered almost-conqueror of Canada grew surly and obnoxious in return.

Gentleman Johnny's Doubts

In Burgoyne's camp at Fort Edward on the east side of the Hudson, second thoughts were the order of the day. In the flush times of July, Burgoyne had written Sir William Howe assuring him that he would need no assistance to reach Albany. Howe had blithely informed Burgoyne that he had no intention of offering any help in the first place; he was off to Philadelphia. Now Gentleman Johnny, with his army shrunk to 4,600 rank and file, plus about 800 Canadians and a mere 50 Indians, informed Lord George Germain that if he did not have specific orders to reach Albany, he would retreat to Canada. Germain had written in his general orders for the campaign that Burgoyne was to "force his way to Albany." But no one would have blamed Burgoyne for disregarding instructions issued 3,000 miles away, six months before the real situation he was facing. Burgoyne was looking for ways to spread the blame as he began to realize the road to Albany had some forbidding bumps in it.

Without his Indian scouts, Burgoyne had no idea where the Americans were. Crossing the Hudson on September 13 on a bridge of boats near Saratoga (present-day Schuylerville), the British commander groped southward in slow, cautious marches. Not until September 18, when an American patrol fired on a group of his soldiers who were digging up potatoes on an abandoned farm, killing and wounding twenty of them, did Burgoyne realize the rebels were close. Although he still had only the dimmest idea of the American position on Bemis Heights, Burgoyne decided to attack it the next day.

Gentleman Johnny divided his army into three columns. Brigadier Fraser, with the light infantry of both the British and German regiments, swung wide to the right, hoping to attack the entrenchments on Bemis Heights from the flank and rear. Burgoyne took charge of the center, with four British regiments numbering about 1,100 men. Along the riverbank marched General Riedesel with about the same number of Germans, plus six companies of the British Forty-seventh Regiment to protect the army's supplies and bateaux.

It was a risky, even foolhardy plan, revealing the contempt in which Burgoyne and his senior officers still held the Americans. Separated by as much as a half-mile of woods, the advancing columns would be forced to communicate through messengers and signal guns. An alert aggressive enemy could easily defeat them separately. But Burgoyne was presuming the Americans would

LEFT *New Jersey-born Jane McCrea was engaged to a loyalist officer in Burgoyne's army. She was killed by Indians who quarreled over who should get the credit and money for finding her. The Americans publicized her death, hoping that it would turn out the militia.*

remain as passive as they had been at Ticonderoga. He thought Fraser and his men stood a fair chance of seizing undefended high ground to the west, from which British heavy guns—Burgoyne had forty-two of them—could wreak havoc on the American defenses.

If the battle had been left to Horatio Gates, that might have happened. He favored staying inside Kosciuszko's fortifications and letting the British attack Bunker Hill style. Benedict Arnold, who had been given command of the army's left wing, argued furiously against this idea. He urged a fight in the woods against any attempt to outflank them. Gates grudgingly consented to send Morgan's 400 riflemen and 250 light infantrymen under Major Henry Dearborn to contest the British maneuver. Gates also agreed to let Arnold support them with men from his wing of the army if they were needed.

Around 1 P.M. Morgan's men collided with scouts from Fraser's column and sent them flying with a volley that killed a number of officers. The riflemen pursued the British into a ravine not far from a clearing called Freeman's Farm, after a loyalist who had fled to Canada. The frontiersmen collided with four times their number of British, who blasted them with musketry from front and flank. Twenty were taken prisoner, and the rest fled past Morgan, who burst into tears, thinking his regiment was ruined. But the riflemen soon regrouped around him in response to his signal, an imitation of a wild turkey call.

Fearing Morgan was in trouble, Arnold sent two New Hampshire regiments, former fugitives from Ticonderoga, to his support. They spread out to Morgan's left as Burgoyne and his four regiments emerged from the woods on the north side of Freeman's Farm. By this time Arnold was on the battlefield. With the instinct of a born tactician, he saw a chance to drive a wedge between Burgoyne and Fraser, wreck the British plan of attack and possibly destroy the enemy army. But Fraser detached several companies to support Burgoyne, and in the center the Twentieth Regiment dropped back and swung west to counter the American thrust. The Yankees were beaten back, and the battle turned into a slugging match between Arnold's men and Burgoyne's British regiments,

LEFT *General Burgoyne addresses the Indians, urging them to join his army. The war split the Iroquois confederacy. Most joined the British. The Oneida and Tuscarora sided with the Americans.*

with Freeman's Farm as the prize ring.

Within an hour Arnold poured in seven Continental regiments and a regiment of New York militia. Back and forth through the tall grass the two sides surged, the British trying to close with the bayonet but repeatedly beaten back by American musketry. The Sixty-second Regiment, exposed to fire from flank and front when the Twentieth Regiment fell back, took fearful punishment. On horseback, Burgoyne exposed himself recklessly to rally his men, ignoring whizzing bullets from Morgan's marksmen even when they shot his aide out of the saddle a few feet away from him.

The Americans repeatedly charged the British artillery, which filled the air with screaming grapeshot. Several times Arnold's men seized the guns but were driven back by a bayonet charge before they could turn them on the British or drag them away. It was, Massachusetts Brigadier General John Glover said, "one continual blaze [of musketry] until dark." Arnold whirled up and down the line, shouting encouragement, leading some of the charges personally. Samuel Downing, a soldier who followed him across Freeman's Farm, said: "There wasn't any waste timber in him, and a bloody fellow he was. He didn't care for nothing; he'd ride right in. It was 'Come on boys'—t'wasn't 'go boys.' He was as brave a man as ever lived."

Between charges, Arnold rode back to General Gates's tent inside the Bemis Heights fortifications a mile and a half away to beg for more troops. Gates repeatedly refused to give him another man. On the battlefield Burgoyne and other senior officers were close to panic by the end of the afternoon. The Sixty-second Regiment was on the brink of collapse. In the artillery every officer and four-fifths of the gunners were dead or wounded. At 5 o'clock Burgoyne sent a frantic call for help to Riedesel on the riverbank.

After another angry exchange, General Gates ordered Benedict Arnold to stay inside the Bemis Heights fortifications, claiming his rash attacks were endangering the whole army. From the riverbank Baron von Riedesel once more marched to the rescue of the British. Taking more than 500 men with him, the German major general left the right-flank column unable to defend the precious stores and bateaux. But Gates, who should have been watching closely for this opportunity, did nothing, and the fresh Germans stormed into the American right flank at sunset, beating drums and shouting as they had at Hubbardton. Even more useful were two six-pounders that Riedesel's artillery officer manhandled into action to belch grapeshot at the charging rebels.

Without Arnold's leadership, the Americans faltered and began retreating through the woods. Colonel Philip Van Cortlandt ordered his Second New York Regiment to direct their aim "below the flash" of the British fire, which soon discouraged pursuit. The dazed, exhausted British had no stomach for more shooting, anyway. The four regiments in the center had lost more than 600 men. Only 60 rank and file from the Sixty-second Regiment were still on their feet—the other 290 were dead or wounded. American casualties totaled 319.

TOP RIGHT *Polish-born military engineer Thaddeus Kosciuszko designed the defenses that the Americans constructed for the battles of Saratoga. He also built valuable forts on the Delaware River and planned the fortress at West Point. Liberty was the central idea of his life. His later attempt to lead a revolution in Poland was crushed by Russia.*

Captain Thomas Anburey, who had spent the day with Brigadier Simon Fraser and saw very little action, was put in charge of burying the British dead. This grisly task prompted him to confide to his journal the "astonishment" of the British at the ferocity with which the Americans had fought: "They are not that contemptible enemy we had hitherto thought them, incapable of standing a regular engagement, and that they would only fight behind strong and powerful works."

The next day Burgoyne startled everyone in his army by announcing he wanted to attack again. All his senior officers advised against it. The men were too spent to obey the order. Nevertheless, Burgoyne resolved to resume the offensive the following day. Many in the American army later admitted that if he had done so, he might have won his gamble. Arnold's regiments were also shaken by their losses, and there was an acute shortage of ammunition in the American camp.

The deputy quartermaster general of the Northern army dispatched a frantic letter to Albany: "For God's sake do not let us be under the necessity of retreating for want of lead." Swallowing his detestation of Horatio Gates, Philip Schuyler sent men around the city to tear the sashes out of windows. They melted them into bullets and rushed them to the army.

On the same day—September 20—Burgoyne received a letter that changed his mind about another attack. The writer was Sir Henry Clinton, the general whom Sir William Howe had left in command in New York when he sailed off to attack Philadelphia. Clinton told Burgoyne that he had received reinforcements from England and had enough men to make a foray up the Hudson in Burgoyne's favor. Gentleman Johnny seized on the proposal as heaven-sent. "Even the menace of an attack" would be of "great use," he replied. He begged Clinton to "do it my dear friend, directly." Burgoyne proceeded to entrench Freeman's Farm and high ground north of it and wait for Clinton.

It took Clinton two weeks to get his expedition under way. With 4,000 men and a Royal Navy escort, he captured the thinly held Hudson Highland forts after a sharp engagement with New York Governor George Clinton and 600 militia. Garrisoning the forts, Sir Henry sent one of his brigadiers up the river with 1,700 men. They had orders to "feel for General Burgoyne, to

ABOVE LEFT *Benedict Arnold persuaded Horatio Gates to seize the initiative from the British at the first battle of Saratoga. Here Arnold leads a charge across Freeman's Farm. The jealous Gates did not even mention Arnold's name in his report on the battle.*

assist his operations, and even to join him if that general required it."

This looming British presence on the upper Hudson badly rattled the Americans. They had no idea of the exact size of Clinton's force. Adding to their alarm was the news that, on September 11, Washington's army had lost a major battle with General Howe at Brandywine Creek in Pennsylvania. That meant the British would soon possess Philadelphia. It was logical to assume Howe might have sent Clinton substantial reinforcements to rescue Burgoyne. In the American hospital in Albany, Dr. James Thacher recorded in his journal the "prevalent opinion" that the British could reach the city in five or six hours, and "involve General Gates in inexpressible embarrassment and difficulty by placing him between two armies."

On October 4 Burgoyne was forced to cut by one-third the rations of vile salt pork and moldy flour on which his army was living. Shivering in summer uniforms in the chilly fall nights, his sick multiplied until the hospital cases, including the wounded from Freeman's Farm, numbered 800. The Americans gave the British no rest. "Not a single night passes but there is firing and continual attacks on the advanced picquets," Captain Anburey glumly noted. "The officers rest in their cloaths, and the field officers are up frequently in the night."

American militia under the command of Major General Benjamin Lincoln added to Burgoyne's woes. A 1,500-man column attacked the vital portage between Lake Champlain and Lake George. The Americans captured 243 redcoats, freed 100 prisoners and burned 17 sloops and 200 bateaux. Burgoyne's supply line to Canada went up in those flames.

On October 6—against the advice of his senior officers, who urged him to retreat—Burgoyne decided on another attack. Gates predicted the move, calling him an "old gamester" who was likely to "risque all upon one throw." In fact, before he left London, Burgoyne had bet a sizable amount of money that he would have Christmas dinner in Albany. The next day, with 2,000 hand-picked men and ten cannon, Burgoyne led an exploratory probe of the vulnerable American left flank. If he saw a chance of a breakthrough, he planned to attack the following day with every man left in his army.

In the American camp, a demoralizing quarrel had been raging between Generals Gates and Arnold. Gates had sent Congress a report of the battle of Freeman's Farm that omitted Arnold's name as well as the names of his friends Morgan and Dearborn. Enraged, Arnold burst into Gates's tent and exchanged insults with him. Gates retaliated by

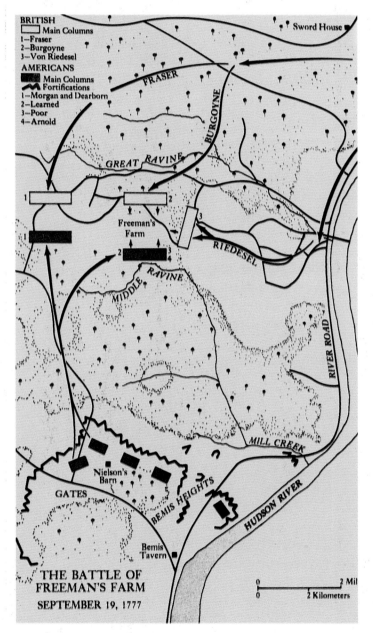

BELOW *This map of the battle of Freeman's Farm illustrates the importance of Benedict Arnold's decision to fight the British in the woods rather than let them outflank the American fortifications on Bemis Heights.*

BRITISH
☐ Main Columns
1—Fraser
2—Burgoyne
3—Von Riedesel
AMERICANS
▨ Main Columns
⌒ Fortifications
1—Morgan and Dearborn
2—Learned
3—Poor
4—Arnold

FRASER
BURGOYNE
Sword House
GREAT RAVINE
Freeman's Farm
RIEDESEL
MIDDLE RAVINE
RIVER ROAD
MILL CREEK
Nielson's Barn
GATES
BEMIS HEIGHTS
HUDSON RIVER
Bemis Tavern

THE BATTLE OF FREEMAN'S FARM
SEPTEMBER 19, 1777

0   2 Mil
0   2 Kilometers

removing Arnold from command of the army's left wing and offering him a pass to Philadelphia. Senior officers were appalled. Several prevailed on Arnold to stay, hoping Gates would relent. But on the day Burgoyne marched out of his camp, the two men still were not speaking, and Gates was in command of the American left wing. Benjamin Lincoln, returned from his militia forays, was put in charge of the right wing.

Arnold used the news of Clinton's incursion to taunt Gates for his failure to attack Burgoyne during the seventeen-day hiatus. He claimed he cared neither for glory nor credit but was deeply concerned that Gates was about to let a great victory slip from their grasp. When Burgoyne's 2,000-man column appeared, Gates realized he could not hunker behind his fortifications without losing face. "Order on Morgan to begin the game," he said.

The British formed a battle line on a long, low ridge about three-quarters of a mile west of Bemis Heights. Burgoyne and his senior officers climbed to the top of a nearby log cabin to peer at the American position through spy glasses. The tall trees beyond Freeman's farm were a wall of impenetrable fall colors, rendering the expedition pointless. While the British debated what to do next and the army's camp women furiously harvested wheat on two nearby abandoned farms, Morgan's riflemen circled wide to hit their right flank.

Gates also dispatched a brigade of Continentals and two Connecticut militia regiments to attack Burgoyne's left wing. Having less distance to travel than Morgan's men, they made contact first, about 2:30 P.M. They quickly cleared skirmishers from the woods on their side of the battlefield and attacked without waiting for Morgan.

The British left wing consisted of grenadier companies commanded by Major John Dyke Acland. The Americans burst from the woods and charged up the slope of the ridge at them. The British met them with a blast of musketry and grapeshot, but as usual most of the metal flew over the Americans' heads. Acland called for a bayonet charge, and the Americans replied with decimating fire that sent the surviving grenadiers fleeing. Acland, shot through both legs, was taken prisoner. The Americans seized a cannon and turned it on the retreating grenadiers and on the 400 Brunswick Germans who held the British center.

By this time Morgan's men were attacking the British light infantry on the other flank, charging from the shelter of the trees "like a torrent" while their sharpshooters did their usual deadly job of picking off officers. As the British changed front to meet them, the riflemen's partners in the first battle at Freeman's Farm, Major Henry Dearborn and his light infantry, appeared and fired a destructive volley. Perhaps remembering Hubbardton, the British light infantry fled, leaving the Germans exposed to attack on three sides. Burgoyne sent an aide forward to order them to retreat, but he was shot out of the saddle, and the Germans fought on.

At this point Arnold entered the battle in defiance of Gates's orders. Taking charge of a Continental brigade that was just entering the fight, he led them up the hill against the Germans in two furious charges that the Brunswickers repulsed with musketry and grapeshot. Seeing the flight of the light infantry, Arnold quickly shifted men to the left and began surrounding the Germans, with the assistance of Morgan and Dearborn.

SARATOGA'S CONFUSING PLACE NAMES

Even in 1777 people were confused by the place names associated with the battles of Saratoga. Eight miles north of the battlefield is the Saratoga of 1777, where Burgoyne finally surrendered his army. Today it is called Schuylerville. Until about 1830 it was known as Old Saratoga. It was renamed in honor of Philip Schuyler, who had a country house and farm there. The reason for the change was the growing fame of Saratoga Springs. That town, famous for its spas and horseracing, is about fourteen miles west of the battlefield and had nothing to do with the battle. The Saratoga National Historical Park is near the modern village of Bemis Heights, where the American fortifications and base camp stood. In some accounts this location is called Stillwater, which is a village three miles to the south, where the American forces camped temporarily before taking the Bemis Heights position. The historical park is twenty-eight miles north of Albany.

The Germans retreated, and the battle teetered toward total rout. Burgoyne, with bullet holes in his coat and hat, his horse shot out from under him, was helpless. Only Brigadier Simon Fraser showed any semblance of command, spurring his horse into the ranks of the fleeing light infantry and rallying them to make a momentarily successful stand. Arnold pointed to Fraser and shouted to Morgan: "That man on the gray horse is a host unto himself and must be disposed of." Morgan passed the order to Tim Murphy, one of his best sharpshooters, who quickly climbed a tree and put a bullet through Fraser's belly.

The brigadier's fall consumed what little heart was left in Burgoyne's ranks, and the survivors ran for the protection of their fortified camp. But Arnold was not satisfied. He wanted to destroy Burgoyne before Clinton arrived to rescue him. For two years he had fought to eliminate the threat of an invasion from the north. He was not going to let the British break off the action to fight another day while he put up with more lectures from Granny Gates about his rashness and insubordination.

Shouting "victory or death," Arnold led the aroused Americans in an assault on the British camp. An appalled Burgoyne, looking over his shoulder, told Captain Anburey, whose company was guarding one of the gates: "Sir, you must defend this post to the very last man!" To Anburey's relief, Arnold's first target was an outlying redoubt in the center of Freeman's Farm that was supported by Canadian volunteers in two stockaded cabins. Routing the Canadians, Arnold and parts of two Continental brigades hurled themselves at the British light infantry and assorted other fugitives manning the walls of the

RIGHT *This seemingly innocent letter enabled General Henry Clinton, the British commander in New York, to communicate with General Burgoyne. Read the words inside the hour glass, and you will discover the message.*

ABOVE **Brigadier Simon Fraser was mortally wounded at the second battle of Saratoga, reportedly by sharpshooter Timothy Murphy. In this painting, his plight stirs pity in his friends, Baron Friedrich von Riedesel, commander of the German troops, and his wife, Frederika. The Baroness nursed Fraser until he died the next day at 8 A.M.**

redoubt. Cannon fire and musketry tore cruel gaps in the American ranks, and they were forced to retreat.

Looking around, Arnold saw another brigade of Continentals arriving on the battlefield, heading for the British right. Riding his horse the length of Freeman's farm, with several hundred British muskets and cannon shooting at him, Arnold seized command of the newcomers and swung them toward another outlying redoubt, defended by Germans under Lieutenant Colonel Heinrich von Breymann, the survivor of the Bennington rout. Arnold rode his horse through a rear gateway with the Continentals swarming behind him, shouting and shooting, while men from Morgan's and Dearborn's regiments poured over the front walls. Breymann started sabering men who tried to run away, and one of his own soldiers shot him dead. Another German got off a final shot at Arnold, breaking the thighbone of the same leg that had been wounded in the assault on Quebec.

A writhing Arnold was carried back to Bemis Heights in a litter. The British had lost another 400 men and all ten cannon that they had dragged on their reconnaissance. American losses were around 150. Far more important than these statistics was Arnold's capture of the Breymann redoubt. On high ground, its cannon commanded the British camp, neatly reversing the dilemma the Americans had faced at Ticonderoga. This time, no matter what Gates thought of Arnold's performance, he tacitly admitted his approval by rushing orders from his tent to hold the little fort "at all hazards."

At 9 P.M. on October 8, after burying Brigadier Fraser, the British began a slow, agonizing retreat, leaving 300 sick and wounded behind them with a letter from Burgoyne begging Gates's mercy. Heavy rain turned the road into a quagmire, forcing the beaten army to abandon wagons with their tents and baggage. The Americans attacked the bateaux following the army up the riverbank, eventually capturing or destroying most of them. It took the British twenty-four hours to cover the eight miles to their old camp north of Fishkill Creek, near Saratoga (now Schuylerville), where the exhausted men fell in the mud and slept in their sodden uniforms.

Soon New Hampshire militiamen, led by John Stark, whom Congress had hastily promoted to brigadier general after hearing the news of Bennington, took up positions directly north of the Royal Army, sealing off its escape route. Counting all the militia in the game, Gates now had more than 14,000 men. He saw that Burgoyne could not tell the difference between a Continental and a militiaman. Any American with a gun in his hand was a menace.

Burgoyne's situation rapidly grew hopeless. While rations dwindled and horses starved to death, the surrounding Americans sniped by day and bombarded by night. The Americans also unveiled a new weapon: about 150 Iroquois Indians whom Philip Schuyler had persuaded to join the war. They made life even more hazardous for British pickets and sentries. Desertions multiplied among Burgoyne's dispirited men. Finally, on October 13, Gentleman Johnny gave up on Sir Henry Clinton and asked Gates for a parley.

Instead of letting Burgoyne propose the first set of terms, Gates nervously asked for an unconditional surrender. When Burgoyne furiously rejected the idea and insisted on the full honors of war, Gates accepted without a demur. Burgoyne, suspecting Gates knew something about Clinton's approach, sparred for time by insisting that the word "capitulation" be excised from the terms. Instead he offered to sign a "convention" that would permit his troops to return to Europe with the promise that they would not be used again in the war. The jittery Gates accepted this demand, although it would permit the British to send fresh troops whom Burgoyne's men would replace in England or Ireland. Perhaps Gates knew—or hoped—Congress would find ways to circumvent the agreement, which they eventually managed to do.

More suspicious than ever, Burgoyne noticed large bodies of militia marching off from Gates's army and wondered if Clinton's approach was causing panic. He suddenly demanded the right to count the American force to make sure it was the same size it had been when he opened negotiations. Gates angrily rejected this silly idea, explaining that some militia were simply going home when their time was up, in their usual style.

Burgoyne asked his senior officers if he could honorably break off negotiations at this point. They unanimously told him he could not—and added that they no longer had any confidence in their men's readiness to fight. After a few more hours of hesitation, Burgoyne signed the convention.

On the same day, October 16, 1777, Sir Henry Clinton's expedition attacked and burned Kingston, where the New York state government had been meeting, and sailed up the Hudson to Livingston Manor, forty-five miles below Albany and eighty-five miles from Saratoga. Militia swarming on both banks—and the navy's doubts about navigating the river—discouraged the British from going further. From the start, Clinton had neither the manpower nor the burning desire to risk much to rescue Burgoyne. Sir Henry knew he was in line to succeed Sir William Howe as commander-in-chief, an event that Burgoyne's surrender made almost inevitable.

On October 17, Burgoyne's men marched out and stacked their arms in a meadow north of Fishkill Creek. Wearing his full-dress uniform, Gentleman Johnny approached Gates, raised his hat and bowed. "The fortune of war, General Gates, has made me your prisoner," he said.

"I shall always be ready to testify that it was not through any fault of your excellency," Gates

THE LINE OF IRELAND

As early as 1763, when Charles Carroll was studying in London, he predicted that America would one day be independent.

In Virginia's Shenandoah Valley there is a gravestone that reads: Here lies the remains of John Lewis, who slew the Irish lord, settled in Augusta County, located the town of Staunton and furnished five sons to fight the battles of the American Revolution.

Those words are an apt summary of the Irish role in the Revolution. They responded en masse to the call for resistance to England. With more than 300,000 of them in the colonies, they had a major impact on the war. They ranged from frontiersmen such as the Lewises to Charles Carroll of Maryland, one of the wealthiest men in America.

With a fortune to lose, Carroll signed the Declaration of Independence without the slightest hesitation. In a letter to a friend, he explained his decision. He said the moment the Americans admitted the British "had the right to tax us in all cases...the most abject slavery and the deepest distresses would follow overnight."

That was not logic or abstract belief—that was Irish blood talking. The Irish had seen first hand what the British Parliament could do to a defeated country.

Throughout the war, the Irish demonstrated their commitment to the American cause with their blood. On the memorial tablets of the Bunker Hill monument are Daniel Callahan, George Shannon, and many other Irish names. The Pennsylvania Brigade, one of the largest units in the Continental army, was known as the Line of Ireland. Well over half its officers and enlisted men were backcountry Irish. Testifying before Parliament in 1779, Philadelphia loyalist Joseph Galloway said half of Washington's army was Irish. It was only a mild exaggeration.

Major General John Sullivan of New Hampshire was the son of a schoolteacher from County Limerick in Ireland. Commodore John Barry, often called "the father of the American navy," was born in Tacumshane, Ireland. Major General Stephen Moylan, son of a Catholic merchant from Cork, served as a Washington aide and later as quartermaster general of the Continental army. His self-designed uniform included buckskin breeches, a bear-skin hat, a red waistcoat—and a bright green coat.

Equally worth remembering, are the Irish soldiers who served in the French army under Count de Dillon. They played a heroic part in the unsuccessful attack on Savannah in 1779. A happier story is the achievement of the Irish regiments in the Spanish army. They played a major role in the Spanish assault that captured Florida from the British in 1780-1781. They were led by Lieutenant Colonel Arturo O'Neil. Among the officers were Captains Juan Hogan, Eduardo Nugent and Pedro O'Reilly.

replied. Later the gleeful Gates wrote to his wife that "Burgoyne and his great army have laid down their arms...to me and my Yankees." With New England's politicians behind him in Congress, Gates thought he was now in a position to supplant George Washington as the American commander-in-chief. He made this clear by reporting his victory directly to Congress, only casually mentioning it to Washington in a letter on November 6.

Fighting for Philadelphia

While Gates was triumphing over Burgoyne in the North, Sir William Howe was assailing George Washington's army in the battle for Philadelphia. Instead of coming up the Delaware, which the Americans had blocked with several strong forts, Howe decided, against the advice of his officers, to approach his goal via Chesapeake Bay. The summer winds proved contrary, and the change in plan added three weeks to his voyage. Many of his army's horses died, and his men suffered severely aboard the crowded unhealthy transports. Not until August 28 did Howe get his army assembled at the Head of Elk, at the northern end of the Chesapeake. His by-now-numerous critics pointed out that he was not much closer to Philadelphia than he had been three months ago in New Jersey.

As Howe began his sixty-mile march to Philadelphia, he issued a proclamation urging all loyal Americans to rally to his side. The results were dismal. In village after village, houses stood deserted. It was not long before he realized his dream of recruiting a loyalist army in Pennsylvania was a chimera. As they advanced, the Germans and not a few British soldiers in his ranks began looting the empty houses, alienating hundreds who might have at least considered rallying to the King's cause.

George Washington positioned his 12,000-man army along Brandywine Creek, twenty-six miles from Philadelphia, and challenged Howe to battle. Weakened by the detachments to Gates, the American force was almost one-third militia. Washington had no intention of committing his men to an all-or-nothing general engagement. There was a huge swath of Pennsylvania behind them in which to retreat. But he could not let Howe capture the American capital without a fight.

Unfortunately, Washington was again operating in a countryside totally unfamiliar to him and his army. Decent maps were nonexistent. Howe decided to try to repeat his success on Long Island. He ordered one-third of his army, mostly Germans, to demonstrate against Washington's center at Chadds Ford, while he swung his best troops around the Americans' left flank and attacked their rear.

Washington was well aware of this possibility. He planned to hurl the bulk of his army across Chadds Ford and cut up the demonstrators. But confusing and then conflicting reports reached Washington as the Germans blasted away with cannon and muskets. First he was told Howe was on the march. Then some local militiamen assured Major General John Sullivan, in command on the critical left flank, that the report was untrue. As Washington hesitated, a final frantic report reached him from the unlucky Sullivan. Howe was across the Brandywine and would soon be at the American rear!

Accompanied by a recently arrived French volunteer, twenty-year-old

WOMEN AT WAR: A Gallery of Revolutionary Portraits

Martha Washington—She shared many of the hardships of the war with her husband, journeying north each year to preside at General Washington's winter quarters at Valley Forge, Morristown and other sites. A consummate hostess, she entertained Congressmen and French diplomats with unfailing skill.

Betsy Ross—While this Philadelphia seamstress's role in making the American flag is a myth, she was a dedicated patriot who gave two husbands to the cause. Her first spouse was killed in an explosion in 1776; her second was captured aboard a privateer and died in a British prison, leaving her with two small children to support.

Sibyl Ludington—When the British attacked Danbury, Connecticut, in 1777, sixteen-year-old Sibyl, who lived just across the New York border in Fredericksburg, mounted the family horse and roused the local militia to resist them. She covered forty miles in her midnight ride, banging on doors with a stick as she passed the isolated farmhouses.

Deborah Sampson—In 1782, at the age of twenty-two, Deborah enlisted in the Continental army as Robert Shurtleff. Stationed at West Point, she was wounded in a skirmish but managed to conceal her sexual identity. During another stay in the hospital, a

doctor learned she was a woman. She was honorably discharged and after the war was granted a pension.

Mary Katherine Goddard—One of the first women to publish an American newspaper, she took over *The Baltimore Journal* from her brother and ran it during the difficult years of the war. Paper was scarce, and she sometimes had to reduce its size, but she seldom missed an edition. Her mother, Sarah Updike Goddard, had published another Baltimore paper in the 1760s. Six of the forty papers in America had women publishers.

Esther Reed—Wife of Joseph Reed, adjutant general of the Continental army and later a political leader in Pennsylvania, Mrs. Reed launched "the Association" in 1780. Its goal was to help the starving, poorly clad American army. Its members raised more than $7,500 in gold dollars, the equivalent of $250,000 in depreciated American paper dollars.

Sarah Franklin Bache—When Esther Reed died in the fall of 1780, the Association was taken over by Benjamin Franklin's daughter. They used the money to buy linen and in December sent Washington 2,200 shirts for the soldiers.

Frederika von Riedesel—Daughter of a Prussian lieutenant general, Baroness von Riedesel and her three daughters accompanied her husband, Baron von Riedesel, the commander of the German troops in General Burgoyne's army. Her vivid journal of her adventures in the American wilderness is one of the most important documents of the Revolution.

Patience Wright—Born in New Jersey, she was a gifted sculptress in wax. In 1772 she moved to London and opened a wax museum that was famous for its lifelike figures of William Pitt, Benjamin Franklin and George III. During the war she travelled to Paris and tried to persuade Franklin to join her in a scheme to launch a rebellion in England.

Betty Zane—Living with her brother near Wheeling, West Virginia, in 1782, this courageous sixteen-year-old was the heroine of the siege of Fort Henry, one of the last battles of the Revolution. Surrounded by Indians, the Americans were running low on gunpowder. Betty offered to get some from a nearby house. She dashed to the house, dumped a barrel of powder into a tablecloth and lugged it back to the fort through a shower of bullets.

TOP LEFT **George Washington's** *private nickname for Martha was "Patsy." Washington wore a ring on his finger containing her portrait in miniature.*

BOTTOM LEFT **Nancy Hart's** *Georgia home was invaded by five British soldiers who demanded a meal. She got them drunk, relieved them of their guns and sent her daughter to summon nearby American militiamen. Seizing a musket, Hart held the soldiers at bay until they were taken prisoner. Georgia named a county after her.*

ABOVE *When* **Lady Harriet Acland's** *husband was wounded and captured in the second battle of Saratoga, she was rowed downriver to the American camp to nurse him. He recovered but was later killed in a duel. She married a minister who had been a chaplain in Burgoyne's army.*

RIGHT **Mercy Otis Warren** *was the sister of James Otis. She wrote poems, satirical plays and a three-volume history of the Revolution. John Adams said her writing "had no equal that I know of in this country."*

Marquis de Lafayette, Washington galloped to the sound of the guns. They met Sullivan's men falling back in disarray. Lafayette sprang off his horse and tried to rally them. He got a bullet in the leg and accomplished little except to display his reckless courage. Back at Chadds Ford, with a thunderous crash of cannon and muskets, the Germans attacked the American center, which Washington had weakened to meet Howe's column.

The American army was soon in full retreat. But unlike the battle of Long Island, it was not a panicky rout. Washington's rear guard fell back from one patch of woods to the next one, fighting hard until the oncoming British forced them out of their cover. Howe's men were tired. They had marched more than seventeen miles before they went into action. Without cavalry, because so many of his horses had died on the voyage to the Chesapeake, Howe abandoned the pursuit as darkness fell.

Twelve miles beyond the battlefield, Washington found Lafayette, weak from loss of blood, trying to organize some Continentals to defend a bridge over Chester Creek. Washington ordered him to a hospital and summoned his personal physician, Dr. James Craik. "Take care of him as if he were my son," he said. This lanky, effervescent young nobleman had already won a niche in Washington's carefully guarded affections.

Attack at Dawn

For the next four weeks, Washington and Howe maneuvered through the web of rivers and creeks around Philadelphia. The British commander repeatedly tried to trap the American army or some part of it. On September 21, in a night attack using the bayonet, his light infantry caught an American division by surprise near Paoli, killing or wounding more than 150 men. The Americans called the clash a massacre because many men were killed while trying to surrender. But most of the time Washington, marching and countermarching his men more than 100 miles, skillfully zigzagged west, keeping his army between Howe and Reading, a main American supply depot. Finally Howe abandoned hope of forcing Washington to accept an all-out battle and marched into undefended Philadelphia.

Congress, warned just in time by Washington's aide Colonel Alexander Hamilton, fled to York, Pennsylvania. An angry John Adams, more and more disillusioned with Washington, raved about the need for a general of "active, masterly capacity" who would "save this country." Washington, with 8,000 Continentals and about 3,000 militia, headed toward Philadelphia, hoping to prove he was that man. Most of the British army was camped in the suburb of Germantown. He decided they were ripe for a "stroke."

Washington concocted one of his most daring plans. He divided his army into four columns and hurled them at the British in a dawn attack on October 4, 1777, three days before Burgoyne's last-gasp assault at Saratoga. The Americans came whooping out of a dense fog and routed British outposts. The Continentals in the two center columns drove 1,000 yards and seemed on their way to tearing the British apart. But the fog, which had covered their advance, swiftly became a fatal disadvantage.

American units fired on each other, and many regiments lost contact with their commanding officers. Six British companies under the command of a

ABOVE *Benedict Arnold's leg was broken by a musket ball during his assault on a key enemy redoubt in the second battle of Saratoga. Arnold ignored General Horatio Gates's order confining him to his tent.*

fighting colonel named Musgrave turned a large stone house owned by loyalist Benjamin Chew into a fortress that distracted and disrupted the Americans' rear. Several regiments stopped to assail it rather than maintaining the momentum of the general attack. Major General Sullivan's division ran out of ammunition. Soon confusion turned to panic in many regiments, and by 10 A.M. the Americans were in retreat once more. The battered British, with more than 500 men dead or wounded, made no attempt to pursue them.

A Cordial to the Dying

For the Americans in Paris, 1777 oozed to a close in an atmosphere thick with hopelessness. The British blockade of America seemed impenetrable. Almost none of the war materiel Silas Deane and Caron de Beaumarchais had purchased with King Louis XVI's money reached Washington's troops. None of the promised cargoes of wheat and tobacco had reached France to finance the American mission. Arthur Lee, who had joined Benjamin Franklin in France as a member of the diplomatic team, displayed a letter from his brother, Richard Henry Lee, predicting that without an early French alliance and an immense loan, independence would soon be a lost cause.

British spies were everywhere. When Franklin presented Foreign Minister Vergennes with a request for an additional loan of 14 million livres, the French diplomat informed him that the British ambassador, Lord Stormont, had warned him that the request was coming and sternly advised against giving the Americans another sou.

Late in November came the news that the British had captured Philadelphia. For Franklin it was an especially cruel blow. All his property—not to mention his daughter, her husband and his grandchildren—were in the enemy's hands. But the patriarch refused to allow his personal anguish to disturb his public style. At a dinner party, a Frenchman said mockingly: "Well Doctor, Howe has taken Philadelphia."

"I beg your pardon, sir," Franklin replied. "Philadelphia has taken Howe."

There was truth as well as wit in this answer. Philadelphia was, from a strategic point of view, useless to Howe. The Delaware River was a thin, tenuous lifeline on which the British had to depend for supplies. They were surrounded by a sea of hostile Americans. Philadelphia was a symbolic conquest, not a real one.

But diplomats deal in symbols, and to the American mission the news was disheartening. On November 27, they gathered for a grim conference. Silas Deane wanted to demand an immediate alliance from the French—or the Americans would begin negotiating a settlement with the British. Franklin refused to throw in his hand so recklessly. He feared France would "abandon us in despair or in anger." Arthur Lee sided with Franklin. The meeting broke up with the glum hope that the French would at least pay the interest on their debts and keep them out of prison.

Less than a week after this dismal meeting, an American ship arrived in Nantes reportedly carrying important dispatches from Congress. Franklin, Deane, Lee and their French friends, Beaumarchais and Chaumont, gathered at Franklin's house in Passy to await the courier.

ABOVE *After General Burgoyne surrendered at Saratoga, General Horatio Gates invited him to refreshments in his tent while Colonel Daniel Morgan and other American officers looked on. Gates ordered his troops to remain silent throughout the ceremony to make sure no insults were flung. Later, Gates had to provide Burgoyne with a dragoon escort to prevent him from being tarred and feathered by farmers who had lost friends and family to his marauding Indians.*

The moment they heard the rattle of a chaise on the cobblestones outside the house, they rushed out. Thirty-year-old Jonathan Loring Austin of Boston, secretary of the Massachusetts Board of War, barely had time to introduce himself before Franklin asked: "Sir, is Philadelphia taken?"

"Yes, sir," replied Austin.

Franklin's great head drooped. With a sigh, he turned away. He had gone perhaps two steps toward the house when Austin said: "But sir, I have greater news than that. General Burgoyne and his whole army are prisoners of war!"

The news, in Silas Deane's words, was "like a sovereign cordial to the dying." With shaking hands, Franklin ripped the dispatches from Austin's bags. Beaumarchais leaped into his carriage and thundered toward the center of Paris with the news. He declined to slow down for a curve and found himself upside-down in a ditch. For the next week he spread the glad tidings with his arm in a sling. At Passy Franklin, Deane and Lee worked day and night preparing dispatches that spread the news to other European countries. But their most important letter went to Count de Vergennes in Versailles.

Eight days later Franklin, Deane and Lee played the secret-service game of changing carriages and sneaking out back doors to meet Vergennes and his undersecretary in a house a half-mile outside Versailles. There they found the Count was almost as impressed with Washington's attack on the British army at Germantown, only twenty-three days after his defeat on the Brandywine, as he was by Burgoyne's surrender. But the Frenchman was still inclined to play a cautious game. He said he could not discuss an alliance without consulting the King of Spain, Louis XVI's Bourbon uncle. Their "family compact" forbade them to enter into wars or alliances without mutual approval.

Franklin saw this could lead to dangerous foot-dragging. He had already sent Arthur Lee to Spain, and the Spanish declined even to let him into the country. Franklin decided to build a fire under the French—and swiftly converted George III into his carrier of kindling wood. The news of Burgoyne's disaster had panicked Prime Minister Lord North. He persuaded a reluctant monarch that the time had come to offer massive conciliation to the Americans. He ordered the chief of the British secret service in France, an American named Paul Wentworth, to talk to Franklin and Deane.

The canny old philosopher told Deane to agree to meet Wentworth. Franklin knew the French secret service would instantly report this decision to Vergennes, who would wonder if the Americans were about to negotiate a reconciliation with the British. Within twenty-four hours, Vergennes's undersecretary was on Franklin's doorstep announcing that France had decided not to wait for word from Spain. Doubting this, Franklin told Deane to meet Wentworth anyway. Well-rehearsed by Franklin, Deane performed like a master diplomat, stonewalling the spy's offers of lavish "honors and emoluments" from the King if he became a cooperative peacemaker.

On December 31, 1777, Franklin learned that word from Spain had arrived—and it was a resounding no. King Charles III was not inclined to fight for American independence at present. Five more days passed with nothing but silence from Versailles. Franklin moved up the pressure another notch—he agreed to meet with Wentworth.

On January 6, 1778, Franklin spent two hours with the spymaster, who tried flattery, argument, and appeals to history. Franklin's reply was independence or nothing. Wentworth produced an unsigned letter from William Eden, head of the British secret service and one of George III's most devoted friends, declaring England would fight for another ten years rather than grant America independence.

"America," Franklin snapped, "is ready to fight fifty years to win it."

The next day a baffled Wentworth went back to London, and Franklin added a final touch to his scenario. He neglected to report to Vergennes that he had seen the spy. The jittery foreign minister, remembering how faithfully Franklin had reported previous British overtures, convened the French council of ministers—the equivalent of the British cabinet—and warned them that England was close to enticing the Americans back into the imperial fold and it was time for France to act. The council voted unanimously for an alliance.

On February 5, the details of the treaty were finally worked out, and Franklin and his fellow envoys were invited to the Ministry for Foreign Affairs for the signing. Edward Bancroft noticed that Franklin wore a suit of Manchester velvet that was vaguely familiar. He finally remembered where he had seen it—it was same outfit Franklin had worn when Solicitor General Wedderburn humiliated him before George III's Privy Council. Silas Deane asked Franklin why he was wearing the suit. "To give it a little revenge," he said.

The treaty of alliance meant war between England and France. But

BELOW *The Marquis de Lafayette was wounded at the battle of Brandywine trying to rally retreating American troops. His father had been killed fighting the British when Lafayette was two years old.*

ABOVE *This German print portrays Louis XVI receiving Benjamin Franklin, Silas Deane and Arthur Lee at the French court after they signed the treaty of alliance. Within a few months, England declared war on France.*

Franklin, with his triple-decker mind, was already thinking of peace. With Edward Bancroft as his emissary (an ironic use of a double agent) he leaked the news of the treaty to his banker friend Thomas Walpole, who had been one of his partners in the projected colony in Illinois. Walpole promptly leaked it to Charles James Fox, the most explosive debater in Parliament.

When the House of Commons convened on February 17, 1778, Lord North introduced "conciliatory acts" that granted America the terms Franklin had suggested two short years before in his negotiations with Lord Dartmouth: the repeal of all the obnoxious legislation back to 1763, the recognition of the Continental Congress and the virtual independence of America within the framework of the empire. Fox allowed North to pose as a peacemaker for the better part of two hours. He even remained silent when the prime minister declared his concessions "were from reason and propriety, not from necessity."

Fox rose and congratulated Lord North for joining the opposition. Then he pinned the prime minister to his bench by asking whether America had signed a treaty with France within the last ten days.

Waspish Horace Walpole described the ensuing scene: "Lord North was thunderstruck and would not rise.... [Edmund] Burke called on his Lordship to answer to the fact of the treaty. Still the Minister was silent till Sir G. [George] Saville rose and told him that it would be criminal to withhold a reply, and a matter of impeachment."

Lord North finally struggled to his feet and admitted he had heard "a report" of the treaty. In fact, a copy was on his desk, courtesy of double agent Edward Bancroft. But admitting it would also have meant confessing that his conciliatory proposals were not inspired by "reason and propriety" but by frantic necessity.

Franklin was hoping to make a fool of Lord North and bring down his administration. Thomas Walpole had already talked to William Pitt, who was prepared to take over the government and bring home the troops. North revealed his desperation by begging George III to let him resign. Beaumarchais, who had secret agents in England, predicted Pitt would be prime minister within the week.

Upping the pressure, Franklin sent Jonathan Loring Austin to London, where he was soon dining in public with all the leading members of the opposition. Franklin was sending a message that he was as willing to do business with Pitt, Burke, Fox and company as he was loath to talk to emissaries from Lord North. On February 26, 1778, he wrote to another member of the opposition, David Hartley, that if England sent "wise and honest men" to talk to him, she could obtain peace with America and avoid a war with France.

But George III was a very stubborn man. Late in 1777 he had taken the precaution of giving Lord North £20,000 to settle his debts. This made the pliant prime minister his personal slave. With a similar use of royal funds and

The American assault at Germantown was disrupted by 120 British light infantrymen who turned a large stone house belonging to loyalist Benjamin Chew into a fortress. The Americans attacked the house with cannon, muskets and battering rams, losing dozens of men. But they could not penetrate its thick walls or solid doors.

favors, the King kept his grip on his majority in Parliament, in spite of fulminations from the Franklin-favored opposition.

The massive majorities of the past were gone, as more and more independent country gentlemen began to wonder where the King was taking the country. Early in March 1778 North won a vote on a new budget by only six votes. But the King was banking on something else that would temporarily restore his power: England's profound hatred of her traditional enemy, France.

On March 20, 1778, King Louis XVI formally received Franklin and his fellow envoys at Versailles. A week before, Count de Vergennes had notified Ambassador Stormont of the existence of the treaty of alliance, and the French ambassador in London had handed a similar note to the British foreign secretary. For his visit to Versailles, Franklin carried his performance as a simple republican to the level of consummate daring by appearing without a wig, sword or any other accoutrements to his simple brown suit, spotless white stockings and shirt, and plain shoes with silver buckles. The sight sent the royal chamberlain, the man in charge of approved court dress, into shock. For a moment he seemed to consider a protest as Franklin strode serenely into the King's dressing room. There Louis XVI greeted him with a lack of ceremony that perfectly matched the tone Franklin had set.

"Firmly assure Congress of my friendship," the King said. "I hope that this will be for the good of the two nations." Franklin assured him of Congress's gratitude and pledged their "faithful observance" of the terms of the treaty, which bound America not to accept peace with England without France's consent.

The following day a sullen Lord Stormont slunk out of Paris without paying his respects to the King. It was practically a declaration of war. In England the opposition gathered around William Pitt for one last attempt to bring down the North ministry. Desperately ill, the Great Commoner was all but carried into the House of Lords. He revived miraculously and began an excoriation of Lord North and George III that has seldom been equaled in the history of parliamentary oratory. As the King's friends seemed on the brink of rout, Pitt collapsed and was carried out of the chamber a dying man. The opposition was left in disarray, and Lord North bumbled on in the service of his relentless master. A few months later the British and French fleets clashed in the English Channel. The struggle for American liberty had become a world war.

ABOVE **William Pitt's collapse in the House of Lords was one of the most dramatic moments in British politics. Ironically, Pitt was trying to keep the American colonies within the empire. He never favored independence.**

Protracted Victory

A grim George Washington reviewed his starving army at Valley Forge in 1778. American harvests had been bountiful. There was no shortage of food. Congressional mismanagement, graft, speculation and civilian indifference were responsible for the ordeal.

"The play, sir, is over."

—Marquis de Lafayette

The American army starves at Valley Forge and Morristown. London is shaken by huge riots. The British shift the war to the South and score startling victories. The continental dollar collapses, and the American army shrinks ominously. With the aid of France, victory at Yorktown rescues the Revolution. George III considers abdication. George Washington resigns, amazing the world.

Joseph Plumb Martin, the young Connecticut militiaman whom we last saw fleeing up the east side of Manhattan, enlisted in the Continental army early in 1777. After several months of garrison duty in the Hudson highlands, his regiment joined Washington's main army in time to fight at Germantown. Then they were ordered to defend one of the forts the Americans had built to bar the British from the Delaware River and complicate General Howe's supply problems in Philadelphia.

It was, Martin later wrote, "in the cold month of November," and he had "not a scrap of either shoes or stockings to my feet or legs." The fort was on aptly named Mud Island, on the west side of the Delaware—a piece of oozing slime on which a man could not lie down without becoming soaked to the skin. The British pounded the fort with heavy guns, virtually leveling the walls each day. Each night, under the stern direction of a French engineer, the Continentals rebuilt them. At one point no fewer than six ships of the line blasted the defenders. Martin saw five men killed by a single cannonball. After three terrible weeks Washington ordered the depleted garrison to evacuate the wrecked fort.

Martin's regiment retreated to a winter camp Washington had set up at Valley Forge, twenty miles from Philadelphia. There they encountered another enemy: hunger. Night after night they dined, as Martin put it in his wry way, "upon a leg of nothing and no turnips." Even water was scarce. One night Martin paid another soldier three cents for a drink from his canteen. Most of the army was barefoot. "They could be tracked by their blood on the rough frozen ground," Martin recalled.

A Connecticut surgeon left this reaction to Valley Forge in his diary:

"I am sick—discontented—and out of humour. Poor food—hard lodging—Cold weather—fatigue—Nasty cloaths—hasty cookery—vomit half my time—smoaked out of my senses....What sweet felicities have I left at home; A charming wife—pretty children—good beds—good food—good cookery—

ABOVE *This gun-wielding woman attests to the guerrilla war that raged in the West and South.*

LEFT *Baron Friedrich von Steuben and George Washington stroll past the huts in which the soldiers lived at Valley Forge. Although the Baron spoke no English, he drafted—with Alexander Hamilton's help as a translator— a program that transformed the American army. One historian called it "the most remarkable achievement in rapid military training in the history of the world." Washington made him inspector general of the army.*

all agreeable—all harmonious. Here all confusion—smoke and cold—hunger and filthyness—a pox on my bad luck."

Contrary to myth, Valley Forge was not an example of American poverty. The soldiers starved because the Congress had allowed the army's supply system to fall into chaos. Elsewhere in America people were feasting on one of the best harvests in memory. But no one seemed to know how to get food to the army. It was the beginning of an ominous decline in the relationship between the soldiers and the Congress.

One of the heroes of this wintry ordeal was the Marquis de Lafayette. At Washington's request, the Congress had given him command of an army division. Soon everyone was admiring the way this nobleman, one of the richest men in France, shared the hardships with his men. Although it must have revolted his French palate, he ate the same unsalted "briled beef" and spent his own money to buy them warm clothing. His men began calling him "the soldier's friend." Lafayette was awed by the Continentals' commitment to the cause. "The patient fortitude of the officers and soldiers," he later wrote, "was a continual miracle that each moment renewed."

Lafayette proved himself even more valuable to Washington in the ugly little intrigue known as the Conway Cabal. While Washington wrestled with the almost insuperable problems of feeding his men, General Horatio Gates, the victor over Burgoyne at Saratoga, made a run at seizing command of the American army. He was backed by several disgruntled Congressmen and an

ABOVE *As their uniforms disintegrated, many soldiers at Valley Forge had nothing to wear but their blankets. "No pay, no clothes, no provisions, no rum," the soldiers sometimes chanted. But desertions were relatively few.*

ambitious Irish-born, French-trained volunteer, Major General Thomas Conway, who had preceded Lafayette to Philadelphia.

Conway tried to lure Lafayette into the plot by proposing that he take command of an expedition to conquer Canada. Flattered at first, Lafayette turned savagely against the Irishman when he discovered Conway and Gates were trying to destroy Washington. He warned the general to beware of the conspiratorial duo. Gates did not seem to realize that his attempt to take credit for Saratoga was forever tainted by his failure to get within a mile of the fighting. Almost everyone in the army, even Gates's admirers from New England, knew the real hero of that crucial victory was Benedict Arnold.

When Gates tried to persuade Daniel Morgan to join him in his campaign to unseat Washington, the ex-wagoner told him never to mention "that detestable subject" to him again. "Under Washington and none but Washington will I serve," he roared. Finally, Washington wrote Gates a blunt accusatory letter. Gates denied everything and vowed he was totally devoted to Washington's leadership. The Conway Cabal soon collapsed.

Another foreign volunteer made an important contribution to the army during the Valley Forge winter. Recruited by Benjamin Franklin in Paris, Friedrich Wilhelm Augustus, Baron von Steuben, began giving the Americans some of the military professionalism he had learned in the Prussian army of Frederick the Great. Steuben's claim to being a Baron was shaky, and his assertion that he had been a lieutenant general under Frederick was totally bogus. His highest rank had been captain. But he knew how to train an army.

Steuben banned what he called "the miserable British sergeant system" of drilling the men. He insisted on officers' doing the job—an idea that at first struck many of these gentlemen as beneath them. Even Washington, trained under the British system, had told his officers to drill their men only as a "disagreeable necessity." The Baron insisted it was the only way to build up the discipline and mutual confidence that would enable the Americans to maneuver on the battlefield.

Steuben began by drilling a model company of 100 men. They soon reached such a state of perfection that others strove to imitate them. Simultaneously, he wrote *Regulations for the Order and Discipline of the Troops of the United States*, a book that soon achieved the status of a classic in the American army. Again and again, Steuben urged an officer "to gain the love of his men" by putting their needs first—making sure they had decent food and clothing, visiting them when sick or wounded.

Although Valley Forge was defended by a chain of strong redoubts, it was vulnerable to attack by the 15,000-man British army in nearby Philadelphia, especially when the American army's numbers sank to 4,000 men. But Washington once more kept General Howe befuddled with an artful disinformation system that leaked vastly exaggerated reports of his strength to the British high command. As the snow began to melt, someone spotted a British agent watching the Steuben-trained Continentals march past with confident precision. The Americans decided to let the spy go back to Philadelphia and tell Howe they had become a truly professional army.

BELOW *Necessity forced George Washington to issue this proclamation, empowering his soldiers to seize food from farmers around Valley Forge. The Americans paid for it in depreciating Continental dollars. In Philadelphia, the British paid hard money—and had no trouble procuring all they could eat.*

No one rejoiced more wildly than Lafayette when the four-month ordeal of Valley Forge ended on April 30, 1778, with the news that Benjamin Franklin had signed a treaty of alliance in which France recognized the independence of the United States. One account has the Marquis rushing to Washington's headquarters and planting kisses on the startled commander-in-chief's cheeks.

Retreat from Philadelphia

Washington gave Lafayette command of a mobile force of 2,200 men with orders to advance to Barren Hill, halfway to Philadelphia and to watch the movements of the British army. Spies had reported that General Howe was resigning as commander-in-chief and that his successor, Sir Henry Clinton, had orders to abandon the American capital and withdraw to New York.

Washington's spies were correct. The British were in a panic. A French fleet was on its way to America. If it barred access to the Delaware, the Royal Army and Navy might be trapped. Clinton also had orders to detach 8,000 men to protect the West Indies and Florida from French depredations as soon as he reached New York. The possibility of the new commander's launching an offensive in America evaporated—plunging Sir Henry into fits of gloom.

Lost in the confusion were the peace commissioners whom Lord North

ABOVE *Baron von Steuben begain drilling a 100-man model company at Valley Forge. A former member of the Prussian general staff, the Baron knew more about training an army than any officer in the American or British forces. His language was vivid. When he tired of cursing the trainees in German and French, he would order his aide to curse "dese badauts" [idlers] in English.*

had dispatched to America to offer the concessions he had so evasively described in Parliament. They were thunderstruck to discover the British were about to evacuate the American capital, utterly destroying their bargaining power. They cursed Lord North and begged Clinton to delay the evacuation until they approached the Congress. He refused. The new British commander also refused loyalists pleas to let them try to negotiate a deal with the Congress that would permit them to stay in Philadelphia unmolested. They were told to cram their effects aboard the fleet that was departing for New York. So many of these frantic people rushed to take advantage of this offer that Clinton realized there would not be room aboard the transports for his army and its baggage. He decided to march overland to New York.

On June 18, 1778, Clinton crossed the Delaware and started his trek across New Jersey with a baggage train twelve miles long. Washington gave Lafayette command of a 4,000-man advance guard with orders to strike hard whenever the British looked vulnerable. Major General Charles Lee, recently exchanged after a year as a captive, asserted his seniority over the "boy general" and compelled Washington to put him in charge of this force. On June 28 Lee had a chance to cut off the British rear guard at Monmouth Court House, on the edge of the New Jersey pine barrens. His attack was confused and halfhearted, and when the rear guard counterattacked, Lee, convinced that Americans could not stand against British regulars, retreated.

An infuriated Washington rode to the front, dismissed Lee and took command of the battle. He managed to check the opening British assault until the entire American army was on the field. Clinton accepted this offer of a general action and threw his best troops into the fray. In searing heat the Americans withstood a series of headlong British attacks that continued until sunset. Monmouth proved the worth of Baron von Steuben's reforms. Watching the Continental regiments maneuver under fire, Alexander Hamilton later said it was the first time he realized the value of military discipline. During the night Sir Henry Clinton continued his torturous retreat to New York, leaving the battlefield to the Americans, who promptly claimed a victory.

The French Arrive—and Depart

On July 9 a strong French fleet appeared off the American coast, commanded by a distant cousin of Lafayette's, Charles Hector Theodat, the Count d'Estaing. Final victory—the destruction of the British army and fleet—seemed just over the horizon. Lafayette was Washington's inevitable choice as liaison to the Count, who spoke no English. The Americans expected the French admiral to fight his way into New York Harbor and attack Lord Howe's fleet, which d'Estaing outgunned, 850 to 534. But Howe planted his ships of the line just inside the narrow entrance to the harbor, where they would fire destructive broadsides at each French ship as she entered. D'Estaing lost his nerve and claimed his big ships drew too much water to make the attack.

A disappointed Washington proposed a joint operation against the 3,000-man British garrison in Newport, Rhode Island. They had been there for a year, almost forgotten in the campaigns against Burgoyne and Howe. The British had seized the seaport in late 1776 to give the fleet a deep-water harbor that would not freeze. D'Estaing agreed to cooperate, and Washington put

Major General John Sullivan in command of 4,000 Continentals, with orders to call out New England's militia. He asked Lafayette to help coordinate the operation and gave him command of one of the two divisions of the army.

Lafayette found himself trapped between two worlds. Sullivan was jealous of the Marquis and rebuffed his military advice. The Marquis was infuriated by d'Estaing's officers' condescending attitude toward the New England militia, whom they compared to "Tartar hordes." Worse, the French could see no difference between the militia and Sullivan's two tattered Continental brigades. The plan called for d'Estaing to land 4,000 marines who would cooperate with the Americans. Lafayette was driven half frantic settling arguments over who was going to have the honor of attacking first and other punctilios.

On August 9, 1778, the day after Sullivan had ferried his army from the mainland to the north end of Newport's Aquidneck Island, the French discovered that Admiral Howe's fleet was approaching from New York. Admiral d'Estaing sallied seaward to meet the enemy. Before the fleets could exchange more than a few fusillades, a tremendous gale scattered and badly battered them. D'Estaing's captains persuaded the admiral to withdraw to Boston for repairs, abandoning the Americans—and Lafayette—on Aquidneck Island. The hotheaded Sullivan virtually accused the French of cowardice. Lafayette exploded and almost challenged Sullivan to a duel.

The militia, disheartened by the French withdrawal, went home. When Sullivan tried to withdraw his Continentals, the British attacked, and the Americans found themselves in the inglorious position of fighting for their lives with their backs to the water. Among the heroes of this inconclusive clash was the First Rhode Island Regiment, which had 125 African-Americans in its ranks. On the night of August 30, Sullivan got the battered Continentals back to the mainland—just in time. On September 1 Sir Henry Clinton reached Newport with 5,000 troops.

The net effect of the Rhode Island adventure was massive American disillusionment with the French. Washington urged Lafayette to "afford a healing hand" to the wounded egos on both sides. The Marquis did his best to paper over the fiasco. But he could do little about the way d'Estaing's officers were insulted in the street by angry Bostonians. Nor could he stop the admiral from sailing off to the West Indies to fight the British for control of the lucrative sugar islands.

Lafayette was enormously depressed by the allied failure at Newport. He tried to persuade Washington to let him recoup by leading an expedition to conquer Canada, but this idea received an absolute veto from Washington. Firmly in charge of the war, Washington had no intention of wasting Continentals on another northern adventure. Instead he suggested that the Marquis return to France, where he might persuade his countrymen to send the Americans more substantial aid than d'Estaing's sail-by fleet.

Protracted War's Boomerang Effect

Gradually the Americans realized that the war was not over. As George III had hoped, the entry of the French on the American side had given the British a new reason to fight on. Moreover, England, with its mature economy and its sophisticated tax system, had the resources to do it. Americans, on the other

ABOVE *This painting in the heroic mode portrays Washington charging to the front to take command of the faltering American army at the battle of Monmouth in 1778. The Steuben-trained Americans fought the astonished British to a draw.*

hand, found themselves confronted by an invisible enemy that began to erode their confidence and sap their war effort: the depreciation of their money. By the end of 1777, the Congress and the states, most of which also printed their own currency, had issued $72 million in paper dollars. But they did not lay any taxes to support this paper avalanche. They had bet on a short war. Washington's strategy of protracted war forced decisions on the lawmakers that they lacked the power or the courage to make.

The four New England states, with their stern ideas about ordered liberty, tried to stem the raging inflation by voting to fix prices and wages by law. In February 1777 the Congress suggested other states should follow their example. New York, New Jersey and Pennsylvania complied, but no other state paid the slightest attention to the idea. Many patriots found price controls "inconsistent with the principles of liberty." By June 1778 the Congress was recommending that all attempts at controls be abandoned. The public had reached

this conclusion well before the politicians.

Congress's nonleadership on this vital issue was all too typical of its performance as the war continued. The members allowed much of their time and energy to be absorbed by internal feuds and quarrels. Gradually a rudimentary party system emerged, with the four Southern colonies tending to vote as a bloc, frequently in opposition to the four New England colonies, which also hung together. The five middle colonies gravitated piecemeal toward one or the other bloc, depending on the issue.

A quarrel that revealed the alarming fissures in Congressional unity erupted over Washington's request for half pay for life for Continental army officers. This was a direct imitation of the British system—but Washington could see no other way to retain a stable officer corps, especially when inflation began eroding the value of an officer's pay. The four Southern States, along with Maryland and New York, supported the proposal. The four New England states, still stoutly determined to rely on militia, persuaded Pennsylvania, New Jersey and Delaware to join them in opposing it. After much wrangling, the Congress reached a compromise in the spring of 1778: half pay for seven years after the end of the war.

But the issue was by no means settled. The New Englanders still insisted the policy would "debase human kind" and vowed to oppose the supposed greed of the "gentlemen of the blade." By and large, the Congress was incapable of creating a consistent policy on anything. The president had no executive power. Committees were transitory. Decisions could be unmade by any member reviving an argument that everyone thought was settled. The fear of giving the Congress too much power, lest it menace liberty, had produced a legislature with no power at all—a recipe for disaster. Delegates demonstrated their disillusion with the way the Congress worked—or failed to work—by voting with their feet. They resigned in droves or went home as often as possible.

Roiled Britannia

England was also displaying signs of strain. The first cracks in the imperial foundation showed in Ireland, where the loss of American markets for woolens and other products had triggered a deep recession. Banks and merchants went bankrupt at an appalling rate. For the first time, the Anglo-Irish Protestants began to feel almost as aggrieved toward the English as the oppressed Roman Catholics did. Irish trade was severely restricted to avoid competition with Scottish and English merchants. Lord North, hoping to improve the situation, persuaded the House of Commons to pass five resolutions, virtually giving the Irish freedom to trade with any part of the empire. The roar of rage from Scotland and England forced the prime minister to retreat. But the English had, in

TOP LEFT *This unflattering caricature of Charles Lee was done by the Polish engineer, Thaddeus Kosciuszko. After his poor performance at the battle of Monmouth, he insulted Washington, was court-martialed and suspended from the army.*

the words of one historian, "confessed their sins" in public. The infuriated Irish retaliated by forming companies of "Volunteers."

Ostensibly, these amateur soldiers were being drilled to repel a French invasion. But no one had any doubt that they might also become agents of an American-style rebellion. The British army in Ireland had been drained of almost every effective soldier to support the war in America. Even more mind-boggling, the Irish announced they would henceforth refuse to import English goods and products. In the House of Commons, Lord Rockingham pointed out the ominous parallel to the Americans' method of expressing their discontent. By October 1779 the Volunteers' numbers had swelled into the tens of thousands—all, wrote one observer, with "a spirit favorable to republicanism and independence."

In England a similar movement began to take shape as the economy felt the impact of the loss of America's trade and landowners grew increasingly upset by the soaring land tax and the plunging price of grain. In the fall of 1779, the landed gentry and small farmers of Yorkshire formed an association that petitioned the King to sweep out corruption and restore confidence in the government. The association echoed many of the things Edmund Burke and other opposition leaders were saying in Parliament. Soon no fewer than forty of these county associations were in business. With the gleeful support of Charles James Fox, they formed "committees of correspondence," with headquarters in London. The committees called for a general assembly of delegates to meet in London early in 1780. Would they become an anti-Parliament? The possibility of a revolution at home began to acquire unnerving reality.

With the opposition hammering him each day in Parliament and with Ireland and England rumbling volcanically beneath his feet, Prime Minister Lord North began to crumble. George III by this time had established a covert system to keep his distracted spokesman in the game. The King encouraged John Robinson, North's chief assistant, to write to him directly, letting him know what the prime minister was thinking and doing. Robinson also leaked information about North to his friend Charles Jenkinson, secretary of war. Jenkinson regularly passed on Robinson's letters to the King and served as a sort of sub rosa adviser to George III on a host of matters, not unlike Lord Bute, the King's "dearest friend" of yore.

Along with the Irish Volunteers and the English county associations, there was the added worry of the French and Spanish fleets. Their combined armada seized control of the English Channel in June 1779 and

TOP RIGHT *It took Count Charles d'Estaing, vice-admiral in command of the French fleet sent to America, 87 days to cross the Atlantic. He missed a chance to bottle up the English fleet in the Delaware River. He went on to worse failures at Newport and Savannah.*

BELOW *Dr. Benjamin Rush wrote Patrick Henry an anonymous letter urging him to join the conspiracy to oust George Washington. Henry sent the letter to Washington, who recognized Rush's handwriting. Rush hastily resigned from the army. He was a signer of the Declaration of Independence.*

THE STORY OF MOLLY PITCHER

Molly Pitcher was a nickname given to several courageous American women who joined their husbands in the front lines during battles. Best known is Mary Ludwig Hays, whose husband was a member of the First Pennsylvania Artillery. At the battle of Monmouth in 1778, with the temperature close to 100 degrees, she brought water to her husband's battery. When he was wounded, she took his place in the gun crew. Joseph Plumb Martin of Connecticut saw her in action. In his war memoir he wrote: "While in the act of reaching for a cartridge, a cannon shot from the enemy passed directly between her legs without doing any other damage than carrying away all the lower part of her petticoat. Looking at it with apparent unconcern, she observed it was lucky it did not pass a little higher, for in that case it might have carried away something else." According to one version of the story, Mary was presented to Washington after the battle, and he praised her courage. For decades American artillerymen offered a toast to Mary:

...Drunk in a beverage richer
And stronger than was poured that day
From Molly Pitcher's pitcher.

Margaret Corbin was another Molly Pitcher. During the British attack on Fort Washington, she took her husband's place when he was killed beside his cannon. She was soon hit by three bullets, leaving her unable to use one of her arms. In 1779 she became the first woman to receive a military pension from Congress.

Both these women were camp followers. Hundreds of women joined the army with their husbands and worked as nurses, washerwomen and cooks. Most did so from necessity, having no other way to support themselves. It was a hard life, and their services seem to have been barely tolerated. General Washington repeatedly called on his officers "to permit no more [women] than are absolutely necessary, and such as are actually useful" to follow the army. But Washington tacitly admitted their usefulness by permitting them to draw the same rations as soldiers.

In 1822 Mary Hays was also voted a pension. She had spent seven years in the ranks beside her husband.

for two weeks rode unchallenged off the great naval base of Plymouth. The outnumbered English fleet, commanded by a doddering admiral named Sir Charles Hardy, fled to Spithead and cowered in this sheltered anchorage between the Isle of Wight and the Hampshire coast. The commissioner of the Plymouth dockyard later confessed that he did not expect to be in charge of it "in ten hours longer." Frantic navy captains wrote letters begging the government to replace Hardy with Lord Howe. But American Secretary Lord George Germain opposed him because of his moderation toward the Americans.

For a while, it looked more and more likely that the French would achieve their dream of a successful invasion of England. But the French-Spanish fleet was commanded by an admiral as old and indecisive as Hardy. Ravaged by typhus and other diseases, the armada eventually limped back to Brest without firing a shot. The opposition used this piece of near-miraculous luck to excoriate Lord North for the nation's unpreparedness to meet the threat of invasion—and for allowing the enemy fleet to get away without a challenge.

As Parliament opened its fall 1779 session, Lord North all but collapsed. In a frantic letter to the King, the prime minister said he had been "miserable for ten years in obedience to your Majesty's commands" and begged permission to resign. The King would not even consider it. On November 28, 1779, while talking to John Robinson, North broke down. In a letter to Charles Jenkinson marked "most private," Robinson described the scene:

"He told me…that he was sensible that every one was leaving him and were plotting to desert him and overturn the King's Government, but why would they do that, why need they do it when he said [they need] only come and take his place, he was ready to quit to any proper Administration that could be formed, but that he could not form one, as he was the Man they all run at, that he saw clearly that he should be deserted [by Parliament] on some question…[and] it would endanger the King, that the dread of all this and that he should be the Cause of it distress'd him beyond Measure, that his Duty, His Honour and Every tie of regard, required him to state this to His Majesty and that it preyed on his mind so much as [to] render him incapable of anything, he had no Decision, he could attend to no business.…He then my dear sir, fell into such a scene of Distress, I assure you as made my heart bleed for him and drew tears from my eyes…."

Jenkinson, one of the hardest of the hard-liners, sent this appalling description of a prime minister in despair to George III with the comment: "I look upon all this as nothing permanent but as a disease of the mind."

Widening the War

In America the British army remained on the defensive in New York. But Washington's army was not strong enough to dislodge it without the help of a friendly fleet. The plunging value of America's currency made it almost impossible to bear the expense of a large army. Washington could only maintain a kind of siege in New Jersey and in Westchester County to prevent the British from foraging for food for their men and hay for their horses.

Elsewhere in America the British were less quiescent. In northern New York and western Pennsylvania, loyalist raiders and Indian allies struck savagely at exposed American settlements. On July 3, 1778, some 400 loyalists

MONEY

This paper money was printed by Congress. It was worth two-thirds of a dollar.

Before the Revolution, Americans suffered from a constant shortage of cash. The British would not allow them to set up a mint and refused to permit any large exports of their own silver coinage to the colonies. The Mother Country also insisted that money owed to it be paid in pounds sterling. This sucked hard money (coins in gold or silver) across the Atlantic.

The Americans were forced to rely on the Spanish milled dollar, known as the peso duro—a silver coin about the size of a modern silver dollar. Five of these were worth $5.00.

French money came in the livre, worth about twenty-five cents, the ecu, worth two livres, and the louis d'or, worth $5.25. Portuguese gold coins called joannes were called "joes" and were worth $8.00 and $16.00. Coins from Germany, Holland, Italy, and the Netherlands also circulated.

There was never enough of this hard money, and the American colonies frequently resorted to issuing paper money in the decades before the Revolution. In 1764 the British banned all further issues, because some colonies— notably Rhode Island and South Carolina—printed too much, and it tended to depreciate.

When the Revolution began, financing it with paper money came naturally to the Americans. But the war lasted too long and they printed far too much money By 1780 it took 600 Continental dollars to pay for goods worth one Spanish silver dollar. The phrase "not worth a Continental" became part of the day's slang.

Henry Hamilton, was known as "the hair buyer" because he paid Indians well for American scalps.

With Indian war parties everywhere, Clark was able to recruit only 175 men when he returned west to launch his offensive. Undaunted, he floated his minuscule army down the Ohio and marched overland to Kaskaskia, in the Illinois country. Mostly inhabited by French, the village and its neighboring hamlets surrendered without a fight.

Using presents shipped up the Mississippi by the American agent in New Orleans, Clark managed to pacify the thousands of Indians in his vicinity, who could have annihilated him any time they chose. Hearing about this American effrontery, hair buyer Hamilton counterattacked and seized the town of Vincennes, in Indiana. He planned to convert it into a base and lure the Indians back to his side with lavish gifts. With snowdrifts burying the woods and fields and with the rivers in flood, he never dreamt that Clark would attack him.

The Virginian took the offensive with a mere 127 men, half of them French volunteers lured by the promise of *liberté*. Wading through chest-deep, freezing water, with their drummer boy floating on his drum beside them, Clark's mini-army reached Vincennes in February 1779. Hamilton was holed up in the town's fort with seventy-nine men and twelve cannon. Clark frightened him into surrendering with a gesture of pure terror. He had captured five Indians with American scalps on their belts. Executing the warriors in full view of the fort, Clark vowed Hamilton and his men would die the same way if they did not capitulate immediately. The hair buyer gave up, and Clark marched him back to Virginia, where he was treated with surprising moderation as a prisoner of war.

I Have Not Yet Begun to Fight

In Europe Ambassador Benjamin Franklin went back to playing admiral—this time with a fighting Scotsman named John Paul Jones. In April 1778 commanding the sloop *Ranger*, armed with only eighteen cannon, Jones captured seven British ships, raided the Scottish harbor of Whitehaven and defeated a Royal Navy sloop in a fierce one-hour fight. England was thrown into an uproar. "Where is the British navy?" the newspapers screamed.

Franklin arranged for Jones to get a bigger ship, which the Scot named the *Bonhomme Richard* in the ambassador's honor. The *Richard* carried forty cannon and a crew of 380 from eleven different nations. Almost all the officers, however, were American. Franklin made Jones a commodore and put four other ships under his command. In mid-August 1779 they circled the British Isles, capturing seventeen merchant ships and taking more than 500 prisoners. The British were thrown into an even greater uproar.

Next Jones launched a moonlight attack on a huge Baltic convoy carrying timber and other vital supplies purchased in northern Europe for the British fleet. A frigate, the *HMS Serapis*, and a sloop, the *HMS Countess of Scarborough*, were escorting it. Captain Richard Pearson, commander of the *Serapis*, ordered the convoy to flee and attacked the *Bonhomme Richard*, while the *Countess of Scarborough* took on another Jones ship, the thirty-three gun *Pallas*.

John Paul Jones knew he was in trouble. The *Serapis* not only had more and bigger cannon. She had copper sheathing on her bottom, which made her much

THE INDIANS' REVOLUTION

In 1776 there were about 200,000 Native Americans living east of the Mississippi, making up 85 different "nations" or tribes. Their initial reaction to the conflict between England and America was bafflement—and neutrality. "We are unwilling to join either side," the Oneida nation of the Iroquois Confederacy said early in 1775. "For we love you both, old England and new."

The English had other ideas. Lord George Germain, the secretary of state for America, ordered the King's northern and southern Indian superintendents to lure the tribes into the conflict. In self-defense, the Continental Congress, which had initially urged the Indians to remain neutral, declared it was "highly expedient" to recruit Indians. In this contest the Americans, short of money and trade goods, were at a great disadvantage.

North and South, the two largest Indian confederations, the Iroquois and the Cherokee, took up the hatchet against the whites. In the Ohio Valley, the Shawnee and other tribes also joined the war. The Indians were motivated not only by the cloth, guns, ammunition and other trade goods the British showered on them. They resented the relentless pressure of the Western settlers on their ancestral lands. It was easy for chiefs to overcome the advice of cautious sachems and lead the young warriors into battle.

The result was disaster for the Indians. The arms-bearing portion of a nation is generally about 10 percent of its population. This means that the total number of warriors the Indians could field was roughly 20,000. Many large tribes, such as the Creek, remained neutral. Historians estimate about 13,000 warriors fought for the British in the course of the conflict.

The Indians won many minor victories against isolated frontier settlements, but they could do little against the overwhelming forces the Americans mustered in retaliation.

In 1776 Georgia, South Carolina

Thayendanegea was war chief Joseph Brant's Mohawk name.

and North Carolina sent 4,000 men against the Cherokee, and Virginia added a 2,000-man column. They routed the Indians and smashed and burned their villages, forcing them to sign a humiliating peace. Only a handful of warriors, led by an indomitable chief named Dragging Canoe, continued to resist. In 1778 his band too was routed and scattered by 900 Virginia and North Carolina militiamen.

In the North, the competition for loyalties split the Iroquois Confederation, a league of six nations that was the most sophisticated Indian polity on the continent. General Philip Schuyler, the commander of the northern Continental army, enlisted 300 Oneida and Tuscarora on the American side. The rest of the league, led by the brilliant, charismatic Mohawk chief, Joseph Brant, fought for the British, smiting the Americans with terrible ferocity at Cherry Valley and other outposts.

In 1779 the Americans retaliated with overwhelming force, sending Major General John Sullivan at the head of a 4,000-man army into the

heart of Iroquois country. Unable to field more than 1,000 warriors, the Iroquois fled to Canada, leaving their prosperous towns to be burned and their fields and orchards to be laid waste by the grim Americans. It was the end of the Iroquois Confederation. In their rage, the losers turned on the pro-American Oneida and burned their villages the following year.

The bitter border war continued, especially in the Ohio Valley. In 1780 a column of 150 Tories and 1,000 Shawnee captured two American forts on the Licking River and killed more than 100 Americans. George Rogers Clark led 1,000 riflemen into the heart of Shawnee country and burned the tribe's "mother town" of Chillicothe, in Ohio.

In 1782 came word that the British had abandoned the war. Most Indians were stunned. Many thought they were winning and bitterly denounced their former allies. An Iroquois chief told the British commander at Fort Niagara that it was "an act of...injustice that Christians only were capable of doing."

Soon American commissioners rode boldly into the Indians' villages and declared they were conquered subjects. When a Shawnee protested, "God gave us this country...it is all ours," he was curtly dismissed.

This attitude led to another series of bloody encounters—until the Congress recommended in 1787 that its representatives drop their "language of superiority and command" and deal with the Indians "more on a footing of equality." Thereafter, the American government attempted to follow this policy. But the tidal wave of Americans moving westward had no enthusiasm for it. Again and again the settlers' hunger for land rendered treaties null and void. In their view the Indians had joined the wrong side in the Revolution, and they had no right to equal treatment.

By and large this unspoken will of the people, sustained by frontier memories of bloodshed and death, prevailed for another century.

In the summer of 1776, two Cherokee and three Shawnee kidnapped 14-year-old Jemima Boone, Daniel Boone's daughter, while she was canoeing with two friends on the Kentucky River. This romantic painting does not come close to telling the true story. The feisty young women did everything in their power to delay their captors. They fell down, complained of foot injuries and refused to mount a horse the Indians stole. Boone and his men soon caught up with the harassed warriors, routed them with a blast of gunfire and rescued the captives.

faster than the *Richard*. In the first or second broadside, two of Jones's eighteen-pounders blew up, killing many men and wrecking the battery. Jones decided his only chance was to grapple the *Serapis* and storm her with a boarding party.

As the *Serapis* cut across the *Richard*'s bow to fire another broadside, Jones rammed her. For a few minutes the ships were locked together, and the over-confident Pearson called: "Has your ship struck?" (By striking, or hauling down her colors, a ship signaled she had surrendered.)

"I have not yet begun to fight!" Jones roared, giving the future U.S. navy one of its favorite sayings.

Backing off, Jones circled his adversary and this time laid the *Richard* alongside the *Serapis* so close that the muzzles of their cannon were almost touching. "We've got her now!" Jones bellowed. But his plan to win the battle with a boarding party failed. The British beat them off. Jones's men in turn beat off the *Serapis*' attempts to board.

A full moon poured golden light across the calm sea. On the cliffs of nearby Flamborough Head, thousands of British had gathered to watch the battle. For the next two hours, locked in their deadly embrace, the two ships blasted away at each other. The *Serapis*' heavier guns soon knocked out all but three of Jones's cannon. One of these the commodore was forced to load and fire himself.

The men in the *Richard*'s rigging were deadly shots, and the *Serapis*' gunners soon abandoned all the cannon on the open main deck. From the gun deck, beneath the main deck, the British ship's eighteen-pounders continued to blast shot through the *Richard*'s hull. Jones's three cannon were on his main deck and he was able to concentrate his fire on the *Serapis*' mainmast. The battle became a race between the swaying mast and the *Richard*'s perforated hull.

As the *Richard* began filling with water, one of Jones's officers rushed up to him and shouted: "For God's sake strike!"

"No, I will sink, I will never strike!" Jones shouted. He released British prisoners from the merchant ships he had captured and ordered them to man the pumps to keep the *Richard* afloat.

By this time half the *Richard*'s crew were killed or wounded. The chief gunner

ABOVE LEFT *These emaciated Americans were typical of the prisoners held aboard decommissioned British hulks in Wallabout Bay off the Brooklyn shore. Some historians estimate as many as 11,500 men died aboard these fetid death traps. Other British prisons, such as the Van Cortlandt Sugar House in New York, were almost as lethal. Americans generally treated British prisoners well. But many loyalists were abused in patriot jails.*

lost his nerve and ran aft to haul down the flag, shouting: "Quarters, for God's sake!" (Quarters was another term for surrender.) Jones threw his pistol at the gunner and knocked him unconscious.

"Sir, do you ask for quarters?" Pearson called.

"I haven't as yet thought of it," Jones bellowed. "But I'm determined to make you strike!" To prove his point he blasted another cannon shot into the *Serapis's* mainmast.

One of Jones's topmen crawled onto a *Serapis* yardarm and dropped a hand grenade through a hatch into the powder supply on her gun deck, causing an explosion that knocked out most of her cannon. More shots from Jones's guns struck the huge mainmast, making it tremble ominously.

The *Serapis* still had four guns firing—one more than Jones had left—but Captain Pearson decided there was no hope of defeating this stubborn Scotsman. He hauled down his flag, and the battle of Flamborough Head was over. A half-hour earlier, the *Countess of Scarborough* had surrendered to the *Pallas*.

As Jones's men took over the *Serapis*, her mainmast snapped and went into the sea. But her copper-covered hull was intact, and the commodore abandoned the sinking *Richard*. He sailed the battered *Serapis* to neutral Holland, where the news flashed through Europe: The Americans had beaten a British frigate in stand-up battle in England's home waters.

BELOW *John Paul Jones's moonlit struggle with the* HMS Serapis *was complicated by the presence of a French captain, Pierre Landais, who tried to sink Jones so he could claim credit for the victory. George III called Jones "a pirate...a rebel subject and a criminal." Jones named his ship* Bonhomme Richard *after Benjamin Franklin. It was the ambassador's French nickname.*

Waiting for the Admiral

None of these minor triumphs moved the Americans any closer to a decisive victory—nor did they stop the Continental dollar's downward slide, which caused growing unrest in the American army. The Congress, back in Philadelphia and enjoying a bountiful social life, seemed immune to this worry. The city was prosperous, thanks to a steady flow of goods smuggled from the West Indies and the infusion of hard money from the French loans that Franklin had obtained. A distraught Continental officer wrote from the American capital: "People here are fast asleep. It's as perfect a peace as it was in '73." Another patriot compared America to a great beauty who had landed a husband: "We have grown careless in our dress and sluttish in our manner."

The news that Spain had entered the war as France's partner—although without recognizing American independence—contributed to the politicians' wishful thinking. They ignored the fairly obvious fact that Spain's only motive was the hope of regaining Gibraltar, to which the Spaniards soon laid siege. It did not seem possible that the British could hold out against such mounting odds. In September 1779 the Congress sent John Adams to Europe to negotiate a peace treaty with Britain.

In the army, grim realism prevailed. Washington and his men began hoping desperately for the return of Admiral d'Estaing and his fleet. The Frenchman had won important victories in the Caribbean, capturing the sugar islands of Grenada and Dominica. It seemed logical for him to come north to escape the hurricane season and join the Americans in an all-out attack on New York. Washington raised everyone's hopes with a call for 12,000 militia from five nearby states.

Instead the admiral decided he could erase his American embarrassments with a quick victory over the British garrison in Savannah. He appeared off that city on September 4, 1779, and demanded its surrender "to the arms of the King of France." The British commander, General Augustine Prevost, requested twenty-four hours to respond and used the time to draw his scattered forces together until he had a respectable defending army of 3,200.

Still, the odds seemed to favor d'Estaing and the Americans. His fleet numbered 2,000 guns, and he had more than 4,000 troops, including a black regiment recruited in Haiti. But the Americans under Major General Benjamin Lincoln were able to muster only 600 Continentals, 750 militia and 250 cavalry led by the Polish volunteer, Casimir Pulaski. The French admiral reluctantly consented to a siege. When it went slowly, he grew impatient. The sailors in his fleet were dying of scurvy at the rate of thirty-five a day. His captains were warning him of disaster from a wandering hurricane. He ordered a frontal assault at dawn on October 9, 1779.

General Prevost's men had been given ample time to construct rugged defenses backed by plenty of cannon. When the allies attacked, the British met them with withering storms of grapeshot and musketry, killing Pulaski and several other ranking officers. As the assault faltered, the British counterattacked and drove many of the Americans into nearby swamps. D'Estaing was wounded twice trying to rally his shaken troops. In an hour the allies lost more than 1,000 men, and a disgusted d'Estaing returned to his ships and sailed home to France. What was left of the American army retreated to Charleston, where anxiety reigned.

In the fall of 1775, the British Parliament passed the Prohibitory Act, which declared that all American ships and their cargoes were open to seizure and confiscation by British men-of-war, "as if the same were the ships and effects of open enemies." The Americans retaliated by filling the seas with 1,151 privateers. The term is a shortened version of "private man-of-war." The Congress or the individual states issued "letters of marque" to private individuals who hired the crews, provisioned and armed the ships, and split the profits from the sale of any ships they captured.

In the course of the war, American privateers captured more than 600 British ships worth an estimated $18 million. While these losses undoubtedly made the British wince, historians doubt that the "rage for privateering" helped the American war effort. For one thing, it drained off manpower from the regular U.S. navy, where crews received only 50 percent of the profits of a capture, the rest going to the government. Privateering also absorbed fighting men who might have volunteered for the Continental army. Although some privateers fought notable battles with Royal Navy ships, most of them lacked the firepower to resist capture when a patrolling man-of-war spotted them. Many a privateering sailor found himself in a British prison, his dreams of big money cruelly shattered.

In New York the news of d'Estaing's repulse had an electrifying effect on Sir Henry Clinton. The poor showing of the Continentals and militia—and the courage displayed by the numerous loyalists in Prevost's army—suggested that the victory that had been eluding the Royal Army might be found in the South. "I think this is the greatest event that has happened [in] the whole war," Sir Henry said. "I need not say what will be our operations in consequence."

Funny Money

On the American side, the news of the French admiral's defeat and his departure for Europe destroyed the illusion that the war might end soon. That realization sent Continental currency into the abyss. The cost of basic commodities such as wheat, corn and beef doubled in two months. Confronting bankruptcy, the Congress stopped printing money. By this time, according to one calculation, there were 200 million paper dollars in dubious circulation. Since it now took, in Washington's words, "a wagonload of money to buy a wagon load of provisions," the army soon began to run short of food. The Congress, recognizing that the states could achieve nothing by printing more of their own money, urged them to supply the army "in kind." This meant they were expected to ship tons of food over the wretched roads of the day, without money to pay teamsters or buy forage for their horses.

Washington instantly recognized the fatal deficiencies of the system. The Congress was abdicating its responsibility for the army and passing it along to the states. In words that would acquire prophetic force, he warned: "Unless the states will…vest [Congress] with absolute powers in all matters relating to the great purposes of the war and of general concern…reserving to themselves all matters of local and internal polity, we are attempting an impossibility and very soon we shall become (if it is not already the case) a many-headed monster."

Well aware of the Americans' problems, thanks to his numerous loyalist spies, Sir Henry Clinton withdrew the garrison from Newport and left New York on December 26, 1779, with 8,700 of his best troops. His destination was Charleston, South Carolina. Behind him in New York he left about 10,000 men under General Wilhelm Von Knyphausen, the commander of the German troops in America. That was more than enough men, the British commander calculated, to cope with Washington's weak army. In fact, there were now more loyalist Americans in the British army than Washington had in his Continental line.

In the American winter camp at Morristown, New Jersey, the lowest temperatures and the most terrific blizzards in living memory numbed the bones of the half-starved soldiers. Washington began warning his mentors in the Congress that the army was on the point of dissolution. His men were eating "every kind of horse food but hay," he told one Congressman.

For days at a time, the men lived on a sickening compound of buckwheat, rye and Indian corn that they pounded into "firecakes" and heated on their crude stoves. Clothing was in equally short supply. One captain wrote a friend: "Many a good lad has nothing to cover him from his hips to his toes save his blanket." Nathanael Greene, who had taken on the thankless job of quartermaster general, looked out his window at the snowbound army on January 4,

1780, and exclaimed: "Poor fellows...more than half naked and two-thirds starved. A country overflowing with plenty are now suffering an army employed for the defence of everything that is dear and valuable to perish for want of food."

Inflation continued its rampage. In May 1780 one American officer paid $850 "for a bad supper and grog and a night's lodging" for himself, three others and three servants, without breakfast. Another soldier wrote: "An ordinary horse is worth 20,000: I say 20,000 dollars." The pay and subsistence for a captain was $480 a month; for a lieutenant, $126.60. In 1776 dollars, the captain was living on $13 a month and the lieutenant on $3.50.

The War Goes South

Meanwhile, Sir Henry Clinton was winning one of the biggest victories of the war at Charleston, South Carolina. Landing thirty miles south of the city in February, 1780, he soon crossed the Ashley River and began a siege. Inside Charleston the defending American general, Benjamin Lincoln, was wedded to Washington's strategy of keeping an army intact at all costs. Washington had reinforced Lincoln's army with Continentals from Virginia and North Carolina, as he had helped Gates's army at Saratoga. Lincoln wanted to abandon the city, but the South Carolinians—led by former firebrand Christopher Gadsden, now lieutenant governor—insisted he could and should defend the place. A mild-mannered man anxious to prove not all New Englanders were hostile to the South, Lincoln was reluctant to force the issue. While he hesitated, British cavalry routed militia defending the last escape route, and Clinton began surrounding the city with a ring of steel.

Soon heavy British guns were pounding Charleston, setting houses on fire and terrifying civilians. One cannonball hit the statue the city had erected to William Pitt after the repeal of the Stamp Act. It knocked out of his hands a stone tablet that represented the Magna Carta, the cornerstone of English liberty. Outside the city Governor John Rutledge tried in vain to muster militia for an attack on the British rear. By May 6 the Americans had enough food for only five more days of resistance. After another ferocious artillery bombardment, the South Carolinians reversed themselves and urged Lincoln to ask for terms. Lincoln surrendered the city on May 12, 1780. More than 5,500 men became prisoners of war, including 2,500 irreplaceable Continentals.

The Return of King Mob

The victory at Charleston had immense consequences in England, where the year 1780 had begun to acquire some of the characteristics of Armageddon. The county associations rained petitions on the King and Parliament, demanding an end to corruption and in many cases opposing the war in America. The Westminster Association, reflecting London's long-running hostility to George III, added that "the Crown has acquired great and unconstitutional influence, which, if not checked, may soon prove fatal to the liberties of the country." In the House of Commons, Edmund Burke backed the association movement with a bill that would require the King to reveal for the first time all the meaningless jobs and job holders on his civil list and cut £120,000 from the royal slush fund. Isaac Barré, the godfather of America's Sons of Liberty, called for the appointment of a select committee to study the public accounts.

Lord North, recovering from an initial panic that had produced another attempt to resign, adopted a strategy of delay and belittlement of the association movement. He sneeringly questioned whether the petitioners represented the people and resisted the idea of a public examination of the civil list because it would be "unsettling." Meanwhile, the leaders of the association movement began quarreling among themselves. Some of them favored radical ideas such as annual elections of Parliament. Only a comparative handful of counties sent delegates to the much-heralded London convention.

Soon ministry supporters such as historian Edward Gibbon were telling each other that "the rumours of a Civil War subside every day." Parliament, as irked by these extralegal challengers as they were by the Continental Congress, defeated Edmund Burke's bill by more than forty votes early in March 1780. Lord North coolly decided to coopt the critics by introducing a bill that would give the administration the power to investigate itself.

But the county associations continued to exert a powerful influence. On April 6, 1780, John Dunning, one of the lawyers who had represented Franklin before the Privy Council, rose in the House of Commons and introduced a motion that virtually echoed the associators' petitions: "Resolved, that the influence of the Crown has increased, is increasing and ought to be diminished." North denounced the motion as an "abstract proposition" that was "altogether inconsequential." A ferocious debate about the whole history of North's ministry, the American war and the new war with France erupted. At its close, Parliament supported Dunning's resolution by a vote of 233 to 215.

Once more North asked George III's permission to resign. Once more the King refused, saying the motion was aimed not at North but at himself. He was right. By this time a great many people had realized that the depressed, bumbling prime minister, who at one point during a debate broke down and wept in the House of Commons, lacked the will to sustain the disastrous war. George III relentlessly propped up North because to lose him would, in the King's black-and-white view of things, "end in evil."

George III seemed to be a prophet when John Dunning pressed his luck and introduced a resolution proposing that, until the proper balance between the King and Parliament was restored, the House of Commons could not be dissolved. This had ominous echoes of the previous century, when the Long Parliament of 1641 had rejected Charles I's attempts to dismiss them and started the English Civil War. Dunning was soundly defeated. Too many members shuddered at the possibility of a replay of that national disaster.

Watching these parliamentary gyrations, the mostly disenfranchised Londoners became more and more angry. By June they were looking for almost any excuse to vent their rage. They found it in a Scottish fanatic named Lord George Gordon, who was a virulent anti-Catholic. In 1778 Parliament had passed almost unanimously a measure to restore the civil rights of English Catholics. The fear of the Stuart kings and popery had long subsided. But when a similar law was proposed for Scotland, it led to riots in Presbyterian Edinburgh and other cities and the formation of a Protestant Association. In 1780 an English Protestant Association was formed in London, and Gordon was proclaimed its leader. He had been active in the Scottish agitation and

REVOLUTION IN BLACK

James Forten could have become the first president of Liberia. He preferred to remain an American citizen.

In 1780, fourteen-year-old African-American James Forten went to sea as a powder boy aboard the U.S. navy warship *Royal Louis*. He worked beside the men on the booming cannon as they won a fierce battle with the British warship *Lawrence*. But on her next voyage, the *Royal Louis* encountered three enemy warships and was forced to surrender.

Forten feared he would be sold into slavery on the British sugar plantations of the West Indies. Although he was a free African American, he knew the British often disposed of black captives that way—making as much as $1,000 a man. Fortunately, the captain of the British ship had his son on board. The boy was about Forten's age, and they became friends. The captain offered to take Forten to England and pay for his education—if he would give up his allegiance to the United States of America.

"No," Forten said. "I was captured fighting for my country. I will never be a traitor to her."

Forten was sent with the rest of the *Royal Louis*'s crew to the British prison ship the *Jersey* in New York harbor. On the crowded lower decks, the air was foul, and there was very little food. Forten spent seven months on this death ship. His hair fell out, and he was reduced to a skeleton by the time the war ended and he was released.

In 1776 one of six Americans was black—and 99 percent of them were slaves. Most of these African Americans lived in the South—but in some Northern states, such as New York and New Jersey, there were thousands of slaves. North and South, they reacted to the Revolution with hope and excitement.

They were stirred by the announcement of several British commanders, notably Lord Dunmore, the royal governor of Virginia, that they would be freed if they deserted their masters and volunteered to fight for the King. They were equally aroused by Thomas Jefferson's Declaration of Independence, which proclaimed the war a struggle for liberty.

The British soon dropped their early promise of freedom to runaways. It had outraged the numerous loyalist slave owners in the South and triggered protests in London from Englishmen who viewed "with indignation and horror" black slaves' being encouraged to revolt against white masters. As operators of a slave system on their West Indian islands that far surpassed American slavery in brutal exploitation unto death, the King's men could hardly pose as emancipators.

Not until 1779 did the British, desperate for manpower, return to the policy of offering freedom to blacks. The British commander, Sir Henry Clinton, justified it as a war measure. He argued that every slave who deserted to the King weakened the American cause. He defended himself against the accusation that he was fostering a race war by pointing out that Americans were using blacks as soldiers and sailors.

After some initial hesitation because of Southern objections, free blacks were accepted into the Continental army. When states began drafting men from the militia into the regulars, many whites sent slaves as substitutes, promising them freedom if they served honorably. By 1779 about 15 percent of the Continental army was African American. Large numbers of blacks like James Forten also served in the Continental navy and aboard privateers.

In 1777 Rhode Island fielded a 125-man black regiment with white officers. The Rhode Islanders fought well in several battles. Massachusetts also debated creating an all-black regiment but decided to mix blacks into their white regiments. In 1779 the Continental Congress, at the urging of Henry Laurens of South Carolina, voted unanimously to recommend

WHEREAS the NEGROES in the counties of Bristol and Worcester, the 24th of March last, petitioned the Committees of Correspondence for the county of Worcester (then convened in Worcester) to assist them in obtaining their freedom. THEREFORE, *In County Convention, June 14th, 1775.* RESOLVED, That we abhor the enslaving of any of the human race, and particularly of the NEGROES in this country. And that whenever there shall be a door opened, or opportunity present, for any thing to be done toward the emancipating the NEGROES; we will use our influence and endeavour that such a thing may be effected, *Attest.* WILLIAM HENSHAW, Clerk.

This protest against slavery in Massachusetts was published in June 1775.

that Georgia and South Carolina raise 3,000 black soldiers by offering them freedom. Laurens had been persuaded to back the idea by his idealistic son, Colonel John Laurens, who saw it as both a war measure and a step toward the elimination of slavery. But the proposal was rejected by Laurens's fellow Southerners, who feared arming that many blacks.

When the British shifted the war to the South from 1780-82, an estimated 20,000 South Carolina slaves joined the Royal Army, some voluntarily, others rounded up in raids to deprive the Americans of manpower. Additional thousands of slaves joined the King in Georgia, North Carolina and Virginia. Among them were seventeen slaves from Mount Vernon, who deserted to a British warship when it appeared in the Potomac near the plantation in 1781.

German Captain Jonathan Ewald said the British army in North Carolina in late 1780 had so many African-Americans attached to it that it resembled "a migrating...Tartar horde." Each officer had "three to four Negroes and sometimes one or two Negresses as cook or mistress.... Each soldier had his Negro to carry his food and his bundle. This disorderly train was followed by about 4,000 more Negroes of every age and sex."

Some of the runaways were organized into fighting units and won their freedom when the war ended. But most of these men and women met hard fates. At Yorktown, when the British army was trapped by the Americans and ran short of food, Ewald reported "all our black friends, who had been freed and dragged away to prevent them from working in the fields, and who had also served very well in making entrenchments, were chased toward the enemy. They trembled at having to go back to their former owners." Ewald deplored this "act of cruelty" and wished the British "had thought earlier to save them."

In British-held New York, Charleston and Savannah, many blacks were considered war booty and ended up on the

In this painting of Lafayette at Yorktown, the slave who became James Lafayette is acting as his groom. He soon went to work as a daring double agent. Lafayette was a passionate foe of slavery. He exhorted his American friends to end it as soon as possible.

cruel sugar plantations of the West Indies, enriching British officers who sold them. Many more succumbed to diseases that swept unsanitary army camps. Others were returned to their masters under article six of the peace treaty between Great Britain and America.

In spite of this ambiguous turmoil, the African Americans who fought for liberty on the American side changed many white minds about slavery. By the time the war ended, Vermont, Massachusetts and New Hampshire had abolished the institution, and Pennsylvania, Rhode Island and Connecticut had voted plans for gradual emancipation of their slaves. In 1862 historian George Livermore wrote a book on black participation in the Revolution that reportedly influenced Abraham Lincoln's decision to issue the Emancipation Proclamation. The President gave Livermore the pen with which he signed that charter of African-American freedom.

had developed an acute dislike of George III, whom he accused of being a secret pro-papist hungry for absolute power.

Unstable and possibly insane (he talked of decapitating the King), Gordon was a magnetic orator, and he soon had thousands of signatures on a petition to repeal the Catholic Relief Act of 1778. Remembering Lord North's sneering comments on the Yorkshire Association's signers, Gordon announced that he would not present his petition to Parliament with fewer than 20,000 signers beside him. On June 2, 1780, he led an estimated 60,000 people to Parliament to perform this ceremonial task.

At first the multitude was well behaved, but when Parliament voted to postpone considering the petition for four days, the associators went berserk. They rampaged through London, smashing up the Catholic chapels of foreign embassies. Next they attacked and demolished the biggest brewery in the city, which was owned by a Catholic, and drank its contents. When Parliament again postponed a decision, the violence escalated to unparalleled proportions.

The rioters stormed Newgate prison, set it afire and released the inmates. They sacked and destroyed the house of Chief Justice Lord Mansfield, the judge who had jailed John Wilkes, and narrowly missed killing that virulent anti-American Lord Sandwich, first lord of the admiralty, on his way to Parliament. Prime Minister Lord North was another target. Twenty grenadiers turned his Downing Street house into a fortress, but he was attacked on the street and was in serious danger until a member of Parliament rescued him with a drawn pistol. Finally, proving that some of them at least had revolution in mind, the rioters launched a determined attack on the Bank of England but were beaten off by troops.

For a week the mob rampaged through London, emptying other prisons and looting any house or store that looked promising. Replicating the Boston experience, not a single London magistrate had the courage to read the Riot Act, which would have authorized the use of troops to restore order. As the violence

LEFT *In June 1780, London was swept by immense riots. Mobs attacked the Bank of England, the prime minister's residence and the homes of many other prominent politicians. Here rioters burn the Kings Bench Prison after liberating its inmates. They gave Newgate Prison the same treatment. George III ordered the army to restore order.*

escalated, the opposition reformers became as appalled as the stand-patters in the government. Edmund Burke called for martial law, and that famous inciter of earlier riots, John Wilkes, went into the streets with a gun to fight for law and order.

George III decided to take personal charge of the situation. He summoned Lord Jeffery Amherst and ordered him to send in the army. The soldiers fought a series of pitched battles with the rioters, gunning down hundreds of them. Not until June 28 did Edward Gibbon inform his wife that "all tumult had perfectly subsided." The government said 458 people were killed or wounded, but unofficial reports put the toll much

higher. All concerned were badly shaken by the upheaval—but the political losers were the opposition. They were damned in Parliament and in the press for encouraging the idea of associations and petitions. Edward Gibbon commented that "the flames of London…admonished all thinking people of the danger of an appeal to the people." The King, as the only man in the government with the courage to act, won widespread praise.

Into this muddle of fear and reaction came Sir Henry Clinton's news of Charleston's surrender, the capture of thousands of American troops and the apparent collapse of resistance in South Carolina. With the civil government of Georgia restored and its assembly doing business under the royal governor, James Wright, the hopeless situation in America suddenly seemed transformed. Lord George Germain looked forward to "the recovery of the whole of the southern provinces in the course of the campaign." Optimism soared even higher as details of the collapse of the Americans' currency reached London through loyalists arriving from New York. Benjamin Franklin's ex-friend, Joseph Galloway, assured everyone from George III to Lord George Germain that most Americans were disgusted with the Congress and could barely wait to reaffirm their allegiance to His Majesty. George III decided it was the perfect time to spring a new election on the discouraged, defensive opposition.

The Forgotten Victory

On June 8, 1780, while London was being ravaged by the Gordon riots, the British army in New York, encouraged by the news of Charleston's surrender, decided to launch a surprise attack on Washington's seemingly demoralized army in Morristown. Loyalists had convinced the German commander, Wilhelm von Knyphausen, that he had a chance to become the man who ended the war. Thirteen days earlier the entire Connecticut Continental brigade had mutinied at Morristown and attempted to march home. Only the leveled muskets of regiments from other states had stopped them. Desertion had reached

TOP RIGHT *Lord Jeffery Amherst, British commander in the Seven Years War, led the army that smashed the 1780 riots. He had refused to serve in America.*

alarming heights in all units. On May 25 Washington had hanged a soldier who had sold more than 100 forged discharges to deserters so they could go home without fear of punishment by local authorities. With Continental money worthless, the states were finding it impossible to raise men. A bounty in paper dollars was a joke.

With 7,000 men, Knyphausen hoped to seize the passes through the Watchung Mountains in a night march and then descend on Washington's 3,500 Continentals, rout them and seize all their artillery and baggage, which was stranded in Morristown for want of horses. With the Southern army in Clinton's hands, the war would be as good as over.

Various things went wrong with this grandiose plan. An American patrol bushwhacked the advance guard, wounding the general in command and delaying their march until dawn. The militia turned out in surprising strength, and the New Jersey Continental brigade, stationed east of the mountains, made a fighting retreat that gave Washington time to get his men into the vital passes and onto high ground beyond the village of Springfield.

Eventually, the enemy was forced to retreat, after burning most of Springfield and Connecticut Farms (now Union). Although it was a victory that left the loyalists discredited, the experience did not seem very triumphant to most of the Americans who fought in this forgotten battle. Washington's aide Alexander Hamilton was disgusted. "Would you believe it," he wrote to a friend, "a German baron at the head of 5,000 men, in the month of June insulted and defied the main American army with the commander-in-chief at their head with impunity and made them tremble for the safety of their magazines forty miles in the country."

Colonel Ebenezer Huntington of Connecticut was even more vehement. Writing to his father, he denounced his "cowardly countrymen who flinch at the very time when their exertions are wanted, and hold their purse strings as though they would damn the world rather than part with a dollar to their army....I wish I could say I was not born in America. I once gloried in it but now am ashamed of it."

LEFT *In this painting of the 1780 London riots, the whole city seems to be ablaze. For a while England seemed on the brink of revolution. Even ex-agitator John Wilkes seized a gun and joined the struggle to restore order. More than 500 rioters died.*

A young militiaman, Ashbel Green, surveyed the battlefield the day after the clash. Looking around him in the morning sunlight, Green saw nothing but "gloomy horror—a dead horse, a broken carriage of a fieldpiece, a town laid in ashes, the former inhabitants standing over the ruins of their dwellings, and the unburied dead, covered with blood and with the flies that were devouring it." He was filled with melancholy. He was ready to say: "Is the contest worth all this?"

Partisan War

In the South a new kind of war was taking shape, far more savage and personal than anything fought in the North. It had actually begun before Clinton captured Charleston, with a minor clash between Georgia loyalists and rebels at a place called Kettle Creek. Surprising the loyalists as they were rounding up cattle for the British army in Savannah, the rebels routed them and took seventy captives. They condemned these men as traitors and hanged seven of them.

After Charleston fell, the civil government of South Carolina collapsed. Governor John Rutledge fled the state, the legislature disbanded and the courts ceased to function. The British fanned out across the state, setting up forts garrisoned by regulars and loyalists. "It is agreed on all hands that the whole state of So. Carolina hath submitted to the British government," wrote one glum Rhode Island Congressman. "I shall not be surprised to hear N. Carolina hath followed their example."

The social and political divisions between the mostly Scottish and Irish backcountry settlers and the lowland planters now returned to haunt the Carolinas. The lowlanders had led them into the war, and many backcountry people sided with the British in the hope of humbling the haughty aristocrats.

But some South Carolinians refused to submit to royal authority. Many of them were Presbyterians who feared their freedom to worship would be taken away from them if the British won the war and established the Anglican Church as the official religion. Joseph McJunkin was one of these holdouts. He had risen from private to major in the militia regiment from the Union district of South Carolina. After the fall of Charleston, he and some friends hid gunpowder and ammunition in hollow logs and thickets. But in June 1780 they were badly beaten by a battalion of loyalist neighbors and fled across the Broad River. At a Presbyterian meetinghouse, they met fugitives from other districts and debated whether to accept British protection. McJunkin and a few others vowed they would fight on. Finally someone asked those who wanted to fight to throw up their hats. "Every hat went up and the air resounded with clapping and shouts of defiance," McJunkin recalled.

A few days later these men met Thomas Sumter, a former colonel in the South Carolina Continentals who had fled west when the loyalists burned his plantation. "Our interests are the same," he told them. "With me it is liberty or death." They instantly elected him their general.

Elsewhere men coalesced around another South Carolina Continental officer, Francis Marion. Still others followed Elijah Clarke, who operated along the Georgia border. These partisan bands, seldom numbering more than 500 men and often as few as fifty, struck at British outposts and supply routes and attacked groups of loyalists whom the British were attempting to arm and train. Their hopes rose when they heard that the Congress, determined to regain South Carolina, had assigned Major General Horatio Gates, the hero of Saratoga, to march to their rescue.

Lost: A Whole Army

The Congress had not consulted Washington in the choice of Gates. But the American commander-in-chief loyally gave his devious rival 1,200 Maryland and Delaware Continental troops, among the best in the army. They were led by another foreign volunteer, the veteran soldier Baron Johann de Kalb, who had come to America with Lafayette. Summoning 1,800 militia from Virginia and North Carolina, Gates was confident of victory. But he soon demonstrated that he had failed to grasp Washington's doctrine that militia should be used only as auxiliaries to a regular army.

On August 16, 1780, outside the village of Camden, South Carolina, Gates put his militia in the front line with his regulars as a 2,500-man British army led by Charles Lord Cornwallis approached. Gates also ignored the half-starved condition of his men—the American supply system had broken down once more.

After a brief artillery duel, Cornwallis ordered a bayonet charge. As the howling regulars emerged from the gunsmoke, the militia ran without firing a shot. Wheeling, the British attacked the 1,200 Continentals from flank and front, overwhelming them in spite of their heroic efforts to make a stand. De Kalb died fighting beside his men. Gates fled with the militia and did not stop galloping until he was in Charlotte, sixty miles away. Even there he did not feel safe and with a few survivors of the rout kept retreating until he was at Hillsboro, 200 miles from the nearest British bayonet. It was a performance that destroyed his reputation as a general.

Whom Can We Trust Now?

The sum of America's 1780 woes was by no means completed by this avalanche of bad news from the South. In the North, Washington struggled to conceal his latest disappointment with the French alliance. Lafayette had returned in the spring with the exciting news that his King was sending an army of 10,000 men and a fleet to support the American cause. When the fleet arrived, it proved much too small to tackle the British fleet in New York, and the troops barely numbered 5,000. They were led by an affable but cautious soldier, Jean Baptiste Donatien de Vimeur, Count de Rochambeau, who settled them in and around Newport and grew more and more pessimistic about their chances of getting back to France alive.

The French general and his officers were dismayed by the barely breathing revolution. Washington had only 3,000 men in his army. The Continental dollar was at 60 to 1. Rochambeau brushed off Washington's proposal for a joint attack on New York, calling it a fantasy of "expiring patriotism." After trying to do business with Lafayette as an intermediary, the two men decided to meet in Hartford, Connecticut, on September 20, 1780. The conference was cordial but inconclusive. Rochambeau declined to budge from Newport. He cited his King's orders to keep his troops away from the Americans, lest there be a breakdown of discipline. Washington, forced to confess he had no

THE SECRET WAR

Espionage played a crucial role in the American Revolution. With both sides speaking the same language and loyalties frequently blurred and uncertain, the chance to spy was irresistible. The harsh fate of American spy Nathan Hale prompted Washington to centralize intelligence operations in army headquarters. In late 1776, spies helped him win crucial victories at Trenton and Princeton.

Soon the American commander and the man who became his chief of intelligence, Major Benjamin Tallmadge of Connecticut, were running networks of spies, using ever more sophisticated methods—cipher codes, invisible ink, double agents, disinformation.

Two of the most important American agents operated inside British-held New York. Robert Townsend was a merchant, and Samuel Woodhull a Se-tauket, Long Island, farmer. Their code names were Culper Jr. and Culper Sr. As a cover, Townsend wrote violently loyalist articles in *The New York Royal Gazette*. He picked up information from British officers and their mistresses and sent it to Woodhull via a courier named Austin Roe.

Woodhull would hang a coded signal on his clothesline, which was visible through a spyglass to Americans on the Connecticut shore. A crew of picked oarsmen would row across Long Island Sound by night, collect Townsend's letters, and rush them to Washington, who would apply a "sympathetic fluid" that revealed the secret messages.

Probably the Culpers' greatest coup was their report that the British planned to assault the French army as soon as it disembarked in Rhode Island in 1780. Washington aborted the plan by leaking his intention to attack the weakened British garrison in New York.

The Culpers were by no means the only American spies in New York. A huge Irish-American tailor, aptly named Hercules Mulligan, sent Washington invaluable information. Mulligan's "handler" was Washington's aide Colonel Alexander Hamilton.

One of the deepest agents was Samuel Rivington, editor of the unctuously loyal New York Royal Gazette. He stole the top-secret signals of the British fleet, which the Americans passed on to the French. This intelligence coup may have helped America's ally win several naval battles.

When the British occupied Philadelphia in 1777, Washington honeycombed the city with spies. The most successful was Lydia Darragh, an Irish-born Quaker who worked as a midwife and undertaker. The British requisitioned one of the rooms in her house for a "council chamber" in which they discussed their war plans. By lying with her ear pressed to a crack in the floor in the room above the chamber, Mrs. Darragh was able to hear a great deal. Her husband wrote the information on scraps of paper in shorthand and Lydia hid them in large cloth-covered "mould

Benjamin Tallmadge was George Washington's spymaster. Here he sits in postwar tranquility with his young son. No man knew more about the dark side of the conflict. In his old age he wrote a book claiming the Americans had won the war through the intervention of divine providence.

buttons." Wearing the buttons, her fourteen-year-old son wandered into the countryside and met his brother, a lieutenant in the American army. The brother snipped off the buttons and the information was soon in Washington's hands.

On the British side, Major John André became director of intelligence late in 1777. Before he made the mistake of going up the Hudson to confer with Benedict Arnold, André had some intelligence triumphs. His most successful agent was Ann Bates, a former schoolteacher who married a British soldier during the Royal Army's sojourn in Philadelphia. Disguised as a peddler, Ann wandered boldly through the American army's camp, counted the exact number of their cannon, overheard conversations at Washington's headquarters and accurately predicted the American attack on the British base in Newport, Rhode Island, in 1778.

Washington concocted several plans to kidnap Benedict Arnold after he deserted to the British. But they all misfired. The British in turn plotted to kidnap Washington. A 1780 warning from Hercules Mulligan aborted the most ambitious of these plans.

The intelligence war ended on a wry note. In 1783 Sir Guy Carleton, the last British commander in New York, began sending George Washington reports from his secret service predicting a plot to assault loyalists and loot the city. Washington made sure his troops arrived within minutes of the British departure, and there was no disorder.

Washington and Benjamin Tallmadge took special steps to make sure their agents were protected. The day after the British sailed home, the American commander had breakfast with Hercules Mulligan—a way of announcing that the Irishman had been a patriot. He also paid a visit to Samuel Rivington. There was reportedly a distinct sound of gold coins clinking in the bag Washington handed the Tory printer.

idea how many men he might raise for 1781, could only urge the French general to request more men and a bigger fleet.

On his way back from Hartford, a discouraged Washington decided to visit West Point. He had recently given Major General Benedict Arnold command of the post. Arnold had taken almost a year to recover from his leg wound at Saratoga. Washington made him military commander of Philadelphia, where his touchy temperament soon had him quarreling with Congressmen, who expected soldiers to be deferential. Before long a full-blown feud was in progress. It ended with several Congressmen accusing Arnold of using his position to make money as a businessman. Washington was forced to order a court-martial, which found Arnold guilty of two minor offenses. Washington gave him the mildest of reprimands and offered him his choice of jobs. He was somewhat surprised when Arnold chose West Point. Washington thought so highly of his battlefield talents, he wanted him to command one wing of the Continental army. Since there was little likelihood of a battle, and the fortress was vital to the control of the Hudson, the commander-in-chief gave Arnold the appointment.

The widowed Connecticut general had recently married a beautiful twenty-year-old, Peggy Shippen of Philadelphia, daughter of a family that included both patriots and loyalists. Peggy was a coquette, popular with Washington's young aides. Unknown to everyone, she was also a traitor. During the British occupation of Philadelphia, she had grown close to handsome Major John André, the adjutant general of the British army. It was easy for her to persuade her husband, brooding over the way the Congress had persecuted him, that he had a brighter future in a British uniform than he would ever have in the disintegrating American army.

While Washington was conferring with Rochambeau, Arnold was having intense conversations with Major André at a loyalist's house not far from West Point. After settling on a princely price for his treachery (£6,000) he handed André everything the British needed to know for a swift conquest of the fortress. But when André attempted to return to the British ship that had brought him up the Hudson River, he found it had retreated downriver after being harassed by cannon fire from vigilant militiamen guarding the shore. This unexpected development forced André to return to New York by land. En route, he was intercepted by three wandering militiamen who were probably

hoping to rob him. They forced him to strip and found in his boot confidential papers from Arnold.

The militiamen hustled their captive to an American outpost. The officer in charge sent André's papers to Washington, who was on his way from Hartford. The harried outpost commander inexplicably sent the prisoner to Arnold under guard, with a letter asking him to deal with this suspicious stranger. By happy chance, Major Benjamin Tallmadge, now Washington's chief of intelligence, visited the outpost. Tallmadge immediately realized the

ABOVE *The British called Francis Marion "the Swamp Fox" because of his fondness for taking refuge in South Carolina's many watery quagmires. A colonel in the Continental army, Marion became a brilliant guerrilla leader after Charleston surrendered in 1780. One British officer complained that he "would not fight like a gentleman or a Christian." Here, Marion and his men cross a swollen river.*

FAR LEFT *The Count de Rochambeau had been in the French army for 38 years when he was given command of the French expeditionary force to America. Level-headed and patient, he had orders to consider George Washington his superior officer. He obeyed the letter of this command but did not hesitate to push ideas that Washington disliked, such as the march to Yorktown.*

truth and ordered the prisoner returned, whereupon André admitted his identity. But the guard continued to West Point with the letter to Arnold. Realizing that his plot was blown, Arnold told his wife what had happened and a few hours before Washington's arrival at West Point fled downriver to the British sloop that was still waiting for André. The traitor got a surly welcome when he revealed that André had been captured.

Not long after Washington reached West Point, the messenger with André's incriminating papers caught up to him. It took Washington only a few minutes to figure out what the papers meant. "Arnold has betrayed us!" he cried. "Whom can we trust now?"

War Without Mercy
In the South, after Camden, the British decided to get tough with partisans such as Sumter and Marion. They declared that anyone who had signed a parole (a promise not to take up arms again), as thousands of militiamen captured at Charleston had done, and violated it by joining one of these guerrilla bands would be executed without trial if caught. Anyone who refused to serve in the King's militia would be imprisoned and his property confiscated. At a convention of loyalist militia regiments on August 23, 1780, the delegates resolved to apply these orders ruthlessly.

For the rest of 1780, a savage seesaw war raged throughout Georgia and South Carolina. Elijah Clarke besieged Augusta with a mixed band of Carolinians and Georgians. Forced to retreat by British reinforcements, he left behind about two dozen badly wounded men. The loyalist commander of Augusta, Thomas Browne, wounded in the siege, hanged thirteen of these men in the stairwell of his house, where he could watch them die from his bed.

A South Carolina rebel named Reed was visiting a neighbor's house when the man's wife saw two loyalists approaching. She advised Reed to flee, but

Reed said they were old friends and went out to shake hands. The loyalists shot him dead. Reed's aged mother rode to a rebel camp in North Carolina and displayed his bloody wallet. Twenty-five men leaped on horses and soon executed the murderers.

Seventeen-year-old James Collins became an "outlier," a fugitive living in the woods, after loyalists raided his settlement on the Broad River. "Women were insulted and stripped of every article of decent clothing they might have on," he said. "They even entered houses where men were sick of the small-pox…dragged them out of their sick beds into the yard and put them to death in cold blood in the presence of their wives and children."

In this sanguinary warfare, the rebels knew the back roads and forest tracks. Francis Marion's men were so expert at retreating into swamps that they earned him his nickname, "the Swamp Fox." But the British had some potent retaliatory tactics. The rebels could do little to prevent the destruction of their homes and property. If a man went into hiding when the British or loyalists summoned him to serve in their militia, all his crops and livestock were liable to seizure, and his house might be burned, leaving his family destitute. This bitter and discouraging truth became more and more apparent as 1780 waned. Without a Continental army to back them up, Sumter and other partisan leaders found it hard to persuade men to keep fighting.

The British had another weapon: Banastre Tarleton. This red-headed twenty-six-year-old cavalryman had begun his career in America with a flourish, capturing Major General Charles Lee in 1776. A lieutenant colonel by the time he reached South Carolina, Tarleton headed the British Legion, a 550-man quick-strike force that operated on the fringe of the main army. He soon became famous for the ferocity of his attacks and the amazing speed at which he and his green-coated horsemen traveled. On May 6, even before Charleston surrendered, he surprised the American cavalry at Lenud's Ferry and virtually wiped them out. Pursuing the Third Virginia Continentals, who had escaped the British net at Charleston, Tarleton covered 105 miles in fifty-four hours and destroyed them at Waxhaws on May 29. After Camden, he caught up with Sumter's band at Fishing Creek on August 18 and killed or captured 400 of them in another smashing charge. When Sumter raised more men, Tarleton caught them again at Blackstocks on the Tyger River. The battle was a draw, but Sumter was badly wounded, and his men went home.

The Green Dragoon

"Sumter is defeated," Tarleton wrote Cornwallis, now the British commander in the South. "His corps dispersed. But my Lord I have lost men—fifty killed and wounded." The war was becoming more and more disheartening to Tarleton. Deepening his black mood was news from home. His older brother had put him up for a seat in Parliament in the surprise election George III had sprung on the opposition. The voters had rejected him. They admired his courage—he was a national hero—but the American war was not popular in his home city of Liverpool.

Tarleton's political defeat was symptomatic of the overall results of the Parliamentary election, which had been held in early October 1780. With the usual combination of "gold pills," as George III referred to a bribe offered one

THE DEATH OF ANDRÉ

Major John André was, George Washington admitted, a "man of first abilities." That made it extremely difficult to condemn him to death by hanging for his part in Benedict Arnold's plot to surrender West Point to the British. The candor and courage with which the major admitted his role in the plot wrung the hearts of the officers on the court-martial board that tried him. But the board had no choice but to report that he "ought to be considered a spy from the enemy and…suffer death." André charmed Alexander Hamilton and other young officers of Washington's staff, who begged the commander-in-chief to make an exception to the rules of war. But Washington was acting under the eyes of the American people and he had to confirm the court martial board's sentence. Only one hope of sparing André remained—to exchange him for Benedict Arnold. Washington sent an officer under a flag of truce into the British lines with this message. But the British were also acting in the public eye. To surrender Arnold would destroy any hope that his example would begin a wave of defections from the American cause. The offer was glumly refused. Washington set in motion a plot to kidnap Arnold from British-held New York, but André's candor made the court-martial so brief that it never came close to fruition. On October 1, with a hand that, according to one version, visibly trembled, Washington signed the order sending André to his death at noon the following day. With drums beating, the handsome young major was escorted to the gallows, where he died with a gallantry that sent tears flowing down the cheeks of every witness.

member; control of rotten boroughs; and patronage the King had won another majority. But it was not the solid phalanx he had commanded until Saratoga demolished the nation's optimism. There was an edginess, a fragility, in Parliament's mood.

The Old Wagoner to the Rescue

In America the Congress, chastened by Horatio Gates's performance at Camden, humbly asked Washington to select another general who might salvage something from the wreckage of the cause in the South. Washington chose Nathanael Greene. This thirty-eight-year-old former Quaker, who walked with a slight limp, had become Washington's right-hand man in five years of war in the North. He was a firm believer in Washington's doctrine of the need for a regular army to stimulate the militia to turn out.

When Greene arrived in Charlotte, North Carolina, on December 2, 1780, he found little to encourage him. There were only 800 Continentals equipped and fit for duty in the American camp—and provisions for only three days. The army had scarcely a horse or wagon and not a dollar of hard money in the military chest.

There were two rays of hope in the gloom. The first was a militia victory at King's Mountain, South Carolina, on October 7, 1780, which put a large dent in British plans to create a loyalist army in the Carolinas. The rebel Americans, their ranks bolstered by several hundred "over mountain men" from Tennessee, had destroyed a 1,000-man loyalist force led by Major Patrick Ferguson, the British inspector of militia for the Southern provinces. King's Mountain taught the British what Washington had learned in 1776: Militia, unless they were supported by a regular army, could not be depended upon.

The second piece of good news was Daniel Morgan's return to the war. Irked by the Congress's failure to promote him, the Virginian had resigned in 1779. He had emerged from his sulk when he saw the South sliding into

RIGHT *The Southern army under Nathanael Greene, joined by militia under leaders such as Francis Marion, attacked a British army at Eutaw Springs, South Carolina, on September 8, 1781. At first the Americans seemed to have victory in their grasp. But a British counterattack forced Greene to retreat. However, British losses were so heavy that they fell back to Charleston, abandoning the rest of the state to the Americans.*

British hands. Studying his maps, Greene began to think Morgan might be the key to frustrating Lord Cornwallis's plan to conquer North Carolina in the winter of 1781. He decided to give Morgan more than half of his tiny band of Continentals, with orders to march into the Carolina backcountry and inspire the militia to stay in the war.

Taking with him the remnants of the American cavalry under Lieutenant Colonel William Washington, the commander-in-chief's young second cousin, Morgan began his campaign with two small victories. Washington's horsemen routed a group of loyalists at a crossroads named Hammond's Store and forced them to surrender another fort with a clever ruse, a wooden cannon. Soon the British were hearing rumors that Morgan intended to attack the British fort at Ninety Six, a key loyalist stronghold in the South Carolina backcountry.

Banastre Tarleton was Cornwallis's answer to this strategy. He rushed an order to his cavalry leader: "If Morgan is anywhere within your reach, I wish you to push him to the utmost." Tarleton obeyed with his usual speed. Scooping up a British regiment on garrison duty along the Broad River and another regiment that was marching to reinforce Ninety Six, Tarleton headed for Morgan's men, ignoring January rains and floods that turned the roads into gumbo.

With 600 Continentals and barely 400 militia, Morgan had no choice but to retreat and send out urgent calls for help. Tarleton, driving his men day and night, grimly gained on him. On January 16, 1781, Morgan halted his weary men at the Cowpens, a lightly wooded tableland not far from the Broad River, where local farmers pastured their cattle before driving them to market. He spent the night resting his men and describing his battle plan. He was going to position his Continentals on a slight rise in the center of the Cowpens. Behind them, out of sight, he would post William Washington and his eighty horsemen. Forward, among the trees, he would distribute 150 Georgia sharpshooters. Closer to the Continentals he would post a line of about 300 North and South Carolina militia. Both partisan groups were told to give the enemy two or three volleys and then retreat behind the Continentals.

Knowing the fear Tarleton's reputation inspired, Morgan repeatedly assured the jittery militiamen that the "Old Wagoner" would crack his whip over "Benny" in the morning. "Just hold up your heads, boys, give them three fires, and you will be free," Morgan assured them. "Then when you return to your homes, how the old folks will bless you and the girls will kiss you."

In the dawn, after an all-night march, Tarleton attacked in his usual headlong style. The Georgia sharpshooters emptied so many saddles that his cavalry fled to the rear. The Carolina militia's muskets wreaked even more havoc as the British infantry surged forward, bayonets leveled. When the militia ran for safety after delivering their promised volleys, the British cavalry, looking for revenge, tried to cut them up. William Washington led his horsemen into the fight and routed the green-coated dragoons. Swinging around, Washington charged the British infantry from the rear while the Continentals hit them with a volley from the front and followed it with a bayonet charge.

With half their officers dead or wounded, Tarleton's exhausted regulars disintegrated. Most of them threw down their guns and surrendered; others took to the woods. Tarleton, after desperate attempts to rally them, clashed briefly

"AFRICAN-AMERICANS NEVER RESISTED SLAVERY ON SO MASSIVE A SCALE AS OCCURRED DURING THE REVOLUTIONARY WAR YEARS. THIS IS THE MOST MASSIVE RESISTANCE MOVEMENT IN THE HISTORY OF NORTH AMERICAN SLAVERY."

Sylvia Frey
Professor of History,
Tulane University

RIGHT *Banastre Tarleton and the green-coated dragoons and infantry of his British Legion terrorized the South for more than a year. Described by one historian as "cold-hearted, vindictive and utterly ruthless," he was the best cavalryman of the war. This glamorous portrait was painted after the war, when Tarleton became a member of Parliament.*

with William Washington and fled. It was a stunning, all-but-total victory, and it lifted the people of the Carolinas from despair to new, miraculous hope.

Nathanael Greene immediately began applying Washington's strategy on a wider scale. He urged Sumter and the other partisan leaders to join his army to give battle to Cornwallis in North Carolina. "The salvation of this country don't depend upon little strokes nor should the great business of establishing a permanent army be neglected to pursue them," Greene told Sumter. "Partisan strokes in a war are like the garnish of a table, they give splendor to the army and reputation to the officers but they afford no national security....It is not a war of posts but a contest for States." The egotistic Sumter did not respond to this summons, but many other partisan leaders did, and Greene soon had more than 4,000 men in his army.

Morgan, crippled by sciatica and rheumatism he had acquired in Canada's subzero cold in 1775, was forced to retire again, but Greene took over the defense of the Carolinas. Using the same mingling of Continentals and militia, and deploying his amateur soldiers in much the same way as Morgan had at Cowpens, he met Cornwallis at Guilford Court House on March 15, 1781. In some of the most savage fighting of the war, Greene inflicted 532 casualties on the Earl's 1,600-man army—and withdrew, leaving the battered British no alternative but retreat to the North Carolina coast. Instead of following Cornwallis, Greene marched into South Carolina, where he soon gave battle to the British garrison there with similar results. "We fight, get beat, rise and fight again," he said, in a classic formulation of George Washington's strategy, which steadily eroded loyalist morale and British strength.

Mutiny in January

In the North, the total collapse of Continental currency forced Washington to distribute his army all over New Jersey and New York. He maintained his headquarters at New Windsor, New York, about a mile from the Hudson River town of Newburgh. This stopgap temporarily improved the Continentals' food supplies, some of which were now being purchased with notes issued by the first American bank, founded by Robert Morris in Philadelphia. But it put many of the regiments beyond the aura of Washington's personal leadership. On January 1, 1781, the Pennsylvania troops camped at Morristown drank enough rum to express their exasperation at endless months of bad or no rations and no pay. At nine o'clock that night, they mutinied, killed two captains who tried to stop them, and began a march on Philadelphia to settle accounts with the Congress.

Major General Anthony Wayne blocked their path with the New Jersey Continental line and rushed word to Washington and to the Congress. The politicians reacted with raw panic and prepared to flee, but Washington insisted that under no circumstances should the Congress cut and run. They would have to stay and face

BELOW *Rhode Island's Nathanael Greene was handpicked by George Washington to rescue the South from British control. Masterfully combining his small Continental army with militia, he cleared the South of British regulars without winning a single major battle.*

At King's Mountain,
South Carolina, American militia
annihilated a loyalist militia army,
killing their British leader, Major
Patrick Ferguson. "Over-mountain
men" from Tennessee played a key
role in this victory, which wrecked
British plans to arm the loyalists.

these angry men, lest the soldiers take out their grievances on the citizens of Philadelphia in an orgy of looting and violence. Washington prepared to rush to Morristown to appeal to the Pennsylvanians—until his staff warned him that if he left the regiments camped at New Windsor, there was a very good chance that they too might mutiny.

Anthony Wayne and two of his colonels spent the next six days pleading and arguing with the Morristown mutineers. They were encouraged when the men said they "spurned the idea of being Arnolds" and arrested two spies whom Henry Clinton had rushed to them with an offer of back pay in gold if they joined the British army. Finally Wayne persuaded the mutineers to hand over the spies for hanging—in return for a promise from Joseph Reed, president of the executive council of Pennsylvania, to give the mutineers everything they demanded: back pay, better provisions, the discharge of half of their number who had served three years, and furloughs until April for the other half. The Pennsylvania Continental Line, once one of the most dependable units in the army, dissolved before Washington's appalled eyes.

A few weeks later the New Jersey Continental Line mutinied in similar fashion. This time Washington reacted with severity, seizing four of the ringleaders and executing two of them. But he knew that he could not repeat this performance. The Continental army was obviously nearing collapse. As the spring of 1781 began, Washington wrote in his diary a cry of soldierly despair: "Instead of having magazines filled with provisions, we have a scant pittance, scattered here and there in different states….Instead of having the regiments completed, scarcely any state has an eighth part of its quota in the field….And

At the end of the battle of Cowpens, the British cavalry leader, Banastre Tarleton, met the American cavalry commander, William Washington, in a head-on clash. In this 1845 painting, Tarleton is on the black horse, Washington on the white. His black slave boy trumpeter saved Washington by wounding the British officer on Tarleton's right. The artist has the colors wrong. The British should be in green coats, the Americans in white.

instead of having the prospect of a glorious offensive campaign before us, we have a gloomy and bewildered prospect of a defensive one...."

A Traitor's Rampage

Making matters worse, if possible, Sir Henry Clinton dispatched Benedict Arnold with 2,000 men to raid Virginia. The traitor, now a British brigadier, sailed boldly up the James River to Richmond, routed the few militia that turned out and sent Governor Thomas Jefferson and his wife and children fleeing into the countryside. Arnold burned the public buildings, tobacco warehouses and other property and marched upriver to Westham, where he destroyed the foundry where Virginia made its muskets.

Setting up a base in Portsmouth, Arnold was reinforced in March and again ascended the James, burning the state shipyard, many ships and huge quantities of tobacco. Once again he easily brushed aside the scattering of militia who turned out to oppose him. A desperate Governor Jefferson begged Washington for his "personal aid." If the commander-in-chief appeared in Virginia, Jefferson was sure the militia would rise and drive Arnold into the Chesapeake. The harried governor did not seem to realize that if Washington rushed up and down the continent, trying to repel every minor British incursion, he would soon look foolish.

Clinging to his doctrine that Continentals would inspire militia, Washington dispatched the Marquis de Lafayette and 1,200 regulars to Virginia. The Marquis was promised French army and navy support from Newport. This venture swiftly turned into another allied fiasco. The British navy tangled with the French squadron off Cape Henry. Although the French admiral had the better of the contest, he lost his nerve and sailed back to Newport.

Washington ordered Lafayette, waiting in Annapolis, to move south without the French. The Marquis's mostly Northern troops considered the Southern climate lethal and promptly mutinied. The Marquis hanged a deserter and offered to let everyone else go home. He proudly reported that no one took him up on it. One reason may have been the small fortune he spent out of his own pocket to buy new summer uniforms for his troops. Unfortunately, Lafayette's appearance in Virginia worked no miracles. Although there were 50,000 militia on the rolls, the state's constitution had given the government almost no power to force them to turn out. Once more America's fear of impinging on personal liberty was creating impotence and chaos.

Reinforced by Major General Anthony Wayne with a newly recruited Pennsylvania line, Lafayette had enough men to turn back another British foray to Richmond. But in April the odds suddenly shifted heavily against him. Into Virginia from North Carolina, after resting and refitting his army at Wilmington, marched Charles Lord Cornwallis in an extremely disgruntled mood. Instead of following Nathanael Greene's army back into South Carolina, the Earl had decided Virginia was the key to subduing the South. En route he complained bitterly to the British general who had replaced Benedict Arnold at Portsmouth that he was "tired of marching about the country in quest of adventures." He too was weary of the protracted war.

Combining his army with the forces Sir Henry Clinton had sent to Virginia, Cornwallis now commanded more than 7,000 men. Lafayette could do nothing but retreat before this host. "I am not even strong enough to get beaten," he groaned to Washington. Looting and burning, the British rumbled into the heart of the Old Dominion. While Lafayette stayed just beyond his grasp, Cornwallis sent a revived Banastre Tarleton and his cavalry racing sixty miles to seize Governor Thomas Jefferson at Charlottesville. Jefferson was warned just in time by hard-riding Jack Jouett, who spotted Tarleton on the road and beat him to Charlottesville by a few hours, thereby earning himself the title of Virginia's Paul Revere. Jefferson fled into the woods as Tarleton's horsemen pounded up the path to his hilltop mansion, Monticello.

A dragoon shoved a pistol into the chest of one of Jefferson's slaves and threatened to fire unless he told where his master had gone.

"Fire away then," the slave said.

The dragoon let the man live and joined his comrades in enjoying the comforts of Monticello. Incredibly, although they numbered only 250, Tarleton's troopers stayed eighteen hours without a single local militiaman's challenging them. They did little damage to the mansion or the farms, unlike Lord Cornwallis, who occupied another Jefferson plantation—Elk Hill, on the James River—around the same time. Here, in Jefferson's words, is the havoc the Earl wreaked: "He destroyed all my growing crops of corn and tobacco, he burned all my barns, containing the same articles of the last year, he used…all my stock of cattle, sheep and hogs for the sustenance of his army and carried off all the horses capable of service; of those too young for service he cut the throat; and he burned all the fences on the plantation, so as to leave it an absolute waste."

The False Dawn of Peace

Shortly after Banastre Tarleton departed, Jefferson received a letter from the Congress, offering him a place in an expanded diplomatic mission to France to negotiate a treaty of peace. The ex-governor—his troubled term had expired—must have wondered what planet the Congress was inhabiting. But the politicians, under the influence of the French ambassador in Philadelphia, the suave Duke de la Luzerne, were dealing with bleak reality as they saw it. The peace that the Americans were expected to negotiate would be far short of the independence of the thirteen colonies.

In February 1781 the Count de Vergennes had begun putting out feelers to create a summit conference of European powers in Vienna. The foreign ministers

BELOW **In this old print, Americans expressed their outrage at Benedict Arnold's treason by burning him in effigy, while a traveling theater portrays the two-faced Arnold yielding to Satan's wiles. Arnold received £6,000 from the British even though his scheme to surrender West Point failed.**

of Austria-Hungary and Russia would act as mediators and propose to the Americans a settlement that would have been "lacking in delicacy" if the French had suggested it. The reason: It would have been a blatant violation of France's treaty of alliance with the United States. The Americans would be urged to accept a truce with England in which each side would claim the territory its armies controlled. For the British that would include all of Georgia and South Carolina and possibly North Carolina and Virginia, where they occupied the principal ports and had marched into the interior more or less unchallenged. George III could also claim northern New York, where the loyalists and Indians were still spreading terror with the tomahawk and scalping knife, and much of the southern end of that crucial state, in and around New York City.

Allowing the British such a large foothold in the heart of the rebellion was tantamount to abandoning the Americans to eventual conquest. But the war was a disappointing stalemate, and France was running out of money. The Count was a realist, and he thought he could prevail upon his equally realistic friend, Ambassador Benjamin Franklin, to go along with this plan. Just to make sure, he had Ambassador de la Luzerne persuade the Congress to instruct John Adams and the other American diplomats in Europe to do whatever the French foreign minister told them.

Outside New York Washington clung to the dwindling hope that Rochambeau would obtain enough reinforcements to join him in an attack on the city. Rumors of Vergennes's projected peace conference made him all too aware that 1781 was likely to be the last campaign of the war. Washington did his utmost to persuade the French to attempt "one great decisive stroke" that would expel the enemy from the country and enable "the independence of America [to be] established at the approaching negociations." But Rochambeau soon reported that instead of a promised 6,000 men, he was going to receive only another 600.

At a May conference in Wethersfield, Connecticut, the French general resisted attacking New York. Even with the help of the French fleet from the West Indies, he doubted their two small armies were strong enough to crack the

JEWISH PATRIOTS

Isaac Franks enlisted at seventeen. Captured on Long Island, he escaped and served until 1782.

There were about 2,500 Jews in America when the Revolution began. Almost all responded to the Declaration of Independence by embracing the patriot cause. Francis Salvador served in the South Carolina Provincial Congress and died fighting the pro-British Cherokee Indians in the backcountry.

Solomon Bush of Pennsylvania was a lieutenant colonel in the Continental army. He told his friend Henry Lazarus in Virginia that he was determined "to revenge the wrongs of my injured country."

David Franks was a businessman in Montreal. When the Americans invaded Canada in 1775, he lent them money and joined the cause. He became a major in the Continental army and Benedict Arnold's aide. A court of inquiry cleared him of guilt in Arnold's treason. In the closing years of the war, Franks's language skills made him a valued part of the American diplomatic team in Paris.

Best known of the Jewish patriots was Haym Salomon. Born in Poland, he came to New York in 1772. Although he early identified himself as a Son of Liberty, he stayed in New York during the British occupation, working as a commissary supplying the German troops. He also was involved in feeding the numerous American prisoners of war in the city. Almost certainly he was an American spy. He was imprisoned twice by the suspicious British. In 1778 he fled the city with his wife and child and went into business as a banker in Philadelphia, working closely with American financier Robert Morris to keep the fragile finances of the republic afloat.

In the 1780s when American currency became worthless, Salomon often lent money to members of the Congress, such as James Madison, interest-free. "I never resort to it [borrowing from Salomon] without mortification," Madison wrote to a friend in Virginia, "as he obstinately rejects all recompense."

After the war, Salomon led the fight against a Christian "test oath" for public office holders in the Pennsylvania Constitution. He deplored this policy which "disables [Jews] to be elected by their fellow citizens." The state soon repealed this un-American clause.

In 1790 Jacob Cohen, president of the Charleston, South Carolina synagogue, Beth Elohim, addressed a letter to George Washington. He said the new federal government's commitment to liberty had raised Jews from the "state of political degradation and grievous op-pression" which they faced in almost every other part of the world.

"Peculiar and extraordinary reason have we...to be attached to the free and generous constitutions of our respective states, and to be indebted to you, whose heroic deeds have contributed so much to their preservation and establishment."

city's formidable defenses. Instead he suggested a campaign in Virginia to help "the poor Marquis." Washington dreaded the thought of marching his mostly Northern army south, fearing the men would mutiny or desert in droves. He held out for New York, and Rochambeau became so testy that one of his officers wrote a letter to Ambassador de la Luzerne, accusing the French commander of insulting Washington. The British captured the messenger and gleefully published the letter in *The New York Royal Gazette*.

Theoretically, Washington was Rochambeau's commander. But he had no authority over the French fleet, either in Newport or in the West Indies. Neither did Rochambeau. On both sides throughout the war, admirals had to be persuaded to help generals. But as a fellow Frenchman, Rochambeau had access to the mariners, and he proceeded to write a crucial letter to the commander of the West Indies fleet, François Joseph Paul, Count de Grasse. He told him the enemy was "making his strongest efforts in Virginia" and that Washington's army was too weak to attack New York. Chesapeake Bay, he said, was where "we think you may be able to render the greatest service." If this turned out to be untrue by the time de Grasse arrived, in another two days he could be off New York. In a second letter Rochambeau urged de Grasse to bring troops and money. The Americans "were at the end of their resources."

The Quarrelsome Generals

In Virginia an equally important behind-the-scenes drama was taking place. Sir Henry Clinton and Lord Cornwallis began a vehement and ultimately venomous quarrel over the Earl's decision to invade Virginia. Clinton thought Cornwallis should have stayed in the Carolinas. Cornwallis at first tried to be polite, but he thought, with some reason, that he was a far better general than Clinton and could end the war if he were given a free hand. Back and forth the letters flew, with nasty comments multiplying on both sides. Clinton finally ordered Cornwallis to retreat to the coast, send half his army to New York and occupy the tobacco port of Yorktown as a base for future operations in Virginia. Cornwallis dutifully obeyed, but when he reached Yorktown, he informed Sir Henry that he would have to keep the troops because he would need every man to fortify the place adequately before winter.

Lafayette, knowing nothing of this quarrel, was baffled when Cornwallis began retreating to the coast. He followed him at a cautious distance until the Earl started crossing the James River at Green Spring Farm. Hoping to cut up the British rear guard, the Marquis attacked—only to discover that Cornwallis had kept most of his army concealed in trees along the north side of the river. Lafayette ordered a hasty retreat, but the clash cost him more than 200 men. Instead of pursuing the shaken Americans, Cornwallis crossed the river and continued his march to the coast. Lafayette immediately fired off letters to Paris, claiming he had forced Cornwallis to evacuate all of Virginia north of the James River. With the peace conference looming, the Marquis was operating as a combination general and publicity man. "It will look well in a gazette," he told Nathanael Greene.

In the North the French army finally left Newport and joined Washington's diminished Continental force at Dobbs Ferry, New York. The Americans were awed by the splendid white uniforms of the French regiments. The two armies reconnoitered and marched and countermarched around New York City for a month, but Sir Henry Clinton's troops met every probe with storms of musketry and cannon fire. On August 14, 1781, into their camp rode a messenger from the French admiral in Newport. He had just received word that Admiral de Grasse was coming to America from the French West Indies with twenty-nine warships and 3,000 troops. But he was heading for the Chesapeake, not New York.

Washington first reacted with dismay. Only a clairvoyant could have foreseen that this was the crucial card, the play that was to change the game from stalemate to triumph. The French had disappointed Washington so often, one can hardly blame him for wavering. A victory in New York would erase the stain of his defeat there in 1776 and would unquestionably guarantee American independence. A march to Virginia, on the other hand, might very well ruin his army and accomplish nothing—if the British fleet snatched Cornwallis and his army to safety.

The Great Gamble

Washington decided he had no alternative but to march south. De Grasse was not bringing enough troops with him to make an attack on New York feasible, even if Rochambeau could be persuaded to cooperate. Within a day the commander-in-chief was writing to Lafayette, telling him of the decision and urging him to block a British retreat into North Carolina. Next he turned to the problem of preventing Sir Henry Clinton from attacking the allied army on the march. He rushed orders to build ovens in New Jersey, to give the impression he was creating a base camp for an attack on Staten Island. When he crossed the Hudson and began the march south, he brought along some thirty large flatboats

ABOVE *This 1781 broadside reports that Lord Cornwallis is retreating from North Carolina after his hard-won victory at Guilford Court House. The Americans spread such favorable news to keep up patriot morale. Washington asked the Congress for money to carry a printing press with his army. The lawmakers turned him down.*

on wheels, again suggesting plans to attack New York. On August 18 he ordered a detachment toward Sandy Hook, as if he were thinking of capturing the British fort there to make it easy for a French fleet to enter New York Harbor.

Inside New York, Brigadier Benedict Arnold begged Sir Henry Clinton to give him 6,000 men. He guaranteed he would destroy the allied army, strung out in a long vulnerable line of march. But Clinton, convinced that the rebellion was expiring, declined to take any risks. He cited the "bold persevering militia" of New Jersey, who had shot up the British army that invaded the state in 1780. As August dribbled away, Arnold could only rage to fellow loyalists that "none of his propositions of service are listened to."

As their troops—2,500 Americans and 5,000 French—headed south, Washington and Rochambeau had several serious worries. At Newport were 1,500 tons of salt beef, reserve provisions for the French army. They would need this meat to feed their soldiers when they reached Virginia. Also at Newport was the French heavy artillery, which would be needed to bombard the British defenses at Yorktown. Washington and Rochambeau asked the French naval commander at Newport, Admiral Jacques Melchior Saint Laurent, Count de Barras, to transport these necessities to Virginia.

The admiral replied he would do no such thing. He was senior to Admiral de Grasse and had no interest in serving under him in the Chesapeake. Barras was going to cruise off Newfoundland and attack British fishing boats. Frantic pleas from Washington and Rochambeau changed his mind, and he grudgingly loaded his eight-ship squadron and headed south on August 23. Four days later Washington learned from coast-watchers that the British West Indies fleet had arrived in New York with thirteen ships of the line, joined forces with the seven-ship squadron in the harbor and put to sea on August 31. The chances of their destroying Barras and the precious salt meat and cannon were all too good.

On September 2 the allied column marched through Philadelphia in blazing heat, raising dust like a smothering snow. The proximity to the Congress stirred mutinous thoughts in the American regulars. They demanded an advance on their back pay—in hard money. Washington borrowed enough gold coins from the French army to give a month's wages to all ranks except those who "lost to all sense of honor...had deserted the standard of freedom at this critical moment." Those words indicate that some of his worries about desertion were coming true. The feeble condition of the Congress could not have raised his spirits: Five states had not even bothered to send representatives to the national legislature.

From Philadelphia Washington rode overland to Chester, while Rochambeau and his staff went down the Delaware by water to view the forts that had done so much to block British use of the river in the fall of 1777. When their ship reached Chester, the Frenchmen were treated to an amazing sight. General Washington was on the dock. He had his hat in one hand and his handkerchief

TOP RIGHT *Six-feet-two-inch French Admiral Count de Grasse was an impatient man with an explosive temper. But he kept his self control long enough to trap the British army at Yorktown. Defeated and captured by the British in April 1782, he played a key role in the peace negotiations between England and France.*

in the other and was swinging them in wide, whooping circles. When Rocham-beau came down the gangplank, Washington threw his arms around him and shouted the glorious news: A messenger had just arrived from de Grasse's fleet. He was in the Chesapeake with all his ships and the 3,000 troops. The soldiers were already ashore. Cornwallis, still in Yorktown, was trapped!

After a stop at Mount Vernon, where Washington had the pleasure of play-ing host to Rochambeau and his staff, the two generals resumed the journey to Yorktown on September 12. A messenger from Lafayette met them on the road with disturbing news. De Grasse had abandoned his blockade of the Chesapeake and put to sea to give battle to the English fleet when it appeared on the horizon. Washington must have wondered if they were about to replay the 1778 Newport fiasco. Would the French fleet sail away and leave the soldiers exposed to attack by a reinforced British army? They could only ride on and hope for the best.

Indecision at Sea

Fortunately for the future of the United States, the British fleet was com-manded by a third-rate admiral named Thomas Graves. Although he had the wind in his favor, Graves did nothing while de Grasse's fleet frantically tried to get out of the Chesapeake and form a battle line. Some French ships had to sail almost ten miles, tacking several times, to emerge from the great bay. "The fifth of September was a moment of ambition for me," Graves admitted later. But he did nothing to improve the moment with a headlong attack, in the great tradition of the British navy. Instead he went from missing opportunities to making blunders, giving his fleet contradictory signals that prevented half of them from firing a shot in the ensuing battle.

On their part the French, eager to settle old scores, fought with ferocity and badly mauled several of Graves's ships. The next day the two fleets cruised within sight of each other, but Graves had no stomach for another attack. Nor did he pay any attention to his second in command, Sir Samuel Hood, who urged him to take advantage of his copper bottoms, outsail de Grasse to the Chesapeake and force the French to fight their way back into the bay. When de Grasse disappeared over the horizon, Graves did nothing but order a frigate to follow him. The frigate's captain soon reported that de Grasse had returned to the Chesapeake—where he had been joined by another eight line-of-battle ships, giving him an overwhelming numerical superiority.

While Graves dithered, Admiral de Barras had slipped into the great bay with the precious provisions and siege guns. Graves asked Admiral Hood what they should do now. Hood replied that he did not know what to say "in the truly lamentable state [to which] we have brought ourselves."

The Siege Begins

In Williamsburg Washington was taking charge. He conferred with Admiral de Grasse and persuaded that volatile sailor to extend his stay on the American coast from two weeks to six weeks, if necessary. That gave the allies until the end of October to bag Cornwallis. On September 28, after building to the utmost his reserves of food and ammunition, and calling out 9,000 Maryland and Virginia militia to bolster his Continentals, Washington ordered the army down the road to Yorktown.

HOW WASHINGTON WON THE WAR

If we imagine statistics that might have been kept if George Washington were a boxer or quarterback, the figures are not very flattering. In seven years of fighting the British, from 1775 to 1782, he won only three clear-cut victories—at Trenton, Princeton and Yorktown. In seven other clashes he either was defeated or at best could claim a draw.

How did General Washington win the war? He won it by devising a strategy that was superior to British strategy. In war, strategy is the overall plan a general follows; tactics refer to how he fights his battles. At first the Americans and the British had the same illusory strategy. The war would be won in one huge battle—a "general action" that would decide everything.

After his defeat on Long Island in 1776, Washington realized he could not hope to win on those terms. The British had a bigger, better-trained army and a huge fleet. While everyone else wrung their hands and lamented that the war was lost, Washington kept his head and devised a new strategy. Henceforth, he wrote to the Congress, the war would be "defensive." Americans would "avoid a general action" and never put "anything to the risque." Instead they would "protract the war."

Lieutenant General Dave Richard Palmer, the former superintendent of West Point, has called this letter "a masterpiece of strategic thought, a brilliant blueprint permitting a weak force to combat a powerful opponent."

A vital corollary to this strategy was Washington's determination to keep a regular army in the field. In another 1776 letter he called it "an army to look the enemy in the face."

In 1778 Washington's second in command, British-born Major General Charles Lee, challenged Washington's strategy. He called for abandoning the regular army and resorting to "partisan war"—what today's soldiers would call guerrilla war. Washington refused even to consider the idea. Without a trained regular ("Continental") army to support them, he saw that the militia—the part-time soldiers—would hesitate to fight.

While the British army floundered after the Continental army, vainly pursuing a general action, Washington retreated or remained on the defensive—and struck when and where the British least expected him. In the later years of the war, General Nathanael Greene applied the same strategy in the South. Slowly but surely, the British Parliament grew weary of the seemingly unwinnable war. Washington's victory at Yorktown thus became the knockout blow.

ABOVE **A 400-man American assault column led by Colonel Alexander Hamilton, under the overall command of the Marquis de Lafayette, seized key British Yorktown redoubt number ten in a night attack. French infantry captured nearby redoubt number nine. Cornwallis's surrender became inevitable.**

In the ranks was Joseph Plumb Martin, who had left his Connecticut regiment to become a sergeant in an elite corps of sappers and miners. He described the march with the wry humor of a veteran soldier: "We prepared to move down and pay our old acquaintance, the British, at Yorktown, a visit. I doubt not but their wish was not to have so many of us come at once as their accommodations were rather scanty. They thought, 'the fewer the better cheer.' We thought, 'the more the merrier.' We had come a long way to see them and were unwilling to be put off with excuses."

In Yorktown Cornwallis had toyed with attacking the allied army in Williamsburg or on the march. At the very least, his troops expected him to fight hard for the outer ring of forts and redoubts they had built with immense toil in the summer heat. To the dismay of his men, Cornwallis abandoned these outer fortifications after only a few light skirmishes and withdrew into his inner lines. He had received a letter from Sir Henry Clinton, promising him that 5,500 men and a reinforced British fleet would sail from New York on October 5. It behooved Cornwallis to conserve his men until Clinton arrived. Then at last might come that "single battle that will give us America."

In spite of de Grasse's deadline, Washington decided to proceed with a siege. The memory of the hasty frontal assault at Savannah in 1779 haunted him. On the night of October 6, with rain drizzling, Joseph Plumb Martin and his sappers and miners prepared to dig the first trench. A tall man in a black cloak appeared out of the murk and asked them if they had seen the engineers who were supposed to lay out the lines of the trench. They did not recognize the man at first. With a gasp they realized it was Washington, sharing the risk of a British surprise attack. The engineers soon appeared, and for the rest of the night the diggers made the dirt fly.

In the dawn the chagrined British found the Americans working behind a solid barricade of earthworks, anchored by two strong redoubts on each flank. The "great trench" ran from the head of Yorktown Creek, near the center of the peninsula, and swung in a long arc to the high bank of the York River, where it came within 600 yards of two advanced British redoubts, numbered nine and ten. A deep ravine cut by Yorktown Creek made it unnecessary for the allies to dig their way across the entire peninsula. On the allied left, this natural obstacle hemmed in the British more effectively than any manmade ditch. With a forest of French masts behind them on the water, Cornwallis's men knew they were trapped.

By October 9 gun emplacements were completed in the trench, and the heavy cannon were dragged into position. At 3 P.M. Washington put the match to the touchhole of the first big gun and sent a twenty-four-pound ball whistling through Yorktown. For the next six days, the siege guns pounded the British fortifications day and night. Cornwallis was stunned by the power and ferocity of the bombardment. He had assured his men that the Americans had nothing but light field artillery in their army. It never occurred to him that the British navy would permit Admiral de Barras to transport the siege guns from Newport.

At first the guns concentrated on Cornwallis's headquarters, the three-story Georgian house of "Scotch Tom" Nelson, and swiftly reduced it to a shattered wreck. Looking for other houses the British might be using, they consulted Virginia's governor, Thomas Nelson Jr., Scotch Tom's grandson. "Fire on that one over there," he said, pointing to another handsome brick dwelling.

"Whose house is that?" asked Lafayette, who happened to be in the battery, watching the bombardment.

"Mine," Nelson said.

In New York, meanwhile, the British army and navy were locked in frantic argument. Admiral Graves had developed serious doubts about the advisability of attempting to fight his way past the French fleet to deliver Sir Henry Clinton and his reinforcements to Cornwallis. He feared that he and his ships would be destroyed piecemeal in the ensuing struggle. Rather than issue a flat refusal, Graves delayed the sailing date, claiming that several of his ships were still repairing damage from the battle with de Grasse on September 5.

By October 14 the allies' trenches in Yorktown were only 200 yards from Cornwallis's fortifications. Blocking the allied soldiers' path were redoubts number nine and ten. Washington decided to carry them by storm. He assigned number nine to the French and number ten to the American light infantry, commanded by Lafayette. Baron Antoine-Charles Viomenil, the haughty nobleman in charge of the French assault, grandly informed Lafayette he would be happy to send him reinforcements if he needed them. The American attack, led by Colonel Alexander Hamilton, succeeded so swiftly that Lafayette had the "unspeakable satisfaction" of being able to rush an aide to the Baron, asking if he needed reinforcements to secure redoubt ten, which was still resisting.

By morning the redoubts were connected to the American trench lines, and the engineers were constructing artillery batteries inside them. The guns would be able to pour round shot and shells into the forward British trenches, making it impossible for any soldier to survive in them.

Soon almost 100 guns would be pounding the British at point-blank range. The moment was approaching, faster than anyone expected, when the enemy, with his guns silent and his walls breached, would be stormed. On October 15 Cornwallis wrote Sir Henry Clinton a despairing letter, reporting the capture of his two advanced redoubts: "We shall soon be exposed to an assault in ruined works, in a bad position, and with weakened numbers. The safety of the place is therefore so precarious that I cannot recommend that the fleet and army should run great risk in endeavoring to save us."

There was no danger of that happening. Admiral Graves continued to find reasons for delaying his departure from New York. On October 13 the fleet was supposed to sail—when a tremendous thunderstorm swept over the harbor. Terrific gusts of wind snapped the anchor cable on one of the ships of the line, smashing her into another ship and damaging both of them. Once again the admiral decided he could not leave until the damage was repaired.

In Yorktown Cornwallis decided on a daring gamble that might rescue his army without Clinton's help. Across the York River in Gloucester was a British outpost guarded by only about 750 French troops and some Virginia militia. Perhaps remembering Washington's escape from Brooklyn Heights, Cornwallis decided to ferry most of his army across the river on the night of October 16 and break out of the Gloucester lines at dawn. By forced marches, living off the country, they would head north to the mouth of the Delaware, where they could easily contact British headquarters in New York.

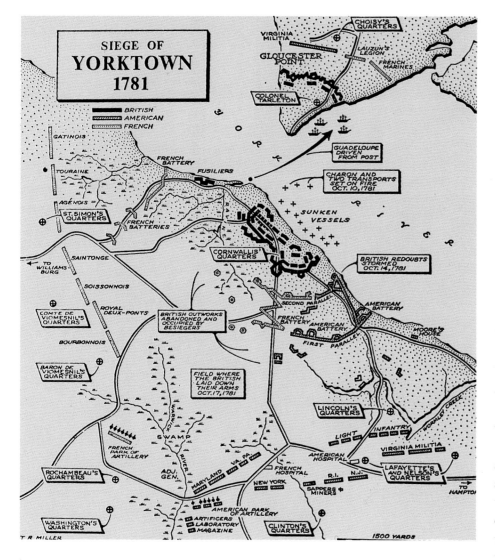

SIEGE OF
YORKTOWN
1781

▬▬▬ BRITISH
▬▬▬ AMERICAN
▬▬▬ FRENCH

GATINOIS
TOURAINE
AGÉNOIS
ST. SIMON'S QUARTERS
FRENCH BATTERY
FUSILIERS
FRENCH BATTERIES
TO WILLIAMS BURG
SAINTONGE
SOISSONNOIS
COMTE DE VIOMESNIL'S QUARTERS
ROYAL DEUX-PONTS
BOURBONNOIS
BARON DE VIOMESNIL'S QUARTERS
SWAMP
FRENCH PARK OF ARTILLERY
ROCHAMBEAU'S QUARTERS
ADJ. GEN.
WASHINGTON'S QUARTERS
T R MILLER

VIRGINIA MILITIA
GLOUCESTER POINT
COLONEL TARLETON
CHOISY'S QUARTERS
LAUZUN'S LEGION
FRENCH MARINES
GUADELOUPE DRIVEN FROM POST
CHARON AND TWO TRANSPORTS SET ON FIRE OCT. 10, 1781
SUNKEN VESSELS
CORNWALLIS' QUARTERS
BRITISH REDOUBTS STORMED OCT. 14, 1781
SECOND PARALLEL
FRENCH BATTERY
AMERICAN BATTERY
AMERICAN BATTERY
MOORE'S HOUSE
BRITISH OUTWORKS ABANDONED AND OCCUPIED BY BESIEGERS
FIRST PARALLEL
FIELD WHERE THE BRITISH LAID DOWN THEIR ARMS OCT. 17, 1781
LINCOLN'S QUARTERS
LIGHT INFANTRY
VIRGINIA MILITIA
MARYLAND VA PA
AMERICAN HOSPITAL
LAFAYETTE'S AND NELSON'S QUARTERS
NEW YORK
FRENCH HOSPITAL
R.I. N.J.
SAPPERS & MINERS
TO HAMPTON
AMERICAN PARK OF ARTILLERY
ARTIFICERS
LABORATORY
MAGAZINE
CLINTON'S QUARTERS
1500 YARDS

ABOVE At the tip of a peninsula, Yorktown became a trap for Cornwallis's army. He assumed the British would retain naval superiority and rescue him if he were attacked.

As the allied guns continued their relentless pounding, Cornwallis relieved the British light infantry in the front lines and marched them to the water's edge. There they boarded sixteen heavy flatboats manned by sailors of the Royal Navy. They were joined by the elite Foot Guards and the better part of the Royal Welch Fusiliers. It took at least two hours to make the trip back and forth across the broad river. Around midnight the boats returned, and a second contingent embarked. About ten minutes later a tremendous storm broke over the river. Within five minutes there was a full gale blowing, as violent, from the descriptions in various diaries, as the storm that had disrupted the fleet in New York.

Shivering in the bitter wind, soaked to the skin, the exhausted soldiers and sailors returned to the York shore. Not until 2 A.M. did the wind moderate. It was much too late to get the rest of the army across the river. Glumly, Cornwallis ordered the guards and the light infantry to return. About 7 A.M. Cornwallis; his second in command, Brigadier Charles O'Hara; and their staffs went to the forward trenches and morosely studied the sweep and scope of the allied bombardment. The commander of the artillery informed them that there were only 100 mortar shells left. The sick and wounded multiplied by the hour. Cornwallis asked his officers what he should do. Fight to the last man? Every officer told him that he owed it to his men to surrender. They had done all that was expected of them, and more. Silently, Cornwallis nodded his assent. He turned to an aide and dictated a historic letter.

"Sir, I propose a cessation of hostilities for twenty four hours, and that two officers may be appointed by each side…to settle terms for the surrender of the posts at York and Gloucester."

An hour later, atop the ruined parapet in the center of the British lines appeared a small red-coated figure beating vigorously on a drum. Lieutenant Ebenezer Denny of Pennsylvania, on duty in the American lines, said: "Had we not seen…the red coat when he first mounted, he might have beat till doomsday. The constant firing was too much for the sound of a single drum."

A moment later a red-coated officer with a white handkerchief appeared

Washington and Rochambeau led their two armies from Williamsburg down the road to Yorktown on September 28, 1781. Here, two miles from the British lines, they divide the responsibility for the siege between their forces. Rochambeau stands on Washington's right, giving an order. Washington had about 9,500 Continentals and militia. French troops numbered 8,800.

outside the British parapet and began walking toward the American lines. The drummer boy climbed down the wall and accompanied him. Where before there had been thundering cannon and trembling earth, there was suddenly, unbelievably, silence. Every allied gun ceased firing, and there was only the sound of the drummer boy beating. "I thought I never heard a drum equal to it," Denny said. "It was the most delightful music to us all."

Washington refused to allow Cornwallis to dicker over the terms. He was all too aware that a relieving British fleet might appear at any moment, prompting Admiral de Grasse to abandon the siege and sail out to meet it. Nor did he allow the Earl to insist, à la Burgoyne, that his troops could return to Europe. The 7,157 soldiers and 840 seamen were prisoners of war, and they were going to stay prisoners of war. At 11 A.M. on October 19, Cornwallis signed the final draft of the surrender document. Washington and Rochambeau waited in captured redoubt number ten for the text to be returned. They signed it there, and Washington ordered an aide to write above their signatures: "Done in the trenches before Yorktown in Virginia, October 19, 1781."

At about the same hour in New York, the British fleet, with 6,000 soldiers crammed aboard the men-of-war, finally cleared the harbor and began the voyage to the Chesapeake. "The stake is great," Sir Henry Clinton wrote to a friend in England. He had somehow convinced himself that Cornwallis's intact army would be waiting behind impregnable fortifications to join him for an all-or-nothing battle.

Upside Down

Later that day the British marched out to surrender in a meadow about a half-mile down the Williamsburg Road. At their head rode their second in command, Brigadier Charles O'Hara. Cornwallis could not bear to perform this final obeisance to the rebel Americans. The British regimental bands reportedly played an ironic tune. It was an old English air to which many songs had been written. One set of lyrics was called "When the King Enjoys His Own Again," but by far the most popular version was "The World Turn'd Upside Down."

Cornwallis was not the only Briton who found the surrender mortifying. Lafayette noticed that as the British passed down the lane formed by the American and French armies, every captive soldier had his eyes riveted to the right, toward the French, trying to blot out, by a physical gesture, the existence of the ragged Americans on the other side of the road. The Marquis snapped an order to his light infantry division's musicians. With a swoop of drums and a squeal of fifes, they exploded into "Yankee Doodle." As if on a string, every British head jerked in the opposite direction and they stared against their will into the impassive faces of their ex-subjects.

At the front of the British column, Charles O'Hara persisted in ignoring the Americans by offering his sword to Count de Rochambeau. The French general directed O'Hara across the road to Washington. There O'Hara stammered out an excuse for Lord Cornwallis's absence. Washington coolly instructed O'Hara to surrender his sword to Major General Benjamin Lincoln, the American second in command. Lincoln directed him to a nearby field, where the British piled their muskets.

THE PRICE OF LIBERTY

There were 1,331 engagements on land and sea during the eight years of the American Revolution. Among the states, New Jersey saw the most fighting, with 238 clashes; New York was second with 228. During this long, sprawling conflict, 6,284 men were killed in action, approximately 10,000 Americans died in camp of diseases such as smallpox and dysentery, and about another 8,500 men died as prisoners, bringing the total number of war-related deaths to 25,324. The William Clements Library of the University of Michigan, which assembled these figures during the 1976 bicentennial, stresses that they are very conservative.

James Thacher, a doctor in the Continental army, proposed a total of 70,000 deaths. Yet even the modern rock-bottom estimate reveals, when compared with deaths in other wars, that the price of liberty came high. The Revolutionary dead represented 0.9 percent of the American population at 2,640,000 white and black Americans. This number of deaths as a percentage of the population makes the Revolution the second-most-costly war in American history. Only the Civil War had a higher death rate—1.6 of the American population at that time. In World War II, the percentage was 0.28. Put another way, of the estimated 200,000 men who served in the militia or the Continental army at some point during the war, 12.5 percent died. Only the Union troops in the Civil War had a higher death rate—13 percent.

After the ceremony an American colonel wrote: "I noticed that the officers and soldiers could scarcely talk for laughing and they could scarcely walk for jumping and dancing and singing as they went about." Lafayette was equally exultant. He dashed off a letter to a friend in Paris announcing: "The play, sir, is over."

Washington gave aide Tench Tilghman the honor of taking the news to Congress in Philadelphia. It took the Marylander two days of hard riding on hired horses. When the Congress finished rejoicing, Tilghman asked them to pay for his trip. The Congress collectively hemmed and hawed. They could not do it. There was not one dollar of hard money in the national treasury. Finally, each member contributed something out of his own pocket, and the messenger of victory was saved from arrest for debt.

At around the same time, off the mouth of Chesapeake Bay, Admiral Graves, Sir Henry Clinton, and the rest of the British army and navy heard the news from loyalists who came out to the fleet in small boats. Graves swung his ships around and returned to New York where Clinton found a letter from Cornwallis reporting the surrender waiting for him.

By the time the news reached London, the city had lived through nine days of agonizing suspense. A frigate from New York had reported that Lord Cornwallis was trapped but held out the hope that Clinton and Graves might rescue him. On November 25 a Frenchman arrived from Paris with word that the Earl had surrendered. Later in the day the commander of the British sloop *HMS Rattlesnake*, a captured American privateer, brought dispatches from Admiral Graves, written off the mouth of the Chesapeake, confirming that the worst had happened.

BELOW *Brigadier Charles O'Hara, Lord Cornwallis's second in command, led the capitulated British army in the surrender ceremony at Yorktown. Lord Cornwallis could not bear to see his 7,157 regulars become captives. Later in the day, Washington gave a dinner for the general officers of the three armies.*

The responsibility of informing Lord North fell on the American secretary, Lord George Germain. Accompanied by two other ministers, he drove to 10 Downing Street and told the prime minister. "Oh God," North said, pacing up and down. "Oh God. It is all over. It is all over."

A Stubborn King

Actually, there were several scenes left in the drama. Parliament met the following day. The King spoke from the throne without saying a word about Yorktown. George III was obviously inclined to soldier on. The next day he wrote Lord North that he was delighted by the support some members had given his speech. It showed him that the House of Commons "retains the spirit for which this Nation has always been renowned...I do not doubt that if measures are well concerted a good end may yet be made to this war."

The King was living in never-never land. Britain was now fighting without a single ally. Russia, Prussia, Sweden, Denmark, Portugal and Austria had formed a League of Armed Neutrality that defied the British navy's insistence on searching ships of all nations for war materiel. Even Holland, Britain's traditional Protestant partner, had become an enemy when she tried to join the league, and England had declared war on her late in 1780. Parliament soon made it clear that the architect of this disastrous conflict, Lord George Germain, had to be jettisoned if George III hoped to retain any influence in the House of Commons. It took Lord North several months to persuade the King to agree to this, but Germain was finally tossed off the government's quarterdeck.

By that time it was too late for such stopgap measures. On February 22, 1782, the opposition proposed an address to the King, declaring that "the war in America be no longer pursued for the impracticable purpose of reducing the inhabitants to obedience by force." The motion lost by one vote. The following week, after some intricate infighting over the budget for the coming year, the motion won, 234 to 215.

North immediately tried to resign again. This time the King realized he had to go—but he tried to find another prime minister who could rally enough diehards to continue the war. This soon proved to be impossible, and Charles James Fox moved in for the kill. He announced he would submit a motion of no confidence that would force Lord North to resign no matter what the King said or did. A delegation of independent country gentlemen informed the prime minister that they were going to vote with the opposition.

When Lord North told George III of this desertion by men who had supported him throughout the war, the King wrote out an act of abdication. In its way it is a moving document, the statement of an earnest man who was so convinced that he was always in the right that he could not bear being defeated. Lord North replied with a letter in which he told the King some hard truths about English liberty that George had too long ignored: "In this country, the Prince on the Throne cannot, with prudence, oppose the deliberate resolution of the House of Commons." He reminded the King that his royal predecessors, including his grandfather George II, had yielded more than once in similar situations to prevent "terrible mischiefs" that could result from the clash of "two branches of Sovereign Power." North assured the tormented monarch that he would "lose no honor" if he yielded now, "having persevered as long as possible in what you thought right."

The King pondered this advice—and decided not to abdicate. But he was far from reconciled to North's departure. With great bitterness, George III warned the prime minister that if he resigned without royal permission, he would "forfeit my regard." When North sent him another letter of resignation, George III still refused to accept it. North resigned anyway, one jump ahead of Parliament's vote of no confidence. Loathing every minute of it, the King let the opposition form a ministry and begin negotiating with the Americans.

The Perils of Peace

Making peace turned out to be almost as difficult as making war. The instructions a supine Congress had sent to Europe—that America's negotiators were to do nothing without the consent of France—put Benjamin Franklin and his two associates, John Jay and John Adams, in a dangerous bind. France had her own territorial goals, notably in the West Indies. Spanish politicians were making noises about claiming control of the Mississippi and title to all the territory between the Alleghenies and the great river.

Franklin, who conducted the first round of negotiations alone, had no intention of playing second fiddle to the French, no matter what the Congress said. He had declared a year before that he would never yield a drop of the Mississippi. "A neighbor might as well ask me to sell my street door," he said. Moreover, his relationship with Vergennes was good. When he told the French foreign minister that he was going to try for the best possible bargain with the British, the Count made no objection.

The seventy-six-year-old ambassador's opening gambit was nothing short of breathtaking. He informed the chief British negotiator there were four necessary articles to the treaty of peace: 1. Recognition of American independence and the withdrawal of all British troops. 2. An agreement on the Mississippi as the western boundary plus the right to use the river. 3. A return of the Canadian boundary to the Great Lakes. 4. The right of Americans to fish in freedom and safety on the Newfoundland Grand Banks. To these four Franklin added several "advisable articles"—the chief one being the cession of Canada to the United States. He also urged the British to issue a public apology to the people of the United States to restore genuine peace between the two nations.

When Jay and Adams entered the negotiations, matters grew confused. Both suspected the French to the point of paranoia, and this inspired the English to drag their feet and try one last time to divide the two allies. During this wasted interval, victories on other fronts toughened the British stand. The garrison of Gibraltar beat off a combined French-Spanish assault, and a British fleet, led by Admiral Lord Howe, slipped through the blockade to bring the fortress enough food and ammunition to survive for another year. In the West Indies the British thrashed de Grasse's fleet and captured the admiral.

The revitalized British brushed aside the idea of apologizing for the war, refused to cede Canada, insisted on the payment of all prewar American debts to British merchants, and demanded compensation for the loyalists whose homes and property had been seized by the rebels. The Americans conceded Canada and the debts, but reimbursing the loyalists was unacceptable. Franklin maintained that they deserved nothing. They had gambled their estates against the rebels' estates and lost. As the situation teetered toward stalemate, Franklin proposed an article requiring Parliament to compensate the Americans for all the seaports the British navy had burned and for the houses their troops had plundered in the previous six years. The English swallowed hard and agreed to a compromise. The Congress would ask the states to restore or at least make some compensation for the seized property of loyalists who did not bear arms in the war or otherwise make themselves obnoxious to the American cause. Since the Congress's influence with the states was close to zero, it was a gesture that meant nothing, and everyone knew it.

The terms settled, the Americans signed the agreement without consulting the French. This was perilously close to violating America's treaty with France and unquestionably ignored the negotiators' instructions from the Congress. While Jay and Adams exulted over this display of American independence, Ambassador Franklin had the task of soothing the Count de Vergennes's extremely ruffled feathers. He not only managed this feat with his usual finesse, but he persuaded the irked foreign minister to agree to one last loan of 6 million livres.

ABOVE *The Treaty of Paris, signed in September 1783, ended the war between the United States and England. Two months later, the British army and navy evacuated New York.*

Early in 1783 the French and the British agreed on terms. Vergennes, pointedly reminding the Americans of the courtesy they had not offered him, invited Franklin to sign the document with him. Franklin smoothly swallowed the implied rebuke and signed without a murmur. Only one thing mattered to him. The war was over. Later that day, when he arrived at the home of the Duke de la Rochefoucauld for dinner, he threw his arms around this staunch supporter of America and exclaimed: "My friend, could I have hoped, at my age, to enjoy such happiness?"

Angry Soldiers and Careless Congressmen
In America George Washington found himself coping with a new threat to

liberty—the Continental army. In their winter camp near Newburgh, some forty miles north of New York City, the embittered soldiers, still unpaid by the bankrupt Congress, brooded on their country's ingratitude. Washington himself admitted their back pay extended, in some cases, six years. One historian has estimated the missing money totaled $6 million. The officers had also been voted pensions. Now a bankrupt Congress could not deliver, and the states were claiming that they had no obligation to make good on federal promises.

Some of the officers came up with a simple solution: Make George Washington King of America. He was the only man around whom the whole nation would rally. They were probably encouraged by the way a number of people, such as Major General Henry Knox, referred to him in their letters as "the father of the country." In May 1782 Continental Colonel Lewis Nicola asked Washington if he would consider becoming King George I of America. Nicola admitted that the title would be hard for Americans to swallow and some term "apparently more moderate" might be necessary.

Washington replied with a blazing rebuke. He told Nicola that "no occurrence in the course of the war" had given him "more painful sensations." Nicola and his small circle desisted, but a larger band of conspirators—working with wealthy speculators out to make a killing and Congressmen who dreaded disunion—were soon hatching a far more insidious plot. The army, they agreed, would refuse to disband when and if the peace treaty was approved by Parliament and the Congress. The soldiers would insist that the Congress get the power to raise enough money from taxes or tariffs to pay them. This access to revenue would theoretically add backbone to the union—and redeem all the promissory notes the speculators were holding. The plotters hoped to trap Washington between his loyalty to the army and his frequently stated desire for a stronger federal government, forcing him to lend his prestige to their cause.

The leaders of the conspiracy circulated an unsigned letter calling for a mass meeting of officers. Next came another anonymous letter, calling on fellow soldiers to do something about a country that "tramples on your rights, disdains your cries and insults your distresses." Washington's reaction to these "Newburgh addresses" was immediate and fierce. He condemned the unauthorized meeting and announced his determination to "arrest on the spot the foot that [is] wavering on a tremendous precipice." Washington saw that if the army got away with bullying Congress, it would set an example that would cause America endless tragedies in the future.

On March 13, 1783, Washington met with his officers in a large building, called the Temple. It was used as a church on Sundays and as a dance hall on other occasions. The commander-in-chief gave a passionate speech, pleading with the men, "as you value your own sacred honor," to ignore the anonymous letters calling for a march on the Congress. He urged them to look with "utmost horror and detestation" on any man who "wishes, under any specious pretenses, to overturn the liberties of our country." The men listened, but their faces remained hard. They were still angry. Washington closed with a plea that the soldiers conduct themselves so that their posterity would say: "Had this day been wanting, the world had never seen the last stage of perfection to which human nature is capable of attaining." Still, the resistance in the room remained almost palpable.

Then Washington drew from his pocket a letter from a Congressman, assuring him that the Congress was trying to respond to the army's complaints. After a moment's hesitation, he pulled out a pair of glasses. Only his aides had seen him wearing them for the previous several months. "Gentlemen," he said. "You will permit me to put on my spectacles, for I have not only grown gray but almost blind in your service."

A wave of emotion swept through the officers. More effectively than all Washington's exhortations, this simple statement of fact demolished almost every man in the hall. Many wept openly. Washington read the Congressman's letter and departed, leaving the men to make their decision without him. They voted their thanks to the commander-in-chief, repudiated the anonymous letters and expressed their confidence in the Congress. The worst crisis yet in the brief history of American liberty was over.

I Now Take Leave of You

When the final peace treaties reached America in November 1783, the British army evacuated New York and sailed home. By that time most of the Continental army had been discharged. Joseph Plumb Martin described his departure in June 1783: " 'The old man,' our captain, came into our room…and…handed us our discharges." The men received "settlement certificates"—essentially promissory notes for their back pay—from the Congress. Most sold them to speculators to get money to buy decent civilian clothing. To Martin's surprise, on the day he departed, he felt "as much sorrow as joy." After having lived with his comrades "as a family of brothers," he found it hard to say goodbye.

Washington and his few remaining officers had a similar experience. They rode into New York City on the day the British departed. Several days later they said farewell at a dinner at Fraunces Tavern. As tears flowed, Washington said: "With a heart full of love and gratitude, I now take leave of you. I most devoutly wish that your later days may be as prosperous and happy as your former ones have been glorious and honorable."

Crossing the Hudson, Washington rode south to Annapolis, Maryland, where the Congress was now sitting. Several months earlier they had been chased out of Philadelphia by a riotous mob of recent recruits for the Pennsylvania Continental Line, demanding back pay. Only twenty members representing seven states were present. Around noon on December 23, 1783, Washington walked to the Maryland State House, where he was met by Charles Thomson, the secretary of the Congress since 1774. He escorted the general to the chamber where the Congress was meeting.

"Sir," said the latest president, Thomas Mifflin of Pennsylvania, "the United States in Congress assembled are prepared to receive your communications."

Washington rose and bowed; the members of the Congress took off their hats as a sign of respect but did not return the bow—as a sign of the authority of the civil over the military. With hands that trembled slightly, Washington read his prepared statement.

Happy that the United States was now a "respectable nation," he resigned "with satisfaction the appointment I accepted with diffidence." He urged "the favorable notice" of the Congress for his aides, especially those who had served him until this final day. When he reached the passage in which he commended

ABOVE *Washington embraces his artillery commander, Major General Henry Knox, at his farewell dinner with his officers at New York's Fraunces Tavern. Major Benjamin Tallmadge said he had never witnessed "such a scene of sorrow and weeping. The simple thought that we should see his face no more in this world seemed to be utterly insupportable." The tavern still stands on the corner of Broad and Pearl Street. Built in 1719, it is the oldest surviving building in Manhattan. Washington hired "Black Sam" Fraunces as his steward when he became President in 1789.*

ABOVE **This John Trumbull painting of George Washington resigning his commission hangs in the Capitol in Washington D.C. The president of the Congress, Pennsylvanian Thomas Mifflin, a long-time foe of the commander-in-chief, answered Washington's emotional statement in a speech written for him by delegate Thomas Jefferson of Virginia. Spectators thought Mifflin's reply lacked feeling.**

"the interests of our dearest Country to the protection of Almighty God," his voice dwindled and he had to struggle against an impulse to weep. "The whole house felt his agitations," his ex-aide James McHenry, now a Maryland Congressman, wrote in a letter to his fiancée.

Regaining his self-control, Washington continued: "Having now finished the work assigned me, I retire from the great theatre of action, and bidding an affectionate farewell to this august body under whose orders I have so long acted, I here offer my commission and take my leave of all the employments of public life."

"The spectators all wept," McHenry wrote, "and there was hardly a member of Congress who did not drop tears."

The scene evoked so many memories—the hairbreadth victory at Trenton in 1776, the winter agonies of Valley Forge and Morristown, the improbable salvation of Yorktown. The spectators also recognized the immense significance of this relinquishment of military power. It guaranteed that American liberty would never become a mere slogan mouthed by a dictator. It was a reality whose meaning would expand and deepen, thanks in large part to this extraordinary man, George Washington.

Around the same time Benjamin West, the gifted American painter who had moved to London before the Revolution, discussed the close of the war with George III. The King asked West what he thought Washington would do now. West predicted he would resign and return to private life. "If he does that, sir," the King exclaimed, "he will be the greatest man in the world."

George III's words were an oblique admission that the King and his fellow aristocrats, with their narrow conception of a liberty that gave them the exclusive power to rule, had begun to understand the epochal nature of the revolution that American liberty had created, not merely for the Americans, but for men and women everywhere.

Liberty Versus Union

Trenton, site of George Washington's 1776 victory that rescued the Revolution, gave the newly elected President one of his most stirring receptions on his inaugural journey to New York.

"Let us raise a standard to which the wise and honest can repair."

—George Washington

Embittered loyalists flee to Canada. American liberty imbues the arts and education with the spirit of freedom. But the thirteen states find it hard to unite. An ex-soldier named Daniel Shays leads a revolt in Massachusetts. A troubled George Washington agrees to preside at the Constitutional Convention. Liberty is reconciled with power.

American liberty had survived the challenges of war. But could it meet the demands of peace? The eight-year seesaw conflict had convinced many people that a strong union was essential to the survival of American liberty. Far and away the most important and most influential of these federal-minded Americans was ex-General George Washington. As one of his last official acts, he sent a circular letter to the governors of the thirteen states, urging them to give the Congress the power it needed to create a genuine union. He warned them that a failure to solve this fundamental problem would make Americans "the sport of European politics, which may play one state against another." Grimly, he reminded them that it was not yet decided "whether the Revolution must ultimately be considered as a blessing or a curse."

No one paid much attention to Washington's admonition. The steep decline in the Congress's power, so evident in the closing years of the war, accelerated without the threat of a British army and navy to inspire even a feeble unity. After wandering from Princeton to Annapolis to Trenton in search of hospitality, the Congress settled in New York. More often than not, the national legislature could not muster a quorum. Delegates often sat around for weeks waiting for missing members to appear.

With no hope of acquiring the power to tax, the Congress tried to persuade the states to authorize them to collect a duty on imports. After years of negotiation, twelve states agreed. But New York, prospering as a port of entry for New Jersey and Connecticut as well as for her own merchants, said no. Under the Articles of Confederation, all thirteen states had to agree to any amendment to the federal government's powers. The campaign for an "impost" collapsed and with it Congress's last hope of solvency. As a result, the United States had no army to repel an invader or suppress internal insurrections. England displayed its contempt for the weakling federal government by refusing to withdraw its troops from six forts on American soil in the West. Spain prohibited Western settlers from shipping farm produce and other exports from New Orleans. Lacking a navy, the United States could do nothing about Arab

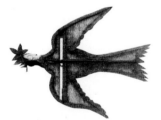

ABOVE *George Washington placed this dove-of-peace weather vane above Mount Vernon shortly before he left "with anxious and painful sensations" to become the first President of the United States.*

LEFT *James Madison, the Father of the Constitution, looks the part in this Gilbert Stuart portrait. When he was elected to the Continental Congress in 1779 at the age of 29, one delegate said he looked "no bigger than half a piece of soap." But his intelligence and appetite for hard work soon made him a legislative leader.*

THE FATE OF THE LOYALISTS

Loyalist refugees endured bitter privations in the Canadian wilderness. New York state made $3.6 million selling confiscated loyalist property. There were 21 loyalist regiments in the British army.

Most of the United States rejoiced at the glad tidings of victory. But one group of Americans was plunged into despair—the loyalists. No one knows the exact number of these dissenting Americans. The best estimates range between 75,000 and 100,000. At least 60,000 and perhaps 80,000 left the United States during and after the Revolution—a larger exodus, on a per-capita basis, than the flight of royalists from France after the French Revolution.

Contrary to myth, loyalists—a name they gave themselves—were not all wealthy aristocrats. Among the loyalists who fled Boston with the British army in 1776 were 382 farmers, traders and mechanics. Most of those who could afford it retreated to England, where they experienced massive disillusionment. Samuel Porter of Salem, seeing the prostitutes thronging London's streets, dubbed England "Sodom." They hated the climate. Several commented caustically on having to wear winter clothing in August. Worst of all, they were desperately homesick.

Some loyalists tried to return to America immedi-ately after the signing of the peace treaty in 1783. Prosper Brown of Saybrook, Connecticut, was seized by a mob in New London, hung by the neck aboard a dockside ship, whipped with a cat-o'-nine-tails, tarred and feathered, and thrown on a boat to New York. At the settlement of Ninety Six, in the South Carolina backcountry, a loyalist named Love was hanged by his embittered ex-neighbors. With the passage of time, however, most people relented, and many loyalists who had not actively fought against the Revolution were able to return unmolested.

When it became apparent that the Americans had no intention of honoring the clause in the peace treaty calling for compensation for loyalist losses, the British Parliament appointed a commission that examined 4,118 claims from loyalists who had had their property confiscated and their houses wrecked or looted by the rebels. Eventually the royal government paid out almost £3.3 million to the claimants.

A few loyalists won pensions or government jobs. But there were not enough places on the civil list; the standard British solution to loyalist pleas was a grant of land in Canada. Most—about 35,000—settled in Nova Scotia. Along with grants of land, the Crown gave them warm clothing, farm supplies and equipment, and cash grants for the first two years. Overall the British spent an estimated £30 million to succor the loyalists.

At first life was desperately hard for the Nova Scotia refugees. "We have nothing but His Majesty's rotten pork and unbaked flour to subsist on," one Connecticut loyalist cried. Filer Diblee, once a prosperous lawyer in Stamford, Connecticut, became so depressed he cut his throat, leaving his wife, Polly, and their children to plead for help from her loyalist brother in London. Many Southerners soon retreated to the Bahamas and other West Indian islands.

More than 3,000 ex-slaves who had joined the British also settled in Nova Scotia. After seven years they were so disgusted by the local government's failure to give them decent land—and its insistence on segregating them and in several cases re-enslaving them—that 1,000 blacks persuaded the Crown to transport them back to Africa, where they helped create the British colony of Sierra Leone.

No matter where they went, most loyalists remained American to the end of their days. No one summed up the divided state of their souls better than Massachusetts's leader of the lost cause, Thomas Hutchinson. Not long before his death, he wrote in his diary: "I would rather die in a little country farmhouse in New England than in the best nobleman's seat in Old England."

pirates who made a specialty of capturing American ships and soon destroyed the country's Mediterranean trade. There was also no way to repay the millions the nation had borrowed from France and Holland to finance the war for independence.

Washington found this failure to maintain America's public credit particularly painful. "To be more exposed in the eyes of the world and more contemptible than we already are, is hardly possible," he wrote to a friend.

A Brooding King

In England George III was foremost among the many Englishmen who did not wish the Americans well. For a while he could not bear to hear "the United States of America" spoken in his presence. At times he told himself he was better off without such troublesome subjects. "Knavery seems to be so much the striking feature of [the Americans], it may not in the end be an evil that they become aliens to this kingdom," he told one man. George roundly announced that he would never receive an ambassador from the new republic and would "ever have a bad opinion of any Englishman who would accept of being an accredited minister to that revolted state."

But the King was no longer in control of the situation. Other men on both sides of the Atlantic decided it might be a good idea to exchange diplomats so that some sort of communication could be established between the two countries. On June 1, 1785, George III was forced by the protocols of state to receive the first American ambassador, John Adams, the man who had persuaded the Continental Congress to vote for independence.

Adams told what happened in a long letter to John Jay. After making three ceremonial bows, he informed the King that the United States "wished to cultivate the most liberal and friendly intercourse between your Majesty's subjects and their citizens." He was also instructed to extend his country's "best wishes for your Majesty's health and for that of your royal family." Adams added that he personally would be "the happiest of men" if he could help restore "an entire esteem, confidence and affection, or in better words the old good-nature and good-humour between people who, though separated by an ocean, and under different governments, have the same language, a similar religion and kindred blood."

The King, Adams reported, was "much affected" by these words. Replying with a tremor in his voice, he said that Adams's language was "so extremely proper and the feelings...so justly adapted to the occasion, that I must say that I not only receive with pleasure the assurances of the friendly dispositions of the United States, but that I am very glad the choice has fallen on you to be their minister." His Majesty went on to insist that he had done nothing "in the late contest" but what he thought himself "indispensably bound to do, by the duty which I owe to my people." He admitted that he was "the last to consent to separation" but he would now be "the first to

BELOW *In 1785, John Adams presented his credentials as the first American ambassador to George III. The King was surprisingly cordial. On a later occasion he was rude to Thomas Jefferson.*

meet the friendship of the United States as an independent power."

Relaxing a trifle, the King remarked that he had heard Adams was not particularly fond of the French. Although somewhat embarrassed, "Honest John," as Adams sometimes called himself, was unable to deny the truth. "That opinion, sir," he said, "is not mistaken; I must avow to your Majesty I have no attachment but to my own country."

"No honest man will have any other," the King replied.

There were times when George III's innate decency triumphed over his narrow mind. But these moments of moral clarity were relatively few. When John Adams brought Thomas Jefferson to court, the King ostentatiously turned his back on the author of the Declaration of Independence. George still took personally those fierce accusations that Jefferson had included in the closing paragraphs of his manifesto.

In 1788 George III suffered a severe mental breakdown from which he never completely recovered. For several months he hurled hateful denunciations at Queen Charlotte and made indecent remarks about one of her ladies-in-waiting. He refought lost battles and issued orders to imaginary generals and prime ministers. Frequently he lamented the loss of his American colonies.

For almost two centuries historians speculated that the King may have been mad throughout the Revolution. Other scholars blamed his breakdown on the humiliation of losing the colonies. In this century medical historians have traced the royal madness to an inherited metabolic disorder, porphyria, which produces many symptoms of manic depression. Although this new information explains the physical cause of the King's disease, it does not alter the personal and political regrets and anguish he revealed during his madness.

BELOW *In Maryland and Virginia slaves grew tobacco under the supervision of overseers. In South Carolina they grew rice and indigo. Cotton did not become a major crop until after the Revolution. Virginia freed all the slaves who had served in the American army or navy.*

Liberty's Ferment

In the United States one of the things that held the Congress together during the postwar years was the vast swath of Western wilderness between the Alleghenies and the Mississippi. By persuading Virginia and other states with often overlapping claims to cede everything to the federal government, the Congress hoped to be able to sell huge tracts to land speculators who were organizing companies in several states. Fortunately, some members of the Congress had more meaningful visions of the future of this enormous territory. One was a returning delegate from Virginia, Thomas Jefferson.

The author of the Declaration of Independence was the driving force behind an ordinance that the Congress passed in 1784, dividing the territory into ten rectangular sections, each of which would become a future state when its population reached 20,000. This vision of an expanding union evolved into the Ordinance of 1787, which provided different population figures and shapes for the emerging states. But it had at its heart a stipulation that Jefferson warmly approved: "There shall be neither slavery nor involuntary servitude in the said territory." This simple statement, which barred slavery from the future states of Ohio, Indiana, Illinois, Michigan and Wisconsin, was the most significant achievement of the postwar Congress. It was encouraging evidence that liberty would remain a dynamic force in American life.

There were many other signs of liberty's impact on slavery. In 1781 a slave named Quok Walker sued for his freedom, pointing out that the Massachusetts state constitution said: "All men are born free and equal." He won his case, and slavery ended in Massachusetts. In the other New England states and in Pennsylvania, where Quakers had been agitating against slavery for decades, a policy of gradual manumission began. All children born of slave parents were declared free. On September 22, 1783, Lemuel Haynes became the first African-American to be ordained as a Congregational minister. Later in the year, James Durham became the first member of his race to begin practicing as a licensed physician. In Boston, Phillis Wheatley, a young African-American who had been educated and freed, celebrated the end of the war with a poem, "Liberty and Peace."

In Virginia the Methodist Church urged the legislature to begin a gradual emancipation program, basing its petition on the Christian religion and the state's Declaration of Rights. The lawmakers rejected the proposal unanimously. Because of the huge numbers of blacks in the South, most Southerners did not believe slavery could be ended without exposing the region to a race war. But Virginia freed all slaves who had fought in the Revolution and joined Delaware and the Northern States in banning the slave trade. Between 1775 and 1800 the number of free African-Americans rose from 14,000 to

TOP RIGHT *Brought to America as a slave at the age of eight, Phillis Wheatley was educated and freed by a Boston merchant, John Wheatley. She learned to speak, read and write English in sixteen months and published her first poem at the age of 13. Her 1773 book of poetry was widely praised in Europe and America.*

ABOVE **Americans often saw Liberty as a woman. In this 1792 painting by Samuel Jennings, she is a teacher, urging Americans to learn the arts and sciences. The artist obviously assumes that Africans will participate in this new democracy of knowledge.**

100,000. "There is not a man living," George Washington wrote to Robert Morris in 1786, "who wishes more sincerely than I do to see a plan adopted for the gradual abolition of [slavery]."

Another example of liberty's ferment was the enthusiasm for educating women. While their husbands were fighting the war or sitting in state legislatures or the Congress, many women were forced to raise children, run farms and sell crops and cattle, relying on their own judgment. This experience led to large leaps in feminine self-confidence. Abigail Adams had long criticized "the trifling narrow contracted Education of the females" in America, as she put it in one of her letters to John. In the 1780s, with the war over, women—and some men—began doing something about it.

In 1786 Timothy Dwight announced that he had opened his Connecticut school to girls as well as boys, promising to teach both sexes "belles lettres, Geography, Philosophy and Astronomy." Soon, in the words of Yale's Ezra Stiles, a "spirit of academy making" spread through the country. Many of these schools were open to young women or created specifically to educate them. Before the war, parents expected a girl to acquire only good work habits. Now many began to see it as their "republican duty" to educate their daughters. When John Jay's wife, Sarah, sent their daughter to the Moravian Seminary for Young Ladies in Bethlehem, Pennsylvania, considered the best girls' school in the nation, she told the young woman that training her mind would give her "the satisfaction of rearing a family agreeable to your wishes." A New Hampshire woman who sent her daughter to a local academy exclaimed: "What an advantage the youth of the present have, compared with former times."

All the arts profited from liberty's growth, especially the theater, which Sam Adams and his fellow Puritans in the Congress had banned during the war. When some people tried to continue the ban, supporters of the theater argued that no government should have the authority to intrude on the freedom of citizens to enjoy themselves. "The same authority which proscribes our amusements may…dictate the shape and texture of our dress or the modes and ceremonies of worship," warned one Philadelphian.

In 1787 Royall Tyler excited audiences with *The Contrast*, the first successful American play. Tyler invented a character who would reappear in a thousand other dramas: Brother Jonathan, the comic stage Yankee. The playwright used him to mock the Puritans: "Ain't the playhouse the shop where the devil hangs out the vanities of the world upon the tenterhooks of temptation?" Jonathan asked, looking down his long disapproving nose.

Perhaps the greatest example of liberty's expanding power was the Virginia legislature's approval of Thomas Jefferson's Statute for Religious Freedom. This landmark legislation guaranteed every citizen the freedom to worship in the church of his or her choice—and ended state support for the Anglican (Episcopal) church in Virginia. Jefferson had first proposed the idea in 1776, but fierce opposition forced him to set it aside. He was in Paris serving as American ambassador when the statute passed, thanks to the unremitting efforts of his fellow Virginian James Madison.

Troubled Times

While liberty was expanding private lives, it was creating serious problems in the shaky American confederacy. The sovereign states began to act like thirteen independent countries. Rhode Island churned out millions of dollars of worthless paper money that her citizens forced local merchants to accept for debts—and tried to palm off on creditors in neighboring states. Other states, such as Maryland, edged toward similar schemes. New York laid import duties on every farmer's rowboat that crossed the Hudson River with produce from New Jersey. Pennsylvania played the same game on the state's western border until someone described New Jersey as "a barrel tapped at both ends." Massachusetts was levying duties on imports from England and other European countries and selling the goods at inflated prices in Connecticut and New Hampshire. One infuriated New Jersey politician predicted the victimized states would soon go to war against their oppressors.

After a brief burst of postwar prosperity, the United States experienced its first economic depression. The British, playing the states off against each other as Washington had feared, persuaded some to charge no import duties and then dumped huge amounts of goods into their stores, driving prices down and throwing shoemakers, dressmakers and other artisans out of work. New England was especially hard hit by the British decision to bar American ships from the West Indies. Farm produce glutted the market. The shipbuilding industry, which had once launched dozens of vessels a year for English buyers, collapsed. Compounding the problem in Massachusetts was the high-tax financial policy of the state legislature, which was controlled by eastern merchants determined to pay off the state's war debt.

Enter Daniel Shays

As 1786 began former Continental army Captain Daniel Shays was an unhappy man. He had fought at Bunker Hill, Saratoga and Stony Point. Now he was living from day to day, constantly fearful of losing his small Massachusetts farm. At one point he was unable to raise $12 to pay a debt. All around him men were losing their farms because they could not pay their taxes or their bills to local storekeepers. In two years, more than 4,000 men had been prosecuted for debt in Worcester County. No less than 80 percent of the inhabitants of the county jail were debtors. Was this the liberty for which they had fought? Shays asked himself.

Shays and a group of like-minded men,

BELOW *Former Continental Captain Daniel Shays' army attacked the federal arsenal in Springfield, hoping to seize weapons and cannon. They were driven off by local militia. Similar unrest swept other states as America grappled with its first economic depression.*

such as former Continental Major Luke Day, decided to solve their problem the way they had defeated taxation from another distant body, the British Parliament. They began organizing companies of men and drilling them with guns on their shoulders. When judges showed up to open the county courts, they were met by an angry mob and hastily left town. The protest movement swiftly spread to other Massachusetts counties and found vocal supporters in New Hampshire, Connecticut and Rhode Island.

The governor of Massachusetts, James Bowdoin, banned unlawful assemblies and called on the militia to disperse the protesters. He was backed by Samuel Adams, who took a dim view of this adaptation of his revolutionary techniques. The protesters responded by threatening to overthrow the Boston government. The alarmed governor called on the Congress for help.

Bankrupt as usual, the Congress voted to ask the states to raise $530,000 for an army. Twelve of the thirteen supposedly united states ignored the request. Only Virginia sent money. Without cash, Massachusetts could not enlist a man. In desperation, one Virginia delegate urged George Washington to rush to Massachusetts and use his influence to calm the rebels. Washington's reply was a growl: "Influence is no government."

Massachusetts was forced to ask wealthy private citizens to donate enough money to raise an army of 4,400 men. With former Major General Benjamin Lincoln in command, they slogged west on snowy roads. The insurgents decided to attack the federal arsenal at Springfield, which held 15,000 muskets and numerous cannon—more than enough weaponry to start another revolution.

Fortunately, the man in command of the arsenal was unintimidated by the radical rhetoric Daniel Shays and Luke Day showered on him. Backed by 400 loyal militia, he beat off their attack with several salvos of cannon fire. Benjamin Lincoln's force arrived in time to cut off Luke Day's retreat and accepted his surrender. Shays fell back thirty miles, determined to carry on the war. Lincoln took a leaf from Washington's Trenton book and marched all night through bitter cold to surprise the rebels' camp. Most of them surrendered; Shays fled to a neighboring state. Bands of Shaysites continued a guerrilla war through the spring of 1787, burning stores and factories and kidnapping merchants and judges. A pitched battle with loyal militia near Sheffield, Massachusetts, left 100 men dead or wounded.

Shays' Rebellion was not an isolated phenomenon. From New Jersey to South Carolina, other groups of disgruntled Americans staged similar protests. In York, Pennsylvania, a mob prevented the sheriff from selling cattle seized for taxes. Maryland's Charles County courthouse was closed down by another mob for similar reasons. In South Carolina judges fled the Camden courthouse under a rain of threats and insults. In Virginia a mob burned down the King William County courthouse, destroying all the records on which taxes were based.

Hearing reports of these disturbances and watching the feckless Congress

TOP RIGHT *Former Major General Benjamin Lincoln led a 4,000-man army to suppress Shays' rebellion. The soldiers were paid by wealthy merchants. The Congress was broke.*

trying to cope with them, George Washington became more and more dismayed. "I am mortified beyond expression," he told one correspondent, "when I view the clouds that have spread over the brightest morn that ever dawned upon any country." To another friend he exclaimed, "Good God! Who besides a Tory could have foreseen or a Briton predicted such a situation?"

"There are combustibles in every state," a worried Washington wrote to James Madison, the young Virginian whose abilities as a politician and political thinker had already impressed him. He urged Madison to persuade the Virginia legislature to issue a call for reform of the federal government. "Let us look to our national character and to things beyond the present moment," Washington wrote.

Virginia's summons inspired a meeting at Annapolis in the fall of 1786 to discuss the mounting chaos. Only twelve delegates from five states showed up, but James Madison prodded them into issuing a call for another convention of all the states to meet in Philadelphia in May 1787. Congress, understandably jealous of its dwindling powers, was not enthusiastic—until Shays' Rebellion escalated to the brink of civil war. The Congressmen seconded the motion but primly stipulated that the "sole and express purpose" of the meeting would be to revise the Articles of Confederation.

The Grand Convention

Soon James Madison informed George Washington that he was one of seven delegates chosen to represent Virginia at this yet-unnamed convention. Should he go? Washington feared he could risk his prestige in such a venture only once. What if the states ignored the Congress and failed to send delegates? What if the delegates who showed up failed to agree? It would make a bad situation far worse if people decided not even George Washington could rescue the foundering ship of state.

Some of the ex-general's most trusted advisers, such as his former artillery commander, Henry Knox, urged him to stay home. For two months Washington brooded and pondered. Finally something deep within him said yes. "To see this country happy is so much the wish of my soul," he told Knox, "nothing on this side of Elysium can be placed in competition with it." On May 9, 1787, he stepped into his coach and began the journey to Philadelphia.

Before he left Mount Vernon, Washington hurled a final challenge at James Madison. "My wish," he wrote, "is that the convention may adopt no temporizing expedients, but probe [our] defects...to the bottom and provide radical cures." It would take three and one half exhausting, harrowing months, but Washington would get his wish—and then some.

The Two Giants

In Philadelphia Washington's first order of business was to call on eighty-one-year-old Benjamin Franklin. The patriarch had returned from France in 1785 and had been elected president of the Executive Council of Pennsylvania, in effect the governor of the state. He had strongly backed the call for a constitutional convention, and he was as worried as Washington about its outcome. "If it does not do good, it must do harm," he told his successor in France, Thomas Jefferson. "It will show we have not wisdom enough among us to

"IN 1783, THE AMERICANS HAD VERY LITTLE SENSE OF NATIONAL IDENTITY. IF YOU READ THE DECLARATION OF INDEPENDENCE, OUR FOUNDING DOCUMENT, CAREFULLY, YOU'LL NOTICE THAT THE "U" IS LOWER-CASED. THIS MEANT THEY WERE A SERIES OF INDEPENDENT STATES THAT WERE TEMPORARILY UNITED."

Ronald Hoffman
Director, Omohundro
Institute of Early American
History and Culture

govern ourselves." He undoubtedly reiterated this opinion to Washington, as they conferred in the small interior courtyard of Franklin's house, beneath his favorite mulberry tree.

It was a toss-up which of these men was more famous. Another man in Franklin's place might have seen this conclave as his last chance for additional glory. Instead the older man sounded the note of compromise and conciliation he would strike again and again throughout the proceedings. He assured Washington that he looked forward to nominating him as president of the convention. On the evening of May 16, he invited him and the other delegates to dinner, tapping a cask of English porter in their honor.

Father of the Constitution

The next day the Virginia delegates began a series of daily meetings at which James Madison swiftly emerged as their leader. At first glance, the thirty-six-year-old graduate of the College of New Jersy (later Princeton) did not look like a leader—or a young man whom the soldierly Washington would befriend. Barely five feet six, with sensitive, pale-blue eyes and a small, delicate mouth, Madison was bookish almost from birth. While other young Virginians spent their time riding, hunting and drinking, Madison stayed in his wealthy father's library, reading. His delicate health prevented him from serving in the Revolutionary army. But the brilliance and boldness of his political thinking had won him election to the Congress, where his calls for a stronger federal government had attracted Washington's attention.

By the time Madison came to Philadelphia, he had spent a good deal of time at Mount Vernon and had thoroughly absorbed George Washington's ideas on what the federal government needed. These could be summed up in a single word: energy. Washington also made it clear that this energy had to include the power of "coercion." Happily, Madison was in complete agreement with both requirements. He had in his luggage a plan that would realize Washington's vision of an "indissoluble union of states under one head."

An Assembly of Demigods

The delegates who gathered in what we now call Independence Hall—the same Pennsylvania State House where the Continental Congress met in 1776—were all leaders from their home states. Of the fifty-five who eventually attended (only seven states were represented at the opening session), forty-two had served in the Continental Congress, and thirty had been in Washington's army. In Paris Thomas Jefferson, when he read a list of their names, called them "an assembly of demigods." Few of them felt either godlike or optimistic about the future. Some glumly noted that Rhode Island had not even bothered to send delegates. The New York delegation consisted of Alexander Hamilton, who passionately wanted the convention to succeed, and Robert Yates and John Lansing Jr., who had orders from Governor George Clinton to obstruct and denounce any proposal that threatened New York's status as a semi-independent state.

Benjamin Franklin was ill on the opening day, but he directed financier Robert Morris, another member of the Pennsylvania delegation, to nominate Washington as president of the convention. Washington was duly installed and

ABOVE *An American dragoon, left, confers with an officer. As of June 2, 1784, the Continental army was disbanded, except for 80 privates who guarded stores of ammunition and weapons at Fort Pitt, West Point and other posts.*

took the chair at the front of the room, facing the delegates, who were grouped around a cluster of green baize-topped tables. The president's chair had a tall, elegant back, with a picture of the sun peeping over the horizon painted on it.

Like the presidents of the Continental Congress, Washington was not free to enter the debates that soon began. Even when the convention met as a committee of the whole to argue off the record, with Washington sitting among the Virginia delegation, he said nothing. But his commanding presence at every session of the convention was a powerful reminder to the delegates that they had gathered to create a stronger central government. They knew how often Washington had called for one during the war. Once the formal sessions ended, we can be sure that Washington mingled with the delegates at various dinners. One historian who analyzed Washington's cryptic diary for the months in Philadelphia noted that sixty nights were unaccounted for in the entries.

At one dinner several men expressed grave doubts about forming a radically new government. Politicians all, they professed themselves bound by the wishes of their constituents, who still liked the undemanding Articles of Confederation. "If to please the people, we offer them what we ourselves disapprove," Washington said, "how can we defend our work? Let us raise a standard to which the wise and honest can repair. The event is in the hand of God."

On May 28 the convention adopted the recommendations of a committee on rules. By far the most important stipulation was secrecy. Years later James Madison said that "no Constitution would ever have been adopted...if the debates had been made public." As politicians, the delegates would never have deviated from their opening stances, whereas in secret discussions, a man could change his mind without embarrassment.

The Virginia Plan

When the delegates met on May 29, Washington recognized Governor Edmund Randolph of Virginia. Handsome and a superb orator, Randolph presented Madison's brainchild, which swiftly became known as the Virginia Plan. It was every bit as bold and radical as Washington wanted it to be. Rather than revising the Articles of Confederation, it called for scrapping them and creating a totally new federal government with a two-branch legislature, a strong executive branch, and a national judiciary with power superior to state courts.

Debate on the Virginia Plan revealed that many delegates could not grasp the subtle mix of power that Madison had brewed. This was a new kind of federalism, directly responsible to the people. They would elect their federal representatives, rather than have them chosen by state legislatures—an unsettling notion to men whose primary loyalty was still to their separate states.

A number of delegates—notably the birdlike Elbridge Gerry of Massachusetts, who talked in agitated bursts interrupted by stammers—wondered if they should even consider the Virginia Plan. Blunt Roger Sherman of Connecticut, a signer of the Declaration, also leaned toward loyalty to the old Congress and its Articles of Confederation. Suave Charles Cotesworth Pinckney of South Carolina was inclined to support Virginia, but only if he was assured that the plan did not clash with the powers of his state's legislature. Washington called for a vote on whether the convention should consider the plan. It carried,

RIGHT *Some of the major players at the Constitutional Convention. Top left is Edmund Randolph, governor of Virginia. To his right is George Mason, passionate opponent of the slave trade. To his right is Elbridge Gerry, dubbed "the Grumbletonian" because he found so much fault with the finished document. On the next level is James Wilson, a brainy but pompous Pennsylvanian whose eloquent arguments were nonetheless convincing. Below him is Charles Cotesworth Pinckney of South Carolina, an Oxford graduate and defender of slavery. On the right is Connecticut's flinty Roger Sherman, who started out dubious about the idea of a new Constitution.*

eleven states to one, with Sherman's Connecticut the lone holdout. Less than a week after they began their labors, the delegates had decided to junk the Articles of Confederation and form an entirely new government.

Large States versus Small States

As June lengthened, Philadelphia's infamous summer weather engulfed the city. Even South Carolinians such as Pierce Butler and his wife found the sulfurous humidity unendurable. Mrs. Butler fled to the "more temperate" climate of New York. Nevertheless, for thirteen days the delegates debated the Virginia Plan—and to Madison's scarcely concealed delight, approved it with only minor changes. Too late, delegates from the small states realized they had been flattened by a political juggernaut. The three biggest states—Virginia, Pennsylvania and Massachusetts—had inveigled Georgia and the two Carolinas to join them to create a 6-to-5 majority. New Hampshire's delegates had not yet arrived.

Smoothly, almost smugly, Madison now proposed one of the essential ideas in his plan. The principle of one state one vote, which had repeatedly paralyzed the Continental Congress, "ought not to prevail" in the new national legislature. Instead, representation would be based on population. This guar-

anteed the large states total control of the new government. The small-state men revolted. Stumpy William Paterson of New Jersey rose to make a ferocious attack on the Virginia Plan.

Paterson warned the large states that they "could unite as they please," but they had better remember that they had no power to coerce the other states. He would submit to a despot, Paterson roared, rather than surrender to such arrogant bullying. Not only would he fight Virginia's presumptions here in Philadelphia but would also go home to New Jersey and rally his state against them.

James Wilson of Pennsylvania, a lawyer with an owlish look and a haughty, ponderous style, told Paterson that he did not care what New Jersey did. Wilson would be satisfied if only a minority of the states united. This arrogance inspired uncouth, untidy Luther Martin of Maryland to side with Paterson. Soon New York, Delaware and Connecticut were also in his camp. Thinly populated New Hampshire, whose delegates were still en route, was certain to back Paterson, too.

On June 15 an emboldened Paterson took the floor to present the New Jersey Plan for reforming the federal government. Each state would have a single vote in the national legislature, which would have the power to coerce the states into obeying its laws. How that coercion was to be achieved Paterson did not say. If this formula did not satisfy the convention, the New Jerseyan had another suggestion: Put the whole country into a "hotchpot" and divide all the lands, north, east, west and south, into thirteen equal parts.

The large-staters sneered at Paterson's plan. Alexander Hamilton added to

ABOVE LEFT *Forty-one-year-old William Paterson of New Jersey was born in County Antrim, Ireland. He was brought to America at the age of two. A short, aggressive lawyer, he was the perfect advocate for the small states in the convention.*

the confusion by attacking both the Virginia and the New Jersey plans. The latter was hopeless, he said, and Virginia did not go far enough. Hamilton wanted a "consolidated" national government that would reduce the states to shadows. Luther Martin, enveloped, in the words of one historian, "in the sour sweet smell of good Maryland rye," raked Virginians in particular and large-staters in general with down-home invective in a speech that lasted two days. Gunning Bedford, a fat, pugnacious lawyer from Delaware, climaxed the small-state counterattack by shouting that there were "foreign powers" who were ready to "take them by the hand."

On Sunday, July 1, a discouraged Washington wrote to a friend in Virginia, fearing the worst. "Everybody wishes, everybody expects something from the convention," he lamented. But it began to look more and more likely that the state governments would refuse to yield their power.

On Monday the small states returned to the fray with a motion by Oliver Ellsworth of Connecticut that each state should have only one vote in the upper house—not yet named the senate. This time the relentless hammering of the small-staters bore fruit. One of the delegates from Georgia, a recently transplanted Connecticut man, switched his vote, and the convention was deadlocked.

Disaster loomed. Roger Sherman of Connecticut observed that they appeared to be at a "full stop." Did anyone have a way out, or should they all go home? Charles Cotesworth Pinckney of South Carolina suggested forming a "Grand Committee" of one man from each state to see if a compromise could be found. As the disgruntled delegates adjourned to celebrate the Fourth of July, Luther Martin reported to the Maryland legislature that the convention was "on the verge of dissolution, scarce held together by the strength of a hair."

Benjamin Franklin, who had said almost nothing thus far, found the Grand Committee the ideal place to wield his formidable diplomatic powers. He seized on an idea that had been proposed by Roger Sherman in an early debate: Each state should have an equal vote in the upper house and proportional representation in the lower house. Shrewdly, Franklin suggested a concession to the large states: All money bills would originate in the lower house. The proposal won the Grand Committee's unanimous support.

On the convention floor, Madison, Wilson and the other large-state spokesmen fought the compromise for days. Madison lost his temper and urged the large states to confederate with or without the small states. But moderate men in the large states, impressed by Franklin's sponsorship, would no longer follow the young Virginian's lead. The Great Compromise, as it came to be called, passed by one vote, saving the convention—and the United States of America—from collapse.

The Puzzle of the Presidency

No longer worried about being swallowed, the small-state men delighted Washington by becoming advocates of an energetic national government. They vigorously supported a resolution giving the new Congress the power to "legislate in all cases for the general interests of the Union." For the first time in a month, the delegates were no longer like two groups of oarsmen in a boat, rowing toward opposite shores.

But there were signs of trouble ahead. Robert Yates and John Lansing Jr. quit the convention in disgust and went home to New York, where they began warning everyone that the large-state men were creating a tyranny worse than George III's. Someone else tried to sabotage the convention by spreading a rumor that the delegates had voted to invite George III's second son to become America's King. This idiotic tale forced Washington to break the rule of secrecy by issuing an off-the-record statement: "Though we cannot affirmatively tell you what we are doing—we [have] never once thought of a king."

But they were beginning to tackle one of the most important tasks confronting them—finding a substitute for a king. In most of the state constitutions written since the Declaration of Independence, Americans had demonstrated their devotion to liberty by giving their governors virtually no power. The chief executive was seldom more than a dutiful servant of the legislature. Everyone agreed that it was time to break this bad habit, but no one was sure exactly how to do it.

The convention's first thoughts about the presidency were chaotic. Madison's Virginia Plan called for the chief executive to be elected by the Congress. George Mason of Virginia thought there should be three presidents. Elbridge Gerry wanted him elected by state governors for a fifteen-year term. Alexander Hamilton thought he should serve for life. Out of this welter of voices, thirty-five-year-old Gouverneur Morris emerged as the man who had the clearest, most coherent vision.

This was no accident. He and George Washington were both living at the home of financier Robert Morris (no relation to Gouverneur). As a result, the six-foot, flamboyant, younger Morris had heard more than any other delegate, except perhaps James Madison, about Washington's thoughts on the presidency.

LEFT *Robert Morris (right) was the leading American merchant and financier of the 1780s. George Washington was his house guest during the Constitutional Convention. They were old and close friends. Morris was an early advocate of a strong federal government. New Yorker Gouverneur Morris was an eloquent spokesman for this idea at the Constitutional Convention.*

On the convention floor, Morris did not mince words. The president, he declared, "must not be the flunky of the Congress. It must not be able to say to him: 'You owe your appointment to us.'"

On the contrary, Morris declared, the president's role should be the people's tribune, their guardian against "legislative tyranny." Morris wanted the nation's chief executive elected by the direct vote of the people. He also insisted that the president should be electable for at least two reasonably long terms. What was the point of electing "a strong man to protect us and at the same time wish[ing] to tie his hands behind him?"

Though his style was often abrasive, Gouverneur Morris remained open to other men's ideas. At first he opposed giving Congress the power to impeach the president. Benjamin Franklin pointed out that this left the people with only one way to get rid of a bad president—assassination. Morris instantly conceded Franklin's point, and impeachment became a safeguard against presidential tyranny.

In the debates on the presidency, Morris spoke more than any other delegate. Ably assisted by James Wilson, he persuaded the convention to give the president a remarkable amount of power. Perhaps most amazing for men who had been spooked in their earlier years by George III, they named him commander-in-chief of the armed forces. One suspects that not a few delegates realized that when Gouverneur Morris spoke, they were hearing advice direct from George Washington. Also, as Pierce Butler of South Carolina pointed out, there sat Washington, the man who was certain to be the first president. There was no need to fear he would became a tyrant.

The Home Stretch

The federal government as we know it began taking shape before the delegates' eyes. Names were pinned down. The Virginia Plan's "legislature of the United States" became "the Congress"—a gesture of respect for the original Congress, still clinging to shreds of its dignity in New York. The House of Representatives and the Senate were christened, and what Madison had called the Supreme Tribunal became the Supreme Court. Specific powers were granted to or withheld from the Congress, the president and federal courts, creating the system of checks and balances that would serve as a perpetual safeguard of America's liberty.

At times the devil got into the details. Charles Cotesworth Pinckney wanted to bar anyone from the presidency who was not worth at least $100,000—well over $1 million in today's money. Franklin remarked that he was opposed to anything "that tended to debase the spirit of the common people." No doubt

TOP RIGHT *Gouverneur Morris lost his leg in a 1780 carriage accident. He said he would gladly pay taxes to free all the Africans in America rather than see slavery tolerated in the Constitution.*

LAFAYETTE STARTS ANOTHER REVOLUTION

Lafayette became hated by both aristocrats and radicals in the French Revolution.

In France the Marquis de Lafayette basked in his fame as "the hero of two worlds." The American adventure had cost him 700,000 livres, but his maternal grandfather had died and left him a huge estate in Brittany, so he was as rich as ever. He and wife, Adrienne, moved into a magnificent mansion on the Rue de Bourbon (today's Rue de Lille), which cost 300,000 livres to buy and furnish. In the library Lafayette hung a framed copy of the Declaration of Independence. Half of the frame was empty. In that space, he told visitors, he hoped some day to see a French Declaration of Rights.

At Lafayette's house, liberals such as his brother-in-law, the Vicomte de Noailles, who had served under General Rochambeau in America, regularly gathered to discuss reforms in France's antiquated absolutist government. But they were not revolutionists. No one set deadlines or issued ultimatums. At Versailles Lafayette became a member of the inner circle around the King, who had appointed him a *maréchal de camp* (brigadier general) in the French army.

Beneath everyone's feet, history was bubbling volcanically. The cost of the war for America had been the coup de grace to France's crumbling finances. Jacques Necker, the brilliant but deceitful minister of finance, had pretended to balance the national books but had secretly paid for the massive military outlays with loans at crushing rates of interest. Louis XVI tried to solve the problem by summoning an Assembly of Notables, mostly bluebloods and clergy who were expected to be a tame parliament. Lafayette was included because he was assumed to be a dependable courtier, loyal to the King.

The notables turned out to be anything but tame. They savagely rejected an attempt by the new finance minister, Charles Alexandre de Calonne, to rationalize the country's taxation by making nobles and clergy pay along with the peasants and the bourgeoisie. To everyone's amazement, Lafayette suddenly began making statements that were remarkably unfriendly to the King and Queen. He criticized their habit of rewarding favorites with huge gifts of land from the royal domain and pensions from the treasury. Next he recommended giving Protestants civil and religious freedom. Then he

said the rich should be taxed and the poor helped. Finally, to the spluttering indignation of the Comte d'Artois, the King's brother, who had favored the assembly, Lafayette said it was time to call the nation's legal parliament, the Estates General, which had not met since 1614. When d'Artois expressed his astonishment, Lafayette replied: "And even better than that."

Lafayette meant he wanted a democratic parliament, not the cumbersome estates, in which the nobles and the clergy would always outvote the rest of the nation, lumped into the third estate. He soon made himself even clearer, becoming the first man in France to use the term "National Assembly."

Unquestionably, Lafayette helped begin the French Revolution with these explosive suggestions, which flowed from his devotion to America's more equal liberty. He had no idea he was triggering a historic upheaval. He thought the crisis would give him an opportunity to become the George Washington of France. But France lacked America's long tradition of representative government and devotion to liberty. The revolution would end with Lafayette an exile and military dictator Napoleon Bonaparte in power.

This American check for $120,000 partially repaid Lafayette for the money he spent during the Revolution.

thinking of his ordeal before the Privy Council in London, he added that the greatest rogues he had ever known were rich rogues. Pinckney's proposal was drowned in a cascade of nays.

Franklin sounded this same note of faith in the people when Gouverneur Morris, whose family owned a huge swath of land north of New York City, proposed that the vote should be limited to people with property. Morris feared the poor would sell their votes to the rich. John Dickinson, another wealthy man, backed him. Franklin again insisted that it was "of great consequence that we should not depress the virtue and public spirit of our common people." The convention agreed with him overwhelmingly.

Elbridge Gerry lectured the delegates on a familiar danger to liberty—a standing army. During a debate in the committee of the whole, he proposed a clause in the Constitution limiting the U.S. army to 3,000 men. According to a perhaps legendary story, this idiocy caused Washington to break his silence. Sitting with the Virginia delegation, he whispered that he agreed with the proposition if Gerry could guarantee that no enemy would ever invade the United States with more than 3,000 men. Another barrage of nays buried the discomfited Gerry.

These and other relatively minor decisions upset a number of delegates. When the convention banned the printing of paper money by any state, Luther Martin threatened to go home. When the number of representatives in the House was limited to one per 40,000 inhabitants, Edmund Randolph announced he was turning against the new Constitution. Elbridge Gerry began making similar negative noises.

Randolph's defection swung a majority of the Virginia delegation against the new government. Rumors of this shift soon leaked back to Richmond, and a wave of dissatisfaction swept the Old Dominion. Shays-style uprisings in the western counties burned courthouses and issued demands for paper money. Similar outbreaks roiled Maryland. With this sort of news jangling everyone's nerves, the delegates plunged into the most divisive topic on their agenda—slavery.

The Odious Issue

Charles Cotesworth Pinckney had already warned everyone that if the convention failed to insert "some security to the Southern states" with regard to slavery, he would be "bound by my duty" to his home state to oppose the final document. In spite of this warning, Northerners boldly challenged the compromise worked out on the number of congressmen each state was entitled to elect. Earlier, the convention had agreed to count three-fifths of a state's slaves as part of its population to give the South a better deal in the House of Representatives.

Revealing how much the ideals of American liberty had changed hearts and minds since 1776, Elbridge Gerry sarcastically asked how the delegates could justify this arrangement. Since blacks were considered property in the South, why not give the North the right to count horses and cattle in computing their representation? Gouverneur Morris suggested that the word "free" be inserted before "inhabitants" in the representation clause. He vowed he would gladly pay taxes to free all the Africans in America rather than see slavery tolerated in the Constitution. He called it "the curse of heaven." Stolid Roger Sherman defended the compromise. He said it recognized a simple if brutal fact.

The country had 700,000 slaves. He might have added that at least twenty-five of the fifty-five delegates were slave owners. Morris's proposal lost 10 to 1.

An even more acrimonious wrangle erupted over meeting Pinckney's demand for a clause in the Constitution forbidding the Congress to outlaw or even to tax the importation of slaves. Delegates were stunned when George Mason, himself a slave owner, condemned "the infernal traffic," which Virginia had banned by a state law, and insisted that the future of the union was involved. People in Western states such as Kentucky and Tennessee were "calling out for slaves for their new lands." If they got their way, they would "fill the country with slaves." With prophetic fury, Mason warned that slavery would bring "the judgment of heaven" on the nation. Echoing Jefferson in 1776, he accused "our Eastern brethren"—New Englanders—of backing the South Carolinians because their ships made huge profits in the ugly business.

The men of the Deep South had a tough answer to this moral fury. Pinckney, John Rutledge and others made it extremely clear that if they did not get their way, Georgia, South Carolina and North Carolina would "not be parties to the Union." Faced with a new threat of collapse, the delegates summoned another Grand Committee. It proposed a compromise that gave both North and South half a loaf. The slave trade would be permitted until 1808, and the Congress would be allowed to regulate American commerce—establish tariffs and embargoes—by a simple majority vote. The South, fearful of New England's monopoly of the sea, had wanted a two-thirds majority on this issue, which would have given it a veto.

Edmund Randolph declared that this extension of the slave trade made the Constitution so "odious" he could never sign it. James Madison and George Mason fought the measure on the floor of the convention. But a

"THE AMERICAN REVOLUTION PRESENTS THE FIRST EXAMPLE OF SLAVEHOLDERS THEMSELVES NOT JUST QUESTIONING SLAVERY'S MORALITY, BUT CONSIDERING DOING SOMETHING TO END THE SYSTEM. IT IS A DEFINING MOMENT IN THE WORLD HISTORY OF SLAVERY."

Christopher L. Brown Omohundro Insitute of Early American History and Culture

LEFT **Many black Americans were swept up in the language of liberty and hoped for an end to slavery. In 1781 an African-American won a lawsuit making slavery illegal in Massachusetts. By 1800 the number of free blacks in the North had risen from 14,000 to 100,000. The famous pottery manufacturer, Josiah Wedgwood, sent this cameo to his friend Benjamin Franklin when he became head of the Pennsylvania Abolition Society.**

majority of the delegates realized that political unity, not moral purity, was their goal. With a hostile Great Britain watching and waiting for the Americans to unravel, the survival of the nation was still very much at stake. Most of the delegates abhorred slavery and hoped it would slowly disappear. The odious compromise was voted into the Constitution.

Who Will Ratify This Constitution?

Now came a sticky point: Should they ask the Congress to approve the Constitution? Virtually to a man, everyone agreed this would be inviting trouble. No legislature would cheerfully vote itself into oblivion. Instead, following the line of reasoning that had motivated Madison and Washington from the start, the delegates decided to send the charter to the people. Each state was urged to call a special convention to ratify the new compact. Again dramatizing their break with the past, the convention voted that the approval of the people of nine states would be enough to launch the new government. The requirement that all states had to agree to major changes had been one of the more ruinous clauses in the Articles of Confederation.

On September 8 Gouverneur Morris was handed the task of giving the Constitution some literary polish. His most important change was in the preamble. The previous draft had read: "We the people of New Hampshire, Massachusetts etc. do ordain declare and establish the following Constitution for ourselves and our posterity."

Morris not only dumped the list of states, he added a masterful summary of the goals of the Constitutional Convention and the entire American Revolution: "We the people of the United States, in order to form a more perfect union, to establish justice, promote the general welfare and secure the blessings of liberty to ourselves and our posterity, do ordain and establish this Constitution for the United States of America."

ABOVE *Alexander Hamilton wanted a consolidated federal government and thought the president should hold office for life. He scoffed at the idea that the voice of the people was the voice of God. But he also opposed the rule of the rich.*

Most of the delegates pronounced themselves satisfied with their joint efforts and were ready to submit the Constitution to the people. But before they could depart, they had to listen to more criticism from dissenters in their midst. George Mason wanted to know why the Constitution did not have a bill of rights like the one he had written for Virginia's constitution. Roger Sherman replied that most of the states had bills of rights already in their constitutions; adding one here would be superfluous. Worn out after three months of day-and-night effort, the delegates agreed with Sherman and rejected Mason's offer to compose a statement of rights in a matter of hours.

Edmund Randolph added an even longer jeremiad against the final document, aiming his strongest barbs at the ratio of one representative per 40,000 inhabitants. This would make the House of Representatives too small, he said, and tempt it to become an oligarchy. Randolph had almost as many nasty things to say about the strong presidency. Elbridge Gerry chimed in with no fewer than seven negative speeches in a single day. These dissents from two of the large states filled not a few delegates with foreboding. Charles Cotesworth

Pinckney rebuked the critics, saying he too had objections but he supported the Constitution as the only alternative to a civil war.

Behind the scenes, George Washington was working overtime to resolve the problem of Virginia's opposition. He and James Madison persuaded delegate John Blair to vote yea, permitting them to register Virginia's approval of the document. This enabled Madison to write in his voluminous notes on the convention: "On the question to agree to the Constitution as amended. All the states, aye.

"And the House adjourned."

The delegates now faced one more tough question: how to present an image of unanimity to the nation. The convention turned to its great conciliator, Benjamin Franklin.

On September 17, with the weather clear and cold, the delegates gathered once more. Their numbers were diminished by the physical wear and tear of the ten-week ordeal and the disapproval of men such as Yates, Lansing and Luther Martin, who had gone home already. Only forty-one voting members were on hand, plus Alexander Hamilton, who had returned from New York to sign the document, although he could not deliver his state's approval on his own.

After a final reading, Benjamin Franklin struggled to his feet with a speech in his hand. He announced that his "infirmity"—a bladder stone—made it difficult for him to stand without pain, so he was asking his friend James Wilson to read the speech for him. This was a shrewd choice. It would do no harm to put honeyed words in the mouth of one of the most obnoxious large-state men.

"Mr. President," Wilson-as-Franklin said, "I confess that there are several parts of this Constitution which I do not at present approve. But I am not sure I shall never approve them. For having lived long, I have experienced many instances of being obliged by better information or full consideration to change opinions."

Franklin's speech urged any member who still had objections to "doubt a little of his own infallibility" and join him in signing the document as proof of their fundamental agreement. Their signatures, he argued, would simply attest to "the unanimous consent of the states present." This idea, suggested by the canny Gouverneur Morris, offered doubters a chance to sign without committing themselves to personal approval—and gave Hamilton a semivote, even though a majority New York's delegation had gone home.

Before anyone could make a decision on this vital matter, Nathaniel Gorham of Massachusetts, chairman of the committee of the whole, rose to urge one final change. He thought the ratio of representation in the House should be altered from one for every 40,000 people to one for every 30,000. He was promptly seconded by Charles Carroll of Maryland and Rufus King of Massachusetts. There was a momentary pause as everyone realized these gentlemen were not coalescing by accident on this relatively minor point. President George Washington confirmed this intuition by making his first and only speech. He endorsed the proposed change because it would remove the fears of "many" delegates about the size of the House of Representatives. It would give him "much satisfaction" to see the motion adopted. The delegates agreed unanimously.

There was only one delegate on Washington's mind—Edmund Randolph. As governor of Virginia, he would have enormous influence on whether the

PAINE AT THE ZENITH

In May 1787 Thomas Paine returned to Europe, arriving, as he had arrived in America, on the eve of a revolution. In a Paris rumbling with hostility to King Louis XVI, he was welcomed as a hero. Three months later Paine visited England and was equally acclaimed by Englishmen who hoped to reform their country's corrupt oligarchy.

As the French Revolution gathered momentum, England's leaders grew hostile to it. Edmund Burke, who had supported America with his oratory in Parliament from 1776 to 1781, wrote *Reflexions on the Revolution in France*, predicting it would end in anarchy and bloodshed.

Tbomas Paine responded with *The Rights of Man*, which swiftly became one of the most popular books ever published. It sold an estimated 2 million copies in England, France and America. Paine called on Englishmen to join France and the United States in a government "of the people and for the people and by the people." As controversy boiled around him, Paine proudly told George Washington that he had "gotten the ear of the country."

With growing recklessness Paine wrote a poem set to the tune of "God Save the King" that was virtually guaranteed to outrage British conservatives.

When Part Two of *The Rights of Man* appeared in 1792, it created an even greater sensation than Part One. It sold an estimated 1.5 million copies and swept England to the brink of revolution. The British government responded with a royal proclamation against seditious writings and began a campaign to discredit Paine. He was burned in effigy in London and many other cities, and a scurrilous biography smeared him.

Meanwhile, the French Revolution was drifting toward mob rule. Paine stubbornly defended it, insisting: "The mob is what the cruelty of government has made it." He toured England making inflammatory speeches to a new

A hostile cartoon of Paine measuring the British crown for a pair of "revolution breeches."

Paine flourished The Rights of Man *like a sword aimed at George III and his fellow aristocrats.*

society, the Friends of Liberty. The British government decided to arrest him. The American ambassador urged Paine to flee, warning him that his American citizenship would give him no protection.

Paine took the advice and fled to France, where he was again hailed as a hero. Elected a member of the French revolutionary assembly, Paine soon found himself in the minority, urging radicals not to guillotine Louis XVI. Paine wanted to send the King into harmless exile. Soon he was almost as unpopular with the French radicals as he was with the British conservatives. After Louis's execution came the radical reign of terror, during which as many as 400 people a day were beheaded in Paris alone.

In England and America there was a huge revulsion against this orgy of bloodletting. Paine, who had done everything in his power to prevent the carnage, was blamed for it. His books, his ideas, his very name became anathema to most Englishmen and many Americans.

ABOVE *George Washington was chosen president of the Constitutional Convention.*
He let others present his call for "an indissoluble union of states under one head."

Old Dominion ratified the Constitution. Clearly moved by Washington's gesture, Randolph apologized for opposing "the venerable names" that were giving sanction to the Constitution. Although he still refused to sign, he said he would "not oppose the Constitution without [outside the] doors."

Alexander Hamilton made a passionate speech, urging everyone to sign. "No man's ideas were more remote" from the plan that had been adopted, he said. But the choice was between anarchy and at least a hope of public tranquillity. Elbridge Gerry still refused to sign. He disliked the idea of asking the people to ratify the Constitution and opposed direct elections to the Congress. The word "people" gave him the shakes. Visions of Shaysites were still dancing through his Massachusetts head.

Except for Mason, Randolph and Gerry, the delegates signed in the spirit of Franklin's motion. As the last few signatures were added to the "engrossed" (copied out on parchment) document, Benjamin Franklin pointed to the painting of the sun on the back of Washington's chair. "I have often looked at that sun...without being able to tell whether it was rising or setting. But now...I have the happiness to know it is a rising and not a setting sun."

Shall We Ratify Tyranny?

Franklin's optimism was premature. As Washington had revealed in his last-minute concession to Edmund Randolph, there was serious anxiety that several key states, notably Virginia, New York and Massachusetts, might not ratify the new Constitution. The signers knew that this was a political problem and momentum was crucial. They immediately tried to create a bandwagon psychology. Franklin led the way, appearing before the Pennsylvania legislature the day after the Constitution was signed to present a copy of it to the lawmakers and urge them to call a ratifying convention as soon as possible.

A substantial minority objected, insisting that there was no hurry. They grew even more vociferous after George Mason published a list of violent objections in a Philadelphia newspaper. Another writer, using the pseudonym Centinel, said the Constitution was the creation of "the wealthy and ambitious," who had gulled Franklin and Washington into endorsing it.

Mason enlisted Richard Henry Lee, who was sitting in the old Congress in New York. When the Constitution was presented to this all-but-defunct legislature, Lee did everything in his power to win a negative vote. But he was outmaneuvered by a number of men who were delegates to the convention and members of the Congress as well. They rose to defend the Constitution and the lawmakers voted to pass the document on to the individual states without comment.

Within a day the news of this resolution was delivered to Philadelphia by a hard-riding messenger, and a majority of the Pennsylvania legislature voted for a ratifying convention to meet on November 21. After three weeks of bruising debate, Pennsylvania ratified the new charter on December 12. Benjamin Franklin led a triumphant procession through Philadelphia's streets to announce the good news from the balcony of the courthouse on Market Street.

By that time tiny Delaware had become the first state to ratify, by a vote of 30 to 0. On December 18 New Jersey ratified 58 to 0. On January 2, 1788, Georgia voted yea by 128 to 40. Every state except recalcitrant Rhode Island had called ratifying conventions. But the opposition, surprised by this first

"THE DEBATE BETWEEN THE FEDERALISTS AND THE ANTI-FEDERALISTS IS WHAT AMERICAN POLITICS IS ALL ABOUT TO THIS DAY—THE QUESTION OF HOW POWERFUL THE FEDERAL GOVERNMENT SHOULD BE."

Bernard Bailyn
Professor of History,
Harvard University

surge, recovered its balance and began a powerful counterattack. The defeated Pennsylvania Antis took to the newspapers to open a wide-ranging assault on the Constitution and the hurry-up tactics of its supporters. Essentially they argued that the Constitution was a threat to liberty. It was going to create a consolidated federal government that would obliterate the states. They accused the "Federalists" of being secret monarchy men. Some followed George Mason's lead and tried to use the compromise on slavery to impugn the signers' moral character.

The Federalists, who were rapidly becoming a political party, hit back hard. One of the doughtiest sluggers was Oliver Ellsworth of Connecticut, who went after George Mason for his high-toned statements on the slave trade. He noted that Mason owned 300 slaves and suggested he wanted to end the trade so he could sell his surplus blacks at higher prices to the Carolinas and Georgia. Ellsworth slammed Richard Henry Lee as an intriguer whose "implacable hatred" of George Washington was well known. In an essay as blunt as his personality, Roger Sherman scoffed at the Antis' claim that the Constitution would annihilate a state's independence and endanger individual liberty. He argued that people of the various states had already granted their legislators the power to make decisions for them, some of which limited their liberty in the name of public order. All the Constitution did was transfer some carefully specified powers to the federal government for the same purpose. The other "unenumerated" powers were retained by the states.

The most forceful voice in this continental war of words emerged in New York. On October 27, 1787, a writer using the pen name Publius began a series of articles that avoided personalities and discussed the principles and ideas of the Constitution with a thoroughness and finesse that won national attention. Eighty-five of these masterful essays appeared over the next several months. In May they were published in two volumes as *The Federalist*. We know now that the writers were Alexander Hamilton, James Madison and John Jay. We also know that their joint effort became far more than an argument aimed at persuading the voters of New York to ratify the Constitution. With these intellects behind Publius's pen, *The Federalist Papers* became a brilliant treatise on the purposes of government, a universal political philosophy adapted to the American scene.

Probably the most famous essay was number ten, in which Madison maintained that American liberty could and would survive and thrive in a continental-sized union of states. Previous thinkers had maintained republican liberty could flourish only in a small state. Madison argued convincingly that the very size of the union would make it difficult for one part of the people to oppress another part. "The influence of factious leaders may kindle a flame within their particular states, but will be unable to spread a general conflagration through the other states," Madison wrote. The Constitution was "a republican remedy for the diseases most incident to republican government."

As 1788 lengthened, it was hard to tell whether these brilliant essays were having any impact. Connecticut seemed to suggest there were grounds for hope. On January 9 Jonathan Trumbull, one of George Washington's former military aides, wrote to him "with great satisfaction" to report that the Nutmeg State had ratified the Constitution 128 to 40. But Massachusetts seemed likely to be

a different story. Elbridge Gerry had been attacking the charter since he returned from Philadelphia. Samuel Adams was making hostile noises. Mercy Otis Warren, one of the brightest women of her time and wife of influential politician James Warren, saw the Constitution as an "aristocratic tyranny."

But the Federalists, learning from their experience in Pennsylvania, took their time about pushing a vote. Meanwhile, they worked on two key figures, John Hancock and Samuel Adams. By expressing sympathy and promising tax relief to the Shaysites, Hancock had been elected governor, and he controlled an estimated fifty votes in the state convention among farmers from the western counties. The Federalists convinced him that if Massachusetts refused to ratify the Constitution, the nation might collapse into warring regions. According to rumor, they also appealed to Hancock's vanity by promising to back him for national office.

For Sam Adams the Federalists used different tactics. Adams's old ally, Paul Revere, staged a mass meeting of Boston artisans and mechanics at the Green Dragon Inn, once the headquarters of the Sons of Liberty, calling for ratification. When the common people of Boston spoke, Sam Adams listened. He soon came out for ratification. To further smooth the waters, the Federalists agreed with the Anti-Federalists that the Constitution needed a bill of rights. They drew up nine proposed changes and allowed Hancock to present them as his creation. Sam Adams, who had not been on speaking terms with his old confederate for a long time, seconded the proposals. In spite of the backing of these two famous revolutionary names, the vote was close enough to give Federalists chills: 187 to 168.

Massachusetts made six states voting yea. Who would be the next three pillars of the new federal house? The first two were easy. Maryland approved by an overwhelming majority. South Carolina was equally enthusiastic. One historian has pointed out an extra-political reason: Roughly half the 149 members of the ratifying convention were related by blood or marriage to the state's signers. But the ninth pillar became elusive. The Federalists lost momentum as their opponents became more and more strident.

In New Hampshire the leading Anti-Federalist, a former loyalist named Joshua Atherton, argued that no honest man should support the Constitution because it countenanced "cruel and inhuman" slavery. By hammering on this point, Atherton managed to deadlock the convention, and the Federalists decided to adjourn until June 18 to give tempers and opinions time to cool.

The next few months were filled with bad news for the Federalists. Rhode Island held a referendum, and the vote was 10 to 1 against ratification. North Carolina elected a convention that was heavy with Anti-Federalists. In New York, two-thirds of the popular vote went to delegates who had spoken out against ratification. Virginia was not much more encouraging; Federalists won eighty-five delegates, Antis sixty-five and twenty were uncommitted.

Moreover, the Anti-Federalists, while continuing to fulminate against the dangers of aristocracy and centralized power, began concentrating on a call for a second constitutional convention to amend the Philadelphia charter. Federalists were convinced that the Antis would send men to this convention with orders to demolish, not amend. They responded by emphasizing their Massachusetts strategy—ratify now and amend later.

REVOLUTIONS BREAK HEARTS

William Temple Franklin served as his grandfather's secretary in France

When Benjamin Franklin left France to return to America in 1785, he agreed to meet with his loyalist son, William, in Southampton, England. William was hoping for a reconciliation. But their conversation was a cold business meeting. Franklin could not forget that William was wanted in America for murder and other crimes committed by the Associated Loyalists, a guerrilla group he formed to raid Americans in New Jersey and Connecticut.

At their Southampton meeting, Franklin presented William with a bill for £1500 that he had advanced to enable him to live stylishly when he was royal governor of New Jersey. Later, in his will, Benjamin left William nothing but a vague title to some land in Nova Scotia, remarking that "the part he played against me in the late war...will account for my leaving him no more of an estate [than] he endeavoured to deprive me of."

William Temple Franklin, William's illegitimate son, was the man in the middle of this quarrel. He returned to America with his grandfather but after Benjamin died went to England to live with his father. They soon quarreled bitterly and Temple retreated to Paris, where he died childless in 1823, extinguishing Benjamin Franklin's hope of founding a notable American family.

June 1788 became the month of decision. Virginia's convention met on the second, New York's on the seventeenth and New Hampshire's on the eighteenth. Although they started latest, the Granite Staters surged to the head of the pack because they had thrashed out a lot of disagreements in their earlier convention—and because Governor John Sullivan had gone from mediocre general to first-class politician. During the months of adjournment, he and his right-hand man, John Langdon, had worked tirelessly to change minds and hearts. On June 21, only three days after the delegates reconvened, the Constitution prevailed 57 to 46.

Nine states having voted yea, the Constitution was theoretically ratified and in force. But everyone knew that without New York and Virginia, this legalism would be meaningless. If Virginia voted nay, George Washington, the presumptive first President, would be an alien. If New York said no, New England would be cut off from the other ratifying states. Heightening the drama, the Virginians gathered in Richmond, unaware that New Hampshire had ratified. They met presuming that the fate of the Union lay in their hands.

The leading spokesman for the Anti-Federalists was Patrick Henry, who had been against the idea of a new Constitution from the start. Now he unleashed on the finished product volleys of denunciation in his bravura style. Many people have called it the most brilliant oratorical performance of his career. For twenty-three days Henry was on his feet almost constantly, several times speaking for an entire day. His goal was to arouse fear of the Constitution in every listener. He portrayed it as a conspiracy of the rich against the poor. He

BELOW *George Washington made only one speech during the Constitutional Convention. He preferred to work behind the scenes for a strong federal government.*

warned people who owed money to British merchants that it would bankrupt them. He told slaveholders it would give the federal government power to free their slaves. Above all, Henry said, the Constitution would destroy everyone's liberty. He dwelt on this threat so vividly that one listener later recalled feeling his wrists to make sure "the fetters were not already pressing his flesh."

George Mason backed Henry with his far-more-modest speaking powers. But he and Henry were staggered by a crucial defection from the Anti-Federalist ranks. When Governor Edmund Randolph rose to speak, he said he favored ratification, because without Virginia there would be no Union. Raising his right arm, he declared he would "assent to the lopping of this limb before I assent to the dissolution of the Union."

Behind the scenes, Randolph did something even more important for the Federalist cause. He received a letter from Governor George Clinton, suggesting an alliance between the Anti-Federalists of Virginia and New York. Clinton urged Randolph to commit Virginia to a call for a second Constitutional Convention. Randolph neglected to show this letter to Patrick Henry, George Mason or anyone else. Instead he sent it to the Virginia legislature, where it lay unread, because all the members were absent, enjoying the oratorical fireworks at the ratifying convention.

James Madison did not even attempt to match Patrick Henry's flamboyant rhetoric. So small he could not be seen by many spectators, and speaking in a voice so low that at first few could hear him, Madison methodically demolished Henry's arguments one by one, pulverizing his loose reasoning and inaccurate historical examples. Calmly, Madison insisted the Constitution should be judged "on its merits solely." The delegates should ask only "whether it will promote the public happiness."

Behind James Madison stood a large shadow: the absent George Washington. Every man in the room knew the man from Mount Vernon was totally committed to ratifying the Constitution as it stood, without any qualifications, amendments or second Convention. But Patrick Henry was almost a match for the former commander-in-chief and his brilliant young confederate, Madison. The backwoods Demosthenes introduced a long series of amendments that he wanted Virginia to submit to other states before the Old Dominion's ratification could become official. This was nothing but the second-Convention idea via the mails. Henry heaped scorn on Madison's assurances of public happiness and called on the delegates to vote with a consciousness that the future of liberty around the world was at stake. "We have it in our power to secure the happiness of one half the human race!" he cried.

As Henry spoke a tremendous storm broke over Richmond. The lightning and thunder reminded not a few men with good memories of the storm that had erupted over Philadelphia while John Adams spoke for independence. Was God telling them to listen to this man, who had sounded one of the first

"THE AMERICAN REVOLUTION IS THE MOST IMPORTANT EVENT IN OUR HISTORY. IT INFUSED INTO OUR CULTURE ALL OF OUR MOST IMPORTANT VALUES, OUR NOBLEST ASPIRATIONS."

Gordon Wood
Professor of History,
Brown University

TOP LEFT *Governor George Clinton of New York was a determined foe of the Constitution. He thought New York was doing nicely without it. Yet he and George Washington remained good friends.*

THE FEDERAL PROCESSIONS

The good ship Hamilton *fired a thirteen gun salute to begin New York's Federalist parade down Broadway.*

In many cities the people celebrated the ratification of the Constitution with parades that became known as Federal Processions. Philadelphia began these political displays on its ratification day, December 12, 1787, with a boat on a wagon, manned by sailors. They rolled through the streets taking soundings until they reached forty fathoms, whereupon they shouted: "Sound bottom, safe anchorage." The majority at the Pennsylvania ratifying convention had been forty.

In Boston some 5,000 men followed another vessel through the streets. Charleston's ship of state was hauled by six snow-white horses. On July 23, 1788, three days before the state was to ratify the Constitution, in order to put pressure on the crumbling Anti-Federalists, New York had one of the grandest parades. It featured a full-rigged thirty-six-gun ship, the *Hamilton*, manned by a uni-

formed crew of thirty and pulled by ten horses. Behind it marched several thousand craftsmen and workers testifying to their belief that the new federal government would stop the British from dumping goods and putting them out of work.

Philadelphia's second parade, on July 4, 1788, outdid New York's in numbers and symbols. It featured the *U.S.S. Union*, a barge captured from *H.M.S. Serapis* by John Paul Jones. Built up as a miniature warship, it had a crew of twenty-five. Groups of marchers carried banners recalling the Declaration of Independence, the French alliance, the treaty of peace, and other great events. Then came a herald, escorted by a trumpeter, flaunting a banner with "New Era" in gold letters. The herald was Richard Bache, Benjamin Franklin's son-in-law, standing in for the ailing president (governor) of the state.

The most popular float was the "New Roof" or "Grand Federal Edifice," a symbol suggested by the poet Francis Hopkinson to represent the Constitution. He had used it to satirize the Anti-Federalists as fogies who clung to the old roof and said the new one would ruin the house. The "edifice" was a dome on thirteen elegantly carved Corinthian pillars. Beside it marched 450 architects, house carpenters, saw makers and file cutters who had built the float.

Behind them came thousands more craftsmen, many carrying the tools of their trades, some holding aloft banners with messages such as "No Tax on American Carriages." The bricklayers' banner summed up the people's view of the struggle for the Constitution—and the entire Revolution—with their motto: "Both Buildings and Rulers are the Works of our Hands."

warnings in defense of American liberty? Or was He urging them to take a new risk to perpetuate that liberty?

Madison and other Federalists—such as the future chief justice of the Supreme Court, John Marshall—opted for the second meaning and answered Henry's pyrotechnics with renewed vigor and even more forceful logic. Finally, the colossus of the Anti-Federalists faltered. Perhaps Henry sensed that the struggle had become a contest between a younger generation, personified by Madison and Marshall, and older men like himself and Mason, who had served American liberty honorably but could not understand this latest evolution of its spirit. Almost admitting defeat, Henry said he would be consoled by "being overpowered in a good cause." He went even further, assuring his listeners that if he lost, "I will be a peaceful citizen."

That same day, June 25, the Virginia convention voted 89 to 79 to ratify the Constitution. They added twenty nonbinding amendments and a bill of rights, which they urged other states and the new federal government to consider. Madison, adopting the Massachusetts strategy, offered no objection to amendments and promised to make a bill of rights the first order of business in the new Congress—a commitment he faithfully fulfilled. A letter from his friend Thomas Jefferson in Paris, strongly urging this safeguard to liberty, played a part in this artful blend of politics and principles.

Federalists rushed a messenger to Mount Vernon to tell George Washington the good news. As word spread along the Potomac, dozens of Washington's neighbors piled into boats and swarmed to Mount Vernon's landing to congratulate him and invite him to a celebration the next day at Alexandria. It was, a delighted Washington wrote Charles Cotesworth Pinckney, the first "public company" to drink a toast to the future prosperity of the new government.

At New York's convention, assembling in Poughkeepsie on June 17, the political tension was as high as Virginia's—and the prospects for ratification looked far worse. When deliberations began, the Anti-Federalists outnumbered the Federalists 46 to 19. The Antis were further buoyed

HAIL AND FAREWELL

This print announced Franklin's death to France. He died on April 17, 1790.

As Benjamin Franklin lay on his deathbed in the spring of 1790, he wrote a farewell letter to George Washington. He congratulated the first President "on the growing strength of our new government under your administration." Then he added a private goodbye.

For my own personal ease, I should have died two years ago; but tho these years have been spent in excruciating pain, I am pleased that I have lived them, since they have brought me to see our present situation. I am now finishing my 84th year, and probably with it my career in this life; but in whatever state of existence I am plac'd hereafter, if I retain any memory of what has pass'd here, I shall with it retain the esteem, respect and affection with which I have long been, my dear friend, yours most sincerely,

Benjamin Franklin

Washington's reply should refute for all time the notion that the father of the country was an emotionless man.

Would to God, my dear sir, that I could congratulate you on the removal of that excruciating pain, under which you labor, and that your existence might close with as much ease to yourself, as its continuance had been beneficial to our country and useful to mankind; or, if the united wishes of a free people, joined with the earnest prayers of every friend to science and humanity, could relieve the body from pains or infirmities, that you could claim an exemption on this score. But this cannot be, and you have within yourself the only resource to which we can confidently apply for relief, a philosophic mind.

If to be venerated for benevolence, if to be admired for talents, if to be esteemed for patriotism, if to be beloved for philanthropy, can gratify the human mind, you must have the pleasing consolation to know, that you have not lived in vain. And I flatter myself that it will not be ranked among the least grateful occurrences of your life to be assured that, so long as I retain my memory, you will be thought of with respect, veneration and affection by your sincere friend,

George Washington

by Governor George Clinton's letter to Governor Randolph. They were confident it would produce an alliance with Virginia and a second Convention, guaranteeing the Constitution's demise. They made no objection when the Federalists, eager to avoid an early vote, asked for a chance to discuss the Constitution point by point in a committee of the whole.

Day after day, Alexander Hamilton and Robert R. Livingston expounded and defended the Constitution before this wall of Anti-Federalist intransigence. "Our arguments confound but do not convince," Hamilton admitted. One frustrated Federalist remarked that the Antis seemed to know the meaning of only one word: "no." Then came the news that New Hampshire had ratified without so much as a quibble. Although the Constitution was now the law of the land, the Antis, still banking on Virginia, remained unmoved. John Lansing said he was ready to let the nine states "make the experiment" without New York.

On July 2 the Anti-Federalists were flabbergasted to learn that Virginia had ratified without any mention of a second Convention. Scrambling frantically for a new strategy, the Antis resorted to the standard arguments against the Constitution—in particular the lack of a bill of rights. Alexander Hamilton sarcastically inquired why this item had suddenly become so important. The New York state constitution lacked one, and Governor Clinton had never seemed disturbed by its absence. The rattled Antis began to split into moderate and die-hard factions.

Armed with a wealth of arguments from his labors on *The Federalist* and his attendance at the Constitutional Convention, Hamilton annihilated speaker after speaker from the Anti-Federalist ranks. For a clincher, Hamilton coolly issued a threat that shook the Clintonites to their shoes. If the convention failed to ratify, New York City and its environs, which had sent an overwhelmingly Federalist delegation to the convention, would secede from New York State, form a separate state, and ratify the compact without them. "And where," Hamilton asked mockingly, "will the Empire State be without its crown jewel?"

The desperate Clintonites retreated to their last line of defense. John Lansing proposed that New York's ratification be "conditional." The state would reserve the right to secede from the Union if its proposed amendments to the Constitution were not accepted. Since Governor Clinton had proposed no fewer than fifty-five amendments, the Federalists found this idea worse than no ratification at all. Alexander Hamilton killed this final attempt to subvert the Union by reading to the convention a letter from James Madison, stating bluntly that the Constitution "requires an adoption *in toto* and *for ever*....Any condition whatever must vitiate ratification."

On July 26 the Clintonites capitulated. Seven of them abstained, and moderates joined the Federalists to ratify the Constitution by a hair-breadth margin, 30 to 27. Seldom had a legislative body had its mind changed so thoroughly. Even the principal Anti-Federalist

BELOW *While Americans struggled to create the Constitution, Thomas Jefferson was in Paris as the American ambassador to France. But he stayed in close touch with the process, thanks to numerous letters from his close friend, James Madison. Jefferson approved the Constitution but felt strongly it should have a bill of rights. He played a large role in persuading Madison to present one in the first session of the new federal Congress.*

ABOVE *While cannon boomed a thirteen-gun salute, President Washington crossed New York harbor in a forty-seven-foot barge manned by thirteen "pilots." He landed at the foot of Wall Street and walked to his house on Cherry Street, surrounded by cheering crowds. Tears of deep emotion streamed down his cheeks. Several times he was forced to stop and wipe his eyes.*

spokesman, an eloquent merchant named Melancthon Smith, voted for ratification. One exultant Federalist wrote that the Constitution had "undergone an ordeal [by] torture, and [had] been preserved, as by fire."

That left only two states still outside the Union—North Carolina and Rhode Island. Both remained recalcitrant. North Carolina refused to ratify until a second Constitutional Convention accepted a bill of rights and other amendments proposed by the state's ratifying convention. This was rejection in disguise. With their history of quarrels between backcountry and seacoast, most North Carolinians suspected all governments. Rhode Island continued to act as if it were operating on the moon.

The Federalists declined to be intimidated by these foot-draggers. They went calmly ahead organizing the first national elections. A reluctant George Washington was chosen President without a single negative electoral vote. Replaying the old Virginia-Massachusetts alliance, the Vice-President was the man who had nominated Washington to be the Continental army's commander—"the Atlas of Independence," John Adams of Massachusetts. With the new government a political fact, North Carolina decided to join it. Rhode Island took a bit longer.

Soon the man who had done so much to sustain and shape American liberty was on his way to New York, the nation's first capital. On a sunny April 30, 1789, on the balcony of Federal Hall, overlooking Wall Street, George Washington placed his hand on a Bible and said: "I solemnly swear that I will faithfully execute the office of the President of the United States and will, to the best of my ability, preserve, protect and defend the Constitution of the United States."

Although it was not in the prescribed oath, Washington added, spontaneously: "So help me God." Then he kissed the Bible.

Robert R. Livingston, the chancellor of the state of New York, turned to the crowd of onlookers. "Long live George Washington, President of the United States," he cried.

The people shouted back the words until they thundered against the surrounding buildings. In the Hudson River, ships' cannon boomed a salute. Above the voices and the guns swelled the peal of massed church bells. American liberty, its essence rethought, its strength restored, was resuming its tremendous journey into the future.

Opening the Eyes of the World

Fifty years after he wrote the Declaration of Independence, eighty-three year old Thomas Jefferson was invited to Washington, D.C., to celebrate the golden anniversary. He was too old and sick to leave his hilltop mansion, Monticello, but he wrote the organizers of the ceremony a letter which turned out to be his last public statement.

Jefferson began by saying how much he wished he could join the "remnant of that host of worthies" who shared the historic struggle for American liberty. He said he was especially proud that his fellow citizens, "after a half century of experience and prosperity," continued to approve the choice they made. Then came prophetic words:

> May it be to the world, what I believe it will be...the signal of arousing men to...assume the blessings of self government...All eyes are open, or opening to the rights of man. The general spread of the light of science has already laid open to every view the palpable truth that the mass of mankind has not been born with saddles on their backs, nor a favored few booted and spurred, ready to ride them legitimately, by the grace of god...For ourselves, let the annual return of this day, forever refresh our recollections of these rights and an undiminished devotion to them.

By the time Jefferson wrote these words, the American Revolution was on its way to fulfilling Thomas Paine's prediction that liberty would expand around the world. The French Revolution was the first upheaval to reveal the idea's explosive potential. Although the struggle ended in Napoleon Bonaparte's military dictatorship, followed by the restoration of the Bourbon kings, it left a legacy of liberty to the French people which they soon proved determined to reclaim.

The rest of Europe seethed with the belief that new more successful revolutions against the *ancien régime* were possible—a faith sustained by America's continued growth and happiness. The Spanish colonies of Central and South America revolted and formed republics on the American model. British liberty fermented until it produced the Reform Act of 1832. This peaceful revolution widened the right to vote, eliminated the rotten boroughs and made Parliament a far more representative legislature.

LEFT *Daniel Boone leads American settlers through the Cumberland Gap into Kentucky. Boone's legendary life became an emblem of America's westward surge under the banner of liberty.*

In America, liberty expanded steadily, creating a new kind of country. Previously, liberty had been handed down from above by a few governments. In America it was the upward, ever-unfolding creation of the people. It inspired the surge west by millions of pioneers, the creation of thousands of new businesses and jobs, the awakening of ambition in millions of men and women.

This dynamic growth of liberty transformed the word democracy—often scorned during and after the Revolution as synonymous with mob rule—into a term of respect. In twenty-eight years, the Republican Party that elected Thomas Jefferson as President in 1800 became the Democratic Party that elected Andrew Jackson.

The steadily deepening understanding of liberty as the sacred watchword of the American nation soon made African slavery incompatible with its goals. The American people endured a terrible Civil War to achieve what Abraham Lincoln at Gettysburg called "a new birth of freedom." For the next hundred years, as America struggled—and often failed—to widen this freedom for blacks and the millions of Irish, Italians, Poles, Jews and other immigrants who poured into the United States from Europe, liberty remained a dynamic force that held out the hope of freeing people from the slavery of subsistence wages and lack of opportunity.

When the American nation emerged as a world power, liberty became the cornerstone of her foreign policy. The determination to defend freedom around the globe against the tyrannies of fascism and communism kept hope alive in millions of hearts and minds through two world wars and the long decades of the cold war.

Liberty remains the driving force of the American nation today. It is the core idea around which equal opportunity and the pursuit of happiness revolve. Without liberty, equal opportunity becomes a mirage, and happiness cannot be achieved. Deepening liberty's meaning and extending its reach will remain at the center of our national mission. Liberty will continue to make America a nation that can welcome people of every race and religion. Greater than any tribal bond or national gene pool, American liberty is both an idea and an ideal in which everyone can participate, whether their ancestors came here three months or 300 years ago.

No one has put it better than John Quincy Adams, the son of John Adams, the man who shared with Thomas Jefferson the responsibility for the Declaration of Independence. "Let us not be unmindful that liberty is power," John Quincy said in 1821, when he was Secretary of State. "The nation blessed with the greatest portion of liberty must in proportion to its numbers be the most powerful nation on earth."

INDEX

Page numbers in *italics* refer to captions.

Adams, Abigail, 1–2, *7*, *75*, 94, *129*, 142, 150, 159, 169, 175, 242, 353
Adams, John, 21, 72–75, *73*, *75*, 79–80, 85, 93–95, 97, 132–33, 143, 147–48, 152, 163, 168–70, 172–73, 175, 176, 181, 195, 199, 235, 242, *265*, 266, 322, 381
    Abigail's correspondence with, 2, 150, 159, 169, 175, 353
    as ambassador, 349–50, *349*
    Declaration of Independence and, 170, 171, 173, *173*
    in peace negotiations, 298, 337, 338
Adams, John Quincy, 384
Adams, Samuel, 54, 65, 72–75, 77–79, *79*, 83, 87, 90, 93–95, *95*, 97–98, 106, 108, 109, 128–29, *129*, 132, 133, 152, 153, 159, 168, 353, 355, 374
Addison, Joseph, 31, 65, 206
Administration of Justice Act, 85
African-Americans, *see* blacks
Albany, New York, 237, 253, 256, 291
Alexander, William (Lord Stirling), 187, 188–89, 196
Allen, Ethan, 129, 130, *131*
Amherst, Jeffery, 46, 48, 104, 305
André, John, 309, 310–11, 312
Arlington, Massachusetts (Menotomy), 121–24
armies:
    U.S., 365
    see also British army; Continental army
Arnold, Benedict, 129–30, *130*, *131*, 132, 153, 154, 157, 158, 166–68, 207–9, *209*, *226*, 238, 243, 251, 253–61, *256*, *257*, *267*, 281, 309, 310, 320, 322, 325
    treason of, 309, 310–11, 312, *321*
Articles of Confederation, 199, 347, 356, 358, 360, 367
arts, 353
Attucks, Crispus, 71, 72, *74*, *76*
Augusta, Princess, 11–12, 18, 40, 41

Bache, Sarah Franklin, 264
Bancroft, Edward, 231, 234, 271
Barré, Isaac, 50–51, *51*, 55, 300
Barrett, James, 114–15, 116–17, 118, 127
Beaumarchais, Pierre Augustin Caron de, *230*, 231, 267, 268, 269, 271
beauty, 25–26
Bemis Heights, 253, 255, *257*, 258, 261
Bennington, Vermont, 246, 249, *250*, *251*, 261
Bernard, Francis, 19, 54–55, 68
blacks, 151–52, 160–62, 163, 284, 298, 302–3, *352*, 366
Bonhomme Richard, 293–97, *297*
Boone, Daniel, *153*, 295
Boone, Jemima, 295
Boston, *39*, 54, 85–88, *88*, 97, 98, 101, 102, 134, 140, 151, *160*, 164, 165, *165*
    riots in, *39*, 52, 54–57, 60, 71–74, *73*, *74*, *76*, 77, *77*, 85
Boston Massacre, *39*, 71–74, *73*, *74*, *76*, *77*, 85
Boston Port Act, 85, 86
Boston Tea Party, 78–80, *79*, 81–82, *81*, 83, 84, 85, 88
Braddock, Edward, 34, *34*, 245

Brandywine, *229*, 257, *270*
Brant, Joseph, 291, 294, *294*
Breed's Hill, *129*, 135–41, *136*, *137*, 145
British army, 74, 93, 101
    American soldiers compared with, 118, 127, *181*
    cost of maintaining, 49–50, 64, 74, 77
Bunker Hill, 90, 135–36, *136*, *138*, *140*, 141–43, 146, 147, 151–53, 182, 185, 187, *187*, 203, 204, 210, 239
Burgoyne, John, 104, 134, 135, 138, 167, 197, 236–40, *236*, *238*, *240*, 242, 243, *243*, 245–47, 249, *251*, 253–63
    Indians and, 250–51, *254*
    letter from Clinton to, *259*
    surrender of, 261–63, 268, 269
Burke, Edmund, 58, 60, 82, 86, *100*, 101, 104, 152, 230, 271, 287, 300, 301, 305, 369
Bushnell, David, 186
Bute, John Stuart, Lord, 11–13, *13*, 15, 18, 32, 38, 39–40, *40*, 41–44, *44*, 46, 52, 58, 63, 287

Canada, 129, *131*, 132, 143, 146, 153–58, *157*, 166–68, 172, 185, 207–9, *209*, 236, 237, 238–42, *238*, *240*, 253, 257, 281, 284
    peace negotiations and, 337, 338
    Quebec, 13, 15, *16*, 85–86, *153*, 154, *154*, 157–58, *157*, 166–67
Carleton, Guy, 153, 154, 157, 158, 166, 167, 207, 209, 236–37, 309
Carroll, Charles, 166, 262, *262*, 368
Cato (play by Addison), 31, 65, 206
Charleston, South Carolina, 181, *182*, 186, 298, 299, 300, 305, 307, 311, 312, *313*
Charlestown, Massachusetts, 135, 136, 137, 138, *138*, 140, *141*, 142
Charlotte, Queene, 18, 35, 242, 350
Chase, Samuel, 166, 173, *262*
Church, Benjamin, 98, 106, 127, 128, 147, 182
Clark, George Rogers, 292–93, 294, 307
Clinton, George, 256, 357, 376, *376*, 379
Clinton, Henry, 104, 134, 137, 140, 163, 181, 186, 188, 194, 235, 237, 256–59, 261, 262, 282–84, 291, 292, 299, 302, 305–7, 317, 320, 321, 323–25, 329, 330, 334–36
    at Charleston, 299, 300
    letter to Burgoyne from, *259*
Coercive Acts, 85–86, 87, 94, 97, 98, 102
Colden, Cadwallader, 55–57
Collier, George, 194, 199
colonial life, 22–29
Common Sense (Paine), 159–60, *160*, 163, 214
Concord, Massachusetts, 105, 106, 109–18, *115*, 119, 120–21, *121*, *122*, 128, 130, 142, 143
Connecticut, 103, 373
Constitution, 367, 372–81, *377*
Constitutional Convention, 356–67, *358*, *375*
Continental army, 132–33, 134, 152, *181*, 197, 200, 202, 327
    blacks in, 151–52, 302
    Congress and, *276*, 280, 299
    death rate in, 334
    discharge of, 340, *357*
    health and morale of, 198, *276*, 279–80, *280*, 299–300, 308, 316

mutiny in, 316–17
number of soldiers in, 181, 235, 308
pay to soldiers and officers in, 286, 339–40
recruitment for, *167*, *181*
Washington appointed general of, 133–34
Continental Association, 95
Continental Congress, 87, 88, 93–98, *93*, *94*, 95, 96, 100–2, 108,
130–34, 143, *147*, 152, 153, 158–59, 166, 168–70, 172,
175, 199, 235, 266, 271, 313, 325, 347, 360
army and, *276*, 280, 299
Bunker Hill and, 142, 143
Canada and, 166–67
Cornwallis' surrender and, 335
Declaration of Independence and, 175–76, 199
feuds in, 286
final debate on independence in, 172–75
Howe's peace commission and, 185, 186, 196, 198, 199,
201, 202
Lee and, 205
money depreciation and, *281*, 285–86, 298, 299
Olive Branch Petition of, 142, 143, 152
postwar, 347, 351
rebellions and, 355–56
war strategy and, 200, 202, 210, 214, 222, 224, 285, 327
Washington given power by, 222, 224
Continental navy, *197*, 302
Cooper, Samuel, 15, 74
Cornwallis, Charles, Lord, 219, 222–23, 224, 308, 312, 314, *314*,
316, 320–21, 323–24, *324*, 329, 330–36, *331*
surrender of, *328*, 334–36, *335*
Cresswell, Nicholas, 162–63, 224
Cushing, Thomas, 77, 98, 101
Custis, George Washington Parke, *223*

dancing, *23*, 25, 27
Dartmouth, William Legge, Lord, 78, 101, 102, 105, 106, 128, 143,
146, 271
Dawes, William, 108–9
Deane, Silas, 229, 230, *230*, 231–34, 267–71, *271*
Dearborn, Henry, 254, 258, 261
death rate, 334
Declaration of Independence, 1, 2, 25, 170–72, *170*, 173, *173*, *174*,
176, 183, 216, 262, 287, 302, 358, 383
Declaratory Act, 64
de Grasse, François Joseph Paul, Count, 323, 324, 325, *325*, 326,
329, 330, 334, 338
de la Luzerne, Duke, 321, 322, 323
Delaware, 35, 173, 372
Delaware River, *179*, 196, 210, 211–14, 215, *215*, 217–19, 238,
255, 263, 268, 279, 282, 283, 326
d'Estaing, Charles Hector Theodat, Count, 283–84, *287*, 298
Dickinson, John, 62, 96, 131, 132, *147*, 159, 168, 172–73, 175, 365
Olive Branch Petition of, 142, 143, 152
doctors, 28
Dorchester Heights, *164*, 165–66, *165*
drinks and foods, 27
Dunmore, John Murray, Lord, 87, 104, 160–63, *162*, 302

East India Company, 68, 75–77, 78, 82
economy, *23*, 35, 63, 354, *354*

Emerson, Ralph Waldo, 118
Emerson, William, 115, 118
emigration, 24, 28–29
espionage, *291*, 309, *309*
ethnic groups, 24, 35

Fairfax family, 30–31, 133
fashion, 25
Fauquier, Francis, 21, 57
Federalist Papers, The, 373
Federal Processions, 377
Ferguson, Patrick, 313, *317*
flags, *132*, 249
Grand Union, 152–53, *154*, 248
Stars and Stripes, 248, *248*, 264
food, 27
Forten, James, 302, *302*
Fourth of July celebrations, *177*
Fox, Charles James, 217, *222*, 271, 287, 336
Fox, Henry, 18, 41, *44*, 217
France, 39, 40–41, *40*, 267–74, 301, 349
American treaty with, 271–74, *271*, 282, 322, 338
Franklin in, 229–35, *231*, *233*, 237, 267–74, *271*, 281,
282, 298
naval forces of, 282, 283–84, 287–90, 308
peace negotiations in, 298, 321–22, 324, 337–39, *338*
Revolution in, 364, *364*, 369, 383
Washington and, 32–34
Francis, Ebenezer, 240, 241
Franklin, Benjamin, 1, *5*, 24, 29, 35–38, *36*, *37*, *38*, 64, 66, 74, 75,
75, 80, 86, 88, 101–3, 128, 130–31, 142, *149*, 158, 166,
174, 297, 322, 366, 374
Constitution and, 356–57, 361, 363–65, 368, 372, 377
death of, 378, *378*
Declaration of Independence and, 170, *173*, 176
Declaration of Independence written by, 142–43, 159
in France, 229–35, *231*, *233*, 237, 267–74, *271*, 281, 282, 298
Howe and, 101, *103*, 186, 199, *201*
Hutchinson-Whately letters and, 77–78
Ireland visited by, 43
Jones and, 293
as Massachusetts's agent, 74–75, 78
in peace negotiations, 337, 338
Pitt and, 101–2
in Privy Council hearing, 8, 80–85, 102, 271, 301, 365
"Rules By Which A Great Empire May Be Reduced To
A Small One," 78
stamp tax and, 50, 51, 57, 60–62, 64
Strahan and, 38, 142
tea tax and, 71, 79
"We Have An Old Mother," 83
Franklin, Deborah, 36, 57
Franklin, William, 35–36, 37, 38, 57, 62, 130, 131, 169,
229, 374
Franklin, William Temple, 374, *374*
Fraser, Simon, 240, 241, 253–54, 256
death of, 259, *260*, 261
Freeman's Farm, 254–55, 256, *256*, 257, *257*, 258, 269–61
French and Indian War, 34, *34*, *37*, 46, 49, 61, 107, *131*,
135, *153*

French Revolution, 364, *364*, 369, 383
Gage, Margaret Kemble, 98, 106–8
Gage, Thomas, 52, 55, 71, 85, 86, 94, 97–101, *98*, 104–10, 126–28,
    131, 134, 135, 147
Galloway, Joseph, 95–97, 100, 103, 130, 131, 305
Galvez, Bernardo de, 307
Gansevoort, Peter, 243, *244*
Gates, Horatio, 238, 242, *242*, 243, 245, 246, 251–53, 254, 255,
    256, *256*, 257–58, 259, 261–62, 263, *267*
    Burgoyne's surrender to, 261–63, 268, 269
    Conway Cabal and, 280–81
    McCrea and, 250–51
    in South Carolina, 308, 313
George I, King, 12, *103*
George II, King, 11, 12, 15, 32, 337
George III, King, 1, 2, *3*, 8, 11–19, *11*, *13*, 30, 32, 39–42, *40*,
    44–46, *44*, *45*, 49, 52, *52*, 58, 61, 63–66, *65*, *66*, 67, 68, *68*,
    70, *70*, 71, 75, 77, 81, 85, 86, *86*, 88, 94, 97–98, 101, 102,
    104–5, 128, 131, 132, 143–46, 152, 153, 159, 169, 182, *185*,
    216, 217, 232, 235–37, 242, 269, 271, 274, 287, 290, *297*,
    301, 336, 343, 349, 362
    abdication written by, 336–37
    Adams and, 349–50, *349*
    breakdown of, 350
    county associations and, 300–301
    Declaration of Independence and, 171, 175
    and French aid to America, 234, 284
    Germany and, 169, 192–93
    Howe's peace commission from, 183–86
    Jefferson and, *349*, 350
    London riots and, *304*, 305
    marriage of, 18, 35
    Olive Branch Petition to, 142, 143, 152
    parliamentary elections and, 100–101, 312–13
    Proclamation of Rebellion issued by, 143, 146, 152
    slavery and, 171, 175
    statue of, 176
Georgia, 175, 291, 305, 311, 322, 360, 372
Germain, Lord George, 146, 185, 186, 198, 199, 217, 234, 236–37,
    238, 253, 290, 291, 294, 305, 336
German soldiers, 169, 187–89, 192–94, *192*, *193*, 204–5, 208, 209,
    214, *216*, 218–19, *220*, 237, 240, 241, 246, 247, 249, 253,
    255, 258–59, 261, 264, 266, 299
Gerry, Elbridge, 166, 358, *358*, 362, 365, 367, 372, 374
Gibbon, Edward, 301, 305
Gist, Mordecai, 188, 189
Glorious Revolution, 12, 43
Goddard, Mary Katherine, 264
Gordon, Lord George, 301–4
Grafton, Augustus Fitzroy, Duke of, 63, 65, 68
Grand Union flag, 152–53, *154*, 248
Grant, James, 105, 187, 188, 219
Granville, John Carteret, Lord, 37, 38, *38*
Graves, Thomas, 326, 330, 335–36
Great Compromise, 361
Greene, Nathanael, 142, 187, 197, 200, 204, 209, 210,
    217–18, 299–300, 313–16, *313*, *316*, 320, 324, 327
Green Mountain Boys, 129, 130, 153, 249
Grenville, George, 44, 45, 46, 49, 50, 51, 58, 60, 62–63,
    64, 75

hair styles, 25, *25*
Hale, Nathan (colonel), 238, 241
Hale, Nathan (spy), 23, 160, 206, 309
    hanging of, 202, 206, *206*
Hamilton, Alexander, 218, *219*, 266, *279*, 283, 306, 312, *328*, 330, *367*
    Constitution and, 357, 360–61, 362, 368, 372, 373, 379
Hamilton, Henry, 292–93, 309
Hancock, John, 25, 75, 81, 108, 109, 133, *149*, 159, 172, *172*, *173*,
    175, 176, 181, 374
Hanover, Duchy of, 12, 18, 192
Harnett, Cornelius, 163–64
Harrison, Benjamin, 172, 173
Hart, Nancy, *265*
Heath, William, 121–23, 124, 126, 210
Henry, Patrick, 24, 51–52, *52*, 93, *93*, 94, 96, 104, 133, 160, *287*,
    375–78
Herkimer, Nicholas, 246, *247*
Hillsborough, Wills Hill, Earl of, 29, 65, 66, 68, *71*, 74–75, 78
Hodgkins, Joseph, 181, 195, 198, 202
Hogarth, William, *43*
Holland, 336, 349
Hopkinson, Francis, 25, 248
horses, 28
House of Commons, 41, *41*, 42, 45, 60–61, 64, 68, 100, 102,
    271, 301, 336
    Ireland and, 286, 287
House of Representatives, 363, 367, 368
Howe, Richard, Lord, 101, *103*, *185*, 201, 211, 215, 337
    peace commission of, 183–86, 196–98, 199, *201*, 202,
    203, 204
Howe, William, 104, 134–41, 146, *164*, 165, 166, 172, 182–85,
    185, 187–88, 194, 195, 198, 203–4, 211, 215, 216, 219,
    235–38, *238*, 245, 253, 262, 282, 290
    Philadelphia campaign of, 237, 239, 245, 251, 256, 257,
    263–67, 268, 269, 279, 281, 282
Hughes, John, 51, 57
Hutchinson, Thomas, 19, 21, 46, 54, 55, 62, 72, 74, *75*, 77–78,
    79, 80, 82, 86, 86

Independence, Fort, 238, 239, 240
Indians, 32, 34, 46–49, *47*, 237, 239, 243, 246, 247, 249, 251, *254*,
    261, 290–91, 292–93, *292*, *293*, 294
    in French and Indian War, 34, *34*, *37*, 46, 49, *61*
    McCrea and, 249–51, *253*
    in Pontiac's Rebellion, 47–48, *48*, 50
Ireland, 42–43, 61, 95, 146, 262, 286–87
Irish soldiers, 262, 287
Izard, Ralph, 82, 84

Jackson, Richard, 37, 38
Jasper, William, *183*
Jay, John, 93, *94*, 96, 169, 170, 337, 338, 349, 353, 373
Jefferson, Thomas, 1, 24, 52, 75, 88, 104, 143, *149*, 160, 173, 176,
    320, 321, *342*, 351, 357, 378, *379*, 383, 384
    Declaration of Independence written by, 170–72, *170*, *173*,
    302, 383
    George III and, *349*, 350
    Statute for Religious Freedom of, 353
Jenkinson, Charles, 287, 290
Jennings, Samuel, *352*

Jews, 322
Jones, John Paul, 293–97, *297*

Knowlton, Thomas, 201, 202, 206
Knox, Henry, *160*, 164, *164*, 165, 218, 339, *341*, 356
Knyphausen, Wilhelm von, 204, 299, 305, 306
Kosciuszko, Thaddeus, 253, 254, *255*, 286

Lafayette, James, 1, 2, 6, *303*, 364
Lafayette, Marquis de, 1, 266, *270*, 279–84, *303*, 308, 320, 321,
    323, 324, *328*, 330, 334, 335
    French Revolution and, 364, *364*
language, 28
Lansing, John, Jr., 357, 362, 368, 379
League of Armed Neutrality, 336
Lee, Arthur, 128, 267, 268, 269, *271*
Lee, Charles, 134, 181, 203, 204, *204*, 205, 209, 210, 211, 283,
    286, 312, 327
Lee, Ezra, 186
Lee, Richard Henry, 88, 96, 104, 131, 148, 162, 169, 267,
    372, 373
Lennox, Sarah, 18, *18*
Leslie, Alexander, 105–6
Lexington, Massachusetts, 108–13, *112*, *113*, *114*, 118, 120–23,
    127, 128, 130, 142, 143, 151, 152
liberty, *352*, 383–84
    British tradition of, 42–43
Liberty Bell, 174, *174*
Lincoln, Abraham, 303, 384
Lincoln, Benjamin, 243, 247–49, 257, 258, 298, 300, 335, 355, *355*
Livingston, Robert R., 157, 169, 170, 379, 381
London, 216–17, 335
    riots in, 301–5, *304*, 306
Longfellow, Henry Wadsworth, *108*
Long Island, 183, 187–88, *190*, *196*, 235, 327
Louis XV, King, 13, 45, 232, *232*
Louis XVI, King, 159, 231, 232–33, *232*, *233*, 234, 267, 269, *271*,
    274, 364, 369
loyalists, 348, *348*
Ludington, Sibyl, 264

McCrea, Jane, 249–51, *253*
McDougall, Alexander, 78, *82*, 196
Madison, James, 322, *347*, 353, 361
    Constitution and, 356, 357, 358, 360, 361, 362, 363, 366, 367,
        368, 373, 376, 378, 379, *379*
mail, 88, *149*
Marie Antoinette, 232–33, *233*
Marion, Francis, *311*, 312, *313*
marriage, 26
Martin, Joseph Plumb, 189, 200–201, 279, 329, 340
Martin, Josiah, 163–64
Martin, Luther, 360, 361, 365, 368
Maryland, 103, 169, 173, *350*, 354, 355, 374
Mason, George, 66, 87, *358*, 362, 366, 367, 372, 373, 376
Massachusetts, 94, 95, 97, 98, 100, 101, 104, 105–6, 134, 354, 355
    Constitution and, 360, 372, 373–74
    reports on Lexington and Concord from, 127–28, 152
Massachusetts Committee of Safety, 121–22, 128, 129, *130*, 135,
    136, 137–38

Massachusetts Provincial Congress, 98, 105, 106, 107, 122, 131,
    132, 138, 183
Mecom, Benjamin, 66
medicine, 28
Menotomy (Arlington, Massachusetts), 121–24
Mercer, George, 57, 60
Mercer, Hugh, *223*, *225*
Mercer, William, *225*
Mifflin, Thomas, 147, *194*, 195, 340–43, *342*
Miles, Samuel, 187–88
militia, 98, 151, 152, 181, 197, 202, 246, 263, 302, 308, 311, 327
    defection in, 151, 198, 205, 207, 210
minutemen, 98, 107, 197
money, 290, 354
    depreciation of, *281*, 285–86, 290, 298, 299, 300, 305, 306,
        308, 316, 322
Monmouth, 283, *285*, 286, 288
Monroe, James, *219*
Montgomery, Richard, 153, 154, 157, 158
    death of, *157*, 158, 159
Moody, James, *291*
Morgan, Daniel, 148, 153, *153*, 154, 157, 158, 197, 251, 254, 255,
    258, 259, 261, 268, 281, 314, 316
Morris, Gouverneur, 362–63, *362*, *363*, 365, 366, 367, 368
Morris, Robert, 159, 175, 222, 235, 316, 322, 353, *362*
    Constitution and, 357, 362
Morristown, New Jersey, 305–6
Mount Vernon, 30, *33*, 34–35, 57
music, 24–25

"Nation Makers, The" (painting by Pyle), *229*
Native Americans, *see* Indians
Newcastle, Thomas Pelham-Holles, Duke of, 11, 13–15, *15*, 39, 40,
    42, 63, 100
New Hampshire, 103, 360, 374, 375, 379
New Jersey, 35, 169, 173, 204, 208, 209–11, *213*, 214, 215, *216*,
    217–24, 229, 235, 237–38, 283, 285, 290, 291, 299, 316,
    325, 334, 354, 372
New Jersey Plan, 360–61
newspapers, 46, 86–87, 103, 128, 186, 264
New York, 35, 169, 173, 175, 186–207, *189*, *195*, 209, 235, 239,
    240, 247, 282, 283, 285, 290–92, 298–99, 305, 308, 316,
    322, 325, 330, 331, 334, 347, 354
    Constitution and, 372, 374, 375, 378–81
New York City, 182, 185, 206, 322, 323, 324, 379
    burning of, 202–3, *205*, 206
Norris, Isaac, 174
North, Frederick, Lord, 65, 66, 68, 70–71, *70*, 75, 77, 81, 82, *84*,
    85–86, 88, 97–98, 100, 101, 104, 128, 130, 143, 146, 152,
    157, 217, 269, 274, 282–83, 286, 287, 290, 300–301, *304*,
    336
    collapse of, 287, 290, 291, 301
    and French aid to America, 234–35, 271
    resignation of, 336–37
North Briton, 44–46, *45*, 66, 93
North Carolina, 163–64, 313–16, 322, *324*, 360, 374, 381

O'Hara, Charles, 331, 334–35, *335*
Olive Branch Petition, 142, 143, 152
Oliver, Andrew, 52, 54, 55

Ordinance of 1787, *351*
Oriskany, New York, 246, *247*
Otis, James, 19–21, *21*, 46, 57, 71, *265*

Paine, Thomas, 159–60, *160*, 166, 169, 171, 214–15, 369, *369*, 383
Pamela (novel by Richardson), 28
Parker, John, 109, 110–13, 115, 120
Parliament, 12, 42, *43*, *44*, 58, 60, *60*, 61, 62, 63, 65, 68, *68*, 88, 95, 96, 102, *102*, 104, 131, 152, 153, 199, 216, 217, 235, 287, 300–301, 336, 348
    elections in, 100–101, 312–13
    Gordon's petition to, 304
    Wilkes and, 65–67, *67*, 68, 70
Paterson, William, 360, *360*
patriotism, 151, 152
peace treaty, 298, 321–22, 324, 337–39, *338*, 340, 348
Penn, Thomas, 36–37, 38
Penn, Richard, 36–37, 38
Penn, William, 35, 36, 47
Pennsylvania, 35, *35*, 36–38, *47*, 50, 168–69, 173, 175, 199, 257, 285, 290, 351, 354
    Constitution and, 360, 372, 373
Percy, Hugh, Lord, 106, 121, 123, 124, 126, 127, *127*, 128, 135, 204
Philadelphia, 237, 239, 245, 251, 256, 257, 263–67, 268, 269, 279, 281, 282–83, 325
Pinckney, Charles Cotesworth, 358, *358*, 361, 363–65, 366, 367–68, 378
Pitcairn, John, 106, 109, 110, 112, 113, *114*, *116*, 118, 120, 124, 141, 142
"Pitcher, Molly," 288
Pitt, William (Lord Chatham), 11, 13, 15, 19, *21*, 32, 38–41, 44, *45*, 46, 50, 58, 60–65, *62*, 68, *74*, 86, 100, 101–2, *102*, 146, 152, 183, 271, 274, *275*, 300
Plan of Union, 95–96, 97, 103
Pontiac's Rebellion, 47–48, *48*, 50
population, 36, 61
Prescott, Samuel, 109, 114
Prescott, William, 135, 136, 137–38, *137*, 141
presidency, 362–63
Preston, Thomas, 71, 72, 73, 76, 85
Prevost, Augustine, 298, 299
Priestley, Joseph, 82, 103
Princeton, New Jersey, 222, *222*, 223–24, *223*, 225, 234, 237, 309, 327
prisons, British, 296
privateering, 298
Privy Council, 8, 36–37, 63, 68, 74, 80–85, 102, 146, 271, 301, 365
Proclamation of Rebellion, 143, 146, 152
Proclamation of 1763, 48–49
Prohibitory Act, 298
Putnam, Israel, 135, 136, 137–38, 140, 187, *187*, 189, 194, 195, 204, *208*, 210
Pyle, Howard, *229*

Quakers, 35, 36, 37, *47*, 66, 93, 94, 351
Quebec, 13, 15, *16*, 85–86, *153*, 154, *154*, 157–58, *157*, 166–67
Quebec Act, 85–86

Rall, Johann, 205, 214, 218, *220*
Randolph, Edmund, 358, *358*, 365, 366, 367, 368–72, 376, 379

Randolph, Peyton, 88, 104
Reed, Esther, 264
Reed, Joseph, 148, 151, 185, 201–2, *202*, 203, 205, 209–10, 214, 264, 317
religion, 24, 35, 353
Revere, Paul, 28, 66, 67, 78, 94, *108*, 374
    engraving of Boston Massacre by, 76
    ride of, *93*, 108–9, *108*, *110*
Rhode Island, 103, *196*, 283–84, 302, 354, 372, 374, 381
Richardson, Samuel, 28
Riedesel, Frederika von, *260*, 264
Riedesel, Friedrich Adolf von, 240, 241, 247, 253, 255, *260*, 264
Rights of Man, The (Paine), 369
Robinson, John, 100, 287, 290
Rochambeau, Jean Baptiste, Count de, 308–10, *311*, 322–23, 324, 325–26, *332*, 334, 364
Rockingham, Charles Watson-Wentworth, Lord, 58–60, 61, 63, *100*, 101, 230, 287
Ross, Betsy, 248, *248*, 264
Rousseau, Jean-Jacques, 230, 231
Rush, Benjamin, 200, *287*, 355
Rutledge, Edward, 96, 151, 152, 170, 175
    Howe's peace commission and, 199
Rutledge, John, 300, 307, 366

St. Clair, Arthur, 238–42, *239*, 243, 245
St. Leger, Barry, 237, 243, 246, 251
Salem, Massachusetts, 105–6
Sampson, Deborah, 264
Sandwich, John Montagu, Lord, 102, 105, 118, 234, 304
Saratoga, New York, *226*, 253, *255*, 256, 258, *260*, 261–62, *265*, 267, 268, 281
Schuyler, Philip, 143, 153, 207, 238, 242–43, *242*, *243*, 245, 246, 249, 251, 256, 258, 261, 294
Serapis, HMS, 293–97, *297*
Serle, Ambrose, 199, 201
Seven Years War, 11, 15, 19, *21*, 38, 40, 44, 192
Shays, Daniel, 354–55, *354*
Shays' Rebellion, 354–55, *354*, *355*, 356, 365, 374
Sherman, Roger, 170, *358*, 358–60, 361, 365–66, 367, 373
slavery, slaves, 14, *14*, *23*, 24, 31, *33*, 41, 151, 160–62, 163, 302–3, *302*, *350*, 351, 366, 384
    Constitution and, *363*, 365–67, 373, 374
    freeing of, *350*, 351–52, *352*, 366
    George III and, 171, 175
Smith, Francis, 106, 108, 109, 113–14, 115, *116*, 118, 120, 121
Sons of Liberty, *51*, 55, 57, 58, 59, *61*, 66, 67–68, 72–74, 77, 78, *79*, 86, 87, 103, 107, 108
South Carolina, 103–4, 173, 175, 305, 307–8, 311–12, *311*, 313, *313*, 314–16, *317*, 322, *350*, 355
    Constitution and, 360, 374
Spain, 39, 40, *40*, 41, 269, 270, 287–90, 298, 337, 347
spies, *291*, 309
stagecoaches, 28
Stamp Act, 50, *50*, 51–62, *52*, *54*, 55, 57, 58, 59, 60, *61*, *62*, 65, 75, 85, 300
Stanwix, Fort, 243, *244*, 246, 251
Stark, John, 138, 140, 246, 246–47, 249, *250*, 261
Stars and Stripes flag, 248, *248*, 264
Statute for Religious Freedom, 353

Steuben, Friedrich Wilhelm Augustus von, *279, 281, 282, 283, 285*

Stormont, David Murray, Lord, 230, 234, 237, 267, 274

Strahan, William, 38, 101, 142

Stuart, Gilbert, *347*

submarine, 186

Suffolk Resolves, 94–95, 121

Sugar Act of 1764, 49–50

Sullivan, John, 151, 167, 168, 187, 188, 189, 196, 198, *198,* 199, 217, 218, 235, 263, 266, 267, 284, 292, 294, 375

Sumter, Thomas, 307, 316

Tallmadge, Benjamin, 198, *206,* 309, *309,* 310–11, *341*

Tarleton, Banastre, 312, 314–16, *314, 318,* 321

tarring and feathering, 59

taverns, 26, 27–28, *28*

taxation, 49–50, 52, 54, 58, 59, 60, 61, 64, 66, 71, 75–80, 87, 88, 102, 153

Stamp Act, 50, *50,* 51–62, *52, 54, 55, 57, 58,* 59, 60, *61, 62,* 65, 75, 85, 300

Townshend Acts, 64–65, *65,* 66, 67, 68, 70, 71, 74, 75, 77

tea, 71, 75–80, *81*

Thacher, James, 240, 257, 334

theater, 353

Thomas, John, 148, 165, 167

Ticonderoga, Fort, 129–30, *130, 131,* 132, 135, 143, *160,* 164, *164,* 168, 207, 209, 236, 238–40, *239,* 242, 245

Townshend, Charles, 50, 63, 64, 65, *65*

Townshend Acts, 64–65, *65,* 66, 67, 68, 70, 71, 74, 75, 77

transportation, 28

Trenton, New Jersey, *179, 196, 198,* 214, 215, 218, 219, *219, 220,* 222, 224, 229, 234, 235, 236, 237, 245, 309, 327, *345*

Trumbull, Jonathan, 128, 129, 153, 181, *220, 342,* 373

Turtle, 186

Valley Forge, *276,* 279–82, *279, 280, 281, 282*

Vergennes, Charles Gravier, Count de, 230, 231, 232, 233, 234, 235, 267, 269, 270, 274, 322, 337, 338–39

Virginia, 31, 32, 49, 94, 95, 97, 103, 104, 160–62, 199, 292, 320–21, 322, 323–24, 325, 350, 353, 365

Constitution and, 360, 368–72, 374, 375, 378, 379

slaves freed in, *350,* 351

Virginia Plan, 358–61, 362, 363

Voltaire, *47,* 230

Walpole, Horace, 11–12, 13, 40, 70, 271

Walpole, Thomas, 74, 81, 271

Ward, Artemas, 134, 135, 138, 142

Warner, Seth, 238, 241, 246, 249

Warren, James, 143, 159, 168, 374

Warren, Joseph, 90, 94, 98, 106, 108, 121–22, 123, 127, 128, *129,* 134, 135, 138

death of, *129,* 141, 142

Warren, Mercy Otis, *265,* 374

Washington, George, 1, *4,* 21–35, *30, 31, 33, 34,* 49, 66, 87–88, 95, 96, 97, 98, 104, 105, 131, 134, 142, 143, *149,* 152–53, 164–65, 181–82, *198,* 202, 206, *219,* 239, *242,* 243–45, 257, 263, 264, *265,* 279, 280, 282–84, 285, 298, 299, 305, 306, 310, 312, 313, 317–20, 322, 324–25, 347, 349, 353, 362

Adams and, 147–48

appointed general, 133–34

army pay and, 339–40

Canada campaigns and, 153–54, 167, 168

Constitution and, 356–58, 361, 362, 363, 365, 367, 368, 372, *375,* 376, *377, 378*

Continental Congress and, 200, 202, 210, 214, 222, 224

Declaration of Independence and, 176

at Delaware River, *179,* 210, 211–14, 215, *215,* 217–19

at Dorchester, *164,* 165–66, *165*

Dunmore and, 162

early experiences as commander, 147–53

at end of war, 339–43, *341, 342*

Franklin's farewell letter to, 378

Howe's peace commission and, 185–86

kingship considered for, 339

made president, *345, 347, 370, 375, 380, 381*

marriage of, 22, 34–35, *35*

Mifflin and, 147, *194, 195*

militia and, 197, 308

in New York and New Jersey, 182, 183, 186–87, 189, 194–96, 198–207, *208,* 209–16, *211, 213,* 217–24, *220,* 229, 235, 237–38, 290, 291–92, 308, 316

Philadelphia campaigns and, 263–67

plots against, 182, 280–81, *287*

postwar rebellions and, 355–56

Rochambeau and, 308–10, *311,* 322–23, 325–26, *332,* 334

soldiers' mutiny and, 316–17

spies of, 309

Stamp Act and, 57, 58

at Valley Forge, *276,* 279–82, *279, 281*

war strategy of, 285, 300, 316, 327

at Yorktown, *311,* 326, 327, 329–35, *332*

Washington, Lawrence, 30, 31–32, *30, 31,* 34, 133

Washington, Martha, 22, 34–35, *35,* 133, 264, *265*

Washington, William, *132, 219,* 314–16, *318*

Wayne, Anthony, 207, 291, 316, 317, 320

Way to Wealth, The (Franklin), 230

wealth, 22–23

Wedderburn, Alexander, 81, 82–85, 86, *86,* 271

Wedgwood, Josiah, 42, *42, 366*

West, Benjamin, 343

West Indies, 40–41, 49, 95, 231, 282, 284, 298, 303, 323, 337–38, 354

Whately, Thomas, 77–78, 80, 82

Whately, William, 80, 84

Wheatley, Phillis, 351, *351*

Wilkes, John, 44–46, *45,* 65–67, *66, 67,* 68, 70, 81, 93, *102,* 128, 152, 304, 305, *306*

Wilson, James, 159, 169, *358,* 360, 361, 368

Wolfe, James, 13, *16,* 25

women, 26–27, 264, 288, 353

Worcester County Convention, 98

Wright, Patience, 264

Wyoming Valley, 291, 292, *292*

"Yankee Doodle," 123, 125, 334

Yates, Robert, 357, 362, 368

Yorktown, Virginia, 303, *303, 311,* 324, 326, 327, *328,* 329–35, *331, 332*

Zane, Betty, 264

PICTURE CREDITS

ACKNOWLEDGEMENTS

No book of this scope could be completed by a writer alone. I am particularly grateful to Don Fehr, my editor at Viking Penguin, whose counsel and support have been constantly available—and invaluable. I would also like to thank associate publisher Jane von Mehren for her substantial contribution to the finished product. Equally helpful has been the encouragement of a fellow historian and friend, Robert Cowley, editor-in-chief of the *Quarterly Journal of Military History*, who stimulated me to keep writing and thinking about the American Revolution in recent years. My wife, Alice Fleming, herself a writer of many noteworthy books for young people, functioned with her usual dedication as a first reader and editorial adviser. Also important behind the scenes has been the support of my literary agent, Ted Chichak.

This book was produced and designed by Jones & Janello. Amy Janello and Brennon Jones are responsible for its brilliant colors, its astutely deployed art. They have a genius for finding the right picture and knowing exactly where to use it. Backing them up in the search for these visual enhancements of the narrative, Laurie Winfrey and Chistopher Deegan contributed their wide expertise and energy, and Chiara Peacock coordinated a thousand-and-one details. Equally important to the final result was the scrupulous copyediting of Leslie Ware and David Pengilly.

I would also like to thank the staff of Middlemarch Films, in particular, producer/directors Muffie Meyer and Ellen Hovde, visuals researcher Jennifer Raikes, and writer Ronald Blumer, who have been helpful in sharing resources and narrative insights. Overseeing the film effort but also lending enthusiastic support to this book, Catherine Allan, executive producer at KTCA Twin Cities Public Television, comes close to being the indispensable person in the creation of *Liberty!* in print and film.

While I take full responsibility for the judgments and opinions, not to mention the facts, in the text, a wide-angle vision such as this book attempts must necessarily stand on the shoulders of the many scholars who have done pioneering work in the era of the American Revolution over the previous forty years. Any list of these historians would include those who were interviewed for the film version of *Liberty!*: Bernard Bailyn, Jeremy Black, Colin Bonwick, Carol Berkin, Christopher L. Brown, Sylvia Frey, Jack P. Greene, Don Higginbotham, Ronald Hoffman, Claude-Anne Lopez, Pauline Maier, George Neumann, Nicholas Rodger, James Morton Smith, John Shy, and Gordon Wood. They have graciously given me permission to select quotes from these interviews which are placed throughout the book. I would also like to thank David Hildebrand for his expert advice on colonial music and Ronald N. Ollstein, M.D., for sharing with me Revolutionary samples from his collection of autographed free-franked envelopes.

Among the many librarians who helped me with that wonderful zeal that puts them in every historian's debt, I would like to single out Lewis Daniels, head of the Westbrook, Connecticut, library, who worked miracles obtaining books on interlibrary loan from every university in the state during my final summer of work on this book. Henry Blanke, reference librarian at Marymount Manhattan College, gave me similar help in New York, as did Mark Piel and his superb staff at the New York Society Library. I cannot begin to estimate the help I received in previous years from the librarians at Yale University's Sterling Memorial and Beinecke libraries, where I have done most of my research on the American Revolution.

—T.F.

Washington and Lafayette at Yorktown.

A NOTE FROM THE EXECUTIVE PRODUCER

The publication of this book by Thomas Fleming, a companion volume to the PBS series *Liberty! The American Revolution*, is the realization of a long-held dream. Ever since KTCA began developing a television series about the American Revolution, we have envisioned a book which could tell the many stories—political and military, social and cultural—that make up this first chapter of our country's history. All of us who work in television cringe every time an important idea or interesting anecdote ends up on the cutting-room floor because of the constraints of time. It is especially difficult when a story has the immense sweep and international scale of the American Revolution—a period that spans 25 years and several continents. It is therefore extremely gratifying to have as our companion volume a book that is both thorough and highly readable. In addition to author Tom Fleming, I want to thank editors Don Fehr and Jane von Mehren at Viking Penguin, Amy Janello and Brennon Jones of Jones & Janello for designing and producing the book, and Ted Chichak and Jonathon Lazear.

The idea for a television series on the American Revolution came from Gerry Richman, KTCA's vice-president for national production. Toward the end of 1990, Gerry was struck by news reports that *The Federalist Papers*—the writings of America's founders—was becoming one of the most avidly sought-after books in the libraries and bookstores of the former Soviet Union, in stark contrast to widespread voter apathy and cynicism about government in our own country. Gerry felt that a powerful re-telling of the genius and risks that went into the creation of our republic might help Americans rekindle their own appreciation for the system of government that we have.

Like many ambitious series on public television, ours was developed with the early support of several organizations: the National Endowment for the Humanities (thank you to Holly Tank and Jim Dougherty); the Corporation for Public Broadcasting (thank you to Sandie Pedlow and Don Marbury); the Public Broadcasting Service (thank you to Jennifer Lawson, Kathy Quattrone, Sandy Heberer and Glenn Marcus); and the Arthur Vining Davis Foundations (thank you to Dr. Jonathan Howe).

Liberty! would not have been possible without the major support of our corporate sponsor, Norwest Corporation. For their commitment and enthusiasm, a very special thank you to Dick Kovacevich and Larry Haeg.

Credit for bringing the American Revolution to life for television goes to producers/directors Ellen Hovde and Muffie Meyer of Middlemarch Films and to writer Ronald Blumer. From the beginning, we were faced with two problems: how to humanize the people and events of the Revolution and how to visualize an era long before the advent of film and photography. The very original production style Middlemarch created in response to this challenge uses "eyewitness" accounts of the Revolution, taken from diaries, letters and official documents and read by actors directly on camera. Thanks also to editors Sharon Sachs and Joshua Waletsky for their craft and unflagging sense of structure, to producers Smokey Forrester and Jo Umans for making production run smoothly amid thousands of mishaps, to Jennifer Raikes and Holly Gill for their superb research and to casting directors Elissa Myers and Paul Fouquet.

Liberty! owes a deep debt of gratitude to many scholars. Foremost among them is Michael Zuckert, professor of political science at Carleton College, who served as lead consultant for *Liberty!* Michael provided the key historical themes and ideas that form the backbone of the series.

Other scholars whose excitement about the Revolutionary period contributed significantly to our series include: George Abrams, Lance Banning, Bernard Bailyn, Carol Berkin, Richard B. Bernstein, Jeremy Black, Colin Bonwick, Christopher Brown, David Edmunds, Sylvia Frey, Jack Greene, James Haskett, Don Higginbotham, Ronald Hoffman, John Keegan, Peter Kolchin, Claude-Anne Lopez, Piers Mackesy, Pauline Maier, James Merrell, George Neumann, Mary Beth Norton, N.E.M. Rodger, Richard Norton Smith, John Shy, Bernard Vincent, Margaret Washington, Robert Whitworth and Gordon Wood

There are many people at KTCA who worked long hours over several years to bring *Liberty!* to television. Although it is not possible to name them all here, I do want to single out several people: writer/researcher Tim Brady; coordinating producer Erika Herrmann; unit managers Steve Krahnke and Norbert Een; audio and post-production wizards Lisa K. Johnson, Jerry Lakso, Bob Sturm, Mitch Griffin and Bernie Beaudry; and station relations manager Elaine Powell. Thanks to Jay Miller, Denise Fick, Janet Raugust, Bob Perkerwicz, Carl Jacobs and Dan Thomas for their work on the many design elements of the television series and its companion Website. And for their unfaltering support of *Liberty!*, special thanks to Jack Willis, Kevin Martin and Michael Perelstein.

Also special thanks to our partners at Sony Classical including Peter Gelb, Rose Schwartz and Laraine Perri for providing *Liberty!* with a first-rate soundtrack composed by Mark O'Connor and Richard Einhorn and featuring performances by O'Connor, Yo-Yo Ma, James Taylor, Wynton Marsalis and the Nashville Symphony.

Finally, for his wisdom, experience and good humor, a big thank you to our friend and publicist, Owen Comora.

Seal of the United States, 1782.

Catherine Allan
Executive Producer, KTCA
St. Paul/Minneapolis